The Revival of British Liberalism

The Revival of British Liberalism

From Grimond to Clegg

Tudor Jones

First published 2011 by
PALGRAVE MACMILLAN

Palgrave Macmillan in the UK is an imprint of Macmillan Publishers Limited, registered in England, company number 785998, of Houndmills, Basingstoke, Hampshire RG21 6XS.

Palgrave Macmillan in the US is a division of St Martin's Press LLC, 175 Fifth Avenue, New York, NY 10010.

Palgrave Macmillan is the global academic imprint of the above companies and has companies and representatives throughout the world.

Palgrave® and Macmillan® are registered trademarks in the United States, the United Kingdom, Europe and other countries.

ISBN 978–1–4039–4428–3 hardback

This book is printed on paper suitable for recycling and made from fully managed and sustained forest sources. Logging, pulping and manufacturing processes are expected to conform to the environmental regulations of the country of origin.

A catalogue record for this book is available from the British Library.

A catalog record for this book is available from the Library of Congress.

10 9 8 7 6 5 4 3 2 1
19 20 18 17 16 15 14 13 12 11

Printed and bound in the United States of America

To the memory of my parents, Brynmor and Eilonwy

Contents

Preface

This book provides an historical study of British Liberalism spanning the period from Jo Grimond's accession to the leadership of the Liberal Party in November 1956 to Nick Clegg's election as Leader of the Liberal Democrats just over 51 years later in December 2007. The book is therefore a history of Liberal ideas, as they were developed within the British Liberal Party and, later, the Liberal Democrats during that period. As such, it is concerned with organised, party Liberalism, not with philosophical liberalism or with liberal ideology conceived more broadly in cross-party terms. More precisely, perhaps, it could be said that this book is an ideological history of the Liberal Party and the Liberal Democrats since 1956. For its focus is on political ideas not only as they have been propounded in the writings and speeches of Liberal and Liberal Democrat politicians, thinkers and activists, but also as they have been embodied in the policies, programmes and strategies of their parties.

The text of this book was completed before the British General Election of 2010, and the subsequent formation of the Coalition Government, and with it the first direct Liberal participation in government since Churchill's wartime Coalition. That development in itself adds, I believe, increased relevance to the title of this book. It will be left to subsequent studies to assess the record of the Coalition and of Liberal Democrat ministers within it.

To a large extent the methods of the historian of political thought have been employed throughout this study – including detailed attention to such published sources as the books, pamphlets and periodicals which form, together with party policy documents and election manifestos, the main receptacles of British Liberal thought during the period under scrutiny. I have also drawn throughout upon material contained in two of the principal histories of the Liberal Party, parts of which cover the post-1945 period. These are: David Dutton, *A History of the Liberal Party in the Twentieth Century*, and Chris Cook, *A Short History of the Liberal Party*. In addition, this study draws upon unpublished Liberal Party papers and upon my own interviews and conversations with some of the leading Liberal and Liberal Democrat protagonists in the ideological and policy debates of those years.

In researching and writing this book, I have examined, and in some cases uncovered, what I believe to be a rich and varied seam of Liberal writing since the 1950s, one, too, that in some respects has been neglected or undervalued. In quoting widely, and at times extensively, from such material I have tried to let those literary expressions of Liberal thought speak for themselves down the years. I have, however, inserted my own interweaving commentary and in places, of course, my own interpretation and analysis.

I have also quoted at length from Liberal, SDP/Liberal Alliance and Liberal Democrat statements of principles and general election manifestos in the post-1945 period. In the case of the latter, my justification for doing so is that, as Duncan Brack has pointed out, manifestos have held a particular significance for members of the Liberal Party and the Liberal Democrats. The reasons for this are really twofold. First, apart from their main function of conveying their parties' principles and policies to the electorate, election manifestos have also been important tools of communication *within* the Liberal Party and the Liberal Democrats.[1] For as the most public expressions of the parties' political philosophy, namely, Liberalism, with its set of core values and beliefs, manifestos have thus helped to unify those parties, imbuing them with a sense of identity, purpose and direction. This has been particularly important, too, in view of the fact that, unlike their major rivals, the Liberal Party and its successor have lacked a firm base in class or sectional interests. Second, because British Liberals had been out of office since the time of Churchill's wartime coalition, they could not rely on their own governmental record as a source of motivation and party unity. Policy development and debate have therefore 'offered an alternative driving force', which has consequently shaped the organisational structures of both the Liberal Party and the Liberal Democrats.[2] Election manifestos have, again, been the clearest expressions of that process. All of the above comments apply, too, of course, to the parties' periodic statements of principles, which, in the case of the Liberal Democrats, have been referred to as 'themes and values' documents.

Essentially, however, this book remains a history of Liberal ideas since the 1950s, viewed within the context of the major events and developments affecting the Liberal Party and its successor. (These are summarised in the Chronology at the end of the book.) It seeks to demonstrate a clear pattern of continuity of Liberal values, principles and themes, and also, to a large extent, of policy. It describes, too, the manner in which new and often creative ideas and policy thinking emerged during the main periods of post-war Liberal revival and subsequent Liberal Democrat recovery – notably, that is, in the late 1950s/early 1960s, the early 1970s, and after 1990.

Of the SDP/Liberal Alliance decade of the 1980s, however, it can hardly be said that its most striking achievement – in securing the largest third-party vote share in Britain since the 1920s – could be attributed to new policy thinking. There were various reasons for that deficiency, which will be explored later in this study. With regard to one half of the Alliance, I should add that this book does not focus directly on the Social Democratic Party. That ground has already been substantially covered by a previous academic study.[3] Nevertheless, I do consider the writings and pronouncements of leading SDP politicians and thinkers who later became prominent figures within the Liberal Democrats. I also examine at length the concept of a social market economy, controversial within parts of the Alliance, that was developed and promoted by David Owen during the 1980s.

Above all, I seek in this historical study to examine and elucidate the reasons for the revival since the late 1950s of Liberalism in Britain as a political philosophy. In addition, I hope to indicate why it has retained over the past half-century, in many eyes, its force, appeal and relevance as a creed, enduring into the radically changed political and economic climate of the early 21st century.

Acknowledgements

A number of people, concerned in their different ways with the political ideas, events and developments examined in this book, generously granted me interviews during its preparation. In several cases, too, they assisted me with my subsequent enquiries. I should therefore like to express my gratitude to the following: the Rt. Hon. Lord Ashdown of Norton-sub-Hampton, the Rt. Hon. Sir Alan Beith, MP, Duncan Brack, the Rt. Hon. Vince Cable, MP, the Rt. Hon. Sir Menzies Campbell, MP, the Rt. Hon. Nick Clegg, MP, the late Lord Dahrendorf of Clare Market, Dr Richard Grayson, Lord Greaves, Dr Evan Harris, the late Lord Holme of Cheltenham, David Howarth, Simon Hughes, MP, the Rt. Hon. Chris Huhne, MP, the Rt. Hon. Charles Kennedy, MP, Lord Kirkwood of Kirkhope, the Rt. Hon. David Laws, MP, Gordon Lishman, CBE, Lord Maclennan of Rogart, Professor David Marquand, Paul Marshall, Michael Meadowcroft, Richard Moore, the Rt. Hon. Lord Owen of the City of Plymouth, John Pardoe, Lord Phillips of Sudbury, Lord Rennard, Tony Richards, the Rt. Hon. Lord Rodgers of Quarry Bank, the late Lord Russell-Johnston, the Rt. Hon. Lord Steel of Aikwood, Lord Taverne, QC, Lord Wallace of Saltaire, and the Rt. Hon. Baroness Williams of Crosby.

Throughout the course of researching and writing this book, Duncan Brack and Michael Meadowcroft on numerous occasions shared with me their wide-ranging knowledge of contemporary British Liberal history and Liberal/Liberal Democrat politics, helping to clarify many points of detail. I am very grateful for their kind assistance. I should also like to thank Tony Richards, who made valuable comments on the first draft of Chapter 4, which in part covers the period when he and I were colleagues in London during the early 1970s.

My thanks are offered, too, to the staff of the New Bodleian Reading Room in the Bodleian Library, Oxford and the Rewley House Library, Oxford, where I spent many hours of study, as well as to the staff of the Nuffield College Library, Oxford and of the Archives Reading Room at the British Library of Political and Economic Science in London, where I was able to read many Liberal Party and SDP/Liberal Alliance publications and unpublished Liberal Party private papers.

For permission to reproduce material from Iain Dale (ed.) *Liberal Party General Election Manifestos, 1900–1997* (London: Routledge/Politico's 2000), I should like to thank the Taylor Francis Group.

With regard to the practical completion of the book, I should like to acknowledge the helpful advice provided by Amber Stone-Galilee, Politics Editor at Palgrave Macmillan, and her editorial assistant Liz Blackmore, as well as the assistance of Rick Bouwman during the final stages. I should also like to thank Carolyn Gara, who typed the whole of the original text of this book with diligence, patience and good humour. I should like to record my gratitude, too, to Judith Arneil who typed and edited the final draft of the book, and to my friends Joanna Zang and Ani D, who assisted in that process. In a lighter vein, I owe my thanks, too, to the staff of 'Al-Andalus', 'The Rose and Crown', 'Saffron', 'X'ian' and my other favourite haunts in Oxford, who alleviated the solitary routines of research and writing with sustenance, refreshment and good company.

Finally, I should like to convey my gratitude to my friend and colleague, Dr Alex Kazamias, for his continual encouragement whilst I was writing this book, and, more generally, for his friendship and kind generosity of spirit.

Chapter 1
Survival of a Creed: 1945–1956

In the wake of Labour's landslide victory at the 1945 General Election, the British Liberal Party had been left stranded with just 12 MPs, representing rural areas scattered throughout Britain. With a total popular vote of 2.2 million, the Party had overall won only 9 per cent of the national poll. Furthermore, some of its leading figures had been lost in the electoral debris: notably, the Party Leader, Sir Archibald Sinclair, the Chief Whip, Sir Percy Harris, and Sir William Beveridge, principal architect of the British welfare state, and a Liberal MP for barely seven months.

Reading the election results in the national press on the morning in July after the poll, the philosopher Bertrand Russell and his wife, 'while mourning Liberal defeats, especially that of Sir Archibald Sinclair', declared that the party was finished.[1] Many shared their gloomy assessment, which seemed confirmed later that year by the municipal election results of November 1945, when only 92 Liberal councillors out of just 360 candidates were elected.[2]

Plans for reconstruction of the party organisation, directed by Philip Fothergill,[3] Frank Byers,[4] and Edward Martell,[5] did, however, produce some modest structural and financial improvements. By 1947, for example, 500 active Liberal associations in Britain had been established, compared with only 200 just eight months earlier, and party finances were starting to improve by 1949.[6] But prospects for the Party's future remained very bleak.

In these dispiriting conditions, the task of the new party leader, Clement Davies, was to hold together a small, loose and ideologically diverse parliamentary party, some of whom, such as Lady Megan Lloyd George, were sympathetic to the new Labour government, while others, such as Rhys Hopkin Morris, were deeply hostile. As J. Graham Jones has observed, Davies's parliamentary colleagues 'were indeed a "motley group", totally lacking in cohesion, with no common political philosophy or parliamentary strategy, ever ready to dissent, even rebel, some of its members perched on opposing poles of the political spectrum.'[7]

1

Moreover, Davies himself did not exactly inspire confidence in all his colleagues, partly because of his rather chequered political past. MP for Montgomeryshire since 1929, two years later he had joined the Liberal Nationals, the faction led by Sir John Simon which Davies eventually left in 1939, rejoining the mainstream Liberal Party in 1942. His chairmanship of the parliamentary party after 1945 consequently 'led to tension and unease, even dissension, among his colleagues',[8] many of whom expected and desired the imminent return to the Commons of Sir Archibald Sinclair, a development that was never to take place.

The Liberal Party's decline deepened at the 1950 General Election, held on 23 February of that year. 475 candidates were fielded, the most since 1929, but only 9 MPs were elected, with 319 deposits lost. The total Liberal vote increased to 2.6 million but the overall vote share remained static at 9.1 per cent. In only three regions – south-west England, north-east Scotland and north Wales – and in only three urban constituencies, did the Liberals obtain 20 per cent or more of the vote. The Party was once again consigned mainly to 'the agricultural backwaters'.[9]

After 1950 the Party's financial resources were more or less exhausted and the parliamentary party remained disunited. As Roy Douglas has recalled, the divisive factor at that time was 'not disagreement about what a Liberal government should do, but whether they preferred Labour or the Conservatives'.[10] Indeed, Clement Davies went even further in his view of his parliamentary colleagues' disunity, lamenting to Gilbert Murray, the eminent classical scholar, in May 1950 that:

> ... there is no Party but a number of individuals who, because of their adherence to the Party, come together only to express completely divergent views.[11]

Yet Davies defiantly continued to reaffirm the Liberal Party's determination to survive, declaring at the 1950 Party Assembly in Scarborough: 'We refuse to get out. We refuse to die. We are determined to live and fight on.'[12]

His defiance, however, ran in the face of his Party's continuing electoral decline, for if the 1950 campaign had proved a debacle, the 1951 General Election 'marked the nadir of the electoral fortunes of the Party'.[13] Fighting this time on the basis of a 'narrow front' strategy, the Party fielded only 109 candidates. From these, only six MPs were elected, with a total national vote secured of under three-quarters of a million, and an overall vote share of only 2.5 per cent. Of the six MPs, only Jo Grimond in Orkney and Shetland, who had won his seat in 1950, had been returned in the face of Conservative opposition.

In these dismal political circumstances, Winston Churchill, the new Conservative Prime Minister, whose party had won an overall Commons majority of 17 without a simple majority of the national vote in October

1951, offered Clement Davies the post of Minister of Education, with a place in the Cabinet. On the advice of senior colleagues such as Lord Samuel, Davies decided to reject Churchill's offer.[14]

Shortly afterwards, Davies responded to Lord Samuel's praise for his decision, expressed at a National Liberal Club lunch in the leader's honour, by stressing:

> … However small be our numbers, we have a task to perform, and that cannot be performed if we sink our independence and see the party gradually welded into the structure of another party.[15]

Many political historians have argued that, had Davies accepted Churchill's offer, the Liberal Party would probably have disintegrated. Certainly its political independence would have been eroded, if not destroyed, with the Party gradually absorbed within the structure of the Conservative Party, just as the National Liberals had been subsumed following the 1947 Woolton-Teviot Agreement.[16] David Dutton, for instance, has maintained that Davies' decision was 'probably the greatest act of service rendered to his party during 11 years as leader'.[17] In the view, too, of Davies' biographer, Alun Wyburn-Powell, his refusal was '… critical to the future survival of the Liberal Party as an independent political force' and hence a 'defining moment' for the Party.[18] Roy Douglas has also agreed that, if Davies had accepted the Tory offer, '… the Liberal Party might well have broken to pieces'.[19]

Nevertheless, in the first few years of the period that followed – during the 1951–55 Parliament – there were few signs of improvement in the Liberals' fortunes as an independent force. The Party contested only eight out of 45 by-elections, saving deposits only once, though there had been an encouraging ray of light amid this overall gloom, namely, a strong performance by John Bannerman at the Inverness by-election in December 1954, securing 36 per cent of the vote. By 1955 only 1.5 per cent of borough councillors were Liberal, with no representation in major cities such as Birmingham and Liverpool. In terms of organisation, by the same year the number of affiliated Liberal associations had shrunk to fewer than 300, and individual party membership had reached an unprecedently low point by 1953.[20] The Party's financial difficulties, too, remained acute.

But at least the danger of formal assimilation within the Conservative Party had receded, largely because of Davies's decision in 1951, but partly, too, because the Tories had achieved their Commons majority of 17 without any further electoral pacts besides those in place in Bolton and Huddersfield, or without any concession to the Liberals of the promise of electoral reform. Moreover, Davies's parliamentary colleagues in the House of Commons – Jo Grimond, the chief whip, Roderic Bowen, Arthur Holt, Rhys Hopkin Morris and Donald Wade – at least formed a more united and disciplined team than in the period from 1945–51. This was reflected, for instance, in the much higher degree of consistency in their parliamentary voting records.[21]

The 1955 General Election, however, held on 26 May, again produced a disappointing outcome. Fighting once more with a 'narrow-front' strategy, the Party fielded only 110 candidates, of whom only six were returned as MPs, with 60 lost deposits. The total Liberal vote was, as in 1951, under three-quarters of a million, but the overall share of the vote at least rose very slightly from 2.5 per cent to 2.7 per cent. In contrast, the two major parties failed to occupy the first two positions in the poll in only 15 constituencies throughout Britain. A stable pattern of duopoly in an era of class-based voting appeared to have been established, with Labour and the Conservatives sharing 96 per cent of the total popular vote.

But in view of the Liberals' marginal increase in vote share, the 1955 General Election was at least the first since 1929 in which the Party had made any improvement, however slight, on its previous performance. This was evident, too, in the slight increase in the Liberal share of the vote per candidate from 14.7 per cent in 1951 to 15.1 per cent.[22] Moreover, while the 1955 election may not in itself have been a turning-point for the Liberals, at least in its aftermath the first stirrings of modest revival became discernible. Concrete evidence of this was provided in the winter of 1955–56 by by-election results at Torquay in December 1955 and at Hereford in February 1956 where the Liberal share of the vote rose to 23 per cent and 36 per cent respectively.

This revival was not related directly to the leadership of Clement Davies, who was suffering from ill-health at that time. But more broadly, his personal contribution at least to keeping the Liberal ship afloat, to use the kind of nautical metaphor of which he was fond, has since been underlined. Douglas has thus maintained that Davies' 'patient courage in the desolate years had played such a large part in keeping the Liberal Party in existence', and that '... but for the inspiring leadership of Clement Davies, Frank Byers, Philip Fothergill and a few others, the Liberal Party might well have collapsed'.[23] Geoffrey Sell, too, has observed that Davies's 'legacy was that he passed on a separate, independent party further from extinction or engulfment by either of the major parties than when he took up the task'. Davies had experienced 'all the tears and few of the joys of leadership', yet he had 'held the pass during the most treacherous years in the party's history, and in doing so, helped to lay the foundations for the revival that took place under his successor'.[24] The efforts of a small number of dedicated and tenacious individuals within the Liberal Party elite – in Douglas's view, 'perhaps half a dozen',[25] including, notably, Davies, Byers and Fothergill – thus formed a major reason for the Party's survival in its darkest days. These were people who shared an 'unshakeable conviction ... that better days would inevitably return'.[26]

But there were broader political factors, too, which have been cited to explain the Party's survival.[27] First of all, there was the immense value of the British Liberal tradition, for as Dutton has noted, 'the depths of the party's roots in history had been a major factor in keeping it going when so many other factors had pointed towards extinction'.[28] This great asset had been increased, too, by the memory of Liberal parliamentary strength in the recent past. That collective memory had in turn helped the Party to recruit a new post-war generation of well-informed and articulate activists and candidates, drawn, not least, from flourishing Liberal clubs at British universities.[29]

Second, a narrow but enduring Liberal electoral base still existed in a few, mostly rural, constituencies which were geographically and socially insulated from mainstream Britain, with its entrenched patterns of class-based voting for the two major parties. Moreover, these areas of electoral support – notably, rural Wales, south-west England and the West Yorkshire/Lancashire Pennine belt – were all parts of the pre-1914 Liberal heartland, containing 'some vestigial elements of organisation ... in Liberal Clubs, Associations, and a small number of councillors'.[30]

Third, on a more expedient level, local electoral pacts with the Conservatives – most obviously in Bolton and Huddersfield after 1951 – and the abstention of Conservative candidates in a few rural Welsh constituencies in 1951 and 1955, had helped to ensure the survival of the Liberal Party as a parliamentary presence at Westminster and hence as a national organisation. Fourth, as John Stevenson has observed, the Party's structure as a loose grouping of individuals 'tied together by sentiment, friendship and voluntary commitment, was one well-adapted to survival and resisting take-over'. Indeed, 'like some declining Nonconformist sect ... the Party retained something of the character of an "organised moral force" ... flying the flag for values and principles which still had some meaning for its participants'.[31] In addition, the Party's organisational and financial weaknesses at a national level in the late 1940s and early 1950s made it an unattractive object of political takeover and absorption by either the Conservatives or Labour in view of the high price – in terms of disruption and inconvenience – that would have to be paid in return for a dubious political asset.

Finally, the Party retained its unrivalled position as the only significant third party, however small, in the House of Commons. There was no other grouping that could compete with the Liberals for effective third party status. The National Liberals had been gradually absorbed by the Conservative Party after 1947, the Ulster Unionists usually took the Conservative whip, and the Scottish and Welsh Nationalists were not yet electorally successful during this period. The Liberals were thus in a position to benefit from future popular revulsion from both major political parties and hence from the politics of protest.

All these factors, therefore, helped to reinforce the determined efforts of a few senior Party figures in London, as well as those of constituency activists scattered throughout Britain, who between them 'managed to convince themselves at least that the Liberal cause was not lost and that the flame must not be extinguished'.[32] It can thus be fairly claimed that the Liberal Party's 'survival in adversity' was, in Michael Steed's words, 'a tribute to its own belief that what it stood for was important, distinctive and attractive'[33]

Indeed, that collective belief reflected the fact that political ideas and ideological conviction remained important to British Liberals during those bleak years. A major reason for this was that, as Malcolm Baines has noted, they 'did not have a firm base in either class or interest around which they could unite' and therefore 'had to rely on a shared ideological heritage to hold the party together'.[34] Evidence for this view was later provided by a survey of the attitudes of Liberal Party members in Jorgen Rasmussen's 1965 academic study, which found that during the 1950s 83 per cent of respondents had been motivated by ideological beliefs in actively supporting the Party, and that this factor had become by far the most important influence in shaping their allegiance.[35]

This is not to suggest that there was a high degree of ideological cohesiveness about the Liberal Party between 1945 and 1955. Baines has even maintained that there was 'no one unified strand of Liberal thought in this period', and that throughout the mid-20th century 'Liberal ideological thinking was coherent in that it centred on the supremacy of the individual, but was united over little else'.[36]

Nevertheless, some kind of distinctive and firmly rooted doctrinal position, developed in particular in the writings of Elliot Dodds,[37] had been taking shape during the Party's wilderness years. At an official level, this was evident in the depiction, by Clement Davies and others within the small party elite, of Liberalism as a third force, free of class and sectional interests, that offered a middle way between the extremes of state socialism and private monopoly capitalism. Such a view, albeit presented in the more radical spirit of a *third* rather than a middle way, underlay the two most distinctive Liberal policy issues of that period – free trade, admittedly at the time a divisive issue,[38] and co-ownership in industry, of which Dodds was the principal and most effective advocate.

That position was reinforced, too, by the Party's stances on civil liberties, on political and constitutional reform, with a special emphasis on the control and decentralisation of political power, and on international cooperation, with an increasingly European focus. Those last two causes were to be advanced further during the 1960s. But in the meantime, the Liberal Party's struggle for survival in the late 1940s and early 1950s had resulted not only in its hard-won, continuing political independence, but also in the maintenance of a broad ideological scaffolding which could be strengthened and extended in the years of gradual recovery that lay ahead.

Chapter 2
The Advent of Grimond: the Creed Revived: 1956–1959

The first signs of the Liberal Party's post-war electoral revival had become faintly apparent in the winter of 1955–56. In parliamentary by elections at Torquay in December 1955 and at Hereford in February 1956 Liberal candidates polled well, in the latter case obtaining a 37 per cent vote share. Nonetheless, Clement Davies' leadership continued to come under critical scrutiny for its lack of a clear strategy or sustained vision. Furthermore, when in 1955 the Leader was ill and unable to attend the pre-election Liberal Assembly, Jo Grimond had impressed his audience with a well-delivered, authoritative speech that marked him out in the delegates' eyes as someone capable of leadership in the near future.[1]

Davies was approached by both Philip Fothergill and Major-General Grey on the question of his retirement,[2] but appeared in no hurry to resign the leadership. Eventually, however, at the Liberal Assembly in Folkestone in September 1956, in his winding-up speech, he announced his intention to resign in three weeks' time, telling the delegates:

> It is time that the tiller were placed in the hands of a younger man, and that a new voice should be calling upon the ship's company, rallying them to the great cause which we have so much at heart ... Fortunately I can step down knowing that there is a worthy successor waiting ... I step down from the bridge, and go below.[3]

The 'younger man' and 'worthy successor', Jo Grimond, had already left the conference hall by the time Davies made his speech and resignation announcement. As the *Manchester Guardian* commented at the time, Grimond had 'appeared before the assembly as a delegate', and had 'left it as Crown Prince'.[4] Yet in spite of the widespread relief felt within the Party at Davies' belated resignation, together with the hopes for future recovery that were widely vested in his young successor, there was also a shared gratitude for the departing leader's past services to the Liberal Party. For in spite of

Davies' various shortcomings as Party Leader, it was also true, as Michael McManus has noted, that:

> ... He had stepped willingly into the breach for his party at an appalling juncture in its fortunes ... He had subsequently turned down office himself in order to protect the independent existence of his party, and he had never been other than competent, decent and utterly true to his Liberal instincts.[5]

Grimond succeeded Davies as Liberal leader in November 1956 in the middle of the Suez crisis, just as the main contingent of British troops was about to land in the Canal Zone. Suez, a watershed in post-war British history, became the source of growing popular disenchantment with the Conservative government. It also helped to destroy, in many eyes, the image of the Conservative Party of Eden, Butler and Macmillan as the natural inheritor of the best aspects of British Liberalism. The crisis and its ramifications served, too, to distinguish the Liberal Party, under Grimond's new leadership, more clearly from its Conservative opponents.

In the 1956–59 period progress was made by the Liberals on two electoral fronts. The first of these was an improved performance in by-elections, with the Party gaining second place in six out of 19 contested, including a notable result at Rochdale in February 1958, where Ludovic Kennedy won 35.5 per cent of the poll. Even more impressive was the Liberal victory at Torrington in March of that year by Mark Bonham Carter, Lady Violet's son and Asquith's grandson. This was the Party's first by-election gain since 1929. The overall performance during this period was to become a feature of the Liberals' subsequent by-election challenges: that is, the capacity for winning a higher percentage of the vote in certain constituencies than in general elections, although individual, at first only occasional, victories could not always be translated into a major increase in seats at the following general election.

The second area of electoral progress during the first phase of Grimond's leadership consisted of a modest revival of the Liberals' virtually dormant base in local politics. The year 1958 provided the Party with its best local election results since before the Second World War, with 54 borough gains and 59 gains in urban and rural district councils.[6] This was admittedly only a limited advance from a very low baseline of support. In the mid-1950s there were, after all, only about 400 Liberal councillors throughout the whole of Britain, many of whom owed their seats to local pacts with either of the major parties.

In spite of these improvements in its electoral performance, the Party still needed to establish a clearer, identifiable image within the British political system, in place of its appearance as, in David Dutton's words, 'a compromise party which combined the better traits of its larger opponents'.[7] To that end, Grimond sought to reposition the Party through a strong emphasis on new policy formulation. He therefore set up the New Directions policy-making groups between 1958 and 1960, which supplemented three Liberal think-tanks: the Unservile State Group, already established since 1953, the Oxford Liberal Group, founded just after the 1959 General Election, and the New Orbits Group, formed in early 1960, which was designed to act as a focal point for policy thinking by younger Liberals.[8] The Liberal Publication Department, chaired by Arthur Holt in 1957, also published a series of pamphlets initiated by the Parliamentary Party.[9] All this policy-making activity was supported, too, by the creation of a new Party research department, funded by the Rowntree Trust and headed by Harry Cowie. The Party treasurer, Major-General Grey, had resigned his post in 1958 over Grimond's proposal to set up this new body, informing Frank Byers at the time that:

> ... we do not need a new Research Department to discover a new Liberal creed. The one of Peace, Retrenchment and Reform, including Free Trade and a recovery of our civil liberties, is good enough for any Liberal.[10]

During this period the Party newspaper, *Liberal News*, also played a more prominent role in the development and promotion of policy. From July 1957 its masthead carried the slogan, 'the organ of the only progressive Non-Socialist Party', indicating the strategic and ideological direction that Grimond was intending to take. In the spring of 1957 the paper published a series of 18 articles, endorsed by the new leader, covering not only distinctive Liberal issues such as co-ownership, parliamentary reform and international cooperation, but also issues that were to become highly significant over the next ten years or more. These included European integration and innovations in defence policy, such as abandonment of Britain's independent nuclear deterrent and of its land bases east of Suez, with the exception of Singapore.[11] Policy ideas emanated, too, from a new series of pamphlets produced by the Unservile State Group. Its Papers, as they were named, were to appear until the Group was formally disbanded in 1990.

These varied Liberal publications underlined the importance which Grimond attached to the formulation and communication of policy and ideas as an essential part of his attempt to restore the intellectual and political credibility of his Party. Indeed, as Geoffrey Sell has observed, of all the post-1945 leaders of the Liberal Party, Grimond 'had the greatest influence on, and interest in, policy-making', and his contribution to that process was 'to create a stimulating and invigorating climate of opinion, open to new ideas from academics and industrialists inside and outside the party'.[12] Among those he encouraged to participate were the economists Frank Paish, Alan Peacock and Jack Wiseman, and the social policy specialists Michael Fogarty and Alec Peterson.

There was nonetheless an unbroken line of continuity in Liberal thought and policy with the Clement Davies era and earlier. Emphasis remained firmly placed on the importance of key Liberal issues such as co-ownership, free trade, political and constitutional reform, civil liberties and international cooperation. Yet under Grimond's leadership there was a sharper focus on constitutional reform and internationalism – particularly on European integration. In general, he provided, as Sell has noted, 'the main impetus towards a reinterpretation of the party's purpose ... representing and redefining the aims of its social reforming wing'.[13]

In spite of these new directions, the traditional cause of free trade remained a central aspect of Liberal economic policy right up to the 1959 General Election. A resolution reaffirming the Party's commitment to unilateral free trade, and moved in visionary terms by Oliver Smedley, had been carried at the 1958 Liberal Assembly 'as a means to abolishing international tensions and promoting World Peace'.[14] That same year, Nathaniel Micklem, President of the Party, wrote an extended and elegant defence of free trade, in which he sought to refute some of the main objections levelled at that policy. Free trade, he declared, was inseparable from 'a free economy'; it involved '... the opening of our ports to all goods of foreign origin, the abolition of quotas and subsidies as well as of the tariffs upon imported manufactured articles'.[15] In similar vein, the historian Roger Fulford, writing in *The Liberal Case*, published for the 1959 General Election, re-emphasized the elevated status of free trade within Liberal policy and ideology, thereby endorsing a view which had been expressed in Sir Andrew McFadyean's predecessor volume nine years earlier. Free trade, Fulford insisted, 'has always been at the forefront of Liberalism', and the compelling arguments against tariffs, 'those barriers to Free Trade', were, he maintained, essentially threefold. Tariffs distorted the price mechanism, 'and hence the use of resources both inside the country and between nations'; they increased prices; and 'by protecting managements from some of the rigours of competition', they removed 'the spur which goads management on to ever more efficient methods of production'.[16]

As in the Clement Davies era, co-ownership, too, remained a central feature of Liberal policy and ideology during the late-1950s. Its practical implications for industry and the economy continued to be explained in the terms which had been clearly stated in the *Ownership for All* Report of 1948 and in subsequent pronouncements. More broadly, co-ownership (the word gradually being used more than 'co-partnership' after 1948), with its underlying distributist and decentralist principles, continued to be portrayed as a distinctive characteristic of a Liberal society.

The policy was given further theoretical elaboration in 1957 in *The Unservile State*, the first major publication of the Unservile State Group. This consisted of a collection of essays, edited by George Watson. Presenting itself as 'the first full-scale book on the attitudes and policies of British Liberalism since *Britain's Industrial Future* (1928)', it described its central theme as 'the prospects of liberty in the Welfare State'. Although 'explicitly Liberal', the book did not seek to 'define the official policy of the Liberal Party', a task for which it had 'no authority'.[17]

In her essay, 'Relations in Industry', Nancy Seear described the main aspects of co-ownership in terms of the broad definition that had been agreed within the Party.[18] The policy, she stated, involved four things: a share for employees in the profits of an industrial company; a share in ownership through some system of employee-shareholding; a share though joint consultation in the management of a company; and a share in policy-making through some form of representation at board level.[19] Furthermore, the underlying aims of any scheme of co-ownership, Seear argued, should always be, first, 'to contribute towards the wide distribution of private ownership which characterizes a Liberal Society'; second, to blur the status distinction between the 'two sides' of industry 'by creating a situation in which wage-earners are also owners, and personally interested in profits'; and third, 'to make the fortunes of the company a matter of direct personal concern to everyone in it'.[20] These aims were stressed in broader ideological terms by Nathaniel Micklem, who declared that: '... Liberals ... aim at the abolition of the proletariat and the emancipation of workers by making property-owners of them all ...', whereas 'the Socialist denounces private property, which is the bulwark of political liberty, and would virtually proletarianize society'.[21]

In *The Unservile State*, Seear set out the case for co-ownership in the immediate context of the wide inequalities in the ownership of both property and industry that existed in contemporary Britain. Whereas since 1945 there had been 'considerable changes' in the distribution of income from industry, the distribution of power, she stressed, remained deeply unequal since:

> ... the ownership of industry itself, like the ownership of property in general, is still in the hands of a tiny minority, while industrial power is confined to a still smaller number of large owners of industrial capital and a small and highly influential group of managers.[22]

Within this context, the economist Peter Wiles, in his essay on 'Property and Equality', drew attention to an important development that had become a characteristic of these patterns of economic power: namely, the growing divorce of legal ownership and actual managerial control within British industry. Anthony Crosland, too, in his major work of revisionist socialist thought, *The Future of Socialism* (1956), had recently examined this development as an important part of his analysis of the changing configuration of economic power in post-war Britain.[23] But whereas for Crosland the significance, both practical and ideological, of this phenomenon was that it underlined the increasing irrelevance of the traditional socialist emphasis on the need for state ownership of the means of production, Wiles drew a different conclusion. The vast increase in 'absentee ownership' through limited liability, he argued in his essay, meant in practice that 'the absentee shareholder in a modern limited company is the possessor of a mere scrap of paper which entitles him to certain payments by a remote and unknown agent'.[24] In practice, too, the large numbers of absentee shareholders very rarely exercised effective power, that is, by achieving a transfer of directorial control, through a shareholders' vote, from one group to another. The reality, therefore, was that 'with every decade that passes the large corporate body becomes more and more a legal entity separate from its individual "owners" '.[25] Such developments might well, as Crosland argued, have invalidated the traditional socialist case for state ownership of industry, but they also, in the Liberal view, precluded the possibility of attaining the far more valuable goal of popular ownership.

In addition to these restatements of the well-established Liberal case for co-ownership, there were at least two other distinctive themes characterising the political thinking of the *Unservile State* essays. The first of these was an evident desire to emphasise and develop William Beveridge's earlier distinction between a 'welfare state' and a 'welfare society'. Indeed, as George Watson later pointed out, Beveridge's own phrase, a 'welfare society', found its first expression in print in the pages of *The Unservile State*.[26] Elliot Dodds, in exploring the relationship between the concepts of liberty and welfare – the main thread running through the essays as a whole – thus argued that:

> ... while wholeheartedly approving of Welfare (i.e. of some social arrangement that will ensure subsistence and protect the citizen against economic misfortune) our aim is a 'Welfare Society' rather than a 'Welfare State'. We recognize that the State must remain responsible for those for whom other sources of Welfare are not available; but in a Liberal society we should look increasingly to the release and stimulation of private endeavour and voluntary agencies of service and mutual aid to diminish the role of the State. Eventually society, i.e. individuals and groups of individuals, would be able and ready to provide most of its welfare for itself.[27]

In support of this view, Dodds invoked Beveridge's stated purpose in *Full Employment in a Free Society* (1944) 'to propose for the State only those things which the State alone can do or which it can do better than any local authority or than private individuals either singly or in association, and to leave to those other agencies that which, if they will, they can do as well or better than the State'.[28]

A second distinctive theme running through some of the *Unservile State* essays was a clear and unequivocal advocacy of economic liberal ideas, and with it a rejection of certain aspects of state collectivism. Nancy Seear, in considering the application of Liberal principles – notably, a belief in the

primary value of individual freedom and individuality, and a fear of the concentration of power – to economic and industrial affairs, thus stated that:

> ... Liberals normally favour the system of free enterprise with a large
> number of competing firms, and oppose the growth of State-owned
> industry and private monopolies.

She emphasised three major benefits of the free enterprise system: that it
gave 'a wider range of choice to the consumer ...; greater scope to the entrepreneur to develop his ideas, his capital and his energies to best advantage;
and greater opportunity for the worker to choose his employer and his
job'.[29] Seear was thus in tune with official Party thinking at this time since
earlier in 1957 *Liberal News* had published a brief but succinct statement
under the headline, 'The Liberal Party believes in Private Enterprise'. This set
out the grounds for the Party's general opposition to the nationalisation of
industry – namely, that, first, it concentrated 'too much power in the hands
of the State', thereby creating 'new privileges and monopolies'; second, that
it was inefficient; third, that it brought politics 'into spheres from which
they should be absent'; fourth, that it raised questions of capital finance and
price-fixing 'which seem insoluble'; and finally, that 'if carried to its logical
limit it denies the fundamental rights of the individual'.[30]

That view was endorsed in Peter Wiles's *Unservile State* essay, in which he
observed that:

> There are few phases in recent history so difficult to explain as the phase
> of Socialist dominance of British political thought (ca. 1918–50) and the
> fascination and repulsion of the concept of State ownership during those
> years.[31]

Since 1945 nationalisation with compensation had been 'a negligible change',
he argued, within the British economy which had not improved industrial
efficiency. It had, however, excluded 'the hopeful possibility of co-ownership'
and limited 'the beneficent increase of the value of property in private hands'.
Furthermore, no employee or consumer had been impressed by the difference
brought about by the post-war nationalisation measures, which amounted to
'State action that might have been avoided, as a waste of Parliamentary time
and Civil Service skill'.[32]

Wiles also repudiated another central aspect of socialist thought since
1945 – namely, its egalitarian thrust, that is, its emphasis on the principle of
equality of outcome. Liberals, he pointed out:

> ... have never been interested in economic equality as such, whether
> in property or in income. Our concern is with liberty, and our objec-
> tion to *extreme* wealth and *extreme* poverty is based on the recognition

that both are, in their separate ways, violations of liberty – extreme wealth because it confers privilege, extreme poverty because it stunts personality.[33]

This point of view did not, therefore, involve any objection to 'moderate gradations of wealth', which were entirely consistent with the Liberal commitment to liberty. Liberals were, instead, 'offended by economic inequality only when it is so gross that equality-before-the-law and equality of opportunity, i.e. liberty itself, are violated by it'.[34]

Sear, too, underlined this distinction between the socialist and liberal conceptions of equality, maintaining that:

> The Liberal society cannot be an egalitarian society, since freedom includes the freedom to make headway or fall back, and Liberals cannot agree to restrict the energetic in the interest of the leisurely. On the contrary we should try to ensure equality of opportunity, accepting the implications that those who seize opportunities will go faster and farther than those who do not.[35]

Wiles, however, whilst rejecting the goal of greater economic equality, observed that in late-1950s Britain 'inequalities in property ... are gross, unjust and practically unchanged since Edwardian times ...'. Since Liberals were 'outright distributists'[36], their concern was therefore to achieve a wider diffusion of property in order to advance the Liberal goal of popular ownership.

Another, and more unorthodox, expression of economic liberal ideas in *The Unservile State* was provided by the economist Alan Peacock. In his essay, 'Welfare in the Liberal State', his main concern was with the relationship between classical liberal beliefs and contemporary Liberal positions on social policy. 'To what extent,' he asked, did Liberals in the 1950s 'accept the views on social policy expounded by the great Liberal philosophers and political economists of the eighteenth and nineteenth centuries?' What principles, too, could be established to 'determine the scope and the form of State intervention in order to achieve the aims of a Liberal social policy?'. And finally, 'what reforms in our present-day social policy' were suggested by such principles?[37]

Since a Liberal society was 'primarily concerned with the freedom of the individual', Liberals were therefore obliged, Peacock argued, 'to consider carefully to what extent we must assume that such a social policy be accompanied by State provision of social services'. In agreement with Beveridge, Peacock believed that there was 'no doubt' that the fundamental principles of a Liberal social policy were, first, the achievement of 'an equitable distribution of income' through the social security system, and, second, 'the provision of more equal opportunity' through the devotion by the community of 'enough of its resources to provide social services, particularly health and education'.[38] However, like Beveridge, too, Peacock stressed the importance of voluntary action, maintaining that 'the ultimate object of a Liberal society is surely to persuade individuals to recognize their social responsibilities and to carry them out themselves'.[39]

In a Liberal society, therefore, he contended that the State should be the provider of public services only if three conditions were applicable: first, if that was 'the only way of instituting a community service because no voluntary system of charging can be introduced'; second, 'if a "natural monopoly" is likely to grow up because of restricted local demand ...'; and third, if 'State provision is more "efficient" in the sense that it uses fewer resources in order to produce the same output of (say) education or health'.[40] In the case of education, the first of those conditions, he maintained, clearly did not apply, a point that he was to develop in later writings. More generally, and with considerable foresight, Peacock advanced the case for devolution in the administration and control of public services and for greater power for local authorities over public expenditure – for example, in financing the education system by means of local taxation revenues disbursed in the form of grants.

In such ways Peacock was attempting to reconcile a commitment to the principles of Liberal social policy attuned to the world of the late 1950s with an enduring attachment to the individualist and voluntarist attitudes that characterised the Party's classical liberal heritage. Indeed, it was those attitudes which underlay his scepticism about the role of the State as the main provider of public services in certain conditions, a position that was to pervade the debate in British politics on public service reform 40 years and more later.

The advocacy in *The Unservile State* of economic liberal ideas – defence of the market economy, opposition to both nationalisation and egalitarian policies aimed at greater equality of outcome, and a questioning of the collectivist assumption that the State should be the main provider of public services – did break ground with the prevailing Butskellite consensus of the 1950s. The essayists who propounded those ideas – notably Peacock, Seear and Wiles – thus, as Richard Cockett has observed, '... gently tried to nudge the Party in a more individualistic direction'. Yet it is also true that during this period the Unservile State Group 'contained people of too diverse political and economic views to make a coherent political impact'.[41] The Group had, after all, since its formation in 1953, never been committed to a particular school of liberal thought. At the very least, however, the exposition of economic liberal views was ideologically significant in the context of the broadly collectivist tone and direction of British economic and social policy at that time. Certainly *The Unservile State* essays helped to reinforce the Liberal Party's ideological position as marking a third way between state socialism and traditional Conservatism.

The issue and cause of co-ownership which helped to define such a position, and of which Elliot Dodds had been the leading Liberal advocate, was given further theoretical elaboration in 1958 by a pamphlet written by Donald Wade, and entitled *Towards a Nation of Owners*. In advancing the case for what the Yellow Book of 1928 had referred to as 'popular ownership', Wade sketched the historical background against which private property had been vilified in socialist thought. The industrial revolution, he observed, had 'intensified the division of society into a property-owning class and a property-less class', which accounted for the popular appeal of the socialist demand for the abolition of private property and for the transfer to the State of the ownership of all the means of production, distribution and exchange.[42] Yet the socialist case, Wade argued, had rested on several 'grave fallacies', notably, 'the belief that power will no longer be abused when the capitalist system has been abolished'. That was 'one of the great illusions underlying socialist philosophy'. Socialists had 'also believed that the natural desire for ownership would be fully satisfied by the new sense of common ownership ... achieved when all industry passed into the ownership and control of the State', which would in turn provide 'an adequate incentive to replace the profit motive'. That had 'turned out to be another fallacy', since a tiny nominal share in a nationalized industry was 'too remote to have any real meaning, either for those employed in it or for the general public who are theoretically the owners'.[43] A third mistaken belief was that any of the proposed alternatives to state ownership of industry – such as acquisition by the State of shares in private industry (as advocated in the Labour Party policy statement of 1957, *Industry and Society*[44]) would 'lead to a wider distribution of individually owned capital wealth'.[45]

In place of those socialist fallacies, Wade maintained that a positive, alternative approach was needed, 'something that is demonstrably better than Socialism',[46] rather than just the Conservatives' encouragement of the trend towards monopoly capitalism. The Liberal aim, in his view, should therefore '... always be to extend the opportunities of individual ownership to more and more people', and in forms that would be 'more satisfying than the mirage of ownership which nationalization provides'.[47] For 'in the eyes of a Liberal, private ownership of property ... while bringing with it responsibilities, brings also many benefits, tangible and intangible' since it:

> ... satisfies the natural and healthy desire to have something of one's own; and it also benefits the individual owner by enlarging his liberty and increasing his security; for he who has something to fall back on in time of need is in a stronger position and better equipped to face the hazards of life than one who is solely dependent on his wage-packet'.[48]

Wade envisaged a new era in which the Liberal concept of popular ownership would become a reality, and in which the 'proletariat' and the socialist bias against private property – both products of the industrial revolution – would disappear. Workers would 'never again be regarded as a commodity to be hired by the investors of capital', and 'in this new era every citizen' would 'have a 'stake' in the country's prosperity, but in a form that is more personal, namely individual ownership'. The 'advantage and responsibilities of ownership' would therefore 'no longer be the preserve of the few'; rather, they would 'be available to all'.[49]

Wade was thus advancing the case for a third way based on the wide diffusion of property, as Elliot Dodds had done before him, a course presented as distinct from, and superior to, both monopoly capitalism, in which ownership of capital wealth was concentrated in the hands of the few, and state socialism in which ownership of entire industries was vested in a remote State. Wade was also adviser, a year later, to the Liberal Party's 1959 Ownership for All Committee, chaired by Nancy Seear. Its Report sought to bring the original 1938 Committee's statement up to date, 'adapting and extending it to meet the changed conditions of the present time', without repudiating any of its principal recommendations.[50] It focused mainly on the development of co-ownership and employee shareholding, on wider opportunities for saving, and on the elimination of monopoly.

More broadly, the 1959 Report declared that in 'the battle for the right of ownership', which had been the 'essential political struggle of the twentieth century', Liberals 'stood four-square in favour of private ownership, of ownership by persons'. They had therefore opposed the socialist movement to replace private by public ownership which had originally been inspired by 'the central doctrine of Communist and Socialist thinkers throughout the last century' – namely, 'the belief that the private ownership of the means of production, distribution and exchange is the root-cause of major economic and social ills'.[51] Moreover, in this fundamental 'political struggle' the recognition by Liberals of 'the close relationship between property and power' was for them 'a major reason for retaining the system of private property, not for abolishing it, since to hand property over to the State means a concentration of power threatening the very foundation of a Liberal society'.[52] Yet Liberal support for the right to private property was also accompanied by a realisation that the struggle against its enemies could only be won 'if it is waged in defence of a system vastly different from any yet experienced'. The Liberal aim was therefore to achieve 'a widespread diffusion of personal ownership so that all citizens have complete control over something they can truly call their own'. Such a goal was far removed from the existing maldistribution of property in Britain, which was 'scarcely more defensible than it was in the years before the war'.[53]

In defence of its fundamental aim, the 1959 Ownership for All Report cited the Yellow Book of 1928 which, in criticising a contemporary social order divided into 'a small class of owners who lived by owning and a very large class of workers whose labours enriched these owners', had declared that:

The remedy in our view is not concentration in the hands of the State but the diffusion of ownership throughout the community. We stand not for public ownership but for popular ownership. The aim must be not to destroy the owner-class, but to enlarge it.[54]

To that end, the Yellow Book had advocated co-partnership and employee shareholding in industry, both of which had also been favoured in the Party's 1938 Ownership for All Report. The 1948 Liberal Assembly had later approved a more fully developed and detailed co-ownership scheme, which the 1959 Report now updated, stating that its underlying objectives were 'to increase the status and sense of personal significance and responsibility of all and everyone in industry; and to spread more widely the wealth and power that industry creates'.[55] The Report cited contemporary analyses of the largest 500 industrial and financial companies in Britain, which underlined the fact that a comparatively small number of people held directorships in several of those companies, thereby wielding immense power. The implications, too, of the widespread existence of holding companies and interlocking directorships throughout British industry and banking were, the Report added, far-reaching. This interpretation of the pattern of power within private industry and finance was in line with the conclusions of the New Left critique of the concentration of power in the private sector published a year earlier.[56] But the inference drawn from such economic analysis by the Liberal Ownership for All Committee – in favour of popular ownership within a market economy – was clearly very different in ideological terms from the collectivist prescriptions of the New Left.

In furtherance of that goal of popular ownership, *Ownership for All* was also concerned to extend its scope beyond employee shareholdings in industry to embrace both a wider diffusion of personal savings of all kinds, through building societies, pension funds and so forth, and more widespread access to home ownership in a country in which fewer than one-third of all dwellings – 4.8 million out of 15 million – were at that time, in 1959, owner-occupied. The ideological position underlying all these proposals was crystallised in a resolution approved by the Party Council for submission to the 1959 Liberal Assembly. It stated clearly and unequivocally that:

> This Assembly condemns the existing distribution of property as emphatically as the collectivist alternative of nationalisation. It regards the widespread diffusion of ownership as a distinctive mark of a Liberal Society.[57]

In addition to these renewed commitments to co-ownership, the enduring Liberal cause of internationalism was also reaffirmed during the late 1950s. Its focus now, however, was shifted on to the newly established European Economic Community, with its underlying project of European unification. Grimond himself had initially preferred the idea of a free trade area in Europe to that of a customs union. A *Liberal News* policy statement, published in February 1957 with the Party Leader's endorsement, referred to the Inner Six – the member-states that joined the EEC at its foundation in 1957 – as a 'Customs Union', protected by a common external tariff, and to the Outer Seven – those countries which were to establish the European Free Trade Association in January 1960 – as a 'Free Trade Area'. Referring, too, to the 'Common Market' in broad terms as a union of the two groupings, the Party newspaper declared that Liberals 'support the proposal that the United Kingdom should join the Free Trade Area – not the Customs Union'.[58] The statement added that 'the more countries are committed to lowering tariffs while still free to fix the level of their tariffs against countries outside the Common Market, the more likely it is that tariffs all round will be low, so that free trade will be increased'.[59] The recommendation thus appeared to be that Britain should join the European Economic Community *only* if no external tariff were established (which was that organisation's expressed intention) and, secondly, if each country were free to determine or even abolish its own tariffs on goods imported from outside the Common Market.[60]

Such a policy position, however unrealistic in the prevailing circumstances, was at least, as Roy Douglas has observed, 'completely consistent with traditional Liberal attitudes to Free Trade'.[61] It was, however, gradually modified after Grimond changed his initial preference for a free trade area, apparently after being persuaded by his mother-in-law, Violet Bonham Carter, and Lord Layton in 1958 that the EEC offered the more promising approach to European integration and 'that an institutional dimension to European unity was more important than free trade purity'.[62] Early in 1959 the Liberal Party Committee consequently revised the Party's policy position on Europe, advocating British entry into the EEC, regardless of the question of the common external tariff.[63] The issue was not mentioned, however, in the Party manifesto for the 1959 General Election, and it was not until 1960 and thereafter that commitment to EEC entry became a distinctive feature of the Liberal programme. Indeed, it subsequently became, as Michael Steed has noted, the Party's 'most distinctive policy of the second half of the twentieth century'.[64]

Grimond's new leadership had placed, then, as we have seen, a firm emphasis on a clearer and sharper communication of Liberal policy and ideas in relation to both established and emerging themes and issues. But in addition, the late 1950s witnessed a second major change introduced through his initiative – namely, the gradual unveiling of a new strategy involving a realignment of the Left in British party politics. Aiming to create a new radical force which would eventually replace the Labour Party, Grimond first set out this strategy well before the 1959 General Election in his speech to the Liberal Assembly at Southport in September 1957[65] and, more explicitly, in November 1958 at a Liberal Rally in London, where he stated that:

> ... The long-term objective is clear: to replace the Labour Party as the progressive wing of politics in this country, to sweep in not only Liberals,

but Liberal-Socialists and Liberal-Tories. It is certain that in the sixties a fresh tide will flow with new ideas and new leaders. I say to you that has got to be a Liberal tide.[66]

Grimond's strategy of a realignment of the Left – a phrase borrowed from his brother-in-law, Mark Bonham Carter[67] – had thus already been conceived before the Labour Party was riven by its deep-rooted and bitter policy and ideological disputes of 1959–61[68]. As we shall see, Grimond was to relaunch the strategy just after the 1959 General Election, advancing and elaborating it subsequently until its virtual collapse by the winter of 1965–66.

The period from 1957 onwards was also one in which Grimond began to develop and refine his own political ideas, and as Dutton has observed: 'In time he came to dominate his party's thinking in a way that no leader had done since Lloyd George.'[69] For as one of Grimond's biographers has also noted: 'It was in policy rather than in matters of party organization that Jo left his stamp. Ideas were his stock in trade ...'[70]

About half of the Liberals' 1959 general election manifesto, *People Count*, was Grimond's own personal statement.[71] More broadly, in his numerous books, pamphlets and articles Grimond sought to give British Liberalism a new direction and impetus during this period. In a pamphlet, for example, entitled *The New Liberalism*, published early in his leadership in 1957, he outlined his personal vision of a 'humane, civilized' liberal society which would seek 'to free the personal qualities and social forces from which a good society can grow'. But in pursuit of that goal, he stressed, 'we should not rely too much on Government' since, in a liberal society:

> ... Responsibility rests with the people. Government is residual. In a healthy society, it should have a comparatively narrow field. But the field remaining to it is vital.[72]

Grimond was here expressing one of the major themes recurrent in his political thought – namely, a pragmatic and ambivalent attitude towards, even a mistrust of, the State. Throughout his political life, as Peter Barberis has observed, he 'thought that the state should do less but do it better'.[73] Over the years that view was to become more pronounced, though Grimond's mistrust of the State never degenerated into a rigid and doctrinaire anti-statism.

The New Liberalism also outlined two other recurrent themes of Grimond's political thought: a defence of a positive as well as a negative conception of liberty, and an emphasis on the need for political reform. In a liberal society the core value of liberty, he maintained, should be 'not grudgingly given, not a negative absence of restraint, but individual freedom as a positive spur'. Moreover, there was a need for 'a proper balance between individual rights and the claims of the Government, local authorities and other organizations'.[74] To that end, he advocated the reform of Parliament so that it acted as 'the watchdog of individual liberty' and as a body that represented 'the common interest above group interests' – two functions which, in his view, it did not currently perform. To rectify that situation, he called for 'electoral reform, a new Parliamentary committee system and a new Second Chamber'. He also favoured 'an overhaul of local government with the reform of finances of local authorities so as to give them greater responsibility in certain spheres and thereby encourage greater individual participation and enhance the position of the ordinary citizen'.[75] This was to be another major theme of Grimond's political thought: the emphasis on active citizenship and hence on the benefits for both civil society and representative democracy of wider citizen participation.

In another pamphlet, *The New Liberal Democracy* (1958), which appeared after the Liberal by-election victory at Torrington, Grimond outlined his thoughts on his strategy of a realignment of the Left, stating his belief 'that the place of the Socialist Party should be taken by a non-Socialist progressive party'[76] – that latter phrase being very similar to that carried by the masthead of *Liberal News* since July 1957. He further argued that the British party system was based on increasingly outdated class divisions and political issues. The important disputes in British politics were no longer, in his view, between monolithic, class-based partisan blocs, but rather between liberals and author-itarians, or nationalists and internationalists. Grimond appeared unclear, however, about the nature of a future realignment in British party politics. It might involve the establishment of a new form of three-party system, such as had existed between 1918 and 1929. Or it might entail, he thought, if Labour moved in a liberal direction, cooperation between the Liberal and Labour parties, or even the creation of 'a new party of the Left'.[77]

Grimond's first major work of political thought, *The Liberal Future*, was published the following year, in April 1959. It constitutes, in Barberis's words, Grimond's 'most extensive and explicit statement of broad politi-cal philosophy', and while 'in no way a complete theoretical treatise', it includes 'interesting refinements and developments of some of the central tenets of liberalism in the modern age'.[78] Grimond had already attempted to formulate the theoretical basis of his liberal philosophy in a 1953 article on 'The Principles of Liberalism', in which he had stated that:

> Liberalism to me is the political philosophy of British empiricism. It springs from the philosophy of Locke and Hume. A philosophy based on the individual and his experience. A philosophy profoundly suspicious of deities, innate ideas and dogma. A philosophy which finds that all our knowledge comes from experience ...'[79]

'The sheet anchors of Liberalism' therefore seemed to Grimond to be 'the individual and the continual examination of our experience'. This empirical basis thus set Liberalism 'in opposition to all abstractions, whether of the 'noble savage' or 'economic man' type or of the 'oversoul' type'. It also denied to Liberals 'pleasant dreams of an ultimate utopia', and as a consequence:

> No Liberal can believe that anything like communism or social credit, the destruction of private property or all the non-Aryan races or even the advent of compulsory profit sharing or proportional representation are going one day to produce heaven on earth. 'The troubles of our proud and angry dust are from eternity and shall not fail'.[80]

In *The Liberal Future* Grimond firmly espoused the ideal of wider citizen participation within the British political system, advocating once more the wide-ranging programme of political and constitutional reform which he had previously prescribed – including more effective scrutiny of the executive by the House of Commons, a stronger, non-hereditary Second Chamber, devolution to Scotland and Wales, and the revival of local government.[81] But he also stressed the importance of civil society and of participation by individuals within its groups and associations. 'The conditions of good political life,' he pointed out, 'depend not on direct action by the Government but on a good society.' The words 'society' and 'community' had unfortunately acquired, he lamented, 'repulsive overtones', the former reeking 'of the "Tatler", starchiness and class distinctions; the latter of prigs and busybodies and professional Sociologists: both of a stuffy, precious and wholly illiberal world'.[82] But for Grimond 'society' was to be understood in classical liberal terms as 'simply the variety of relationships which individuals feel agreeable and useful'.[83]

Moreover, he asserted in a classical liberal manner, too, not only the primacy of the individual over the State but also the ascendancy of civil society over the State. 'A society,' he pointed out, 'maintains its own organizations apart from government. It is superior to government. Government is its servant'. A hallmark of a society was also, in his view, that it was 'bound together by a general morality which is interpreted in different ways in various institutions, but which rests on the broad pillars of a general agreement'.[84] The atomised, amoral antithesis of civil society, understood in these terms, was for Grimond a proletariat since 'the proletarians are marbles in a bag', maintaining 'no institutions of their own'. A proletariat was defined solely by its relationship with a ruling group, whether that was big business or the State. Within the massed ranks of the proletariat, the subordinate group, it was apparent that:

> ... Other group relationships are feeble. All the horizontal threads are weak. The mass of undifferentiated citizens are not bound together, they are bound to the ruler.[85]

On the question of economic organisation and political economy in general, Grimond turned towards familiar ideological territory: the traditional antithesis between socialism and capitalism, which had been at the heart of political debate since 1918. Here he attacked what he called 'the wild bull attitude towards capitalism' which was characteristic of socialist thought and which implied that capitalism was 'a fundamentally dangerous beast but that it can be put to tolerably good use in the most severe straitjacket', with private industry 'under even more stringent public control'. But in Grimond's view it was 'not capitalism that is the mad bull, but Socialism' since capitalism had not only 'performed remarkable feats in the increase of wealth' but had also 'reformed many of the admitted evils which existed'.[86] Yet for socialists profits – one of the main driving-forces of capitalism – had 'a bad name because they still have the smell of "unearned" usury or the taint of exploitation'.[87] Recent Labour Party policy, he noted, alluding to the 1957 statement, *Industry and Society*, had admittedly proposed that the State should hold equity shares in private industry. But those revisionist socialists who had reached that position should then, Grimond argued, 'accept the success and serviceability of the system', and seek to ensure that it could be 'worked to the best advantage, its virtues admitted, encouraged and exploited'. Such a change in attitude, however, was 'a long way from the mad bull view of capitalism'; it was really 'the end of the road for Socialism and the beginning of Liberalism'.[88]

Grimond's overall judgment, however, on the question of the most appropriate form of economic organisation was an empirical rather than absolutist one since:

> For Liberals ... the Free Enterprise system associated with private property seems the best instrument to hand ... But we emphasize that Free Enterprise is a system, an artificial system, which can be changed.[89]

It was 'a system subject to control and alteration', the aim of which should be 'to increase the prosperity and freedom of choice of individuals, leaving a margin over for the support of communal activities'.[90]

In his defence of a market economy, Grimond also advanced a position which 20 years later would become a much-contested challenge to prevailing economic orthodoxy. He argued that inflation was a problem which should be tackled mainly through monetary policy, and not through state intervention in controlling the growth of incomes, and that:

> ... to ask Unions to moderate their demands below what employers are willing to concede because there is inflation is to cure the symptom and not the cause. It is for Government in the first place to curb currency, credit and its own spending. The Unions may have been guilty of restricting output but I doubt if they can be blamed for causing inflation, except at one remove back.[91]

In defending the free enterprise system, Grimond argued the case, too, for the wider diffusion of property that was at the heart of the Liberal cause and policy of co-ownership. That case was 'political or social as well as economic',[92] since:

> The possession of some property widens a man's choice and gives him more scope to exercise his talents. Personal ownership is one badge of a citizen as against a proletarian. It is a shield against petty tyranny ...[93]

These were beliefs central to what Geoffrey Foote has described as Grimond's conception of 'a republican political economy',[94] based on the wide dispersal of property ownership among free, independent citizens. To realise that ideal, Grimond wanted to bring about 'the transition from an industrial oligarchy to an industrial democracy'.[95] But in the oligarchic conditions which prevailed throughout much of British industry, he recognised, as Peter Wiles had done in *The Unservile State*, the significant new development of the growing divorce of industrial ownership and control whereby: 'The owners in the sense of shareholders have lost a great deal of their powers. The managers have gained in importance ...'[96]

But whereas Crosland and other revisionist socialists viewed the ideological significance of this development in terms of the erosion of the traditional link between socialist doctrine and the public ownership of the means of production, Grimond was far less sanguine about its wider implications, contending that:

> To Liberals, the splitting of ownership from management is not welcome ... A valid criticism of the present position of joint stock companies is that the risks have been greatly reduced by amalgamations, Government support or an achievement of a near monopoly in their particular line. The managers feel only the effects on their prestige if their company is unsuccessful and the shareholders are little more than rentiers.[97]

The increasing divorce of ownership and control was in fact breaking the chain of responsibility for efficiency in private industry, which was one of the 'checks and balances' of the free enterprise system through which:

> The managers and owners should directly feel the consequences of success or failure. If the managers were to become too like Civil Servants and the shareholders almost negligible the system would work imperfectly.[98]

In contrast, the schemes of co-ownership favoured by Liberals would involve the adjustment of company law to give employees equal status to that of shareholders, with the resulting growth of a body of worker-shareholders. Those changes would create conditions in industry, Grimond maintained, in which '… property can be more fairly spread, unity of purpose achieved and responsibility made real'.[99] As for traditional socialist objections to co-ownership, he observed that: 'Ever since Marx, nothing has been more alarming to Socialists than the disappearance of the proletariat'. Yet that product of the industrial revolution would be one of the casualties arising from the introduction of co-ownership. Indeed, '… there could be no better way of breaking down the worst features of class stratification'.[100]

In the epilogue of *The Liberal Future*, Grimond sought to clarify his position in relation to the ideological dispute within the Liberal Party during the 1950s between classical liberal free traders and social liberals, without referring explicitly to that debate. He made it clear that he did not adhere to that purist school of thought 'which seems to believe that if you free trade, reduce interference by the Government and let the market take its course Liberalism will flourish'.[101] The 'main reason why I do not belong to it,' he explained, was 'that it seems to assume that a Liberal world is in some sense more 'natural' than any other'. Yet the free market – 'to take that as an example of a Liberal institution' – was in reality 'a highly "artificial" arrangement' which depended on 'orderly government, impartial laws fairly enforced and a currency which is to be trusted'.[102] Roger Fulford made a similar point in his pre-election book, *The Liberal Case*, published later in 1959, when he observed that within a market economy '… the limited liability company is not a natural organism – it is a legal creation, and it is certainly not the only structure round which a free enterprise economy could have evolved'.[103]

In contrast to a purist free market position, Grimond appeared to endorse a social liberal approach in arguing that:

> … a Liberal Government must not be frightened to take positive action to promote Liberal conditions. Defence of the weak, help for the poor, eradication of evils, guardianship of scarce resources, maintenance of the coherence of society, the setting of an agenda in those fields where the Government acts, all these are part of its legitimate duties.[104]

Nevertheless, as we have seen, Grimond had also been concerned in *The Liberal Future* to emphasise his support for aspects of the Party's economic liberal heritage so cherished by the free traders. He had firmly defended a competitive market economy and decried the alternative collectivist prescriptions of state socialism – particularly nationalisation of industry. He had also advocated the containment of inflation by monetary policy rather than by governmental controls on incomes.

But as well as positioning himself deftly in relation to this long-running ideological debate, Grimond was marking out new territory in *The Liberal Future* by underlining in its pages the importance of active citizenship. He was, as Foote has suggested, reviving in Liberal terms the idea of 'a republic as an unservile society, where the independence of the citizen was based on the local community within a market economy'.[105] This reinvented form of 'republican politics' placed at its heart the wider participation of the citizen within a more decentralised political system, within the groups and associations of civil society, and within a market economy reshaped and strengthened by the benefits of popular ownership.

As the 1959 General Election approached in October of that year, the Liberal Party, in spite of its organisational and financial weaknesses, was able to field 216 candidates, nearly twice as many as in 1955. The Liberal Party's election manifesto, *People Count*, stressed, like its predecessors since 1945, the Party's unique appeal as one free of class and sectional interests. 'A Liberal vote,' it declared, 'is a protest against the British political system being divided up between two powerful machines, one largely financed by the employers and the other by the Trade Unions.'[106] Moreover, there was a 'vital task to be done,' it continued, 'in building up a Progressive alternative Party'. But so long as Labour remained 'tied to nationalization (which is part of their constitution) and financed by the vested interests of the Trade Union establishment', they would 'never broaden their appeal sufficiently to embrace all the people who want a progressive party in this country'.[107]

The Liberals' commitment to co-ownership was reaffirmed in the statement that: '... This traditionally private-enterprise country must pull together to bring about ownership for all.'[108] The manifesto therefore advocated the encouragement through tax reliefs of co-ownership and co-partnership schemes. But the traditional commitment to free trade was reduced to the bare observation that prices in the shops would be lowered 'if tariffs were reduced step by step ... and price fixing arrangements effectively banned'.[109]

People Count did, however, break new ground in two policy areas. First, it opposed the independent British nuclear deterrent, favouring instead contribution to 'a general Western Nuclear Programme',[110] in effect the NATO nuclear shield provided by the United States of America. Second, the Liberals in 1959 were the first and only party, and Grimond subsequently the only party leader during the campaign,[111] to raise the question of trade union reform. 'Restrictive practices,' the manifesto declared, 'both by management and labour must go. The causes of crippling disputes must be eliminated.' Specifically it was recommended that unions should be 'registered with the Registrar of Friendly Societies in such as a way as to ensure fair elections and prevent victimisation'.[112]

These critical references to the existing operation of British trade unions, with their collective goals and practices, together with criticisms elsewhere in the manifesto of waste in both the nationalised industries and the public services,[113] were all essentially anti-collectivist policy positions. As such, they were more likely to appeal electorally to disaffected Conservatives than to Labour's industrial working-class supporters. Yet it was the latter core Labour voters whom the Liberals needed to attract in order to bring to fruition Grimond's strategy of a realignment of the Left, which largely hinged, after all, on the prospect of the Liberals replacing Labour as the main progressive party in British politics. This was a contradiction at the heart of that strategy which would eventually serve to undermine it over the next few years.

Nevertheless, the Liberals' performance at the 1959 General Election, held on 8 October, was a considerable improvement on 1955. The Party more than doubled both its total national vote, which rose to 1.6 million, and its overall vote share, which was increased to 5.9 per cent. This was in spite of the fact that, as William Wallace has recalled, Party organisation was 'ramshackle and underfinanced', projecting the image of 'a party of enthusiastic amateurs without a real sense of power'.[114] Indeed, because of these shortcomings, the Liberals were unable in 1959, as David Butler and Richard Rose commented in their subsequent election study, to 'mount anything like a full-scale national campaign or join effectively in the exchanges between the major rivals'. As a consequence, they 'appeared in the election as the largest of the minor parties, a federation of independently operating candidates, rather than a broad national movement'.[115]

For all that, an increase in the total Liberal vote to 1.6 million clearly marked an advance. Yet, as in 1955, only six Liberal MPs were returned. The Party's greatest electoral support in 1959 still came from its traditional heartlands – south-west England, the West Riding of Yorkshire, rural Wales and northern Scotland – where the domination of the two major parties had failed to penetrate. What was significant, however, was that, under Grimond's leadership, the Liberal Party was beginning to acquire a clearer political identity, shaped by a firm commitment to traditional causes and by a concern with emerging contemporary issues, and sharpened by Grimond's own emphasis on the value of active citizenship through wider participation. It was the latter idea that was emerging in his political thought, as Sell has noted, as 'the carat of modern Liberal politics', distinguishing Liberalism from both 'the bureaucratic elitism of Socialism and the social elitism of the major strands of Conservatism'.[116] It underlay a distinctive political approach, which, while drawing upon the economic liberal as well as the social reforming aspects of the Party's ideological heritage, could serve to enhance the Liberals' recently rediscovered, post-Suez role as Britain's only non-socialist progressive party.

Chapter 3
Of Progress, Realignment and Disappointed Hopes: 1959–1967

In the immediate aftermath of the 1959 General Election, Jo Grimond turned again to the promotion of his case for a realignment of the Left in British politics. In an interview in *The Observer*, he even appeared to suggest that he wanted some kind of alliance with the Labour Party, for 'otherwise the Left may be in opposition for years and years'.[1] Grimond doubted, however, whether the Labour Party could resolve the deep-rooted policy and ideological disputes – particularly over public ownership and Clause Four of Labour's Constitution – in which it was then embroiled. Alluding to the controversy sparked by Hugh Gaitskell's Leader's speech at the 1959 Labour Party Conference, Grimond commented that:

> ... You can't have a doctrine which is ostensibly founded on the belief of the rightness of Socialism and the wrongness of capitalism ... submitted to the sort of examination which is going on now in Blackpool.[2]

Four months later, after Gaitskell was forced to retreat from his objective of amending Clause Four, Labour's compromise policy document, *Labour's Aims*, which was soon dubbed the 'New Testament', was mocked by Grimond in appropriately Biblical terms:

> The real New Testament was not written because a Gallup poll showed that the Old Testament was unpopular. It was written because there was a fiery new prophet who said what he meant ...[3]

Grimond referred explicitly to Labour's fierce dispute over public ownership in an article in the *New Statesman* published shortly after the 1959 election. Here he tentatively offered a route that might be taken by Labour moderates sympathetic to the prospect of realignment. He drew a clear distinction between those 'fervid state socialists' with whom Liberals could never agree and the bulk of the Labour Party which 'now accepts Keynesian economics – the liberal alternative to socialism'. But he also identified

Labour's continuing commitment to public ownership, its 'central constitutional doctrine', as '... one of the difficulties ... in any revival of a radical movement on the Left of politics'. Historically, too, he noted that it had been '... a grossly over-simplified analysis of the ills of industrial society that led to the conclusion that the cure lay solely in a change of ownership'. There was in fact 'no one simple, glorious formula', and he conceded that it was 'not a matter of scrubbing out nationalisation and writing co-ownership on the banners'.[4]

Grimond made clear, however, that he accepted the view 'that a high proportion of the growing wealth of the country should not only be used for communal purposes within and without the country but also that we should maintain areas of life where the profit motive does not count'. Instead of the established boundary in the economy between state and private ownership of industry, 'a more useful distinction', he believed, lay in 'the possibility of non-profit-making as against profit-making activities'.[5] He had earlier made the same point in *The Liberal Future* where he argued that there was '... undoubtedly a field for public management not always being exercised by the Government'. The choice in this respect was 'not primarily between Free Enterprise and Nationalization', but rather 'between the tasks done for profit and those which are not'.[6] Nevertheless, Labour's traditionally hostile attitude towards private enterprise remained for Grimond a major obstacle in the path of realignment, which would not be feasible ideologically until Labour came to embrace, rather that merely tolerate, a market-oriented mixed economy.

By the spring of 1962 Grimond was offering further justification for his strategy of realignment, arguing that it was based on a more realistic dividing-line in British politics between progressives and conservatives, with the Liberals forming the nucleus of a new progressive grouping. He thus maintained that:

> The divisions in politics fall in the wrong place. The natural breakdown should be into a Conservative Party, a small group of convinced Socialists in the full sense, and a broadly based progressive Party. It is the foundations of the last named that the Liberal Party seeks to provide.[7]

Such a restructuring of party groupings clearly depended on a major split occurring within the Labour Party, something to which many observers did seem possible between 1959 and 1962. Labour's third successive defeat in 1959, and subsequent evidence of a greater number of voters defecting to the Liberals from Labour than from the Tories, an unusual phenomenon in the post-1945 period,[8] led some revisionist socialists to break out in controversial directions. Douglas Jay, for example, even suggested changing the Labour Party's name and raised the possibility of some kind of arrangement with the Liberals.[9] Much later, Roy Jenkins also confirmed the fact that he and Grimond had discussed informally the feasibility of both coalitions and realignment.[10] In reality, however, Liberal advance was to depend more on the growing unpopularity of the Conservative Government after 1960 than on Labour's factional strife. Dissidents on Labour's moderate wing were aware, too, of the Liberals' lack of bargaining power in the wake of the 1959 election.[11]

In addition to this strategy of realignment of the Left, the other major innovation of Grimond's leadership was, as we have seen, his emphasis on the clearer formulation and dissemination of Liberal ideas and policy. This process was developed further after 1959. The New Directions policy groups, for instance, first established by Grimond in 1958, launched a series of pamphlets from 1960 onwards. The New Orbits Group, too, was formed in early 1960 by a joint committee of the two wings of the Liberal youth movement – namely, the Union of Young Liberals and the Union of University Liberal Societies (later the Union of Liberal Students) – acted as a ginger group, promoting new policy ideas and strongly supporting Grimond's realignment strategy.

This sharper focus on the presentation of Liberal ideas and policy was also apparent after 1959 at a more formal organisational level in the activities of the Party's recently created Research Department, headed by Harry Cowie. This became the source of new policy statements on such themes as modernisation of the economy, decentralisation of government, industrial co-ownership, parliamentary and electoral reform, and the reordering of Britain's foreign policy priorities and commitments.

The cumulative effect of all these developments upon the public perception of the Liberal Party appeared at the time to be generally favourable. As William Wallace later recalled of that period:

> The combination of a youthful leader, a set of policies which emphasized the transformation and adaptation of economy, society, and foreign policy, and the novelty and freshness of the Party itself contributed to a distinctive and appealing image ...[12]

Modernisation – economic, political and social – emerged in fact, along with internationalism, as one of the two dominant themes underlying this burst of Liberal thinking and policy-making during the early 1960s. In the first place, it was expressed in a heightened emphasis on the need for a transformation of the British economy and, within it, British industry. This was crystallised, for instance, in a New Directions pamphlet, *Growth Not Grandeur*, published in Grimond's name in April 1961, but, as he later recalled, 'written under the influence of Harry Cowie, possibly at his dictation'.[13] This contained wide-ranging technocratic, and in some cases fairly 'dirigiste', policy proposals for national economic regeneration, which included annual growth targets set by government and designed to co-ordinate the long-term plans of private industry, together with a five-year plan for industrial expansion to be implemented through the creation of 'an independent growth agency similar to the French "Commissariat de Plan" ... with a programme and a staff of experts'.[14]

These prescriptions were based on a diagnosis of Britain's economic ills which, as Andrew Gamble has noted, was at that time rapidly gaining acceptance among British economists.[15] Among the various causes of national economic under-performance cited in that diagnosis were: the undue emphasis by successive British governments on the protection of sterling as an international reserve currency; a commitment to high levels of overseas military expenditure deemed necessary to sustain the illusion of Britain's continuing world power status; the frequent recourse to deflationary and stop-go policies in order to avoid devaluation of sterling; and periodic balance-of-payments deficits, with consequent financial crises.

Endorsing that analysis, *Growth Not Grandeur* maintained that the Liberal Party had long championed the cause of economic and industrial reform in the face of Britain's economic malaise, which was all too evident in 'strikes, high taxation with poor returns, a declining ability to pay our way in the world, insufficient use of our men and machines and a constantly debased currency ...' But neither the Tories nor Labour had 'shown any capacity to push through the necessary reforms', and the penalty that would be paid for such negligence would be Britain's eventual 'decline into a third-rate economy or a third-rate power – the 51st State of America or one of Europe's offshore islands'.[16]

The Liberals' programme of economic modernisation through indicative planning was reinforced, too, by an increased emphasis on the redirection of British foreign policy away from the illusory pursuit of world power status, and hence from its corollary of high levels of overseas military expenditure, towards wholehearted acceptance of a European role. The case for this recommended policy shift was strengthened by the evidence of Britain's poor economic performance – in terms of the rate of growth of both production and exports – during this period compared with the record of the EEC member states.

The case for British entry into the EEC had already been advanced in a written statement agreed in July 1960 by an all-party group of MPs, whose Liberal signatories included Grimond, Clement Davies, Arthur Holt and Jeremy Thorpe. The Liberal Assembly at Eastbourne in September 1960, the best attended since the War, endorsed that case after it had been put by Mark Bonham Carter, presenting it, as Roy Douglas has recalled, 'in terms designed to win support from convinced free traders'. For 'the whole point,' Bonham Carter argued, 'of Britain going into a wider free trade area was that she would be better able to persuade other nations on free trade liberalisation for the benefit of all countries'.[17] The Liberal Party in 1960 thus became the first mainstream British party to support the UK's membership of, and participation in, the European Economic Community. It did so because it was firmly committed not only to its post-Suez concern with modernisation – of Britain's economy, political institutions and foreign policy priorities – but also to the related, and more longstanding, Liberal cause of internationalism, which since the late 1950s had acquired an increasingly European focus.

The interaction of these two dominant Liberal themes of the early to mid-1960s was reflected in a 1962 essay by Mark Bonham Carter, one of the Party's leading advocates of British membership of the EEC. Entitled, 'Liberals and the Political Future', the essay was published in *Radical Alternative*, the first book produced by the Oxford Liberal Group, which had been founded in October 1959 and, chaired by the historian, R. B. McCallum, included Lord Beveridge among its founding members. In his essay, Bonham Carter lucidly explored an issue that had concerned Jo Grimond since the late 1950s – namely, that the process of modernisation so needed in Britain in the second half of the 20th century was being impeded politically by the Labour Party. For the many 'built-in disadvantages' from which it suffered prevented it, Bonham Carter argued, from becoming the radical alternative to the Conservatives.[18]

In the first place, Labour was 'historically a socialist party' and that 'albatross' still hung around its neck, 'scaring away voters and forcing leaders of the party to spend their time defending ideas in which they no longer believe instead of pursuing radical objectives of urgent importance'. In particular, the Labour Party remained committed to nationalisation – an idea that had 'played an altogether exaggerated part in British politics since the war', owing mainly to 'the conservatism of political thought in the Labour Party', together with 'its inflexibility'.[19]

Second, Labour was also, Bonham Carter observed, manifestly a class party; it was 'committed to the idea of the working class as a solid and identifiable unit in the body politic'. But in the light of social change in Britain, that view of 'the homogeneity of the working class' was really 'a wasting asset'; and yet Labour must, he surmised, 'with one half of its mind, actively desire the working class to remain homogeneous and proletarian', since such a condition was, after all, 'the source' of the party's strength. That was 'hardly a progressive point of view'; for it led the trade unions 'to concentrate on the wrong objectives: to prefer workers to be wage earners rather than property owners; to neglect the task of breaking down the barriers which separate staff from shop floor; to pour cold water on schemes which encourage participation and which could help to destroy the distinctions between the various grades in industry'.[20] A third and related disadvantage was that Labour was in reality 'hobbled by its connection with the trade union movement, the source of its finance and among the most conservative forces in the country'.[21] In both the industrial and political wings of the Labour movement many of the unions' established practices, Bonham Carter contended, were in need of radical reform, requiring, for instance, the election of union officers by secret ballot and changing the block-vote system at Labour Party conferences.

Finally, there was the question of the Labour Party's attitude towards Europe. Labour 'looked on the radical experiments which were developing in Europe', Bonham Carter noted wryly, '... with all the jaundiced scepticism of the Football Association towards European teams'.[22] Labour's inability to adapt its ideas and policies in that and other areas was due in part to 'the meagre quality of its intellectual inheritance'. While that might seem, he conceded, 'a strange charge to bring against a party which is generally accused of being dominated by intellectuals', nonetheless the reality was, in his view, that 'the leading Socialist thinkers of the 1920s and 1930s added singularly little that was new to political thought'. For Cole and Laski, in particular, were 'expositors of other people's ideas', who 'translated a vigorous nineteenth-century doctrine into an emasculated form which they thought (wrongly) suitable to the British political climate'. They 'were hardly pioneers', but 'rather teachers who made converts among their pupils'.[23] In contrast, the 'most important contribution to the political thought of that period', Bonham Carter pointed out, had come instead from a Liberal economist, Maynard Keynes. The adoption of his ideas 'helped, as he knew it would, those who wished to develop some kind of managed free enterprise and undermined the position of those to whom capitalism and the profit motive in any form were anathema'. Another Liberal, too, William Beveridge, had been, he added, 'the most influential academic practitioner in the political field', whose social policy ideas, 'by extending the scope and efficiency' of the welfare measures introduced by the pre-1914 Liberal government, had 'helped to protect the individual from the harsher consequences of capitalism and lowered the social and political temperature of the times'.[24]

This assessment of the limited contribution of Labour's intellectuals of the 1920s and 1930s to the climate of British political thought appeared generally fair and incisive, all the more so in comparison with the impact of Keynes and Beveridge upon the whole course of post-war British politics. In 1962, however, Bonham Carter's strictures hardly did justice to the contemporary development of revisionist socialist thought, particularly in the writings of Anthony Crosland and Douglas Jay.[25] Nonetheless, these critical comments formed part of a theoretical explanation of why Labour's 'built-in disadvantages' seemed to Bonham Carter, as to Grimond, to render that party ill-equipped to play the leading role in the modernisation – political, economic and social – of contemporary Britain.

The policy instrument chosen by the Liberal Party in the early 1960s as the technocratic means of achieving modernisation in the economic sphere – namely, indicative planning – was given its most elaborate theoretical justification to date in Liberal terms in a 1963 pamphlet written by Desmond Banks. In a 1963 Unservile State Paper, *Liberals and Economic Planning*, Banks provided a carefully argued defence of 'the underlying Liberal attitude to government planning'.[26] Pointing out that 'Liberal principles are not, in the first instance, economic' and that 'Liberalism is not a theory of economic organisation',[27] Banks maintained that ever since *Britain's Industrial Future* in 1928, the Liberal Party, whilst rejecting the socialist policy instruments of widespread state ownership of industry and central state planning of production, had accepted that the State had certain policy responsibilities in the economy, specifically in respect of the monetary system, transport, power and schemes for national development to tackle unemployment. The Party's current proposals for state intervention in the economy had in fact evolved 'from the ideas of the Yellow Book'. Indeed, they followed 'a logical line from the reforms of the pre-1914 Asquith Government, through the Yellow Book to the modern Liberal programme'.[28]

Whilst tracing this social liberal lineage, Banks stressed, too, the fact that over the years the Liberal Party had adopted both collectivist and individualist proposals in the formulation of its policies. The social security system and state intervention in the economy were clearly examples of the former; measures to spread personal ownership and to attack monopolistic practices were examples of the latter. He pointed out, however, that:

> ... the general development of Liberal thought on economic planning, on the relation of the state to industry has been consistent. It has certainly not been consistent in terms of individualism versus collectivism ... It has been consistent in terms of the basic Liberal principle of the need to see that all action is part of a design to give all men true economic freedom to match political liberty[29]

'Individualism by itself,' Banks observed, 'does not ensure economic liberty', which he defined broadly as embracing the freedom to set up enterprises, freedom from poverty, unemployment and squalor, and equality of opportunity. But on the other hand, 'collectivism without limit ultimately destroys political liberty'. Modern Liberalism therefore sought 'to use a balance of the two to secure economic liberty without destroying political liberty and individual initiative'. Moreover, in addressing that problem, the Liberal Party did so, he claimed, 'with no emotional bias, no doctrinaire prejudices, no clear inhibitions and no sectional interest'.[30]

Banks had thus attempted not only to locate the Liberal Party's current policy commitments within its social liberal tradition, but also to confirm their broad compatibility with its economic liberal heritage. He then proceeded, however, to advocate a set of collectivist proposals which appeared only loosely related to that heritage. Designed to achieve 'a sustained expansion of the economy', in contrast to the effects of the stop-go policies pursued by post-war British governments, the Liberal Party's recently adopted five-year plan for the economy, he explained, would involve the government seeking the voluntary cooperation of industry in reviewing estimated labour requirements, in developing methods of increasing exports to sustain expansion, and in coordinating investment planning throughout the economy as a whole. Furthermore, this planning process would be supervised by a Minister of Expansion, acting as the senior government minister in the field of economic policy, with the Chancellor and Treasury playing a subsidiary role, and with the newly created Ministry of Expansion guiding both the Board of Trade and the Ministry of Labour.[31]

In spite of the 'dirigiste' appearance of such proposals, Banks was concerned to stress that 'the essence of Liberal planning' was 'that it should be in the main indicative and persuasive', with government therefore, as on the Continent, indicating targets, and the methods of attaining them, to private industry, rather than directing and coercing it. Labour, by contrast, believed that further extension of public ownership was intimately connected to its own interpretation of economic planning, and had 'a tendency to rely on controls for control's sake', favouring a directive and coercive, rather than indicative, approach. Furthermore, as 'a sectional Party', like its Conservative opponents, Labour was 'consequently less well placed than the Liberal Party to secure support from all sections of the community'.[32]

In addition, Banks maintained that, since Liberalism was 'essentially internationalist', the Liberal Party did 'not seek any form of planning for expansion on a national basis which cannot be reconciled with the increasing liberation of international trade'.[33] The assumption here was that the Liberal approach to planning could readily be combined with active support for British membership of the European Economic Community, even though that organisation was committed to a Common External Tariff, which would be established five years later, in 1968. But in the context of his advocacy of indicative planning, Banks's related point was that 'much of the Labour hostility to Britain's entry into the Common Market was based on a fear that socialist national planning would be impossible in an international community'. The Conservatives, on the other hand, 'although forced by events to view the prospect of trade liberation with greater favour ... than formerly', were nevertheless, he claimed, 'protectionist by tradition and reluctant and unenthusiastic internationalists'.[34]

In spite of Banks's emphasis on the distinctive character of Liberal economic planning, its overall approach was clearly technocratic and statist, albeit attuned to the modernising mood and climate of the early 1960s. In contrast, however, a significant restatement of an economically liberal approach to social policy had appeared two years earlier in an Unservile State Paper written by the economist Alan Peacock, and entitled *The Welfare Society*. Developing further views expounded in his 1957 *Unservile State* essay, Peacock observed that justification for the welfare state, if not presented in terms of the redistribution of income, tended to be based 'on one of two grounds: the necessity for paternalism because people in the main cannot look after themselves, or the necessity for nationalized social services because nationalization is the most efficient way of providing the services'. But, he continued, '... if we are consistent in our application of Liberal principles we can hardly regard its [the welfare state's] methods as satisfactory in the long run'. Indeed, it was his view that: 'The true object of the Welfare State, for the Liberal is to teach people how to do without it'.[35]

The long-term social policies consistent, Peacock maintained, with 'the principles of a liberal society' might well, therefore, 'be far removed from present practice'. Liberals believed, for instance, 'that individual responsibility can be fostered by the diffusion of the ownership of capital', through encouraging either co-ownership schemes in industry or wider home ownership. To realise that aim, he proposed 'the transfer of ownership of houses and flats from local authorities to the tenants',[36] in effect involving the sale of council homes on a very long lease with local authorities acting merely as ground landlords. The essence of his proposal thus anticipated Conservative government policy and legislation introduced, amid much publicity and controversy, more than 20 years later during the 1980s. As for the funding of public services, Peacock pointed out that in Britain it was 'often assumed that taxation is the only form of finance which is politically or administratively possible'. But while there might be 'much to be said for the view that educational and health services should be operated by the State', that did not, in his opinion, imply 'that they must be financed almost exclusively by taxation'.[37]

Shortly after the promotion of these contrasting policy ideas, Jo Grimond's second major work of political thought, *The Liberal Challenge*, was published in October 1963. While this did not amount to such an extended exposition of his broad liberal philosophy as his earlier work, *The Liberal Future*, it did contain more detailed policy proposals over a wide range of issues, together with further interesting theoretical reflections. His aim, he explained, had not been to write a manifesto or a statement of Party policy, but rather, by 'taking in hand the thread by which Liberals must keep their direction, to think through the political system and find out how it must be changed to suit the modern world'.[38] The contemporary Liberal theme of the need for change and modernisation in Britain was underlined at the outset when, surveying the state of the nation in the early 1960s, he reflected: 'Like some other countries, exhausted from their imperial efforts, we have seemed to settle down into a torpid conservatism fed on dreams of past or future grandeur ...'[39]

In his conception of a Liberal society, Grimond stressed once more the moral primacy of the individual, pointing out that Liberals '... believe that loyalty to human beings must come before any political doctrine: individuals must not be subordinated to "historical necessity", creed, race or the glorification of any nation or state'. Liberals, therefore, 'would oppose to Communism, not another political Utopia of the same sort, but a way of life which is always trying to approximate to an ideal society in which individual states of mind and individual relations are paramount'.[40]

Moreover, for Grimond, Liberalism as an ideology was not primarily a theory of economic organisation. It was 'not about "laissez-faire" or Free Trade or indeed any economic doctrine'; rather it was 'about the broader questions of humanity and society or, if about economics, then about the wider sort of political economy on which Adam Smith wrote'.[41] If, in terms of underlying values, socialism was about the pursuit of equality, then, in his view, 'an equivalent shorthand description of Liberalism' was 'that it is about Freedom and Participation'. Of those three core ideas and values, which were 'fundamental to the Left in politics', Liberals, he maintained, believed 'that Participation at present is the one which needs developing most as far as Britain is concerned'.[42] More broadly, Grimond observed, too, that the adjective 'liberal' denoted something more even than liberty or freedom. It also implied generosity of behaviour and 'lavishness', thereby evoking 'ideas of breadth and lightness, reason and beauty', qualities, contributing to the 'humanity' of Liberalism, which needed to be underlined in the contemporary political climate. [43]

As in his earlier work, *The Liberal Future*, Grimond revisited, too, the major ideological fault-line in European politics since 1918: the choice between socialism and capitalism as forms of economic organisation. Here he clearly reaffirmed Liberal support for the latter, maintaining that 'the competitive system and a free market on the whole seem the best means to wealth, freedom and choice'. But as he had done previously, he also made clear that his view on that central question was an empirical rather than an absolutist one; for competition and the free market were 'means to ends' and had to be 'subordinated to the good of society ...'.[44] Private enterprise, in the Liberal view, 'should contribute to communal as well as individual well-being', and since it could 'only flourish in an orderly community', should therefore be required by the community 'to conform to certain rules, make its payment to common expenditure and assist in a common purpose'. Nevertheless, 'Liberals,' he stressed, 'favour private enterprise. Let that be said unequivocally'; for it was 'an important freedom and a protection for private liberties which will wither if the State takes too much power into its own hands'.[45]

In *The Liberal Challenge*, Grimond sought, however, to reconcile this defence of a market economy with the type of economic planning which the Liberal Party had been advocating since 1960. He insisted that the Party's approach to this issue had 'no edge of hostility to private enterprise in it', and indeed that Liberal planning, among its other tasks, was 'charged ... with the creation of the conditions in which private enterprise can flourish'. That might involve 'experiments in new forms of industrial ownership and management'. In some instances even, he suggested, 'a partnership between public and private control might be fruitful'. In general, it was his pragmatic view that: 'The antithesis between free enterprise and public management is not absolute.'[46]

Grimond was concerned, too, to contrast this flexible Liberal approach with the type of economic planning 'brought into disrepute' by the Labour Government of 1945–50, an approach that 'was confused with nationalization and the ambivalent view of private industry held by Socialists'.[47] Liberals, by contrast, wanted planning 'of a type which relies on fiscal measures, skilful management of currency and credit and the sophisticated techniques of guiding the economy as a whole rather than imposing clamps on this operation or that'.[48]

The trend in Liberal thinking and policy after 1960 towards a technocratic and collectivist approach was nonetheless endorsed in this advocacy of indicative economic planning, even if that policy was presented by Grimond in somewhat muted terms. That trend was offset, however, by his clear restatement of the Liberal case for co-ownership as the remedy for the 'antiquated and self-destructive' attitude towards the 'two sides' of industry. It was a remedy, moreover, applied to the field of industrial relations 'in which Liberal ideas on participation … are particularly relevant'.[49] Schemes for profit-sharing and shared ownership would enable, Grimond argued, employees to take a share in both the main elements in industry, that is, wage/salary costs and residual profits, which at present reflected the distinct and opposed interests of two 'sharply differentiated groups' – the wage and salary earners, on the one hand, and the owners, on the other. That 'sharp division' of interests was the source of friction in industry, which in turn fuelled the demand for nationalisation. Indeed, it was 'because of the fact that the vast percentage of the wealth of the country is owned by a tiny fraction of the population that the capitalist system as at present organized' was, in Grimond's view, 'fundamentally unstable'. The wider participation, through co-ownership, of employees in the companies in which they worked would therefore ensure that more people had an appreciation of how the interests represented by wages/salaries and profits coincided, as well as at times conflicted. That would consequently enable more employees to feel 'an identification with our mixed economy system', thereby fostering industrial harmony.[50]

In *The Liberal Challenge*, Grimond also addressed another enduring Liberal concern and theme, internationalism, in an attempt to consider 'political change in a wider field – in Europe, I hope, and eventually in an even wider embracing frame'.[51] He recognised that the present age was one in which 'the nation state is inevitably shedding its pretension to be the ultimate fount of all sovereignty'.[52] Britain, he thought, 'perhaps more than ever', needed, therefore, to 'clarify her ideas on the political means of pooling sovereignty with other countries',[53] a process that should be accompanied, in his view, by the measures of political decentralisation within Britain which he favoured. Envisaging the possible promotion within Europe, in some way, of federalism (a word, he warned, which 'I think it wise to use as little as possible in this context just because it can mean so many things'[54]),

Grimond considered that it would be necessary 'to release sovereignty downwards as well as upwards'. Scotland and Wales should thus not only be granted autonomy in certain policy areas, but should also be 'allowed representation in the European as well as the British structure of government'.[55] On this question of European federalism, he noted, however, that historically all 'the greatest empires', including the British and Russian, had 'tended towards centralization, until in some cases the reassertion of nationality has disrupted them'. Only, he suggested, 'by developing a new political philosophy and new institutions can Europe avoid the same fate'.[56]

In the final part of *The Liberal Challenge* Grimond developed further the case for his strategy of a realignment of the Left in Britain. In a broad historical overview of the development of the progressive forces in British politics, he observed that state socialism had emerged towards the end of the 19th century as part of a humanitarian response to the social and economic ills that had arisen in the wake of the industrial revolution. Socialist ideas had been embraced in the search for 'some creed which might satisfy morality and a desire for the common good ...'. But in the process, the entire progressive movement had been 'infected by the natural and proper belief that a great deal of good could be achieved by state action'.[57] Yet the State, 'from which so much had been hoped, proved as spurious a god as the supposedly automatic checks of "laissez-faire"'. In fact it had proved at times 'far worse' a god since 'from the elevation of the state above individuals, and from the belief that somehow it could evoke the eternal spirit of a people, flowed the evils of Communism and Nazism and two world wars'.[58] In counterfactual speculation, Grimond wondered, however, whether:

> If there had been no First World War, if there had been a synthesis of Liberals and Labour in 1929, if Guild Socialism or Sydicalism had not been rejected, we might have had a continuation of the main flood of progressive thought. But we did not. Belief in the state and state Socialism dominated politics between the wars. This was to be the main road forward for the Left.[59]

As for the contemporary British Labour Party, it had, in Grimond's view, certain innate conservative tendencies. It had, as Mark Bonham Carter had also noted, 'a vested interest' in maintaining the class system. It was also 'the Party which all too often appears as the champion of the more conservative lobbies in the economy – the protector of obsolete branch lines and restrictive industrial practices'.[60] Those people who, on the other hand, 'went into the Tory Party to make it a Party of progress and reform' had achieved, Grimond maintained, 'no more success than most wives who marry debauched husbands hoping to reclaim them'. The Conservative Party was 'not a home for liberals', and indeed since conservatism was 'an important element in politics', why, he asked, should it be? A Conservative party was in fact 'necessary for the political mixture' in Britain, but it 'should not dominate it,' he stressed, 'as it has done for almost fifty years'.[61]

With regard to the future alignment of British party politics, Grimond speculated in very broad terms, as he had done since the late 1950s, about its likely shape. Three parties were 'perfectly consistent with the British system', but if the two-bloc arrangement were to continue, then 'the natural division', in his view,

> ... would be a Conservative Party faced by two Parties of change, the larger of which would be a liberal, radical Party embracing as well as the Liberal Party some people now voting Conservative and a large part of the Labour Party; the smaller being a Socialist Party.[62]

Grimond was, however, 'under no illusion about the difficulties' that lay ahead, nor about 'the length of the road before the Liberal Party asserts itself as the main progressive force' in British politics. The next general election, due by October 1964 at the latest, would 'only be a step on the way'. He recognised, too, that the historical fact 'that Britain has not suffered revolution, defeat nor occupation has made it harder for her than for her European neighbours to set about the spring-cleaning she needs'.[63] But in spite of this caution *The Liberal Challenge* clearly conveyed, as one of his biographers has observed, 'Grimond's feeling that the carapace of the political system may have cracked, that the essential foundations of a political realignment could be in place'.[64] He subsequently felt emboldened to pursue that strategy a little further, up to and beyond the forthcoming general election.

The year 1962, which preceded the publication of *The Liberal Challenge*, had witnessed a remarkable rise in the Liberal Party's fortunes. In March at a by-election in Orpington, in the heart of the London commuter belt, Eric Lubbock had overturned a Tory majority of 14,760 to win the seat with a majority of 7,855. It seemed an historic breakthrough, and was indeed, as Chris Cook has described it, 'the most sensational by-election since East Fulham in October 1933'.[65] In its immediate aftermath the moniker 'Orpington Man' was subsequently coined 'as a symbol of the upwardly aspiring, professional, suburban middle-class commuter'.[66] In the following May local council elections the Liberals achieved 567 gains, 400 of them from the Conservatives. There were, however, no further Liberal gains in the 16 parliamentary by-elections held in 1962, though the Liberal vote averaged a respectable 28 per cent. Another notable sign of recovery lay in the rise in Party membership, which peaked at 350,000 in 1963, compared with 75,000 ten years earlier.

But in spite of these encouraging developments the two major parties were beginning to challenge or even erode the distinctiveness of the Liberals' credentials and appeal as modernisers and internationalists. The Macmillan Government, though appearing politically tired and under increasing strain, evident, for instance, in the Cabinet reshuffle of July 1962, nevertheless introduced measures designed to modernise and galvanise an ailing economy. Along the lines broadly advocated by the Liberals since 1960, the Conservative government thus implemented a formal, if limited, incomes policy, supervised by a National Incomes Commission established in 1962, and committed itself, too, to indicative economic planning embodied in the National Economic Development Council, founded that same year. In addition, Macmillan applied to join the European Economic Community in 1961, before being blocked by an uncompromising de Gaulle two years later.

Meanwhile, following the sudden death of Hugh Gaitskell in January 1963, his successor as Leader of the Labour Party, Harold Wilson, increasingly positioned himself as a moderniser, favouring change and innovation in the economic and industrial – though not the political – fields. This was epitomised by his speech at the Scarborough Labour Party Conference in October 1963, in which he promoted his vision of a scientific and technological revolution sweeping through Britain. Wilson's skilful elaboration of this theme, which served, too, as a means of containing Labour's deep-seated policy and ideological differences at that time, thus also had the effect, as William Wallace has observed, of emulating, and thereby diluting, 'the Liberal appeal as a modernizing and innovating force in a stagnant society'.[67]

Nevertheless, Grimond made strenuous and eloquent efforts during this period to preserve a distinctive Liberal voice. In a wide-ranging and celebrated speech at the Liberal Assembly in Brighton in September 1963, in which he promised 'to march my troops towards the sound of gunfire', he advanced once more the case for modernising the institutions of a country which had become in many ways a '20th Century Ruritania'. Britain in 1963 remained, he declared, a class-ridden country in which '... to have a title, to have the right background, to know the right people, is more important than to know your job'. 'No establishment in the world,' he observed, was 'so concerned with titles and decorations as is official Britain. Nor is any governing class so concerned with prestige and so anxious about status rating'.[68]

A few months later, in a keynote speech in July 1964, Grimond also launched a 'Liberal Charter for New Men'. Emphasising the need for greater promotion opportunities and higher rewards for people with skills and qualifications, he argued that: 'We shall not get abundance into our generation unless the people who understand and lead the technological revolution – the new men – are given their heads.'[69] This appeal to a rising new middle class was to form much of the basis of the Liberals' 1964 General Election manifesto. In the aftermath of that election, Grimond was to reaffirm the fact that the Liberal Charter was directed at 'the new men and women, the professional and technically trained people, the younger executives and trade unionists [who] do indeed want modernisation',[70] people who regarded the Tories as mired in the past yet who also rejected Labour's state socialist dogmas, what Grimond called the 'dead weight in its luggage'.[71]

This conviction that only the Liberal Party could therefore provide the modernising force that Britain needed, thereby meeting the aspirations of 'the new men and women', was reinforced by Harry Cowie in his *Why Liberal?*, a book published for the 1964 General Election which underlined the Liberals' credentials in terms regularly expressed since 1945: namely, that they were the only British party free of class and sectional interests. 'More and more people,' Cowie claimed, were 'realizing that only a party which has a strong sense of liberal values and no vested interests to protect will create a new spirit of partnership out of our class-ridden society ...'[72] Meanwhile, 'the New Men', he maintained, found themselves 'frustrated and challenged at every turn, not only by the Whitehall machine, but by the established interest groups and the sheer impersonality of modern industrial organization'.[73]

The Liberals' 1964 General Election manifesto, *Think for Yourself – Vote Liberal* clearly echoed those views. Based on the work of the Party's Research Department, headed by Cowie, it offered a wide-ranging policy programme which welded together the themes of modernisation and internationalism and was strengthened at the same time by traditional Liberal commitments. The Liberal Party, the manifesto declared, offered the electorate 'a radical, non-Socialist alternative'. A decisive Liberal influence in the next Parliament, it claimed, would ensure 'that change and growth are stimulated' by the technological revolution, and would also enable Britain to play 'a new and greater part as a pioneer of the new international order that mankind so badly needs' in order to contain the 'giant risks of the nuclear age and the explosive problems of world poverty'.[74]

Re-emphasising the need for modernisation of British institutions, the manifesto maintained that the country had lagged behind since 1945 'because the "Establishment" in politics, in Whitehall, in industry, and the trade unions, has too often been unresponsive to the possibilities of the new age'. To rectify that situation, therefore, it argued, 'the way Britain is run must be drastically reformed; the new men and women who understand modern technology must be given wider opportunities to use their talents; economic growth must become a major aim through more skilful management of the nation'.[75] Moreover, in order 'to give economic expansion top priority', a reorganisation of the machinery of central government was needed with the creation of a Ministry of Expansion 'as the hub of economic management'. A national plan for economic growth should then be drawn up, in consultation with industry and the unions, by the Minister of Expansion and submitted to Parliament for debate and approval.[76]

In his pre-election book Harry Cowie had already attempted, as both Desmond Banks and Grimond had done earlier, to distinguish the Liberal approach to planning from Labour's. Liberals, Cowie pointed out, were concerned with 'the central coordination of forecasts and targets which are made in the different parts of the economy', whereas Labour, by contrast, seemed to 'regard planning as a means by which the State transmits its ideas about rates of growth to industry rather than the other way round'.[77] Nevertheless, the state collectivist and technocratic character of the Liberals' planning proposals since 1960, culminating in the 1964 manifesto commitments, was starkly apparent. The proposed coordinator of the entire planning process, the 'Minister of Expansion', even appeared to bear 'a mildly Orwellian title', as Shirley Williams remarked a year later.[78]

The 1964 manifesto did, however, reaffirm the Party's continuing support for the established Liberal causes of free trade and co-ownership. Britain, it declared, should 'take the initiative in the drive to bring down world tariffs', which would not only 'help to expand world trade', but also, by bringing down production costs at home, thereby 'make our exports more competitive abroad ...'.[79] In support, too, of co-ownership in industry, the manifesto contended that: 'Go-ahead companies have already realised that the alternative to negative control by the unofficial strike is real participation by the employee in the running of his firm'. The Companies Act should therefore be amended 'to give all established employees in public limited companies a status comparable to shareholders'. Employees should be 'given a share in the decisions and profits of the companies in which they work', and should be 'represented on the board of directors, or on a joint supervisory council'.[80] Longstanding Liberal commitments stretching back in the postwar era to 1948 were thereby reaffirmed.

At the 1964 General Election, held on 15 October, the Liberal Party, fielding 375 candidates, won 3 million votes with 11.2 per cent of the total national poll. Only nine Liberal MPs were elected, but this was nonetheless the first increase in the Party's parliamentary representation, and its largest popular vote, at any general election since 1929. The Liberals also gained second place in 54 seats, twice as many as in 1959, and suffered only 53 lost deposits.

The outcome was a setback, however, for Grimond's central political strategy. For as he later recalled, Labour's narrow victory, with a wafer-thin majority of four, 'put paid for the time being to any realignment on the Left'.[81] If, on the other hand, Labour had lost, he considered that 'there would have been strong forces working for a realignment'.[82] Yet the process whereby the Liberals had gained the votes of many former Conservative supporters meant, as David Dutton has noted, that the Liberal 'aim of forming the nucleus of a new opposition to Conservatism could only materialise if the Labour vote declined independently of anything the Liberals did'.[83] In the event, however, Labour's share of the national vote in 1964 increased marginally – by just 0.3 per cent – in comparison with 1959.

Nevertheless, immediately after the election result, Grimond indicated that the Liberals were prepared to support the new Labour government on a limited programme and specified the policies which his Party would back.[84] A few months later, he restated that position after Labour had lost the Leyton by-election, thereby reducing their parliamentary majority to only three; he suggested 'some reasonably long-range agreement with the Government' so as to guarantee stability for a parliamentary programme.[85] In the summer of 1965 Grimond therefore raised the possibility of some kind of formal cooperation between the Liberals and Labour, provided that the two parties could reach some agreement on long-term policy aims. *The Guardian* newspaper had been campaigning throughout the early part of the summer 'for rapprochement between the parties', and its editor, Alastair Hetherington, had even arranged a private meeting between Grimond and Harold Wilson in early August 1965.[86]

In his speech at the subsequent 1965 Liberal Assembly in Scarborough, Grimond sought to defend his approach in both historical and immediate terms. British politics, he declared, had 'been bedevilled all my lifetime by the love-hate relationship of the Liberal and Labour parties', and consequently, in his view, '... it would have been utterly wrong not to have raised the question of at least a working partnership ...'. Moreover, his proposal had created a political situation, he argued, in which '... our teeth are in the real meat and our muscles exerted in the real power struggle of politics'.[87]

This prospect of inter-party cooperation was, of course, not only an essential part of Grimond's realignment strategy, but also a likely consequence of the introduction of an electoral system based on proportional representation to which the Liberals were so firmly committed. It was, however, the strongly held view of Liberal critics of Grimond's strategy, first, that the Liberal Party already constituted a non-socialist progressive party, and, second, that those Labour supporters who favoured that kind of political grouping should therefore join the Liberal Party, instead of Liberals being required to form an alliance with Labour, thereby jeopardising their own political independence.

At the Scarborough Assembly those views were to be vividly expressed. For while, as Alan Watkins later recalled, the delegates, following the Leader's memorable speech, 'were willing to cheer Mr Grimond to the echo ... they were not prepared to follow [him] in believing that the Party's real future lay in a new radical party of the left which excluded fundamentalist socialists'.[88] Rather, many tended to favour more the views of those such as Emlyn Hooson who, in a speech in June 1965, had argued that at that finely balanced moment in British politics '... there is only one course open to the Liberal Party: that is to soldier on in complete independence of any arrangement with Conservative or Labour and to press for policies in which we believe'.[89] At Scarborough many Liberal activists agreed, too, with the Party President, Nancy Seear, when she maintained, in more lurid terms, that:

> For forty years we have prophesied that the country would come to recognise the need for a non-socialist progressive party. We have not

spent these years isolated but undefiled in the wilderness to choose this moment of all moments to go, in the biblical phrase, a-whoring after foreign women ...[90]

This debate in the Party raised by Grimond's proposal for 'a working partnership' with the Wilson Government was sharpened by an awareness of the fact that during the 1964–66 Parliament the Liberals were clearly unable to make political headway. Only on the question of the renationalisation of the steel industry did they appear to play a distinctive and influential role, helping to shelve the issue until after the next general election. Their position in this ideologically contentious policy area had already been set out in the 1964 election manifesto, which stated:

> Liberals want a truce in the dispute over steel which will take the industry out of politics and enable it to get on with the job. We press instead for modernisation of the industry, government help for redundancy, competitive marketing, and a world steel conference to cut tariffs and agree on world rules of competition.[91]

In spite of this limited area of influence, the harsh political reality was that the Liberals did not hold the balance of power in the House of Commons after 1964. Grimond later stated that consequently he did 'not see that much could have been done between 1964 and 1966', and that 'our influence on immediate events was very limited, if indeed it existed at all'.[92] However, he added in retrospect that the Liberals should have campaigned harder during that period for devolution to Scotland and Wales, stamping 'our image upon the demand for less and better government nearer home', and thereby possibly pre-empting the growth of the Scottish National Party and Plaid Cymru.[93] During this period the Liberal Party's restricted room for political manoeuvre was matched by its falling national opinion-poll ratings, which were alleviated only by the consolation of David Steel's by-election victory at Roxburgh, Selkirk and Peebles in the Scottish Borders in March 1965.

The 1966 General Election, to be held on 31 March, once it was called, had brought to an end the short Parliament of 1964–66, during which the Labour government's overall majority had fluctuated between five and only one. The Liberal election manifesto, *For All the People*, like its predecessor of 1964, again stressed the theme of modernisation and underlined the Liberals' unique capacity, as a party free of class and sectional interests, for assuming the necessary role of modernising Britain's institutions. The Labour Party, on the other hand, the manifesto claimed, '... for all their talk about modernisation', in reality, like the Conservatives before them, 'cannot find the answer to our problems' and 'have been unable to implement workable solutions'. The simple reason for that situation was that both major parties had 'their roots firmly in one section of the community or another', with the Conservatives 'both ideologically and financially ... still tied to the interests of capital', and with Labour 'tied to the interests of the Unions, often to the detriment of both'.[94]

After pointing out that Liberal pressure in the 1964–66 Parliament had helped both to shelve the nationalisation of steel and to prevent the nationalisation of small plots of building land, the manifesto argued that the process of modernising Britain's institutions urgently required 'a fresh and realistic approach to economic planning, defence and the machinery of government ...', because only then would 'the wealth be created that can bring about a real improvement in living standards, housing, education and the social services for all the people of Britain'.[95]

To rectify an economic situation in which Britain in 1966 had 'the slowest rate of growth of any developed industrial economy', the Liberal manifesto prescribed some currently fashionable, statist remedies, including 'the formulation, execution and continuous modification of a new national economic plan' by the recently created Department of Economic Affairs, in partnership with a new Parliamentary committee on economic affairs, in order to achieve economic expansion, together with an incomes policy designed to control inflation 'with a minimum of unemployment'.[96]

With the aim of re-ordering Britain's foreign policy priorities, *For All the People* favoured cuts in overseas military expenditure, which accounted for over half of the national debt, and hence the abandonment of 'illusions of military and economic grandeur', including Britain's commitments East of Suez, which had become unrealistic and financially unsustainable.[97] Emphasising instead the other dominant Liberal theme of the 1960s, internationalism, the manifesto urged support for the authority of the United Nations 'in settling disputes between States and policing scenes of international violence', as well as in the search for controlled, multilateral nuclear disarmament. It declared, too, that 'Britain is a European power' and advocated British membership of the European Economic Community 'at the earliest opportunity'. That development would not only be 'of great economic benefit' to Britain, it was argued, but would also make the country 'a pioneer in the first supranational community where States have agreed to share some of their sovereignty'. At the same time, the manifesto reaffirmed Liberal belief in 'the late President Kennedy's concept of the Atlantic partnership between the USA and United Europe', one that 'would wield great power for progress'.[98]

At the ensuing 1966 General Election, on 31 March, 12 Liberal MPs were elected, including, for the first time, Richard Wainwright in Colne Valley, Michael Winstanley in Cheadle and John Pardoe in North Cornwall. This was the largest Liberal parliamentary presence since 1945. However, the total Liberal vote fell by 750,000 compared with 1964 and the Party's share of the national poll fell from 11.2 per cent to 8.5 per cent, albeit with 54 fewer candidates fielded than in the earlier election.

The national outcome of the election – a sweeping Labour victory with an overall Commons majority of 97 – was highly significant for the Liberals in strategic terms. For the size of Labour's majority ended any possibility of a formal arrangement or working partnership with the Liberal Party. As William Wallace later observed: 'The rationale for the Liberal advance of the previous five years, that Labour must lose, had been decisively destroyed'.[99] For Grimond this was a defining political moment, and with 'his vision of a new progressive party in ruins', he began to contemplate retirement as Party Leader.[100] His strategy of realignment, which had appeared gravely undermined by the winter of 1965–66, had now in effect been dismantled by Labour's decisive victory. In its aftermath, as David Butler and Anthony King later recorded, 'it was no clearer than it had been ten years before how the Liberals were going either to form a new radical coalition with elements from both the Conservative and Labour parties, or to supplant Labour as the chief opposition to the Conservatives'. Although, then, under Grimond's leadership the Liberals had increased both their total national vote and their parliamentary representation, they had 'made no strategic advance'.[101]

In Geoffrey Sell's view, Grimond's overriding strategy, to which he had already devoted so much time and energy, had in fact been 'his greatest misjudgement' since it was 'based on a complete fantasy, a will of the wisp'. His attempts 'to woo Labour moderates' had met only 'a brick wall of hostility, reflecting the philosophical difference about the role of the State and the position of the trade unions ...'.[102] Yet his vision of the Liberal Party offering the nucleus around which a new progressive grouping could unite depended either on an irreparable Labour split or else on the Liberals supplanting Labour as the non-socialist radical alternative to the Tories. But the Liberals' main electoral advance, from Orpington in 1962 to the 1966 General Election, had been based on attracting discontented voters away from the Tories rather than on making significant inroads into Labour-held territory. The entire realignment strategy, however, rested both on the importance of that latter development and on Labour's inability to halt its continuing electoral decline.

This, then, was the major contradiction at the heart of Grimond's strategy, one that gave rise, as Michael Steed has pointed out, to 'the most serious mismatch of the party's organisational and political strategies'.[103] For the main thrust of the Liberals' organisational strategy was the need to build up constituency associations and resources in Conservative-held territory, whereas the leadership's political strategy hinged on building up support in Labour-held industrial seats where Liberal organisation in most cases remained weak.

Apart from this major contradiction, and the tensions which it generated, there were at least four additional flaws in the realignment strategy. First, as Sell has noted, it implied, in the Liberal view, 'a realignment of ideas and values as well as ... of political support'.[104] The progressive constituency identified by Grimond was one that was 'impatient with class distinctions and outworn political creeds; eager to press forward with the modernisation of the British economy and passionately committed to British membership of the Common Market'.[105] But progressive voters of that kind were in reality scattered through the electorate, or else remained loyal to a Labour Party which under Wilson's leadership was projecting a modernising and less doctrinaire image. Furthermore, a clear political distinction could be drawn, as Roy Jenkins later commented, between 'the agreeable, civilised radicalism of Grimond and his immediate colleagues, on the one hand' and those voters, on the other, who were 'more Poujadist than radical and voted Liberal to express a general discontent'.[106]

A second flaw inherent in Grimond's strategy was that it implied a widespread process of partisan dealignment within the British electorate – that is, a serious weakening of previously strong and enduring voter identification with one or other of the two major parties. But that process did not become clearly evident in British politics until the 1970s and 1980s – most conspicuously at the general elections of 1974 and thereafter.[107] Moreover, partisan dealignment has arisen historically from the catalytic effect of such factors as generational change, major socio-economic developments and the emergence of new political issues. All of those factors have served to change the voting allegiances of individuals and groups within the electorate. But as Peter Jenkins later observed, realignments in party politics 'of the kind that Grimond had in mind are rare phenomena and usually associated with war, which hastened the demise of the historic Liberal Party after 1914 and ushered Labour to majority power in 1945, or an extension of the franchise, as after 1867, or with the rise of a new class or interest in the land, the Peelite middle classes of the 1840s and the trade unions in the 1880s and 1890s'[108], and with the enlargement, it should be added, of the trade-unionised industrial working class after 1918.

No development of comparable significance was evident in Britain during the 1960s – other than the steady expansion of a largely suburban professional and managerial middle class estranged from the interests of both big business and trade unionism and providing, therefore, a vehicle, as at Orpington, for by-election protest or, as in 1964 and 1966, for disaffection with an apparently out-of-touch Conservative Party. Moreover, by targeting this expanding social group and justifying such a strategic approach in terms of the 'embourgeoisement' thesis widely advanced at that time by sociologists, the Liberal leadership was thereby, as Wallace has pointed out, 'enormously overestimating the speed of generational change'.[109] Nor had any cross-cutting issue of importance emerged as the focus for realignment either of ideas or of political support in British politics. Europe, which was later to assume that role, had not yet fully emerged as a significant electoral issue, and the Liberal theme of modernisation had been partially appropriated by Labour after 1963 with Wilson's celebration of the scientific and technological revolution and all its meritocratic implications, together with his espousal of the merits of 'purposive planning'.

A third flaw in the realignment strategy was that it underestimated the partisan loyalties of politicians and activists in both the Labour and Liberal parties. In the case of Labour, it underplayed the tendency of its moderate wing to remain loyal to their Party not only in the hope of eventual electoral victory, as in the run-up to the 1964 General Election, but also in view of the realities of office in its aftermath. In the case of the Liberal Party, Grimond's strategy was either widely misunderstood or strongly opposed. Its critics insisted, as we have seen, that a non-socialist progressive party already existed in the form of the Liberal Party itself, and they believed, therefore, that the onus was on moderate Labour supporters to join and swell the Liberal ranks. That seemed a defensible position in the finely balanced political circumstances of the mid-1960s, particularly when advanced by articulate advocates such as Hooson and Seear.

Finally, it can be argued that on one level Grimond's strategy was, as Sell has suggested, 'old fashioned' since 'what it was trying to do was to replicate the politics of his childhood before the rise of the Labour Party'. He was seeking 'to reverse what had happened in the 1920s. Instead of Labour, with the aid of left-wing Liberals, replacing the Liberal Party, the Liberals, with the aid of right-wing Labour, would replace the Labour Party'.[110] Grimond thus seemed to regard a realignment of the Left as involving the establishment of a party system based on two main blocs: one conservative and suspicious of change, the other progressive and innovative, though he did always acknowledge the uncertain and unpredictable shape and form that realignment might assume within the British party system.

In spite, however, of these various flaws, as well as the major contradiction, running through his strategy, it may be said in Grimond's defence that he had at least persuaded his Party to consider the importance of inter-party cooperation as a means both of ensuring its own political survival and of bringing it closer to the realities of government, to, in his own words, 'the real meat' of politics. In this sense his initiative anticipated later political developments occurring in more favourable circumstances: notably, the formation of the SDP/Liberal Alliance in 1981 and the foundation of the Liberal Democrats in 1988.

In the post-1959 period Grimond's strategy arguably helped, too, to sharpen the edge of his leadership, providing, as Steed has maintained, 'a good response to those who doubted the point of reviving what had seemed to be a dying party, and one which made it seem more relevant to the future than to its immediate desolate past'.[111] Ultimately, however, the lack of practical feasibility of Grimond's strategy became increasingly apparent, and, in his attempt to pursue and sustain it, he was unable to carry a large part of his Party with him. Partly for that reason, and partly owing to despondency and exhaustion, he subsequently resigned the Party leadership in January 1967.

How, then, does the eventual failure of Grimond's realignment strategy affect an overall assessment of his leadership? One of his successors, David Steel, was later unequivocal in his favourable judgement:

> No single person has done more than Jo Grimond in the whole post-war era to keep alive the values and principles of Liberalism. Without the foundations he laid, nothing in the years ahead could have been attempted.[112]

All the criticisms of Grimond's realignment strategy need, too, to be considered in the light of the wider political impact of 'the first Liberal leader to have a major national profile since Lloyd George'. For Grimond's leadership challenged the dominance of the British two-party system and thereby 'lit the blue touch paper of revived third party politics'.[113]

The influence, however, of Grimond's leadership upon the Liberals' electoral fortunes was significant but limited. As has been noted, the first signs of Liberal revival were evident in the 12 months before he became Leader in November 1956. At that time there were six Liberal MPs, the Party having won only 2.7 per cent of the national poll, with just over 700,000 votes, at the previous General Election of 1955. By the time of his resignation there were 12 Liberal MPs, the Party having won 8.5 per cent of the poll, with 2.3 million votes, at the previous election of 1966, which followed the impressive result of 1964. In terms of organisational advance, the effect of his leadership was more obvious – particularly in the years from 1959 to 1964. During that period party membership rose from 150,000 to 300,000, peaking at 350,000 in 1963; the Party's annual income rose from £24,000 to £70,000, and the number of full-time agents doubled.[114]

But it is in the area which is the particular focus of this study – the development and dissemination of political ideas and, in some cases, their translation into policy – that Grimond's contribution was most conspicuous, as many observers have recognised. Michael Steed has recalled the inspirational effect on his own generation of Liberals of Grimond as a communicator of ideas, of 'a remarkable politician' who employed a 'combination of the skills of a nineteenth-century radical orator with those of a late-twentieth-century television performer'. His 'ideas, personality and skills' drew not only 'a whole generation of new, young people into Liberal activism', but also a large number of academic and industrial advisers, who became involved, directly or indirectly, in policy formulation.[115] Another Liberal prominent in the 1960s and 1970s, Timothy Beaumont, also later emphasised Grimond's decisive 'influence on the intellectual standing' of the Liberal Party. In 1956, Beaumont recalled, Grimond, who was himself 'at heart a maverick intellectual ... found an intellectually run-down party (and with the help of Mark Bonham Carter) lit an intellectual flame which continues to this day ...'.[116]

Indeed, as Peter Barberis has noted, 'in sheer fertility of ideas and published output' Grimond exceeded 'any other Liberal parliamentarian since Lloyd George'.[117] He also came to exert a more dominant influence on the Party's thinking than any other Liberal leader since Lloyd George. In his wide-ranging published writings, which continued to appear on a regular basis long after his resignation as Leader, he gave British Liberalism, as Sell has observed,

> a new direction and purpose ... based on a reassertion of the traditional liberal insistence that ideas and principles are more important than interests, a rejection of class-based politics and of the lingering imperialism of the post-war era, and a belief in the possibility of a realignment in British politics to reflect the real division between progressives and conservatives.[118]

In particular, he offered a distinctive and attractive ideological path for his Party to tread:

> Grimond gave eloquent voice throughout the long night of the Butskellite consensus to a third tradition in British politics, critical of the State but compassionate to the poor, suspicious of big business but enthusiastic for free enterprise.[119]

That 'third tradition' was advanced through the development and communication of ideas and themes that were to characterise Grimond's political thought throughout his life: notably, a positive as well as negative conception of liberty; an emphasis on the importance of civil society and voluntarism as bulwarks against state tyranny and as safeguards of liberty; and a qualitative conception of democracy that stressed the merits of active citizenship through wider participation. This rich blend of ideas helped to give strength and resonance to the central Liberal policy concerns, both traditional and contemporary – constitutional and political reform, the decentralisation of political power, the defence of civil liberties, co-ownership in industry, and international cooperation. Under Grimond's dominant influence that last commitment, highlighted by a firmly European emphasis, had become, along with modernisation, one of his Party's overarching themes of the 1960s, reflecting the political developments, as well as the mood and spirit, of that decade. Through this substantial contribution, then, Grimond, as his successor as Party Leader, Jeremy Thorpe, later acknowledged, had managed to build up, indeed to restore, 'the intellectual credibility' of the British Liberal Party.[120]

Chapter 4
The Rise of Community Politics in Uncertain Times: 1967–1976

The period from 1967 to 1979, covering the years of Jeremy Thorpe's leader-ship, his subsequent political demise and its aftermath, really consisted of three distinct phases of Liberal development. The first, from 1967 up to the electoral debacle of 1970, was one of steady political decline. The second, from 1972 to 1974, was, in contrast, one of a remarkable, largely unexpected revival, marked by five by-election victories in the course of just 13 months, and by the support of six million voters at the subsequent February 1974 General Election. The third phase, from the months following the October 1974 General Election to Thorpe's resignation in 1976 and, beyond that, to the General Election of 1979, was a dismal trough of further decline, marked by the sad, scandal-ridden end of Thorpe's political career, with electoral disaster narrowly averted under the leadership of his successor, David Steel, following a controversial pact between the Liberal Party and an increasingly unpopular Labour government.

The first of those historical phases, the late 1960s, was also one of uncer-tainty over the Liberal Party's strategic role within the British party political system. Was it to strike out as a radical alternative to the two major parties, to what it had depicted as two essentially consensus-bound and conserva-tive forces, a view crystallised in its slogan of the late 1960s, 'Which Twin is the Tory?'. Or was it to present itself as a moderating, centrist influence, interposing itself between two ideologically polarised parties tied to rival class and sectional interests? Thorpe himself, who had been elected Liberal Leader in 1967, clearly appeared to favour the latter, more conventional option, particularly after 1970 when Labour, in the wake of its election defeat, began to move more steadily to the Left.

Overshadowing those strategic questions, however, was the bleak real-ity of the Liberals' declining electoral performance during the 1966–70 Parliament. Deposits were lost in 12 out of 28 by-elections contested, and the local election revival of the early 1960s was not sustained. Disturbingly, too, there was a sharp decline in the number of truly active Liberal con-stituency associations. By April 1970 the Party had full-time agents in only

17 constituencies,[1] and only about a half of Liberal associations were send-ing an affiliation fee to Party headquarters.[2]

The one consolation for the Party during this period was the surprising by-election victory in June 1969 of Wallace Lawler, a populist local Liberal councillor, in Birmingham Ladywood, on a 32 per cent swing from Labour. The significance of this, which was to have longer-term implications, was that the Liberal victory was, as David Dutton has noted, 'the product of grass-roots politics, with local activists led by Lawler himself, patiently building up a well-cultivated local base'.[3] This pattern of local campaign-ing success was also becoming apparent at that time in Liverpool and Leeds.

The late 1960s were also a period marked by the radicalism of the Liberal youth movement, advanced by its two wings, the National League of Young Liberals and the Union of Liberal Students. By 1966 these organisations had replaced the New Orbits Group as the heart of the Party's youth movement.[4] This new generation of radical Liberals was itself a by-product of the wave of student activism in the late 1960s, inspired by counter-cultural influ-ences and fuelled at home by disillusionment with Harold Wilson's Labour governments.

By 1966, at their annual conference, the Young Liberals were advocating policies espoused at that time by the Labour Left – including the withdrawal of American troops from Vietnam; non-alignment in the Cold War, involv-ing British disengagement from NATO and a massive reduction in defence expenditure; opposition to a statutory incomes policy; and workers' control of nationalised industries. Such positions were accompanied by the advancement of mainstream Liberal causes such as active support for the anti-apartheid move-ment in South Africa and for majority rule in Rhodesia.

The emergence of the so-called 'Red Guards' of the Young Liberal move-ment as a significant force within the Party after 1966 widened the rift between Young Liberals and the Party establishment, some of whom depicted the more militant young activists as Marxists in a new guise. In reality, this radical movement generally had closer ideological links with various forms of liber-tarian socialism in both its analysis of capitalism and its decentralist empha-sis, and, in particular, with syndicalism in its advocacy of workers' control and with anarchism in its espousal of the cause of mutual aid. Quite apart from the obvious tensions between some of these views and many traditional Liberal beliefs, the Young Liberals' broad radical approach was, as Ruth Fox and Robert Ingham have observed, 'idealistic but inchoate and ... incapable of providing a coherent and sustainable Liberal programme at the national level'.[5]

In more practical terms, the Young Liberal movement was closely linked, too, to the growth of single-issue pressure groups such as Friends of the Earth, the Campaign for Nuclear Disarmament and the Anti-Apartheid Movement. In the latter case, both of the Young Liberal organisations had formal representation on the National Council of the Anti-Apartheid Movement from 1967 onwards, as well as on the organising committees for the major anti-Vietnam War demonstrations in London in March and October 1968.[6] More broadly, the cause of radical direct-action politics was advanced by the Young Liberals through the building of political links, in the form of joint campaigns, with these various single-issue pressure groups, which in turn provided factual information and resources to enhance the effectiveness of the Young Liberals' activism. In one much-publicised instance, however, this focus on direct-action politics resulted in the controversial, disruptive tactics employed by the 'Stop the '70 [South African cricket] Tour' campaign. After the chairman of the Young Liberals, Louis Eaks, appeared to claim responsibility for those tactics, in January 1970 the Liberal Party's National Executive formally requested, to no avail, that the Young Liberals should remove Eaks from the chair.[7] Nevertheless, two months later he was succeeded, by a narrow margin, by Tony Greaves as Young Liberal chairman.

Meanwhile, in the more settled mainstream of Party debate, the cause of applying economic liberal ideas to social policy, recommended in 1957 by some of the *Unservile State* essayists, was revived in the columns of *New Outlook* by some of the leading Liberal advocates of that approach – notably, Michael Fogarty and Arthur Seldon, with the support of the journal's editor, Richard Lamb. Fogarty argued that in Liberal social policy there was a need to maintain basic and guaranteed state provision for health care and social security, but to combine that 'with meeting the demand for freer choice, competition and participation which goes naturally with people's greater education and affluence today'. The Conservatives, by contrast, were 'throwing out the baby of planned and guaranteed benefits with the bathwater of State monopoly and uniformity', while socialists, on the other hand, still shuddered 'at the thought of independent services, even when they are co-operative and non-profit-making, let alone such things as private housing for profit'.[8]

Shortly afterwards, Arthur Seldon restated his case for vouchers in social policy, arguing that in the 1970s Liberals should seek to offer 'more choice in welfare for everyone' by providing either cash grants instead of free services in kind or else coupons or vouchers to ensure use of the desired services. State aid should therefore 'be given as purchasing power to *consumers* – parents, patients, owner-occupiers or tenants, pensioners – and not as subsidies to *producers*, whether schools (including direct-grant schools), Regional Hospital Boards or Councils'. Seldon summarised this controversial policy aim in a slogan designed 'to crystallise the essence of what social policy ought to be': 'Every citizen a consumer, not a supplicant'.[9] In such ways, Seldon, whose political sympathies still lay with the Liberal Party, wanted to see it 'again pioneering a new direction in social policy as Liberals did in 1908 and 1942'. In the choice between the 'liberal' and the 'paternalist' points of view, he hoped that the Party would 'follow the liberal line pursued by John Pardoe and Michael Fogarty'.[10]

John Pardoe, a Liberal MP since 1966, was indeed promoting economic liberal ideas in the field of social policy during this period, stating that he saw 'no reason why we should not allow and encourage the private sector throughout the whole field of welfare services to widen its scope'. Liberals, he wrote, should realise that 'while they are certainly not capitalists, if that term implies the concentration of capital in the hands of the few, they are marketeers', who believed in the merits of the market economy and in the beneficial use of market forces.[11] Pardoe's views in this area were strengthened by the links which he forged during this period with the free-market think-tank, the Institute of Economic Affairs, and with its co-director, Arthur Seldon. These links, which involved attendance at IEA seminars and lunches, were to be sustained into the 1970s and beyond.[12]

Nevertheless, the hopes which Seldon retained for the future of Liberal social policy – that in its formulation a market-led 'liberal line' would prevail, thereby clearly distinguishing Liberal policy from that of its rivals – were to be sorely disappointed in the years that lay ahead. In the field of economic policy, too, Richard Lamb was frustrated that the Party as a whole, and its parliamentary team in particular, were failing to support economic liberal ideas and policies, embracing instead state collectivist measures such as prices and incomes policies. He argued that: 'If the Liberal Party is to have a firm raison d'etre it must with its tradition and philosophy be the champion of a free market economy and a firmly committed opponent of the Prices and Incomes Policy', and that in this area 'Enoch Powell has stolen the traditional economic Liberal ground laid down so enthusiastically at each Liberal Assembly'.[13]

Lamb had earlier pointed out that his aversion to a prices and incomes policy was shared by leading Liberal economic policy advisers such as Christopher Layton and Frank Paish.[14] But the broader basis for his frustration was the new Leader's perceived unwillingness to give his public support to radical or unorthodox positions on domestic policy issues. It was 'disturbing', too, Lamb noted, 'that serious minded people attracted intellectually to the Liberal Party by Grimond's policies in the early '60s are falling away'.[15] This was a theme taken up by Richard Holme, previously one of Grimond's closest supporters, who observed that:

> Grimond Liberalism was attractive, so attractive that its style, if not enough of its substance, has been appropriated by the Tory and Labour Parties. It was classless with an appeal to the 'new man' – greying slightly at the temples by now; it was modernising in the best pragmatic way, unafraid of institutions and traditions; it was exciting and sometimes irreverent. It was the creature of its times, the finest flowering of the late fifties and early sixties ...[16]

The need for a clearer and more distinctive ideological focus for the Party which many Liberals were now emphasising did, however, receive official support when in May 1968 the Party Council stressed the importance of defining and promoting 'a consistent Liberal ideology', particularly in view of the Party's recent decline in terms of finances, organisation and morale. It therefore instructed the Party's National Executive to write a report on the subject, which should then be debated at the Party Assembly.[17] This undertaking was made just after an abortive revolt against Thorpe's leadership while he was away on his honeymoon. The eventual outcome was the establishment of the Liberal Commission, which in turn produced a 24,000-word report, *Liberals Look Ahead*, in time for the 1969 Liberal Assembly.

Donald Wade, who chaired the Commission, had already recently written a new edition of his own 1961 booklet, *Our Aim and Purpose*, which aimed, in his words, to provide 'an outline of basic Liberal philosophy and an analysis of the Liberal attitude to current issues'.[18] Here he stressed in clear language the primacy of liberty – personal, civil and political – in liberal thought, declaring that:

> The aim of Liberalism is always liberty – and liberty for more people. This constant liberal aim ... springs naturally from something fundamental in liberal philosophy, that is, the belief in the value of individual personality.[19]

In line, too, with the British social liberal tradition, Wade repudiated the doctrinaire anti-statism of some economic liberals. The Liberal Party, he pointed out, had 'never advocated or believed in the doctrine popularly, but inaccurately, known as "laissez-faire"'.[20] Indeed, it was, he argued, 'the proper function of the State to prevent exploitation and to limit privilege'. Moreover, he continued, highlighting as in his previous writings, the distributist aspect of Liberalism, 'one of the best ways to extend and safeguard individual freedom and diminish privilege is through the individual ownership of property, using the term "property" in its widest sense'.[21] Liberals were therefore 'striving for a wider distribution of both power and property'. As in his earlier pamphlet of 1958, *Towards a Nation of Owners*, Wade thus re-emphasised the close link in Liberal ideology between liberty and personal ownership, the latter being viewed as a means to greater independence and security for the individual.

This point was made in the wider context of a restatement of the Liberal policy of co-ownership, of 'Ownership for All', which was presented again as a superior alternative to the socialist idea of state ownership, 'an outmoded panacea' that merely created 'a greater concentration of power' in the hands of the State. Co-ownership would also promote the ideal of 'industrial democracy in a Liberal society' in place of 'the old conventional form of capitalism', under which capital employed labour as if it were some kind of commodity. That Liberal ideal, by contrast, was based on the view that industry 'should be run as a partnership ... between management, employees, those who provide capital and the consumer'.[22]

All this did not imply, Wade stressed, the need for some ideal type or uniform pattern of organisation since 'modern industry is so complex that there can be no one simple formula whereby the old form of capitalism can be transformed by a single legislative act into a new kind of partnership'. For in a dynamic society 'one must expect experiment and change'[23] and the structure of industry would therefore inevitably vary. Wade made the same point in relation to the welfare society, the foundations of which had been laid by Liberals. Since, he observed, 'a Liberal society ... will not be static but ever-changing and progressive', as a consequence 'the form and extent of the social services ... cannot be frozen'.[24]

In *Our Aim and Purpose* Wade also provided a broad analysis challenging and rejecting the conventional view of a linear left-right spectrum in British politics. Political alignments in Britain could be described more adequately, he maintained, in terms of a triangle, with Liberal at the apex and Conservative and Labour at the base, rather than in terms of the misleading image of a semi-circle, in which Liberals were placed firmly in the centre.[25] Wade's analysis was developed in more depth by the liberal economist, Samuel Brittan, in his book, *Left or Right: The Bogus Dilemma*, published in 1968. Brittan argued that '... the left-right spectrum today obscures more than it illuminates'. It was 'misleading as a classification of political differences', and its persistent use in political discussion had 'a positively harmful effect'.[26] Moreover, in line with Wade's point of view, Brittan observed that as a political creed

> ... liberalism is not a middle way between conservatism and socialism, but at the opposite extreme. All the collectivist varieties of socialism, and the forms of conservatism which emphasise authority and obedience, have much more in common with each other than they have with systems of thought which attach a high value to individual freedom.[27]

The entrenched 'Conservative-Socialist division' in British politics therefore hid from public view 'the older and more fundamental argument between liberty and authority'. Since the core value of liberalism was individual freedom, it was for that major reason a political creed distinct from both conservatism and socialism. In Brittan's vivid definition, therefore:

> A liberal is someone who responds neither to authority nor to working-class solidarity, but to the trumpet call in the Second Act of 'Fidelio', announcing the liberation of the prisoners.[28]

Liberals Look Ahead, the 1969 report of the Commission which Donald Wade had chaired, took a broadly similar, but more prosaic, view of the intrinsic character of Liberalism. Essentially it provided a restatement of traditional Liberal values and principles in relation to contemporary issues and problems, developing themes outlined in earlier statements such as Wade's *Our Aim and Purpose* and expressing them in similarly libertarian and distributist terms, though in a greatly extended form. The report did, however, break new ground in, for example, its innovative proposals on environmental policy, which in the late 1960s was just beginning to emerge as an important issue-area in British politics. In general, it was welcomed within the Party at a time of growing internal criticism of Thorpe's leadership that was fuelled by the perception that he lacked his predecessor's intellectual weight or sense of strategic direction.

Much of the 1969 report formed the basis of the Liberals' 1970 General Election manifesto, *What a Life! Show 'Em You Care!*. The manifesto itself, however, lacked a coherent overall theme, merely listing a series of grievances afflicting the British people at that time. Nevertheless, one of the issues that seemed most salient in 1970, shortly after the publication of the report of the Donovan Commission on industrial relations – namely, the need for industrial harmony – was addressed in a reiteration of the key Liberal proposals entailed in schemes of co-ownership or co-partnership. British industry, the manifesto declared, should 'become a partnership between capital and labour, with management responsible to the partnership', and with both 'sides' of industry 'moulded into one team', rather than locked into 'a wrestling match'.[29]

At the ensuing 1970 General Election, held on 18 June of that year, the Liberal Party was largely marginalised, receiving little attention either from the two major parties or from the media. As William Wallace has observed, the election was marked by the 'apparent irrelevance of the Liberals to the central issues' – which were essentially economic and industrial – raised in the campaign.[30] The result itself was, as David Steel later recalled, 'a disaster'[31] for the Party. The number of Liberal MPs was halved from 12 to six, the 332 candidates polled overall just over 2.1 million votes, nearly one-third fewer than in 1964, and the Party's share of the national poll was only 7.5 per cent; 182 candidates lost their deposits, the largest number since 1950. Liberal parliamentary representation outside Scotland, Wales and the West of England was eliminated. As Chris Cook has commented, the outcome 'seemed to set the seal on the revival that had followed in the wake of Orpington'.[32] Furthermore, beyond Westminster the Party retained only a small local government base and offered only a weak presence in most of the big cities, with just a foothold on the councils in Liverpool and Leeds, together with Wallace Lawler's supporters in Birmingham.

It was in this dismal climate that the Party engaged in an anguished reappraisal of its strategy, purpose and future direction. In the view of Emlyn Hooson, one of the six parliamentary survivors, the seeds of the Liberals' electoral disaster had been sown within Grimond's earlier, flawed strategy of a realignment of the Left. The former Leader's vision of realignment, 'a concept little understood by anybody, least of all by its author', had produced, in Hooson's view, a 'long-term emotive effect' that was 'devastating'. For it had conveyed to the electors the impression that even the Liberal Leader himself 'did not conceive of his Party as a vehicle destined to carry him to power, but merely as a means of achieving some kind of re-orientation with the Socialists'. This impression had in turn led to a widespread view 'that the Liberals regarded themselves as some form of superior, enlightened coterie in a tacit, informal coalition of the Left – remembering that Left to most people now connotes Socialist rather than Radical'.[33] Hooson concluded by reaffirming his enduring belief in the Liberal Party's independent identity, declaring that:

> ... There is no reason for its existence, save that it accommodates people of deep Liberal beliefs who see through it a means of achieving greater political power.[34]

A major reappraisal, however, of the Party's strategy and purpose, if not yet of its policies and programme, was imminent in the wake of the 1970 election debacle. Emerging initially from the radical leadership of the Young Liberal movement, its strategic focus was the concept of 'community politics', first developed by Gordon Lishman, vice-chairman of the Young Liberals, and Lawrence Freedman at a Young Liberal strategy session in 1969. It was actively promoted at the post-election 1970 Liberal Assembly in Eastbourne through an amendment, successfully moved by Tony Greaves, the recently elected chairman of the Young Liberals, to a resolution on Party Strategy and Tactics. With the amendment carried by 348 votes to 236, the Assembly thereby endorsed 'a dual approach to politics, acting both inside and outside the institutions of the political establishment'. The strategy contained within itself three elements, the resolution declared, as:

> Our role as political activists is to help organise people in communities to take and use power; to use our political skills to redress grievances; and to represent people at all levels of the political structure.

In addition, the resolution committed the Party 'to build a power base in the major cities of the country ... [and] to capture people's imagination as a credible political movement, with local roots and local successes'.[35]

   The adoption in September 1970 of this 'community politics' resolution was to prove a turning-point in the Liberal Party's strategic and, to a significant extent, ideological development. Strategically, the fundamental aim of community politics was to secure significant political and social change at a grassroots, local community level. Such change was to be achieved by means of local community campaigns and structures, such as neighbourhood councils and cooperative ventures of various kinds. This was a strategy commended, as Wallace has observed, as 'an alternative rationale for political activity within a third party largely excluded from political influence at the centre'.[36] Moreover, the formal endorsement by the Liberal rank-and-file of that strategy, which had been conceived by leading Young Liberals, constituted, as Ruth Fox has observed, 'an achievement unsurpassed by any other political youth group'.[37] However, it was also the case that the Young Liberals' success at Eastbourne 'only served to heighten the differences with the party leadership' since 'the radicals were unconvinced of the potency of parliamentary politics, and the parliamentarians simply did not understand municipal politics, as few of their constituencies had a strong Liberal local council base'.[38]

Ideologically, the principal aim of community politics was to foster a participatory society in which people in local communities could gain greater control over, and hence increased responsibility for, their living and working environments, and thereby achieve a much greater sense of involvement in the decisions affecting their lives. That aim was in turn bound up with the need for popular control of the exercise, and hence the redistribution, of political power. In all these respects, community politics as a political approach was considered by its proponents entirely consistent with the Party's social-liberal tradition.

A number of radical Liberals, actively involved in one or other of the two wings of the Young Liberal movement, were to develop the philosophical basis of Liberal community politics over the coming years. These included, most notably, Lawrence Freedman, Bernard Greaves, Tony Greaves (the two were unrelated), Peter Hain and Gordon Lishman. Much of the impetus behind this thinking derived from the radicalism of the Liberal youth movement of the late 1960s, which was itself part of the wave of Western youth protest and unrest building at that time around issues such as student democracy, the Vietnam War and apartheid in South Africa. That movement was in many cases more committed to direct-action politics than to the processes of conventional politics.

Within the framework of British politics at that time, the young radical Liberals were seeking an alternative to what was perceived as a stale and remote political system dominated by class- and interest-based party politics and by professional political and administrative elites at both national and local levels. As Tony Greaves later recalled, to his own generation of Young Liberals in the mid-1960s 'the established political structure of our parliamentary "democracy" ... seemed remote, out of touch with people, fossilized into irrelevant procedures, and more and more subject to control by the bureaucracy ...'. Democracy itself was 'becoming a ritual divorced from the realities of power, of decision-making and execution'. Moreover, to Greaves and his contemporaries 'state socialism with a far greater amount of bureaucratic control seemed no answer'. But instead, 'the steady growth of "community action" seemed a way of bridging the gap between radical politics and real people, and at the same time actually doing something useful for and with one's fellow people ...'.[39] In similar terms, Gordon Lishman has recalled that the concept and theory of community politics developed, at least in part, as a reaction against 'the relative hollowness of national activism, in the context of British parliamentary politics' during that period. In contrast, community politics, with its emphasis on individual participation and civic engagement, emerged, in his view, both as 'part of a broader Liberal ideological tradition', and as 'a product of its time', and was thus 'a coming together of those two things'.[40]

Community politics drew its strength as a movement from a reaction, in particular, against the perceived indifference, passivity or complacency of the ruling political parties in British cities with regard to the views and needs of individual citizens and local communities. That insensitivity was probably most apparent during this period in decision-making in the fields of housing and urban redevelopment. Community politics was also a critical response to developments in British society, such as the growth of large-scale institutions and organisations, and the steadily increasing bureaucratisation of society, with its centralising and dehumanising effects. In the face of those developments, community politics was therefore, as another of its Liberal practitioners later wrote, 'an attempt to regenerate democracy and recast democratic institutions so that power is driven downwards to the most basic level possible'.[41]

With its emphasis on active participation and its reaction against bureaucratic inertia and authority, the Liberal idea of community politics derived much of its thrust not just from these radical Young Liberal influences but also from the impact of Jo Grimond's leadership from 1956 to 1967, which had itself inspired many of the new generation of radical activists. In his writings and speeches, as we have seen, Grimond had consistently emphasised participation as a distinctive Liberal value, intimately connected to, indeed an aspect of, the core Liberal value of liberty. This emphasis was in turn linked under his leadership to a new strategic focus on the importance of achieving electoral success at a local level, which was viewed as an important condition of the Party's revival and growth at a national and parliamentary level. To that end, the Party, at Grimond's instigation, had established a Local Government Department in 1960, under the direction of Richard Wainwright and Michael Meadowcroft, which was designed to encourage wider Liberal involvement in local council elections and to assist existing Liberal councillors. The tone of this new localist approach was evident in Grimond's observation in 1961 that: 'Every time a local Liberal councillor gets a bus stop moved to a better place, he strikes a blow for the Liberal Party.'[42]

Furthermore, the reaction of young radical Liberals against the growth of bureaucratic control in contemporary society had already been clearly articulated by Grimond. In a 1967 lecture, for instance, he drew attention to the increasing ascendancy of bureaucracy over democracy, and the destructive effects of that process. For whereas 'the characteristic of democracy' he noted, was that 'it is open, mobile, elective and participating ... [and] appreciates argument and dissent', in sharp contrast,

> The characteristics of bureaucracy are that it is secretive, rigid, non-elective, hierarchical. Its motive force is the furthering of the interests of an apparatus, whether ... within the civil service, big business, the professions or even the universities. It does not appreciate mobility or dissent. It is by nature conservative.[43]

Community politics was later commended, too, by its leading theoreticians as an approach consistent with the belief of T. H. Green, Leonard Hobhouse and other social liberal thinkers, in the importance of communal endeavour and freedom of association as means to the self-realisation of the individual, and hence in the values of community and active citizenship, values threatened, or even undermined, by an atomised society created by the forces of large-scale industrialisation. More broadly, community politics was conceived as a contemporary restatement of the emphasis of those New Liberals upon the interrelationship between the individual and the active communities of civil society. The Liberal community politicians of the 1970s could thus cite in support of their approach Joseph Chamberlain's defence, whilst establishing the National Liberal Federation in 1877, of

> ... the principle, which should be at the bottom of all Liberalism, that the best security for good government is not to be found in 'ex cathedra' legislation by the upper classes for the lower, but in consulting those chiefly concerned and giving shape to their aspirations wherever they are not manifestly unfair to others ...[44]

In the most developed theoretical elaboration of the case for community politics, *The Theory and Practice of Community Politics*, written by Bernard Greaves and Gordon Lishman and published in 1980, ten years after its formal endorsement by the Party, Lishman later confirmed the influence of the Liberal tradition upon their own thinking:

> We have not used Liberal thinkers and activists of the past merely as a starting point. Rather we have developed our own ideas, we have discovered common themes in Liberal history, and we have read and interwoven their ideas and approaches with our own.[45]

Community politics had thus emerged, Greaves and Lishman observed, as 'a restatement of Liberalism in a new synthesis to meet the changed perspectives of a new generation', and 'every element in that synthesis', they stressed, had 'a pedigree in the classical Liberal tradition'. *The Theory and Practice of Community Politics* thus reaffirmed its authors' belief in the moral primacy of the individual, which lay at the heart of Liberal ideology, stating that: 'Our starting point is the individual. We want to find ways of enabling and encouraging each person to fulfil his or her potential.' But that overriding goal was to be attained not through the promotion of an 'egotistic individualism', but rather within the framework of a community 'which guarantees liberty and supports interdependence', and hence encourages 'mutual and individual responsibility'.[46]

This principled advocacy of community politics, clearly linking it to the Party's ideological heritage, tended to obscure some of the difficulties engendered by its strategic implications, difficulties which would later rise to the surface. Among these were differences of opinion between Liberals who regarded community politics as a supplement to parliamentary activity and those who considered it a radical alternative to it. The 'dual approach' formally adopted in 1970 did at least attempt to address that question, even if it did not resolve it. There were also latent tensions between the localist emphasis of community politics and the national focus and synthesising responsibilities of the parliamentary party and leadership. Nonetheless, at a time of electoral failure and widespread demoralisation within the Party, the local campaigning style and strategy of community politics, with its concern for wider citizen participation and its emphasis on both political decentralisation and popular control of the exercise of power, had emerged as an approach that was in harmony with the Party's Liberal traditions, and which could provide a distinctive flavour and ethos for British Liberalism in the years ahead.

The adoption of the community politics approach in 1970 was also accompanied by the emergence of two significant radical Liberal publications, which helped to reinforce and sustain its role within the Party's strategy and ideology. These were the periodical, *Liberator*, and a monthly newsletter entitled *Radical Bulletin*. The masthead of the latter declared that its aim was 'to foster communication and promote thought among radicals'. Edited by John Smithson, *Radical Bulletin* during the first half of the 1970s played, as Tony Greaves later recalled, 'a vital and increasingly influential role in pushing the Liberal Party to a more radical and activist stance'. It sought to rally radical Liberals within the Party by 'spreading community campaigning ideas, holding conferences, plotting action at party councils and assemblies, pushing candidates in party elections, encouraging people to go to by-elections, spreading news of local campaigns'.[47]

The influence of these publications, and of the groups gathered around them, was buttressed during the early 1970s by the strength of the Young Liberals as a distinct entity within the Party. At that time they constituted the largest single bloc at Liberal Assemblies, amounting on average to one in four delegates. This numerical advantage, combined with tactical and organisational skills, enabled them to promote their views and agenda effectively. The Young Liberals were not, as we have seen, the sole architects of community politics, but they were, as Fox has pointed out, 'at the forefront of the fight to ensure that it became the party's main strategic focus'.[48]

The Young Liberals also made a significant contribution to the Party's brief, largely unexpected and remarkable electoral revival of 1972–73, during which the Liberals won five parliamentary by-elections in the course of 13 months. This was widely perceived as, to a large extent, a vindication of the community politics strategy. The revival developed against the background of a mounting series of economic and industrial problems which engulfed Edward Heath's Conservative government, whilst the Labour Party was clearly moving Leftwards. The Liberal Party was thus well-placed to take electoral advantage of these developments.

The succession of Liberal by-election victories began in October 1972 at Rochdale, one of the few English seats in which the Liberals were the main challengers to Labour, with the election of the popular local figure, Cyril Smith. Six weeks later, at Sutton and Cheam in the outer London suburbs a 29-year-old Young Liberal, Graham Tope, was victorious after a campaign directed for most of its duration by Trevor Jones, the Liberal Liverpool city councillor and a leading practitioner of community politics. Liberal victories followed in July 1973 on the same day in the Isle of Ely and Ripon, with the election of Clement Freud and David Austick. Four months earlier, at Lincoln, Dick Taverne had fought and won as an independent Democratic Labour candidate, with unofficial Liberal support, following his resignation from the Labour Party. His victory gave credence to the idea, fostered in the columns of *The Times* throughout the winter of 1972–73, that there was mounting popular support for a broadly based party of the Centre. Finally, in November 1973 the Liberals, with Alan Beith as candidate, recaptured William Beveridge's old seat of Berwick-upon-Tweed.

All of this amounted to an upsurge of Liberal support easily outstripping the earlier revivals sparked by the victories at Torrington and Orpington in 1958 and 1962. It represented in fact, as Dutton has pointed out, 'the best Liberal performance since the Lloyd George-inspired revival of the late 1920s'.[49] In all the by-elections held throughout 1973 the Liberals won more votes in total than either Labour or the Conservatives.[50] By August 1973 national opinion polls showed support for the Liberals at 20 per cent.

Moreover, this impressive revival was accompanied by nearly 900 Liberal gains in the 1973 local elections, the Party's best performance at this level since 1945. The most remarkable advance was in Liverpool where, building on foundations laid by Cyril Carr and Trevor Jones, the Liberals became the largest single party on the City Council. A city which had not experienced a Liberal administration since the end of the 19th century thus became the only major English urban authority under Liberal control. This in itself, as Stuart Mole later commented, 'gave the opportunity to test the theory of community politics against the practice of municipal government'.[51]

Trevor Jones, the deputy leader of the Liberal group on Liverpool City Council, was a member of the Association of Liberal Councillors, a campaigning body formed in 1969. He had become the pioneer of a distinctive feature of the community politics campaigning style, namely, the local newsletter *Focus*, which carried news about local issues and campaigns and promoted community action on those issues. Reflecting the widespread appeal at that time of his political style and approach throughout the Liberal Party nationally, Jones had become Party President in 1973.

In addition to the Liverpool advance, the Liberals in 1973 became the largest party in five other local authorities and won control of the council in Eastbourne.[52] These gains provided further evidence that the Party was becoming a far more professional campaigning force. This was exemplified by the tactics and strategy employed in Liverpool by Trevor Jones, 'Jones the Vote', as he was soon dubbed by the media. The linkage between these victories in both by-elections and local elections and the Party's commitment to community politics led Michael Meadowcroft to comment that:

> ... the revival would have been stillborn after Rochdale, but for the community politics strategy – a fact that is even more marked when the local election results are analysed, showing that 48 seats are won in Liverpool with barely any Liberal tradition whereas not a single seat is won in Huddersfield with a Liberal tradition imprinted on almost every flagstone.[53]

Faced with a second miners' strike, Edward Heath called a general election based on the theme, 'Who Governs Britain?', to be held in February 1974, in an attempt to secure a renewed mandate for his government. The Liberals approached the election in an optimistic and buoyant mood, anxious to transform their by-election triumphs into a major electoral breakthrough. The Party fielded 517 candidates, the highest total since 1906. The February 1974 Liberal manifesto, *Change the Face of Britain: Take Power – Vote Liberal*, was drafted by Tony Richards, the Party's Director of Research, and was based on a policy document, *Forward with the Liberals*, largely written by Desmond Banks in 1973.

In a personal message introducing the manifesto, Jeremy Thorpe addressed the 'immediate economic and social crisis' facing the country by stating that the role of the Liberal Party at the imminent, confrontational election was 'to act as a catalyst' in bringing about 'the necessary political consensus' based on both a recognition of the general good and a vision of 'a fairer society'. Every Liberal vote cast at the February 1974 General Election, Thorpe declared, would therefore be 'a nail in the coffin of the old two party system of confrontation and a step toward national unity and reconstruction'.[54] He was thus adapting a theme that had resonated through Liberal election manifestos since 1945 – the Party's unique status as a third force free of class or sectional interests – to meet the crisis-ridden and polarising conditions of the time.

The manifesto itself restated this point:

> The Liberal Party is tied to no sectional interest. That is why we can justly claim that we approach the problems of our country with no doctrinaire prejudices, no class inhibitions and no sectional interests.[55]

Liberals were going into the February 1974 General Election, the manifesto further claimed, advocating 'a fearless programme of economic, social and industrial reconstruction ...'.[56] Among the key priorities of that programme were proposals for a permanent prices and incomes policy to tackle the increasingly grave crisis issue of rising inflation. This would be enforced by tax penalties imposed on those 'whose actions cause inflation' – whether they were companies that raised prices above 'an agreed annual rate of increase', or employers or employees who negotiated increases in earnings higher than that agreed rate.[57]

These highly state-interventionist proposals were partially qualified by some genuflection to economic liberal positions. The next government should, it was added, 'stimulate competition where it can still be made to work, break up and control monopolies, prevent non-productive mergers and stamp out widespread restrictive practices'. The manifesto recognised, too, that 'nationalisation will not solve the problem of high prices or monopolies', and that in too many cases the public, and hence the consumer, had to 'subsidise non-profit-making industries'.[58]

The control of inflation through a permanent prices and incomes policy would be accompanied, too, by measures of 'industrial reconstruction' amounting to a 'new charter for industrial relations'. This would entail schemes for industrial partnership involving all individuals working in an industry rather than merely the 50 per cent of the working population who were trade union members, as in Labour's plans for industrial democracy. The key proposals which had 'been the cornerstone of our policy for over fifty years' were therefore restated: membership of their companies by employees, in similar manner to shareholders, with clearly defined rights; representation of employees at management level through works councils; employee participation in the election of directors at board level; and the right of employees to share in the profits of their companies and in the growth of their assets.[59]

As in the past, industrial partnership was depicted as a remedy for the deep division in British industry, which was reinforced by the two-party system, 'into two camps to the detriment of the community'. Yet in the febrile and adversarial national climate of early 1974 this traditional Liberal policy prescription did seem particularly apposite. So did the claim that Liberal proposals in this area '... would achieve the identification of employees' interests with those of the firm by providing a visible link between the immediate limitation of wage demands and the future prosperity which will be generated for both employees and shareholders as a result'.[60]

Change the Face of Britain also advocated a comprehensive overhaul of welfare policy – including a tax credits system to replace existing means tests and allowances; a guaranteed minimum earnings level; and increased earnings-related retirement pensions.[61] In the field of political and constitutional reform, the manifesto reaffirmed Liberal commitments to decentralisation, given fresh impetus by the advancement of the community politics strategy since 1970, and to devolution. It proposed, too, a Bill of Rights to ensure 'protection from arbitrary interference' in the individual's personal and private affairs and to defend freedoms of speech and assembly, the right to a fair trial, and freedom from discrimination on grounds of race, religion, gender or national origin.[62]

After a vigorous election campaign in which Thorpe effectively portrayed the Liberals as a moderate yet progressive party of the Centre at a time of increasing political polarisation and mounting class conflict, he declared on 25 February that the Liberal Party's primary goal was to form a government but, if that proved impossible, that he would be willing to 'work with any person of moderate or progressive views to get this country back on the rails'.[63] The 517 Liberal candidates in the field resulted in far greater media coverage than in the past, which in turn increased the impact of the national campaign.

Its outcome, on 28 February, was that the Liberals polled over six million votes, with 19.3 per cent of the national poll, yet won only 14 seats – a vivid and cruel illustration of the way in which the first-past-the-post system worked against the Party's interests. It had taken, on average, 432,000 votes to elect each Liberal MP but only 40,000 and 39,000 respectively to elect each Conservative or Labour MP.[64] The Liberal Party would have needed to obtain at least 30 per cent of the national vote in order to have countered the electoral system's anomalous and disproportional effects.

Nevertheless, this was still an impressive Liberal electoral performance. The Party had polled well throughout Britain, particularly in the South East and South West of England. Only four deposits were lost in the whole of England, and for the first time since 1931 a majority of Liberal MPs now represented English constituencies.[65] The failure, however, to win seats in areas such as Liverpool, where the Liberals had built up a solid local council base, underlined the difficulty of converting the post-1970 community politics approach into a national strategy. Throughout the country as a whole the Liberal challenge was directed most credibly against the Conservatives, not Labour. Of the 100 unsuccessful Liberal candidates with the highest percentages of votes, 98 had lost to Conservatives and only two to a Labour opponent.[66]

The ultimate verdict on the workings of the electoral system in February 1974 was delivered 25 years later by Jeremy Thorpe. Recalling the achievement of a Liberal advance from two million to six million votes in the course of just four years, he commented sadly that:

> It was a bitter fact that those four million additional votes gave us only three more MPs. Under any fair voting system, this should have been a breakthrough.[67]

In the aftermath of the February 1974 General Election, in the conditions of a hung Parliament in which no one party had an overall majority, the Liberals, with 14 MPs, had enough representation to exert influence, but not enough to hold the balance of power. The Conservatives had won over 200,000 more votes than Labour but had four fewer MPs (297). Labour, with 301 MPs, were 17 short of an overall majority. In these circumstances Thorpe accepted Edward Heath's invitation to talks in Downing Street to explore the possibility of some kind of arrangement to support his Conservative administration. Thorpe's willingness to discuss such a possibility was consistent both with the Liberal Party's commitment to proportional representation and with his earlier statement that, in the event of the Liberals holding the balance of power, he would be prepared to cooperate with moderate elements in other parties. But his response to Heath's invitation generated a predominantly hostile reaction from Party candidates and activists who had interpreted the Liberals' national vote of six million as in large part a verdict on the Heath Government's failure to tackle the country's acute economic and industrial problems.

In the event, the negotiations were terminated when, it seems, Thorpe, in spite of being offered a place for himself in the Cabinet, failed to extract from Heath any commitment to the future possibility of electoral reform besides the tentative concession of a Speaker's Conference on the issue. In March 1974 Harold Wilson subsequently took office at the head of a minority Labour government.

In the interval before a second general election in 1974, which Wilson was soon expected to call, the Liberals were engaged in a strategic debate over their aims for the immediate future. Should they strive to increase their parliamentary representation in order to hold the balance of power or even to participate in a national coalition government? Or should the Party continue, as many purists argued, on the long march to an eventual Liberal government, even at the price of a lengthy exclusion from office? Thorpe clearly favoured the former strategy, and throughout the eight months between the two general elections of 1974 promoted the aim of campaigning for what he called a 'Government of National Unity'.[68] In June 1974 the Liberal Chief Whip, David Steel, also a supporter of that strategy, announced in a party political broadcast that the Liberals would be 'ready and willing to participate' in a coalition government in the event of another hung Parliament, if the voters gave them the power to do so. Thorpe endorsed that view the same evening, stating in a television interview that the idea of a Government of National Unity 'reflects the views of millions of people'.[69]

The Liberal manifesto for the forthcoming general election, to be held on 10 October, was a shortened version of the earlier February document. Entitled, *Why Britain Needs Liberal Government*, it was again written by Tony Richards. In its introductory section, Jeremy Thorpe committed his Party 'to breaking the two-Party system in which the Party of Management alternates with the Party of Trade Unionism'. Both those interest groups represented 'vital elements in our society', but neither, he stressed, 'should ever be allowed to dominate the thinking of the government of the day'. In a similar spirit, he reaffirmed the Liberals' commitment to the cause of national unity, maintaining that the first priority should be 'to promote a sense of common endeavour and national purpose in government'.[70] Significantly, too, the manifesto itself foreshadowed a major theme of centre-left thinking 25 years or so later – the need for a balance between market incentives and social concern – in its statement that:

> The great issue facing all nations in this century is how to combine the collective activity of the state, necessary for the welfare of the people, with democratic freedoms and an opportunity for individual initiative in economic enterprise.[71]

In terms of specific commitments, the October 1974 manifesto restated the Liberal case for a statutory prices and incomes policy enforced by fiscal penalties;[72] for a radical overhaul of the social security system; for devolution to Scotland, Wales and the English regions; and for industrial partnership. But as in February, the details of policy tended at the time to be overshadowed by questions of overall strategy, such as, in particular, which party to support in the event of another hung Parliament. Nevertheless, the October manifesto and its February predecessor were notable documents because, as Duncan Brack has commented, 'for the first time in a generation their content mattered to the outside world, as neither of the two other parties seemed likely to win a majority'.[73]

The outcome of the October 1974 General Election was a Labour victory with a wafer-thin parliamentary majority of just three seats and with only 39 per cent of the national vote. The Liberals' performance was disappointing. In spite of 102 more candidates than in February, they won 13 seats, with 18.3 per cent of the national poll. Their total national vote fell from 6 million to 5.3 million, and they made only one parliamentary gain, in Truro. In Scotland the Party's standing was eroded by the rise of the Scottish National Party, which won 11 seats, in spite of the Liberals' firm commitment to devolution.

Underlying all this was the harsh electoral reality that the Party had failed in its, admittedly difficult, task of offsetting the loss of fickle and transient support gained in February by attracting a sufficiently large new tranche of disaffected floating voters. An academic analysis of Liberal electoral support later showed that between the two general elections of 1974 the Party lost 2.5 million of its voters and gained nearly 2 million new ones.[74] Furthermore, the Nuffield election study indicated the lack of a clear Liberal political identity in the minds of the voters – either in terms of their perception of the nature of Liberal policies or in the sense of their firm commitment to the Party itself.[75]

On the other hand, the outcomes of both the general elections of 1974 provided substantial support for the thesis that there were long-term trends of class – and partisan – dealignment in British voting behaviour; that is, tendencies towards a weakening of the once-powerful bonds between social classes and their party allegiances, and a related decline in strong voter identification with one or other of the major parties. At the 1951 General Election, for instance, 96.8 per cent of British voters had supported the Conservative and Labour Parties. By October 1974 that vote share had shrunk to 75 per cent. In effect, that meant that whereas in 1951 only one in 30 voters had supported the minor parties, by October 1974 that figure had risen to one in four.[76]

Moreover, the politics of economic decline – the failure of both Conservative and Labour governments since the early 1960s to halt, let alone reverse, Britain's faltering economic performance – was creating a situation favourable to the Liberals. For since the Party had, as Jeremy Thorpe often put it, 'led a blameless life since 1915', in the sense of its lack of involvement in governmental failure, it was therefore able to benefit politically from that dismal reality. Ironically, then, as Dutton has noted, 'the most optimistic of political creeds picked up support in a mood of mounting pessimism'.[77]

Throughout 1975, the focus of the Liberal Party's campaigning efforts shifted, in response to the outcome of the 1974 general elections, to promoting the case for both electoral reform and devolution. But at this time there were also some interesting developments in the Party's ideological debate. John Pardoe, for example, the leading Liberal advocate of a permanent prices and incomes policy, was publicly espousing a more market-driven approach to the British economy as a whole. In an article in *Liberal News*, he broadened his critique of state collectivism, which in the late 1960s he had developed mainly in the area of social policy, to encompass the fields of economic and industrial policy. 'Collectivism,' he declared, 'is the enemy of Liberalism'; for a collectivist approach was 'at best a defensive mechanism' and 'a poor substitute for individual economic freedom and security'. The 'private ownership of property' should, in his view, always remain 'a central Liberal aim' since it was an essential part of the wider Liberal goal of 'popular ownership as opposed to public ownership'.[78]

The Liberal Party, Pardoe maintained, was 'a post-capitalist party' in so far as it sought 'an equal partnership between capital and labour' rather than 'the supremacy of the forces of capital over those of labour'. It aimed to foster industrial conditions 'in which the two partners see that they have a common interest in the system'. But within that reformed, post-capitalist system Liberals were also 'the friends rather than the enemies of market forces' because profit was 'still the best guide we have to industrial efficiency' and the market was 'the best means we have of decentralising economic decision-making'.[79]

Pardoe also questioned the existing boundaries of the mixed economy in Britain, which had 'gone almost unchallenged' for the past 25 years. In its present state, he argued, it 'cannot be said to have worked well'. Investment and exports had been poor, return on capital disappointing, productivity 'dismal' and 'job satisfaction, measured by absenteeism and labour relations, appalling'. The time had come, therefore, for 'a major re-assessment of the structure and purpose of the mixed economy'. In place of 'the convenient myth' of a neat division between a nationalised sector 'somehow accountable to the public' and a private sector 'driven efficiently along by competition and enterprise', Pardoe proposed, as Grimond had done in his writings, a division between 'the administered and the competitive sector'. This would draw a distinction between 'those enterprises which wish to live in conditions of competitive free enterprise and those which want the benefits and protection of monopolistic practices'.[80] The role of government, moreover, was to pursue economic policies which would enable the market to provide firms in the competitive sector with the necessary capital to make a profit. He concluded with the observation, which seemed particularly pertinent in the climate of mid-1970s Britain, that:

> Unless Liberals are prepared now ... to think through to the post-capitalist economy, there can be no doubt that we shall sink beneath the tide of collectivism and central statism which both the Labour and Conservative establishments are quite prepared to inflict on us.[81]

In 1975 not many leading Liberals were arguing in these economically liberal terms and nor, for that matter, were many British politicians generally, certainly not until the widespread promotion of such views within the Conservative Party under Margaret Thatcher's leadership from February 1975 onwards, albeit without the Liberal emphasis on industrial partnership. In a later article, published that year in *New Outlook*, Pardoe returned to these themes. 'In the economic field,' he wrote, 'we have to define the nature of the modern Liberal Economy.' That meant acknowledging the fact 'that in any Economy short of Socialist the desire for profit is a thoroughly desirable thing'. For as Keynes had written in his *Treatise on Money*: 'It is enterprise which builds and improves the world's possessions ... (and) the engine which drives enterprise is ... profit.' As Pardoe had argued earlier, the 'Liberal Economy' could not, in his view, be described as a capitalist one; rather it was 'Post-Capitalist'. But such an economy was 'all the more determined for that to promote and encourage private enterprise'.[82] Recommending, too, as 'the best textbook for the Liberal Economy today' James Meade's work of 1975, *The Intelligent Radical's Guide to Economic Policy*, Pardoe concluded his reflections in unequivocal terms, declaring that:

> Liberalism must be in no doubt where it stands in the battle between individualism and collectivism: whether in its attitude to Trade Union monopoly power, the distribution of power or wealth, or the future shape of the social services ...[83]

In September 1975 the Liberal Party's Standing Committee, the body charged with the development of party policy and chaired since 1970 by Pardoe, produced a brief discussion document on Liberal principles, entitled *Liberalism Today*. In *New Outlook*, Gordon Lishman welcomed its aim of improving the climate of ideological debate within the Party, which, in his view, had been 'remarkably arid over the last few years', perhaps, he suggested, because of 'the limited role which Liberal academics have played in the Party's affairs' during that period.[84] Lishman noted with approval the attempt by Nancy Seear, one of his 'favourite Liberals', to define liberalism in a single mnemonic – the letters PIDL, standing for 'pluralism, internationalism, distributivism, and libertarianism'. He considered that 'a fair description of basic components of liberalism, and certainly more descriptive as a distinctive philosophy that the cack-handed attempts of Standing Committee members to fit a definition into "liberty, equality and fraternity" '.[85] He pointed out, too, that liberalism was 'more concerned with political activity than with political structures' since it was a fundamental liberal belief that 'human fulfilment comes from human activity rather than from political structures or policies imposed by a State, however benevolent'. For that very reason, he contended, 'the community politics idea, representing action as well as policies and ideas' was 'so clearly in the mainstream of liberal thought', and was 'very clearly foreshadowed in the writings of the most important Liberal philosophers'.[86] In support of that claim, he cited the concluding sentence of John Stuart Mill's *On Liberty*, which underlined the 'vital power' of the individual, and declared that:

> The worth of a State ... is the worth of the individuals composing it; ... a State which dwarfs its men, in order that they may be more docile instruments in its hands, even for beneficial purposes – will find that with small men no great thing can really be accomplished; ...[87]

Lishman was thus re-emphasising the central role which community politics, of which he himself was a leading theoretician, had assumed within British Liberal ideology in the first half of the 1970s. It was the liberal 'emphasis on the habits of participation,' he pointed out, that was 'the message of the community politicians in today's Liberal Party'. That did not mean, of course, that they believed 'that the policies and the legislation are unnecessary', but rather that those things were 'only a part of the political process, in which the most important role is played by action and by the education of people, by experience'.[88]

Further evidence of the major influence exerted on Party thinking by the community politics strategy emerged the following year in a book edited by Peter Hain and designed, in his words, to provide 'an analysis of the principles of community politics'.[89] In its introduction, Hain offered his own definition of it as a political approach which aimed to create 'a participatory democracy ... based on a series of self-managed communities through which people can control the decisions which affect them ...', and in which 'power would be exercised from the bottom upwards and resources would be co-operatively owned'. A 'cornerstone' of a participatory democracy of that kind, in Hain's view, 'would be workers control and ownership of industry', to be achieved through 'workers co-operatives within an economically decentralised system'. He distinguished that goal sharply, however, from existing Liberal policy proposals for workers' participation which, he argued, were concerned merely with 'ameliorating the most authoritarian effects of capitalism whilst retaining the system intact ...'.[90] In this respect he was clearly departing from mainstream Liberal thinking, as seemed to be the case, too, with his statement that advocates of his chosen model of participatory democracy wished 'to use the egalitarianism of socialism to underpin a libertarian ethos that rejects all forms of hierarchical organisation'. For the rationale underlying his political vision was, he pointed out, 'ideologically associated' with the libertarian socialist tradition.[91]

On the question of Hain's contribution to the theoretical justification of community politics, Bernard Greaves and Gordon Lishman later wrote that he had 'made a more determined effort than anyone to develop a coherent view of community politics'; yet 'in doing so,' they maintained, 'he argued himself into a position of opposition to some of the principles we set out'.[92] Twenty-six years later Greaves made this point more explicitly, arguing that Hain's presentation of community politics 'related it to a tradition of anarcho-syndicalist political theory, contained a highly contradictory tendency to the imposition of centralised state regulation, and linked it to the advocacy of direct action protest and civil disobedience in deliberate defiance of the law'. Hain had been 'quite right to leave' the Liberal Party in 1977, Greaves concluded, since 'this was not Liberalism'.[93]

The various contributions of these theoreticians of community politics, and, in a different vein, John Pardoe's vigorous attempts to promote a more market-driven approach to economic as well as social policy, clearly indicated that fresh thinking and lively writing on Liberal principles and philosophy were appearing at both grass-roots and parliamentary levels during this period. These developments even suggested that the aridity of recent intellectual debate within the Party, of which Gordon Lishman had complained, was being alleviated. The post-1974 period, was, however, one of further decline for the Liberal Party. This was evident in dismal local election and by-election results in 1976. But above all, it was dramatically underlined by the scandal-ridden termination of Jeremy Thorpe's political career.

Thorpe's downfall had been triggered in early 1976 by two damaging sets of revelations which seriously undermined his position as Party Leader. The first of these was contained in the report of the Department of Trade and Industry into various malpractices committed by the collapsed secondary bank, London and Counties Securities, of which Thorpe had been a non-executive director. The second, more sensational, set of revelations involved an alleged longstanding homosexual relationship between Thorpe and a former male model, Norman Scott, and further allegations, in the ensuing months, concerning elaborate cover-ups and even murder attempts. In the wake of the damage caused by these revelations, Thorpe eventually resigned the Liberal leadership in May 1976. He and three others were later charged with incitement and conspiracy to murder in August 1978, but were ultimately acquitted on all charges in June 1979.[94]

Following Thorpe's resignation from the Liberal leadership, Jo Grimond briefly became caretaker Leader until David Steel defeated John Pardoe in the first British party leadership election determined by the wider membership. Steel became Liberal leader in July 1976. He later recalled that 'the misery through which all of us at the top of the Liberal Party and close to Jeremy lived from 1975 to 1979' was 'difficult to describe'. For Liberal politics 'had been blighted for four years by Jeremy's problems'.[95]

On Thorpe's leadership as a whole, Dutton has commented that in retrospect

> ... sandwiched ... between the clearer, more creative visions of Jo Grimond and David Steel, (it) emerges as a period in which, notwithstanding some electoral successes, the party drifted without a sense of conviction or underlying purpose.[96]

Moreover, in his view, the Liberal revival from 1972 up to, and including, the February 1974 General Election, in which the Party achieved its best electoral result since 1929, 'fed off Thorpe's very real but somewhat superficial qualities'.[97] These included, in the words of his successor, David Steel, Thorpe's 'enormous flair, charisma, showmanship and boundless energy'.[98] Dutton's generally unfavourable, or at best highly qualified, judgement reinforced William Wallace's earlier observation that Thorpe, for all his strengths 'as an organizer, a money-raiser and a public personality', was 'largely uninterested in policy, and not much concerned with strategy'.[99]

Weighing other factors against that view, John Pardoe has stressed Thorpe's gifts as a 'superb communicator', particularly during the period of the early-1970s Liberal revival,[100] while Tony Richards, one of Thorpe's closest aides in 1974, has recalled a charismatic orator who drew huge crowds to public meetings in the election campaigns of that year when 'he was at the height of his powers'.[101] Indeed, in the retrospective view of another sympathetic observer, the first of those campaigns, that of February 1974, was 'one of the most brilliantly argued Liberal platforms of the last century'.[102] Furthermore, in Richards' view, Thorpe's central strategy in 1974, in contrast to the ambiguities and contradictions inherent in Grimond's earlier project of a realignment of the Left, was rooted in a clearer and more realistic view of the conservative mood and temper of the British nation during a polarising and acrimonious period in its history.[103] On Thorpe's political appeal in general, Richard Lamb later commented, too, that Thorpe 'brought eloquence, humour and compassion into politics',[104] while a biographer has described 'a progressive, stylish and popular politician' whose downfall obscured the fact that under his leadership the Liberal Party polled the highest number of votes in its history.[105]

In conclusion, it may be said that, whatever judgements may be made on Thorpe's qualities as Liberal Leader, his downfall in May 1976, coinciding with, and producing, a further downturn in his Party's fortunes, was followed by a leadership contest which, in its formal procedures at least, did justice to the Liberal tradition. For the wide franchise, in the form of an all-member ballot, on which that election was based amounted to a significant democratic initiative in the development of British party politics.

Chapter 5
Liberalism in a Cul de Sac: 1976–1979

Soon after becoming Liberal leader David Steel unveiled his chosen strategy for the Party at the Liberal Assembly in September 1976. It was to be one based on inter-party co-operation, which might involve a pact or even a coalition, as part of the Liberal Party's movement towards power. Steel had already been involved in this process of cooperation on several specific policy issues: in the successful promotion of his private member's bill on abortion law reform in 1966–7; on the question of Kenyan Asian immigration; in opposition to apartheid; and, most recently, in the 1975 national referendum on British membership of the European Community. Moreover, in the aftermath of the Liberals' 1970 electoral debacle he had become convinced that the long-march approach to Liberal revival favoured by many activists was futile and self-defeating since it required the Party, in his words, 'to plod on as before, spending the next ten years building up to a dozen MPs only to face near annihilation again on a sudden swing of the pendulum'.[1]

In his 1975 pamphlet, *The Liberal Way Forward*, Steel had also made clear that his focus on inter-party cooperation was envisaged as a further development of Grimond's earlier strategy of a realignment of the Left in British politics. While seeking, as he later put it, 'to promote some of my own heresies as well as my version of party orthodoxies ...'[2], Steel thus maintained that 'many of the self-styled social democrats would be happier company in combination with Liberals than Socialists'. If, then, 'an opportunity for an effective regrouping of the centre', were to arise, it was important, he stressed, 'that the Liberal Party should not behave like a more rigid sect of the exclusive brethren, but be ready to join with others in the more effective promotion of liberalism'.[3]

Indicating the thinking that underlay his sympathetic view of such a 'regrouping', Steel later remarked that if, in the late 1950s, 'the Labour Party had been as Gaitskell was, the need for and relevance of the Liberal Party at that time would have been largely eclipsed'.[4] The ideological implications of that statement, which Steel's mentor, Grimond, would certainly have questioned, were significant. Indeed, this 'near equation of Gaitskellite social democracy with Steel's own conception of Liberalism', deserved, as David Dutton has observed, 'to be more clearly noted than it was'.[5]

Steel's strategic emphasis on inter-party cooperation was again revealed when, in announcing his candidacy for the Liberal leadership in May 1976, he argued that the Party 'should combine our long-term programme with a readiness to work with others wherever we see what Jo Grimond has called a break in the clouds – the chance to implement any of Liberal policies'.[6] In a newspaper interview a few weeks after acceding to the leadership, he stressed, too, that the Liberal Party had to 'start by getting a toe-hold on power which must mean some form of coalition'.[7]

The ground was thus well prepared in advance by Steel when, in his first Leader's Assembly speech at Llandudno in September 1976, he told his audience that:

> ... if we tell the public that only by voting Liberal in sufficient numbers to prevent one other party gaining a majority, will we achieve electoral reform, and break the Tory-Labour stranglehold, then equally we must be clear in our own minds that if the political conditions are right (which of course they were not in February 1974) and if our own values are retained, we shall probably have – at least temporarily – to share power with somebody else to bring about the changes we seek.[8]

Steel continued by stating that he wanted the Liberal Party to be 'the fulcrum and centre of the next election argument – not something peripheral to it'. If that were to happen, then Liberals should 'not give the impression of being afraid to soil our hands with the responsibilities of sharing power'. Rather, they should be 'bold enough to deploy our coalition case positively'. After stating, too, that he wanted the Party 'to be a crusading and campaigning movement, not an academic think-tank nor minority influence nor occasional safety valve in the political system'[9], he concluded what he later called 'the troublesome part' of his speech[10] in candid terms:

> The road I intend us to travel may be a bumpy one, and I recognize therefore the risk that in the course of it we may lose some of the passengers, but I don't mind so long as we arrive at the end of it reasonably intact and ready to achieve our goals.[11]

The challenging nature of this chosen strategic course was soon clearly demonstrated when a parliamentary pact between the Liberals and the Labour government, headed by James Callaghan, was formed in March 1977. The government, recently embroiled in a major financial crisis, which had been averted the previous year only by a loan from the International Monetary Fund, had by this time lost its slim parliamentary majority in the House of Commons. The pact therefore amounted to a provisional agreement by the Liberals to support the government on confidence votes in return for a consultative role with regard to all major policy initiatives. This was not accompanied, however, by Liberal seats in the Cabinet or by any prior commitment to electoral reform. Nevertheless, the negotiations between Steel and Callaghan which paved the way for the formation of the pact did include legislative proposals for the first direct elections to the European Parliament, to be held in June 1979, with free votes in Parliament on a voting system based on proportional representation.

The pact was subsequently renewed in July 1977 and endorsed by a special Liberal Assembly in January 1978 in the face of the opposition of a substantial minority of party activists. This followed the Commons vote in December 1977 against a regional list system of proportional representation, one of the provisions of the European Assembly Elections bill. The rejection of this proposal by a Commons majority of 87, including the votes of over 100 Labour MPs, understandably fuelled widespread Liberal disillusionment, or, at least, growing unease. The pact endured, however, for 18 months in all, until its formal termination was announced in advance by Steel in May 1978.[12]

In support of the Lib-Lab Pact, it could be said that it provided a decisive break with the adversarial two-party system, and that the logical implication of Liberal support for electoral reform was, as Steel regularly stressed, inter-party cooperation or even power-sharing in a multi-party government. Indeed, Steel's eyes were fixed on the broader picture, for as Dutton has noted, he was 'more concerned with the concept of a pact and the idea of consultation – the toe-hold on power of which he had earlier spoken – than with specific policy commitments'. The pact would therefore, Steel hoped, 'be the first step in a process which, by getting the Liberal Party locked into the governmental machine, would one day lead it, via a formal coalition and proportional representation, to real power'.[13] As two contemporary analysts of the pact favourably commented, Steel had thereby offered his Party 'a direction, a purpose and an ambition'. Within months of becoming its Leader he had placed it 'at the centre of British political life, and had made it too important to be ignored by anybody'.[14]

Against that interpretation, it can be argued that the outcome of the Lib-Lab pact was disappointing and its achievements modest. In terms of policy and legislation, it did not promote much that was clearly 'Liberal', as Jo Grimond, its most severe critic in the parliamentary party, observed – apart, that is, from some limited proposals for profit-sharing in the 1978 Finance Bill. Above all, it did not advance the Liberal cause of electoral reform, as became painfully obvious in the Commons vote of December 1977. On this crucial issue, Steel's critics within the Party, especially those with experience of local government inter-party bargaining, accused him of a lack of toughness and pertinacity.[15] Yet electoral reform was, in Grimond's view, 'the prize, the only prize, which could have justified the pact'. For it offered 'the only immediate way' of strengthening the hand of 'the non-socialist but progressive element in our politics' at a time when the social-democratic wing of the Labour Party no longer seemed to him likely to 'gain the upper hand', something which he had believed possible 15 or 20 years previously.[16]

In Grimond's judgement, therefore, the Lib-Lab pact turned out to be 'a dubious arrangement'[17], both for that fundamental reason, and because, as he warned, it brought for the Liberals guilt by association with an unpopular Labour government. Steel himself later conceded this point, recognising that: 'We were lambasted for simply keeping in office a government which had outstayed its welcome.'[18] This became apparent in the outcomes of both parliamentary by-elections and local elections during this period. In the 10 by-elections held between the formation of the pact and its announced termination the Liberal share of the vote dropped by an average of 9.5 per cent. In the May 1977 local elections, held just two months after the pact was formed, the Party lost three-quarters of its county councillors.[19]

Underlying Grimond's reservations about the pact, however, were more deep-seated ideological concerns. These were increasingly expressed in his writings and speeches during the late 1970s. In his *Memoirs*, for instance, published in 1979, he noted the way in which the Conservatives, under Margaret Thatcher's leadership, were becoming receptive to economic liberal ideas. While they '... did not generate much newly-minted thought' during that period, they were nonetheless, in his view, '... putting together the teachings of the market economists and monetarists in a packet which could be presented as the policy of change and as a challenge to the conventional socialist/capitalist mixed economy bureaucratic thinking of the Establishment'. This was evident, he believed, in the speeches and thinking of Sir Keith Joseph.[20]

On the question of the established boundaries of the mixed economy, Grimond, like John Pardoe, challenged the conventional attitudes of the post-war collectivist consensus. In an article based on a 1976 lecture he argued that Liberals should 'clear our minds about the degree of government intervention and what is meant by "a mixed economy"'. The nationalised industries were 'inefficient, over-manned and wasteful of capital'. Moreover, in the face of these realities, social democrats within the Labour Party were being driven to face difficult economic questions such as the proportion of national income that should be absorbed by government expenditure or what the appropriate mixture of the mixed economy should actually be.[21]

Grimond questioned, too, the Liberal attitude towards the incremental growth of nationalisation in Britain since 1945. State ownership had 'crept forward', he pointed out in his *Memoirs*, 'either by the random acquisition of firms in difficulties or as a means to maintain employment'. But whereas 'socialists could justify this process because in their eyes any extension of state control was welcome', Liberals, by contrast, 'if they were to accept the "mixed economy" should have given much more thought to the principles according to which the state should nationalise and should have produced some boundaries between the free and the nationalised sectors'. In his view, the nationalised industries in Britain were 'not in fact a series of commanding heights, but at best a range of dying volcanoes ... distinguished, not by their current economic importance, but by their historical fame and by the numbers they employed'. Indeed, a crucial factor that had made the British economy 'so difficult to manage' had been 'the incompetence of the nationalised industries coupled with their insatiable demands for capital and subsidies'.[22]

In his 1976 pamphlet, *The Bureaucratic Blight*, Grimond renewed his attack on another favourite target: the bureaucratic attitude which pervaded not just the civil service but many other British institutions – including 'local government, public authorities, nationalised industries, many of the professions, and a great deal of big business'.[23] Whilst he recognised that bureaucracy was needed by management, it should exist, he stressed, in a blend with democracy and individualism. Yet in the Britain of 1976 'the democratic and individualistic elements are too weak and the bureaucratic element too strong'. Politically, that imbalance would lead to only one end, namely 'a highly inefficient socialist state in which freedom and originality are suppressed'.[24] A further malign effect of increasing bureaucratisation was evident in the British economy of the late 1970s, within which '... a smaller and smaller genuinely private sector' was 'being asked to carry on its back a bigger and bigger inefficient public sector' that was characterised '... by over-staffing, mismanagement and unresponsiveness to demand'.[25] This was a point developed at length by two Oxford University economists, Robert Bacon and Walter Eltis, in an influential book published the same year as Grimond's pamphlet and entitled *Britain's Economic Problem: Too Few Producers.*[26]

In *The Bureaucratic Blight* Grimond had delivered a trenchant polemic against what, as Peter Barberis has noted, 'seems in retrospect to have been the apogee of the peacetime "command state"'.[27] In his third major work of political thought, *The Common Welfare,* published in 1978, Grimond presented his radical alternative to that kind of society, to the swollen bureaucracies, entrenched corporatism and centralised statism of Britain in the late 1970s. In its pages he offered what he described in his *Memoirs* as his 'alternate strategy for Liberals'. Instead of 'trying to palliate state Socialism and its bed fellow corporatism', Liberals ought, he argued, to 'reassert more fertile traditions' – namely, those of the free market, cooperation and community development. On those three pillars, supported by 'a new appreciation of the virtues of private property', a modern liberal society could be built.[28]

In *The Common Welfare* one of its main themes, he explained, was his belief '... that people should be actively concerned in promoting communal welfare so that it is not merely "handed down"'. In that way the Liberal goal of a welfare society could be pursued and, at the same time, the social services would become more effective.[29] Underlying that social vision was the ideal of 'the overriding common good' which had been 'an essential of liberal thinking since the eighteenth century'. Yet in contemporary society that liberal ideal, stemming from European and American Enlightenment thought, had 'become confused with state control, corporatism, collectivism', which were 'usually the enemy of the common good'.[30] As a consequence, 'by way of reaction to collectivism', there had developed 'a school of liberal politicians and thinkers who, rightly concerned about our loss of liberty', had been 'inclined to throw out the idea of the common good along with the ideas of state socialism'. It was therefore, in Grimond's view, 'as essential to reassert the notion of the common good, with all the obligations which go with it, as it is to assert liberty and the voluntary character of our acceptance of the common good and the rule of law'.[31]

With regard to the first of Grimond's three pillars of a liberal society, the free market, he identified a number of advantages inherent in that form of economic organisation, about which, in his view, there was 'widespread ignorance'.[32] One of them was the propensity of a market economy to decentralise decision-making, to break it down 'into a multitude of individual bargains'. This 'autonomous and multifarious process' conferred several benefits. In particular, it ensured flexibility, and it limited the damaging effect of wrong decisions to only a part of the economy, imposing the cost of such decisions on those who made them rather than on the public at large. The opposite, however, was the case when mistakes were made in a national plan.[33] Moreover, implicitly endorsing Friedrich von Hayek's notion of a spontaneous, unplanned order inherent in a market economy, what Hayek called a 'catallaxy', Grimond argued that the market was 'not a random, haphazard way of conducting affairs'. For in reality its central mechanism of 'automatic changes of prices, responsive to supply and demand' was 'a much more scientific regulator than haphazard interference by ministers at the request of this or that pressure group'.[34]

But in spite of his recognition of these and other advantages, Grimond qualified his support for a market economy in four main respects, taking into account its 'severe drawbacks and limitations'. In the first place, since the market was 'an artificial creation protected by the laws of the state', such as, for instance, the law giving limited liability to joint-stock companies, the State was therefore 'entitled to regulate it'. Second, there were many human activities, involving public goods in particular, which 'should not be subject to the market'.[35] Third, there was the problem, he noted, of 'the perennial inequality of those who have to operate the market' – evident in the weak position of consumers in the face of monopolies or, in some cases, of employees in the face of employers.[36] Finally, there was 'the basic difficulty facing market economies – that some of those operating in it have, through no fault of their own, far less chance of benefiting from it than do others'. The 'advantage of inherited wealth', for example, was very great, and 'far too many people' still suffered 'from the disadvantage of being born poor in a poor community'.[37]

These qualifications clearly indicated that, as in his previous writings, Grimond continued to hold an empirical rather than absolutist view of the desirable form of economic organisation. Nevertheless, the free market remained, in his view, one of the main pillars of a free society. The others, he maintained, were those formed from the interrelated values of cooperation and community.

In his examination of the co-operative pillar, Grimond had been influenced by the ideas of Robert Oakeshott, who had founded Job Ownership Limited in order to encourage the conversion of existing businesses into cooperatives. Oakeshott had provided a detailed account of independent cooperatives operating throughout Europe in *The Case for Workers Co-ops* (1978), described by Grimond as 'a book which all Liberals should read'.[38] While 'pondering on the means whereby our industrial system might give more satisfaction while retaining its essential freedom'.[39] Grimond had been introduced by Oakeshott to the Mondragon group of workers' cooperatives in the province of Biscaya in the Basque area of Spain. These consisted of more than 60 productive ventures or enterprises operating since the late 1950s and employing about 15,000 people. Their savings and investments were managed by a Basque bank, the Caja Laboral Popular, which played a pivotal role in their operations. The cooperatives functioned as elements in a competitive market system, with wages, for example, fixed by reference to comparable wage-rates in the private sector. In addition, the cooperatives provided welfare services such as sickness and unemployment benefits and pension schemes, and supported schools and hospitals for which people paid or subscribed.

In spite of his admiration for the Mondragon system, Grimond realised that its translation into British conditions would require a radical change in attitudes and practices. It would clearly threaten entrenched vested interests, including employers' federations, trade unions and departments of the bureaucratic State. Not only, however, had the Mondragon cooperatives, Grimond pointed out, been productively efficient, generating at that time sales in excess of £200 million a year, as well as a considerable export trade; they had also significantly reduced tensions between capital and labour, fostering generally harmonious industrial relations.[40] 'The whole operation,' he maintained, was 'a lesson in how to reduce class distinctions and bureaucratic top-hamper'. In short, it was 'socialism without the state'.[41] Since in reality, however, the State was unlikely to wither away, then, in his view, cooperatives like those at Mondragon held out 'a much more realistic solution for a reduction in its power than does orthodox socialism'.[42]

Grimond also regarded the Mondragon system as an illustration of how community development might advance the Liberal ideal of a welfare society, that interrelationship, which Beveridge had favoured and promoted, between individuals, voluntary organisations and the State. In turning, therefore, to consider his third liberal pillar, community action, Grimond examined a number of experiments in community organisation and community services. On a small scale, these could be introduced in small towns or rural districts, but they might have most to offer, he suggested, in large cities. In Liverpool, for instance, the Liberal-controlled city council since 1973 had encouraged the growth of community ventures of various kinds, including coopera- tives and self-management schemes among tenants of both privately rented accommodation and council-owned properties.[43] Community action along such lines was thus viewed by Grimond as closely linked to his second pillar, cooperative enterprise. Both of them covered areas in which individuals could further their self-development, and both provided means of reconcil- ing a market economy with collective endeavour, thereby making the system more acceptable and attractive to more people. A liberal form of collective activity could thus flourish, released from the heavy hand of bureaucratic statism, which undermined not only individual initiative but also the very notion that 'the hallmark of a community is the voluntary acceptance of it by its members'.[44] More broadly, Grimond regarded the ideas of both coop- eration and community as intimately connected to the advancement of the Enlightenment liberal ideal of 'the overriding common good', to the promo- tion of 'the common welfare', which Grimond viewed in broad terms 'as embracing employment, education, health and architecture, and the other activities of a healthy community', and concerning 'all the members of the community and not only the poor or incapable'.[45]

Grimond's three-pillared structure of a liberal society was thus another expression of his earlier conception, evident in particular in *The Liberal Future*, of an 'unservile society', in which the individual citizen's active participation would be encouraged not just within a decentralised political system but also within cooperative enterprises, within local self-managed communities, and within a more competitive free enterprise economy. On another level, this could be viewed as a further development, attuned to the late 1970s, of a Liberal third way, distinct from both state collectiv- ism and market individualism. Nearly 40 years earlier, Elliot Dodds, in his espousal of the cause of co-ownership, had presented it as an alternative to both state socialism and monopoly capitalism. Grimond's own concep- tion of a third way involved an attempt, in his words, to 'reassert the twin legacies of the eighteenth century, the legacy which gave us Mill, Ricardo and the liberal tradition of political economy' and the legacy, too, of the liberal Enlightenment which had inspired, in different ways, Robert Owen, Ebenezer Howard and G. D. H. Cole.[46] In other words, Grimond proposed a progressive synthesis which would combine the revived emphasis on eco- nomic liberal ideas, zealously promoted at that time by Conservatives such as Sir Keith Joseph, with a social liberal concern with the common welfare,

and hence with an emphasis on cooperation and community development. Such a synthesis would include, too, a firm commitment to political
and constitutional reform, advocated in all of Grimond's other writings,
and shared by British Liberals of all kinds. All the elements in this Liberal
third way were clearly distinct, in various respects, from the state socialism which was at that time the dominant ideological tendency within
the Labour Party. With the significant exception of the endorsement of a
market economy, they were also themes that were clearly distinct from the
free-market Conservatism associated with Margaret Thatcher's leadership.
Grimond recalled later the false ideological choices which often seemed
to be posed during the 1970s, and which he had attempted to transcend,
observing that:

> If the positive side of Hayek and other liberal political economists had
> been followed up and married to a defence of the common interests
> which must inspire any democratic society, then we should have had an
> alternative liberal programme. But, unfortunately, the prevailing fashion
> was against these writers when they were at their zenith. It dismissed
> them as 'right-wing', then a damning indictment.[47]

The economic liberal element in Grimond's proposed benign synthesis
found, as he suggested, few leading advocates within the Liberal Party in the
late 1970s apart from himself and John Pardoe, who later candidly recalled
that he 'failed totally to convert the Party' to such ideas during that period.[48]
Apart from their contributions to Liberal thought and debate, and those of
a few others, much of the impetus for fresh thinking within the Party continued to spring from the grass roots – in particular, from the theoreticians
of the community politics approach – rather than be driven, as in the era of
Grimond's leadership, from the leadership level. There was, however, as we
have seen, much common ground shared between the theory of community
politics and the views expressed by Grimond in *The Common Welfare*. There
was agreement, too, between all these prominent Party thinkers on the need
for a clear and coherent restatement of Liberal philosophy.

Gordon Lishman, for example, who became the editor of *New Outlook* in
the autumn of 1977, stressed the importance of Liberal ideology in providing 'the only secure basis for a radical Party which seeks to change fundamentally the society of which it is a part'. He declared that a 'Great Debate'
within the Party needed 'to be re-opened for the health and future of organised liberalism in Britain'. He believed, too, that it would be 'possible to
construct ... a definition of modern liberalism as distinct from "moderation"
and "social democracy"'.[49]

The ideological debate which Lishman desired failed, however, to be
ignited within the Party during the late 1970s. This was due in part to the
party elite's lack of receptiveness to the economic liberal ideas that Pardoe

and Grimond were propounding. But in part, too, the absence of vibrant debate could be attributed to what Lishman has described in retrospect as 'the apparent antithesis between community politics and national activity' which, in his view, was 'not in any way necessary'.[50] That tension stemmed from both scepticism and misunderstanding among the community politicians and parliamentarians alike. Tony Greaves, for example, later doubted whether at that time David Steel had 'any understanding of community politics at all'. Instead, he believed, the Party Leader 'placed it in the context of English local government'.[51] On the other hand, John Pardoe later expressed his own retrospective doubt about 'whether there was any ideological acceptance of community politics within the parliamentary party'.[52] As a consequence, Lishman has recalled, a gap opened up in the Liberal Party between local and Westminster politics during the second half of the 1970s. There was 'no guiding coherence in the middle of the local and parliamentary levels', which he considered 'ought to have been essentially ideological'. There were, in his opinion, some people in the Party who 'did understand the connection' between the two levels of Liberal political activity – notably, Geoff Tordoff, Richard Wainwright and William Wallace – and who could therefore have developed that theoretical coherence.[53] But the acute internal problems besetting the Party during that troubled period, following Jeremy Thorpe's resignation as Leader, combined with the strains created by the continuation of the Lib-Lab Pact, served to distract Party thinkers from that kind of intellectual exercise, however valuable.

For all that, Lishman attempted a further editorial contribution to the dormant Party debate in *New Outlook* in March 1978. There he expressed his general unease about the phrase 'a Liberal society', which he admitted had been widely used by Young Liberals and community politicians in the early 1970s as '... a shorthand way of affirming that the values of liberalism are expressed in attitudes and relationships as well as in policies and institutional power'.[54] He confessed that he always felt 'somewhat uncomfortable with that phrase, "Liberal society"', since it was 'reminiscent of the "socialist society" or any other utopia', suggesting 'a static perfection, which can be achieved and towards which policies, legislation and Government can move'.[55] Liberalism, by contrast, was 'about attitudes rather than systems ... about the process rather than the end'. It was his view, therefore, that:

> To present liberalism, or even to try to comprehend it, without an idea of change, of process, of dynamism is like trying to understand the nature of a peregrine falcon from a still photograph. The essence is in the movement, the flexibility and the style.[56]

Lishman, as Donald Wade had earlier done in his writings, stressed the fact, therefore, that liberalism was not some static entity, a notion 'foisted on our political system by the collectivists', but rather 'a continuing process of debate, of argument, of striving ...'. For while liberalism had its prophets, it had 'no gospel ... no one source ... no single definition ...'.[57]

Two months after the publication of these ideological reflections, David Steel announced the imminent termination of the Lib-Lab Pact. To the surprise of most commentators, the Prime Minister, James Callaghan, postponed his announcement of the date of the next general election, widely expected in autumn 1978, and consequently suffered the damaging effects of the 'winter of discontent', the wave of conspicuous industrial unrest afflicting Britain in the winter of 1978–79. Eventually, in March 1979, for the first time since 1924, the Government fell on a vote of no confidence in the House of Commons.

The Liberal Party approached the impending 1979 General Election in a highly defensive posture, accused by the Conservatives of keeping in office an unpopular Labour government. The Liberals, however, had recently, in March, received the consolation of a by-election victory at Liverpool Edge Hill, with David Alton elected as MP, reflecting the continuing effectiveness of community campaigning in previously Labour-dominated inner-city areas.

The 1979 Liberal election manifesto, *The Real Fight Is for Britain*, largely drafted by William Wallace and Peter Knowlson, the Party's Director of Research, placed its central emphasis on political and constitutional reform, which was presented as the essential condition of the economic and industrial changes so urgently needed in Britain at that time. Arguing in the introduction to the manifesto that political reform was the 'starting point', David Steel stressed that not 'until we break the two-party stranglehold' and 'get away from the adversary class politics which are embedded in our parliamentary structure', could the country 'successfully tackle the problems of economic weakness and industrial mistrust ...'. Electoral reform was 'the key to the lock', which would deprive the Conservative and Labour parties of 'their ability to maintain electoral support by frightening wavering voters with the spectre of a single, unacceptable alternative'. Changing the voting system would also force those parties 'to face up to their own internal contradictions: the unstable coalition within a weakened Labour Party between its nationalising left and its conservative centre; the tensions within the Conservative Party between moderate Tories and doctrinaire free-marketeers'.[58]

In addition to electoral reform, the manifesto itself advocated the rest of the set of political and constitutional reforms which Liberals had consistently championed since 1945: a reformed Second Chamber; devolution to Scotland, Wales and the English regions; a Freedom of Information Bill; and a Bill of Rights.[59] In the economic and industrial fields, it maintained that Britain was characterised by '... an unjust industrial society in which most workers are pitted against management and are denied any share in decision-making or in profits'. It therefore regarded 'a revolution in attitudes amongst all at work through the introduction of Democracy in Industry as the key to reversing Britain's economic decline'. This would involve implementation of the principal Liberal proposals for industrial partnership. In tune, too, with ideas that Grimond had explored in *The Common Welfare*, Liberals would encourage producer cooperatives through the establishment of a Co-operative Development Bank.[60]

On the major area of ideological debate that was then emerging in British politics – concerning the role of the State within the economy – in the light of the revival of economic liberal ideas, the manifesto sought to present a balanced, albeit rather circumspect view, certainly a less radical one that Grimond and Pardoe were expounding. The 'primary aim of government intervention' in British industry was thus depicted as 'the promotion of viable market enterprises'. The role of government was 'to provide a stable political and economic framework, not to dominate the economy'. But the manifesto pledged, too, continuing Liberal support for 'a sustained prices and incomes policy based on wide consultation and enforceable at law'.[61] Pardoe himself, the leading Liberal advocate of that policy, later recognised the tension between its state collectivist character and the economic liberal ideas and policies which he was otherwise promoting. Within, however, the historical context of the 1970s, he has recalled, 'we were all so seared by the terrible problem of inflation', that such a statist policy seemed then, to him and many others, to be a practical necessity.[62]

More broadly, *The Real Fight Is for Britain* also defended on pragmatic grounds selective state intervention in the economy as a whole. It was 'dangerous to pretend,' the manifesto stated, 'that government can be taken out of economic and industrial planning', particularly in view of '... the active involvement of governments of competitor countries in supporting their industries and promoting their own economic interests'. In similar vein, it was argued that, while there was 'no case for further large-scale nationalisation in Britain, [...] attempts to denationalise at present would further disrupt the industries affected'. Furthermore, the Labour government's National Enterprise Board provided, it was claimed, 'a valuable mechanism for assisting new industries and for aiding companies temporarily in difficulty'; but it 'should disengage from them when they regain commercial viability'.[63]

This ideologically cautious tone was perhaps understandable in view of the defensive position in which the Liberals found themselves in 1979, and in the light, too, of the limited advancement of economic liberal ideas within the Party at that time. But the manifesto's overall approach in this area could also be regarded as an unadventurous and conservative response to the gravity of the economic and industrial problems afflicting the nation.

The manifesto did, however, break with consensus politics in two significant respects. First, it recommended a shift in fiscal policy from direct to indirect taxation, proposing a starting rate of income tax of 20 per cent and a top rate of 50 per cent, as well as 'tax incentives for profit-sharing and employee share ownership'[64]. Second, it revealed a clear ecological perspective in its proposals for conservation of scarce resources, especially land and energy, and in its commitment both to reducing waste and pollution and to protecting the natural environment.[65] 'We have a duty,' the manifesto declared, 'to preserve in trust for future generations that which we inherit from the past'.[66]

The outcome of the 1979 General Election, held on 3 May, was a setback for the Liberals, but not a disaster comparable to 1970, which had been widely feared. The Party polled 4.3 million votes with 13.8 per cent of the total poll and 11 MPs elected. In view of the damaging effects both of the Party's association with an increasingly unpopular Labour government and of the long-drawn-out termination of Jeremy Thorpe's political career, there were even some encouraging factors to be taken into account. A substantial block of Liberal voters had been either retained or gained; the Nationalist challenge in Scotland had been blunted; and the Liberals were at last broadening their electoral base, making inroads into the industrial North of England, with three of their 11 MPs victors over Labour.[67] David Steel, as Grimond and Thorpe had done before him, had fought a skilful national campaign, proving himself an effective communicator of the Party's appeal as a positive third choice. The Liberal vote in 1979 remained, however, volatile and unstable in nature, as it had done since 1959. On average fewer than 50 per cent of Liberal voters had remained loyal to the Party at the following general election during that 20-year period.[68] Nevertheless, in 1979 the Liberal Party, as David Steel subsequently remarked, had 'survived the election in better shape than anyone forecast ...'.[69] It had at least avoided the descent into either the desolation of the pre-Grimond era or the profound demoralisation of 1970.

Chapter 6
Liberalism within the Alliance: Denting the Mould: 1979–1983

In the aftermath of the 1979 General Election the Liberal Party did at last engage in the kind of public examination of its values and philosophy which Gordon Lishman and others had earlier called for. At the instigation of Michael Meadowcroft, a special debate on the nature of Liberalism was held at the 1979 Liberal Assembly in Margate, during which speakers addressed, among other concerns, the contentious ideological question which had begun to dominate British politics – concerning the proper role of the State within the economy.[1] William Wallace contrasted the Liberal attitude towards that question with that of what he called '... the terrible simplifiers of the left and right' who had 'gained more strength in both the established parties' and, in the case of the latter, were 'strongly represented' in the new Thatcher government. These polarised groups were either '... demanding more intervention and control', or else desiring 'to roll back the frontiers of the State all the way across the economy'. In view of this rigid antithesis, Wallace recalled a passage from the 1928 Yellow Book which referred to the illusory simplicity 'with which extremists of the left and right sum up these questions in a single sentence, telling us either that the State should cease to meddle with industry, or that the capitalist system should be replaced by Socialism'.[2] In contrast, Liberals, both in the late 1920s and 50 years later, Wallace pointed out, 'insisted on the need for active state intervention in managing the economy, but equally insisted that intervention must not be allowed to slide into state domination'. They accepted the fact 'that markets need to be policed, that abuses of power need to be checked, that those for whom the market does not cater must be helped'. But Liberals, unlike socialists, also believed 'that state power must be checked ... and must be exercised as flexibly and moderately as possible'.[3]

With reference to 'the terrible simplifiers of the right', those such as Margaret Thatcher and Sir Keith Joseph who wanted to curtail drastically the role of the State in economic policy, another speaker, Ian Bradley, examined the widely made claim that Thatcher had appropriated for the Conservative Party 'many of the themes of Gladstonian Liberalism', such as self-help and a belief in minimal government. Bradley did not believe that Liberals could 'escape the fact that there is some truth in this'. But, because Thatcher had 'plundered the Victorian store-cupboard for some of her ideas', there was no reason, he argued, for Liberals 'to ignore what is rightfully our heritage'. Margaret Thatcher had in fact been 'extremely selective' in what she had taken from Gladstonian Liberalism and had 'often misinterpreted' the ideas which she had imbibed. For example, she had 'misread, as a kind of passive, do-nothing notion of laissez-faire, the central Victorian principle of voluntarism', first developed in the 1840s. But in reality, Bradley pointed out, voluntarism had been 'a strenuous call to social action, to reform, to improve and reconstruct society, but to do so wherever possible through the free, spontaneous action of individuals and communities, not through the compulsory action of the state'.[4]

The central points which both Wallace and Bradley were making here were highly relevant to the major ideological and policy debate that had developed in British politics, a debate in which leading Liberals, with a few exceptions such as Jo Grimond and John Pardoe, seemed unwilling to engage. For in the face of the entrenched state collectivism and corporatism of the 1970s, and in the light, too, of the revival of economic liberal ideas since 1975, how, as Wallace had asked, should British Liberals strike a new balance between the market and the State, clarifying 'the boundaries of state control' and 'the necessary limits of individual enterprise'? Or in Bradley's interpretation, which parts of the classical Liberal tradition should be reclaimed in place of the centralised statism of the social-democratic consensus, without adopting the 'laissez-faire' attitudes of a doctrinaire anti-statism?

These important ideological questions had, then, at least been raised within Liberal Party debate in the immediate post-election period. Two months later another, much more widely publicised, debate was ignited by Roy Jenkins's 1979 Dimbleby Memorial Lecture, entitled 'Home Thoughts from Abroad'. Jenkins had left the Labour government in 1976 following his disappointing, unsuccessful bid to succeed Harold Wilson as Labour Party Leader. He had subsequently, in 1977, taken up the post of President of the European Commission in Brussels.

In his Dimbleby Lecture, delivered in London on 22 November 1979, Jenkins emphasised the deleterious effects of the current polarisation of British politics and denounced 'the constricting rigidity – almost the tyranny – of the present party system'. This had led, he pointed out, to disruptive changes of policy direction, to what he called 'queasy rides on the ideological big-dipper', a process exacerbated by the first-past-the-post electoral system.[5] What was needed, therefore, Jenkins argued, within the British political system as a whole was, paradoxically, 'more change accompanied by more stability of direction'. To that end, he called for a fairer electoral system, based on proportional representation, and a 'strengthening of the radical centre',[6] with a new grouping committed to a programme of political, constitutional and social reform and to a political approach through which state intervention and market forces complemented each other. For Jenkins's view on this ideologically contentious question was that:

> We need the innovating stimulus of the free market economy without either the unacceptable brutality of its untrammelled distribution of rewards or its indifference to unemployment.[7]

This, he observed, was 'by no means an impossible combination', which worked well in a number of countries. It meant, too, accepting 'the broad line of division between the public and private sectors' and not constantly threatening those in the private sector 'with nationalisation or expropriation'.[8] A 'strengthening of the radical centre' would promote and sustain that kind of economic balance. More broadly, it could also, he believed, 'bring into political commitment the energies of many people of talent and goodwill who ... are at present alienated from the business of government, whether national or local, by the sterility and formalism of much of the political game'.[9]

As soon as David Steel had seen the draft script of Jenkins's lecture, sent to him personally in advance by its author, he 'realized immediately its political impact' as 'a polished, elegant historic overview of the current state of British politics ...'.[10] After it had been delivered, Steel conveyed to Jenkins his view that the mould of the two-party system might be broken more easily through the combined challenge of two separate but allied parties: the Liberal Party itself and what Steel later described as 'some new organization founded mainly on a massive exodus from the Labour Party but linking up in alliance with us ...'.[11] In effect, that new political organisation would be a social democratic party.

The position of the social democrats within the Labour Party – of, that is, its predominantly pro-Europe, pro-NATO and pro-mixed economy moderate wing – had long been precarious. By the late 1970s they had been increasingly marginalised in the face of the revival of a fundamentalist socialism on the Labour Left, assiduously promoted by Tony Benn and his supporters. With the aid of a quasi-Marxist analysis of monopoly capitalism, the Labour Left had developed an alternative economic strategy based on widespread state ownership and on greater state control of private industry.[12] Social-democratic decline had become even more apparent after Roy Jenkins's departure from British politics in 1976 and following the deaths of Anthony Crosland in 1977 and John Mackintosh in 1978. The declining intellectual influence of social democracy within the Labour Party was symbolised, too, by the demise in December 1978 of *Socialist Commentary*, once the leading revisionist socialist journal.

Nevertheless, Jenkins's 1979 Dimbleby Lecture had, at the very least, pointed towards future political possibilities. With a more specific focus, David Marquand, who had been a Labour MP until 1977 when he joined

Jenkins at the European Commission, tried to disentangle, in an essay in *Encounter* in July 1979, the causes of the growing polarisation within the Labour Party. He, along with other social-democratic politicians and thinkers such as Evan Luard and John Mackintosh, had already begun to develop a critique of the centralist and corporatist tendencies inherent in state socialism.[13] In his 1979 essay, 'Inquest on a Movement', Marquand refined that critique further by identifying as one of the main causes of the decline of British social democracy the dominant influence of the Fabian element in its inheritance, while the decentralist New Liberal influence had been largely neglected. As a consequence, he argued, that pervasive Fabian legacy had in practice led to the degeneration of social democracy into a centralist, bureaucratic form of social engineering.[14]

Marquand emphasised, too, the defensive posture of social democrats within a party which, in his view, had become increasingly left-wing in its composition, proletarian in its ethos and anti-intellectual in its instincts. He concluded gloomily that he did not believe 'that the job of revising welfare-state social democracy can be done within the formal framework of the Labour Party or that active Labour politicians can contribute much to it'. In the same essay he also stressed the need to define the purposes of what he called 'a new-model libertarian, decentralist social democracy', and suggested that a new political vehicle might be needed for that task.[15]

The response of some Liberals to these developments – to the Dimbleby Lecture in particular – had at first been rather lukewarm. A *Liberal News* editorial noted that the content of Jenkins's lecture 'was stated with conviction and supported Liberal aims'. But Liberals, it stressed, were 'not concerned with the formation of a new brand of Social Democrats', and saw 'no need for a new centre party'.[16] Jo Grimond was also guarded in his response to 'Home Thoughts from Abroad', and expressed an unflattering view of Labour's moderate wing, of which Jenkins had once been an acknowledged leader, declaring that:

> The Social Democrats have been discredited. Most of them have put up a poor fight inside the Labour Party and too many have left for lucrative jobs outside.[17]

David Steel, too, drew attention during this period to the enfeebled position of Labour's social democrats, observing that:

> ... the Labour party's intellectual right has lost Roy Jenkins to Europe, Shirley Williams to defeat, John Mackintosh through death, David Marquand to the academic world, Dick Taverne to new party failure and Brian Walden to television. What is left is ill-equipped to oppose the strength of the hard left who at least have a credible if repugnant economic credo on offer.[18]

Steel, however, later recalled that this social-democratic weakness within the Labour Party for him provided grounds for optimism. He was 'very much on the lookout for allies to break out of the Labour Party and link with us'.[19] Labour's changed balance of power thus offered the possibility of that break-out occurring. It strengthened his argument for the formation of a new political organisation which, in alliance with the Liberals, would help to bring about a realignment of the Centre-Left, the ultimate aim of the strategy which he had pursued since 1976.

In April 1980 Steel restated his case for such a realignment in a pamphlet provocatively entitled, *Labour at 80: Time to Retire*. As Grimond had done before him, he dismissed the Labour Party's claims to be an agent of progressive change in Britain. 'Insular, rent by doctrinal schism, owned by the trade unions and devoid of new ideas', Labour, in his view, was 'simply incredible as the vehicle for the transformation of Britain'.[20] The root cause of that political reality, he argued, lay in the historical fact that the early Labour Party had taken 'four wrong turnings'. These were, first, the special power that it had accorded to the trade unions; second, the projection of social class as the basis of the Party's appeal; third, the equation of the centralised State with socialism; and fourth, the Fabian preference for paternal authority over fraternal democracy.

For all those reasons, Steel believed that it was 'structurally impossible for the Labour Party to reform itself ...'[21] In its place, he depicted the Liberal Party as the source of 'a set of ideas around which alternative policies can form ...', drawing upon a Liberal intellectual tradition that brought together the values of 'self-reliance and participation, voluntarism and co-operation and above all community'.[22] All this would provide, in his view, the basis for a 'radical programme ... for political, economic and social change'. The route to its fulfilment, he suggested, would be inter-party cooperation involving some kind of alliance or even coalition. 'A movement of reform coalescing around a resurgent Liberal Party', would thus, he argued, be 'the first step'. But 'a great national government of reform' was where that movement 'should lead', and it should have room in it 'both for socially responsible Conservatives and radical Socialists alike'.[23]

A series of developments within the Labour Party during the course of 1980 appeared to vindicate Steel's strategic vision. In early June Labour's anti-EC Common Market Safeguards Committee issued a statement which claimed that current Labour Party policies and the demands of EC membership were irreconcilable, and which therefore sought to secure at the Labour Party Conference in the autumn of that year a firm Party commitment to withdraw from the EC with no renegotiation and without even a referendum. In response, David Owen, Bill Rodgers and Shirley Williams published their own joint statement in defence of Britain's continued membership of the European Community. This statement by the 'Gang of Three', as they soon became popularly known, ended on a defiant note by declaring that 'there are some of us who will not accept a choice between socialism and Europe. We will choose them both'.[24] That, Owen later recalled, 'was the first indication I had ever given that I would contemplate leaving the Labour Party for a new social democratic party'.[25]

In June 1980 a commission of enquiry on revising Labour's constitution approved proposals for both mandatory reselection of all sitting Labour MPs between general elections and an electoral college for choosing the Party Leader. These constitutional changes had been advocated since 1973 by the Labour Left and were designed to ensure that the parliamentary party and leadership should be accountable to the Labour rank-and-file and hence, in practice, to left-leaning constituency and trade union activists. The official approval of these major changes, which had far-reaching implications for the balance of power within the Party, led David Owen 'to wonder whether the Labour Party was now salvageable'. At that time, however, he was 'still not thinking of a Centre party', but rather, 'was questioning my continued membership of Labour'.[26] For Owen had already expressed his view, shortly after Jenkins's Dimblebly Lecture, that a newly formed Centre party would be 'rootless, brought together out of frustration' and would not only 'soon split apart when faced with the real choices', but could also 'easily reflect the attitudes of a London-based liberalism that had neither a base in the provinces nor a bedrock of principles'.[27]

In the meantime, however, Roy Jenkins restated his case for a new party of the radical Centre in a speech, his first in England since the Dimbleby Lecture, in London on 9 June. He reminded his audience that nine days earlier, on 31 May, at a Special Conference in Wembley, the Labour Party had committed itself to 'a near neutralist and unilateralist position' on defence policy, to 'practical non-cooperation with the European Community leading in all likelihood to a firm proposal for complete withdrawal in the near future', and to 'a massive further extension of the public sector' in the economy, together with plans for the subjection of the private sector 'to a straitjacket far tighter than in any other democratic country in the world'.[28]

More broadly, Jenkins argued that 'the politics of the left and centre of this country are frozen in an out-of-date mould which is bad for the political and economic health of Britain and increasingly inhibiting for those who live within the mould'. The two major parties, resting on organised producer interests, promoted a brand of 'politics based on industrial confrontation', a form of class politics incapable of setting the necessary framework for cooperation in British industry. He concluded by likening his proposed new party to an 'experimental plane' which might well 'finish up a few fields from the end of the run-way'. But it might instead 'soar in the sky', going 'further and more quickly than few now imagine, for it would carry with it great and now untapped reserves of political energy and commitment'.[29]

David Owen, who had spoken out against Labour's unilateralist defence stance, amid booing and heckling, at the special Wembley conference in late

May, later commented that 'Roy's experimental plane was of little interest to me' at that time, and believed that Bill Rodgers and Shirley Williams were also 'extremely reluctant to contemplate ever being part of a Centre party'.[30] Nevertheless, at the beginning of August 1980 Owen, Rodgers and Williams published a wide-ranging policy statement in the form of an open letter in *The Guardian*. Its trenchant conclusion stated that if Labour's governing body, its National Executive Committee, remained

> ... committed to pursuing its present course and if, consequently, fears multiply among the people, then support for a Centre Party will strengthen as disaffected voters move away from Labour. We have already said that we will not support a Centre Party for it would lack roots and a coherent philosophy. But if the Labour Party abandons its democratic and internationalist principles, the argument may grow for a new democratic socialist party to establish itself as a party of conscience and reform committed to those principles.[31]

Two-and-a-half months later, in late September/early October 1980, the Labour Party Conference at Blackpool endorsed the plans, approved in June, for a new electoral college for choosing future Party leaders, together with the principle of mandatory reselection of Labour MPs. These constitutional changes were accompanied by a decisive leftward shift in Labour policy, as Conference approved commitments to unilateral nuclear disarmament, to unconditional withdrawal from the EC, and to an Alternative Economic Strategy involving a substantial extension of both state ownership and state control of industry.

By the time, then, of what, for Labour's moderate wing, had thus been a disastrous conference, many social democrats were contemplating leaving their Party.[32] Any lingering doubts about that course of action were soon dispelled by two further developments. The first of these was the election in November 1980, under Labour's existing procedural rules, of the veteran tribune of the Labour Left, Michael Foot, as Party Leader, succeeding James Callaghan. Roy Jenkins later confessed that the result had left him 'elated' since 'it clearly opened up a much greater prospect of political realignment'.[33] The second major setback for Labour's moderate wing was the confirmation by a special Labour Party conference in January 1981 of the details of the new electoral college for Party Leadership elections. According to these arrangements the largest share of votes – 40 per cent – would be accorded to the trade unions, with the parliamentary party and constituency parties each receiving a 30 per cent vote share.[34]

It was against this background that Owen, Rodgers and Williams, together with Jenkins, who were collectively now dubbed the 'Gang of Four', issued the Limehouse Declaration, at Owen's house in east London on 25 January 1981, to launch the Council for Social Democracy. This soon evolved into the Social Democratic Party, formally established on 26 March of that year.

The gradual loosening, from June 1980 onwards, of the ties that still bound Owen, Rodgers and Williams to the Labour Party, and the consequent emergence of the new Social Democratic Party, were viewed, however, at the time with some degree of scepticism by several influential Liberals. In September 1980 Desmond Banks, for example, confessed that he was 'not sure what the definition of social democracy is' since it seemed to him 'to embrace people who are virtually socialist ... and people who are virtually liberal'. As someone who had been consistently on the social liberal wing of his Party, Banks pointed out that the Liberals had come 'to believe in demand management, incomes policy, public expenditure for public good, the mixed economy, social security and social welfare policies'. In so far, therefore, as Labour's social democrats believed in those collectivist policies, they clearly had 'something in common with Liberals'. But 'while stressing the importance of this positive role for the state', Liberalism as a creed, he added, was also 'very conscious of the damage of too much power at the centre in the hands of the state'.[35]

From a broader historical perspective, Ralf Dahrendorf had argued, earlier in 1980, that social democracy itself was 'on the wane', having begun 'to lose momentum in the 1970s'. 'Historically,' he observed, 'the specifically social democratic contribution consisted in an overriding concern with economic inequality and in a belief in the ability of benevolent governments to solve most problems'.[36] But in addressing 'the economic, social, cultural and political problems of the day', the social-democratic approach had, in his view, 'exhausted its strength'. Indeed, it had also begun 'to produce as many problems as it solves'. For example, the welfare state, 'a necessary condition of freedom for many', was something which 'had its price' since it 'required the setting-up of gigantic bureaucracies which have landed people in a new dependence'. The removal of 'one set of obstacles to liberty' had thus 'created new obstacles to liberty'. How, then, could liberals deal with this paradox: the need to 'maintain the beneficial effects of the welfare state while freeing the individual of bureaucratic bondage?'.[37]

Dahrendorf noted that social democracy had flourished in the period from 1948 to 1973, 'years of unprecedented economic growth even in Britain', involving 'a cycle of improvement which led to the trebling, in some cases the quadrupling, of the gross national product as well as the real incomes of most within a quarter of a century'. But by 1980 economic growth had, for various reasons, 'become very difficult indeed'. Yet social democrats did 'not talk, let alone write on such disturbing themes'. Indeed, social democracy in general had, in his view, 'ceased to be a subject of political thought'. It was 'almost as if all imaginative minds had emigrated to opposition groups'.[38]

'The issue today,' Dahrendorf concluded, was '... what comes after social democracy'. He considered that:

If this is not to be a Blue, Red or Green aberration, it will have to be an imaginative, unorthodox and distinctive liberalism which combines the common ground of social-democratic achievements with the new horizons of the future of liberty.[39]

In outlining its historical decline, Dahrendorf had stated that 'in important respects, social democracy has become yesterday's politics'.[40] Or as he later trenchantly commented, social democracy, and subsequently the British Social Democratic Party, appeared to offer 'a better yesterday'. These were sentiments echoed by Jo Grimond in a lecture delivered in London in October 1980, in which he observed that:

> At this moment there is a temptation to win votes by a rather woolly moderation, or by emphasising that latter-day conservatism which would preserve the accepted tenets of the past thirty-five years – what has been called the doctrine of a better yesterday.[41]

Grimond also restated his view, which had been expressed consistently throughout his writings, but which now chimed with the recent revival of economic liberal ideas in British politics, that:

> The market for economic purposes is by far the best means. Liberals must stress at all times the virtues of the market, not only for efficiency but to enable the widest possible choice.[42]

'The trouble today', however, he noted, was 'not only that the market has been expelled from many of its legitimate fields, but that it has invaded many temples where its presence is illegitimate'.[43]

But Grimond struck a more controversial note when he turned to consider the international position of liberalism in 1980. 'At present,' he pointed out, 'in three-quarters of the world, there is little or no liberalism', and even in Britain it was '... no longer the dominant philosophy'. In such circumstances it was 'no longer a case of defending it, but of regaining ground'. For that purpose allies were essential, just as in the feudal age aid was accepted 'from the better barons, at least for specific battles and on a temporary basis'. In the struggle, therefore, to reassert liberal values against the forces of bureaucratic state socialism allies might even be sought within the Conservative Party; for it was Grimond's view that 'much of what Mrs Thatcher and Sir Keith Joseph say and do is in the mainstream of liberal philosophy'. Indeed, in recognising the need to widen the appeal of liberalism, he stressed the fact that, as a philosophy, it was 'not a private jewel in the exclusive keeping of the Liberal Party, to be hugged to our hearts in case it is stolen'.[44]

Grimond's reference to Thatcher, Joseph and liberal philosophy clearly went against the current of mainstream British Liberal thinking in 1980. But as Ian Bradley had pointed out at the 1979 Liberal Assembly philosophy debate, there was some truth in the claim that Thatcher had drawn, however selectively, on ideas and themes discovered in what he had called 'the Victorian Liberal store-cupboard'. Grimond had merely underlined that historical point more unequivocally, although he concluded, as in the past, with a characteristically pragmatic and empirical view of liberalism. In promoting, he maintained, their fundamental beliefs, albeit in a predominantly illiberal climate, liberals needed to be 'continually ... adjusting our system and institutions to give effect' to those beliefs, which depended 'not upon one form of democracy or economic organisation, but upon keeping in mind the purpose of all human societies, that is, to enable the individual in his or her community to make their own choices and live better lives'.[45]

Grimond and some other Liberal thinkers and writers at this time were thus, either explicitly or by implication, expressing strong reservations about the nature of the social-democratic approach that was beginning to seek a political vehicle separate from the Labour Party. Such reservations were reinforced by a restatement in 1980 of the theoretical basis of the community politics strategy which had become so central to British Liberalism during the 1970s, and which, with its essentially participative and decentralist focus, differentiated itself sharply from the perceived characteristics of British social democracy, at least as it had developed from the mid-1950s to the late 1970s. That restatement appeared with the publication of *The Theory and Practice of Community Politics*, a booklet written by two of its leading theoreticians, Bernard Greaves and Gordon Lishman. It was the most coherent theoretical justification to date of community politics both as a set of ideas and as a strategy. As Greaves later explained, it was produced to fill 'the lack of a clear and easily accessible authoritative statement' describing community politics.[46] In its foreword the booklet's co-authors insisted that community politics was 'not a technique for the winning of local government elections', but rather in their view, '... an ideology, a system of ideas for social transformation'.[47] For such ideas to become a reality, there was, they acknowledged, 'a need for a strategy of political action', and for that strategy to be successful, it needed 'to develop effective techniques of political campaigning'. But those techniques were merely 'a means to an end'. If they became 'an end in themselves', then 'the ideas they were destined to promote' would have been lost.[48] Those ultimate aims were to secure for individuals within their communities greater control over their living environments and a deeper sense of involvement in decisions affecting their lives. Expressed in broader ideological terms, the goals of community politics were thus indissolubly linked to the popular control and wider distribution of political power.

In practice, however, over the past ten years, Greaves and Lishman regretted that some of the strategy's 'most persuasive advocates' had even appeared to be 'dangerously near to presenting community politics in terms of our opponents' caricature of "pavement politics"' and had thereby 'revealed their ignorance of the underlying ideas'.[49] As Lishman put it shortly after the booklet's publication, the theory of community politics had been 'misinterpreted and dismissed by those who insist on seeing community politics as indistinguishable from multiple leaflet delivery tactics at local government elections'.[50] Over 20 years later Tony Greaves made the same point, observing that community politics had often degenerated into 'surveys to help us win elections', instead of serving as a strategy concerned with asking 'what can we actually do to change things in this patch on the ground?'.[51]

Moreover, in Lishman's view, 'the instinctive tendency of Liberals to avoid the grind of hard thought and thorough discussion of issues on philosophy and ideology' had made 'the commitment to community politics little more than a token for a Party which is increasingly obsessed with the minutiae of policy details and the prospect of power to the detriment of the analysis and liberalism which should underlie both'.[52] In contrast, he and Bernard Greaves continued to conceive of community politics in more elevated ideological terms, viewing it as a theory of political and social transformation, since for them ideology was 'a necessary part of political debate, the only guarantee of constant principle, and the unifying and motivating force of a Party'.[53]

Many years later, however, Lishman reconsidered this harsh judgement on the apparent, widespread lack of theoretical understanding of community politics within the Party. He had become 'less convinced about the distortion' involved, about the gap between theory and practice. For in his view, community politics was something 'visceral to Liberals', who consequently 'didn't need to understand the underlying theory' since they realised instinctively that liberalism was a creed that was not only individualist and libertarian but also 'socially generous and participative'.[54]

The theoretical misunderstanding of which Lishman had originally complained was, however, evident, in the view of his co-author, among the parliamentary leadership under both Thorpe and Steel, who 'neither embraced nor understood the community politics strategy'. For in their eyes, it consisted, Bernard Greaves believed, of '... a rather dubious form of local populism; a technique for fighting local government elections and Parliamentary by-elections; an undue emphasis on local government; and a misguided romantic attachment to historic neighbourhoods which had little relevance to the modern world'.[55]

In addition to the view that in practice community politics had often degenerated into an electioneering technique, a further criticism was that it had often, too, become a method of enlisting the aid of elected politicians in order to redress local grievances. This process had thereby superseded the original aim of helping to organise people in local communities 'to take and use power', in the words of the 1970 Liberal Assembly resolution. Only one part of the community politics strategy, the part which emphasised the role of Liberal activists in 'using ... political skills to redress grievances', was thus being implemented.

This was a point also made by Jo Grimond when he argued that the cause of community action and development which he had championed in *The Common Welfare* had in practice usually meant 'raising grievances and pressing for action by an organization, either the state or the local authority, to be financed by national taxation', thereby involving 'a plea for more government and more expenditure'.[56] As he later observed, it was therefore 'important to distinguish between schemes designed to encourage communities to help themselves and schemes which simply prod people to clamour for more public funds and more bureaucracy'.[57]

A third criticism of the practical application of community politics was that its techniques could be, and often were, copied by other political parties. In 1973 Desmond Banks had pointed out that community politics was not in itself a political philosophy. Its underlying ideas and concerns – 'dealing with people's grievances, consulting people's wishes, helping people to take effective action to bring about changes in their environment' – all sprang, he recognised, 'naturally from the Liberal philosophy'. After all, the wider participation of people in their place of work or in their local community was essential for individuals' self-development and therefore inseparable from 'the basic principle of Liberalism', that is, 'a belief in the supreme value of individual personality'. But while an emphasis on the value of participation followed naturally from Liberalism, it was 'not by itself Liberalism', but 'only one strand' of that creed. Moreover, the participative approach fostered by the community politics strategy was not a Liberal monopoly. A political body like the National Front, Banks warned, could 'adopt similar community tactics for electoral purposes and gain support and sympathy as a consequence'. Liberals therefore had 'a two-fold task to perform: firstly, to enable people to participate, and secondly, to persuade them to support Liberal policies ...'.[58] Over 30 years later, Banks's warning was confirmed by Tony Greaves who pointed out that by 2007 in his own political territory in Lancashire the successor to the National Front, the British National Party, had become, apart from the Liberal Democrats, 'the most effective community campaigners'. Indeed, in most of the wards in Pendle, for example, the BNP, through such campaigning, had become the main challengers to the Liberal Democrats at local government level.[59]

At its worst, therefore, community politics could degenerate into a Poujadist manipulation of popular grievances. As Michael McManus has argued, such an approach, in the view of many observers, thereby

> ... debauches and cheapens politics. With its reliance upon negative and oppositional campaigning, 'grumble sheets' and the exploitation of local grievances, it tends to weaken any conception of the 'general good' and reduces politics to a series of unilateral appeals to separate interest groups.[60]

A more general criticism that could be made of community politics as a strategy was that it rested on a questionable assumption about the extent to which a widespread popular desire existed for participation in local community decision-making. Was there not a distinct possibility, some critics asked, that such a desire was harboured by the most articulate and voluble, or simply by those used to involvement on the committees of various voluntary organisations or public bodies, rather than by those most in need of community action? David Steel expressed, albeit in humorous terms, his own concern about this possible shortcoming when he stated that:

> Where I disagree with some of the theoreticians on community politics is that they postulate a society where everybody is going to damn well participate whether they like it or not.

Steel continued:

> This is where the thinking is flawed. The great majority of our citizens may have a particular wish to participate in the organisation of the community at some particular level of their own choosing, but we cannot create a sort of perfect model and say everybody must engage in this, this and this activity and construct society accordingly.

Indeed, he considered the likelihood of that kind of mass participation in local communities to be 'just Utopian'.[61]

A final and more far-reaching criticism centred on the adequacy of community politics as a national political strategy. The dual approach adopted in 1970 had, of course, attempted to address that question by depicting it as a supplement, rather than an alternative, to Parliamentary activity. Nonetheless, a number of problems remained unresolved. In an analysis of community politics published in 1985, David Thomson maintained that '... the ALC and Liberal community politicians' were 'attempting to "nationalise" a campaigning style and political ethos ... which has already achieved success in local politics'. Yet many Liberal strategists, he pointed out, had come to believe 'that community politics is not a coherent national strategy on its own'. For the municipal successes of Liverpool and elsewhere had served only 'to emphasise the paucity of success at parliamentary level in the same places'. Indeed, a 'central danger' inherent in the pursuit of community politics was 'the problem of the Liberal Party being widely seen as "localists" and becoming trapped in the ghetto of local politics'. How, then, Thomson asked, could the Liberals 'break out of this municipal cul-de-sac without weakening the campaigning style and distinctive image that community politics has contributed?'.[62]

While, then, community politics had become 'the dominant political strategy for local government campaigning', effectively promoted by the ALC, particularly since the transfer of its operational base to Hebden Bridge in 1977, it had not become, Thomson noted, the Liberal Party's accepted national strategy. That, as we have seen, had been since 1976 one of inter-party cooperation through pacts and alliances. Those two Party strategies therefore co-existed 'uneasily'.[63] Indeed, since the community politics strategy took an essentially 'long-march' approach to political power, it tended to ignore 'the vital intermediate stage of achieving credibility' through holding the balance of power in Parliament, the goal to which Steel's national strategy was specifically directed.[64] For, as Michael Meadowcroft stressed, there was for Liberals a 'barrier to jump' in order that the voters might perceive them 'as a national party with a consistent viewpoint'.[65] That was particularly the case, he later pointed out, in Leeds, a city with a tradition of being represented by high-profile national politicians, such as Hugh Gaitskell, Denis Healey, Merlyn Rees and Sir Keith Joseph, and where consequently a Liberal MP was widely expected to take up positions on national and international issues rather than act mainly as a 'super-councillor'.[66]

Moreover, the tension between the two strategies was apparent in the different political pressures arising, on the one hand, from the need to respond to the diverse and specific problems of particular communities and, on the other, from the need to develop at a Parliamentary level coherent and consistent policies on major national issues. As Michael Steed commented in 1983, the weakness of the community politics strategy was that it provided 'little guide to the role of Liberal MPs at Westminster (as opposed to their constituencies) or to the logic of voting Liberal in national elections when the colour of the next government is at stake – other than a "plague on both your houses" attitude ...'.[67] Yet, in Steed's view, the reality was that 'too many Liberal Community Politicians found it easier to assume that such an attitude would suffice for a posture, and were without an answer or much influence at critical moments in the party's development, as in 1974, 1977, 1978, or 1981'.[68]

In spite of these various shortcomings, it was nonetheless the case that by the early 1980s a strategy which had been devised in 1970 not only, as Tony Greaves has recalled, 'to define a strand of Liberalism' but also 'to ensure the survival of the Party' at a time when such an outcome appeared highly uncertain.[69] had achieved considerable success at local government level. Whereas in the early 1970s Liberals amounted to only four per cent of Britain's local councillors, by 1985 their share had passed the 10 per cent mark.[70] The Party by then not only had about 2,000 councillors but also assumed a pivotal role in many town halls. More broadly, as Thomson observed, community politics had become 'central to the ethos of the Liberal Party', having made '... a major impact on every part of the Party's activity from policy formation and electoral strategy to campaigning techniques', whilst 'providing a general motivation to activists'. It could thus be said to have 'become both the heart and the brain of the Liberal body politic'.[71]

The establishment of the Council for Social Democracy in January 1981, leading to the foundation of the Social Democratic Party two months later, had been accompanied by an official, broad statement of principles, the Limehouse Declaration, which reaffirmed the principle of political and economic decentralisation that had been emphasised in the late 1970s by some social-democratic politicians and thinkers, notably Evan Luard, John Mackintosh and David Marquand, as part of their critique of the bureaucratic centralism and statism of established Labour thinking and policy. In a 1980 lecture Marquand had developed further that critique by proposing a decentralist strategy for controlling what he called the 'new Leviathan' of the centralised corporate State.[72] In similar vein, the Limehouse Declaration, drafted and signed by the 'Gang of Four' at David Owen's home in east London, underlined the support of their newly established Council for Social Democracy for 'more decentralisation of decision-making in industry and government, together with an effective and practical system of democracy at work'.[73]

It also echoed the sentiments and language of Roy Jenkins's 1979 Dimbleby Lecture in its stated desire for 'more, not less, radical change in our society, but with a greater stability of direction', in its rejection of 'the politics of an inert centre merely representing the lowest common denominator between two extremes', and in its emphasis on the need to combine 'the innovating strength of a competitive economy with a fair distribution of rewards'.[74] The Declaration's concluding sentence, drafted by Jenkins, ended by stating that 'we believe that the need for a realignment of British politics must now be faced'.[75] Those words, Jenkins later recalled, 'gave clear notice that we were moving outside a Labour Party laager'. Furthermore, since realignment could not be 'a purely internal or unilateral act', there being a need for 'somebody with whom to realign ... the most obvious although not necessarily the only people whom this embraced were the Liberals'.[76]

David Owen, however, interpreted the word 'realignment' in a different sense. In his view, it was not used in the Limehouse Declaration as Grimond had used it in the past, namely, to imply a process of 'bringing part of the Labour Party together with the Liberals into one party'. Rather, for Owen it meant that the newly launched SDP, as 'an independent national fourth political party', might act as 'a catalyst', thereby maintaining its independence yet bringing about change in the party political structure.[77] Owen's interpretation gains some credence from the fact that in early March 1981, just before the SDP was founded, the Gang of Four sent a telegram to the vice-presidents of Socialist International requesting that the new party should be permitted to join that organisation. The request, strongly opposed at the time by the Labour Party, was eventually turned down by Socialist International.[78]

Nevertheless, Jenkins later rejected as 'nonsense' the suggestion 'that those who joined the SDP believing that they were joining a pure and exclusive party were sold a false prospectus and subsequently hijacked first into alliance and then into amalgamation with the Liberals'. Indeed, 'part of the central message' of the Social Democratic Party was 'an attack on the sterility of exclusive politics, on the view that any party is a sacred tabernacle with those within it anointed and those outside damned'. But that anti-tribalist attitude was 'not of course the same as advocating an immediate merger with the Liberal Party'. For in 1981, while he was 'committed ... to a close partnership' with the Liberals, Jenkins insisted that he 'had no set view for or against eventual merger'.[79]

Whatever interpretation might have been placed on its concluding emphasis on 'the need for a realignment of British politics', the Limehouse Declaration itself was welcomed by David Steel as part of the development of, in his words, 'an effective non-Socialist alternative to Thatcherism'.[80] David Owen later recorded his resentment that social democracy had been 'redefined' in those terms. 'Socialism,' he observed, was then 'as much a dirty word to the Liberal Party as to the Conservative Party ...', though he conceded that he and his colleagues 'could not thrust the term at our potential friends or allies who did not come from the Left'.[81] Owen's reaction, together with his desire that the SDP, after its foundation, should join Socialist International, thus indicated that in 1981 he drew a clear ideological distinction between social democracy, conceived as a moderate and decentralist form of socialism, and the main currents of British Liberalism.

Owen set out his own ideological position in a clear and developed manner in his first major work of political thought, *Face the Future*. This was one of three extended treatises written by the 'Gang of Three'. Owen's book and Shirley Williams' *Politics Is for People* were published in 1981. Bill Rodgers' *The Politics of Change* appeared the following year. *Face the Future* was Owen's attempt to provide the embryonic Social Democratic Party with a clear political and ideological identity. First published in January 1981, before the SDP's launch and while, in his own words, he was 'still nominally a member of the Labour Party'[82], the book was republished in a revised and abridged edition later that year. It soon became, as David Marquand later described it, 'the nearest thing to a philosophical credo which the new party had'. It consisted of Owen's 'earnest attempt to give policy substance to the co-operative, decentralist, non-statist tradition in British socialism'.[83] In the revised edition, however, several, but not all, of his references to 'socialist' and 'socialism' were changed to 'social democrat' and 'social democracy'.[84]

In drawing on that particular decentralist tradition, associated with British socialist thinkers such as Robert Owen, William Morris and G. D. H. Cole,

David Owen was thereby developing, like Marquand, a critique of the state collectivism and centralism characteristic of Labour Party policy in the early 1980s. As Owen later explained, 'the most important theme of the book was the need to break the grip of bureaucratic corporatism'. 'Early in its history,' he pointed out, 'the Labour Party had chosen the path of Fabian paternalism personified by Beatrice and Sidney Webb; pursuing nationalization and Clause Four state socialism', and this had been an 'historical error bedevilling every Labour Government'.[85]

In *Face the Future* Owen also emphasised his support for a mixed economy, a stance which in Britain at that time remained ideologically contentious on the Left, and yet had become a widely accepted orthodoxy among European social democratic parties. Indeed, in continental Europe the term 'Social Democrat' had become a description, he pointed out, of 'a socialist who worked constructively within the framework of a mixed economy, not against the framework of the mixed economy, as is the more prevalent attitude in Britain within the Labour Party'. For the dominant Labour attitude on this question in 1981 was 'one of resigned acceptance'; it was 'acceptable to defend the mixed economy, but not to espouse it'. 'Much of the deep-seated antagonism to the European Community within the Labour Party' stemmed, Owen noted, 'from its Clause 4 socialists who do not want the mixed economy that Community membership involves'.[86]

More broadly, the overall approach of Owen's *Face the Future*, with its espousal not just of the mixed economy but also of the cause of the decentralisation of political and economic power, together with its advocacy of constitutional reform, could be considered entirely compatible with mainstream Liberal ideas and commitments. Indeed, David Marquand later recalled how many Liberals whom he spoke to during that period were impressed by *Face the Future*, even regarding Owen at that time as 'an ideological soulmate'.[87] This was a view shared by Alan Beith in 1982 when he observed that in their writings or speeches all of the SDP's 'Gang of Four' had presented 'what have been long-standing Liberal policies with a freshness and vigour which Liberals, conditioned by familiarity, do not always bring to these issues'. Moreover, 'the fact that this new thinking' had brought the SDP's leading co-founders 'on to a convergent path with the Liberals' was, in his view, 'what makes the Alliance possible'. When David Owen, in particular, Beith noted, was 'at his most radical – on decentralism of power, for example', he preached 'the pure gospel of Liberalism'.[88]

In a similar spirit, Jo Grimond, reviewing *Face the Future* in *The Spectator*, applauded its author's 'adherence to the ranks of the anti-corporatists'. But he also expressed wider doubts about the social-democratic approach to Britain's current problems. He still believed that Owen's colleagues were 'thinking of the days of Gaitskell', whereas, in Grimond's view, there was 'a need for a new departure in British politics'. In the face of the threats then posed 'to a satisfactory democracy and to our freedom – notably the threat of inflation', he doubted 'if semi-dirigiste policies, palliatives to state socialism, are enough', or indeed 'if that old political nirvana, the middle ground, is any longer there to occupy'. He feared, too, that the kind of strategy which he had advocated in *The Common Welfare* – 'a new political programme based on co-operation, community development and a free market' – might even be adopted by the Tories, 'if they move with determination', thereby making themselves 'the radical element in our politics ...'. In this respect, he regretted that the Liberal Party had 'not made more use of the new thought which now abounds on industrial organisation, the market and the local community'.[89]

Grimond developed these thoughts further in a later *Spectator* article in which he admitted that he was among those who had 'always had doubts about the middle ground, the mixed economy as mixed today and the structure of government and industry'. In contrast, the Social Democrats were, in his view, 'the inheritors of the Gaitskell tradition which believed ... that the framework of government left by Attlee would work perfectly well if only directed by the right hands and heads, essentially spiritual Wykehamists or Fabian head-girls'. Moreover, he observed, the Social Democrats, when in office, 'were not famous for their reforming zeal'. They were 'hardly in the forefront of the battle over workers' participation, co-ops, the break-up of the nationalised industries or home rule for Scotland or Wales'.[90]

Grimond's scepticism about a political approach based on a 'middle way' and on espousal of a mixed economy was rooted, he explained, in an awareness of the sheer scale of the structural problems endemic to the British economy. These included 'the size of the unproductive public sector, the state monopolies and the bureaucratic feudalism of the trade unions', all of which made it 'impossible to run the country on the present mixed economy'. He therefore had doubts over the 'sufficiency' of the current policies of both the Social Democratic and Liberal parties, to 'meet our needs' in the face of such grave problems.[91]

Grimond's doubts were not entirely allayed by the publication in June 1981 of a brief joint statement of agreed principles issued by the two parties. Entitled, *A Fresh Start for Britain*, it contained proposals for political and constitutional reform (including devolution and proportional representation), industrial partnership, and support both for collective security through NATO and for continued British membership of the European Community. The statement also indicated other areas of agreement: on an incomes policy, on a strategy for economic recovery and on measures for environmental protection, including conservation of resources. Although *A Fresh Start for Britain* added little to recent Liberal and SDP statements of principles, it was, as Ivor Crewe and Anthony King have noted, 'of critical importance symbolically' since it 'underlined what the parties had in common' and marked 'the moment at which the two parties formally announced that they were to do business together'.[92]

In his review of the document, Grimond, however, returned to themes that he had explored in his recent writings – including, in particular, the question of the existing boundaries between the public and private sectors within the mixed economy, and the incompatibility of a formal incomes policy with what he had earlier referred to as 'the presuppositions of a liberal society'.[93] While conceding that the statement was 'admirable in many respects', he considered nonetheless that the key unresolved question was

> ... whether its authors are searching for a middle ground – a reformed and diluted variety of étatism, a mixed economy in which the mixture is to be much as now ...; or whether they intend to strike out for a new highly decentralised political economy with drastic changes in our methods of running industry, competition, workers' ownership, and so on; in fact a total alternative to state socialism.[94]

Grimond's reservations highlighted, then, some perceived ideological differences which still, in his view and that of some others, remained between, and indeed within, the parties. Certainly the leaderships of both the Liberal Party and the SDP, in the face of the acrimonious and confrontational climate of British politics at that time, appeared to be rejecting radical ideas on economic and social policy that diverged sharply from the commitments of the post-war collectivist consensus. In their history of the SDP, Crewe and King later underlined the common ground, in policy, strategic and ideological terms, that by 1981 was already occupied by David Steel and Roy Jenkins. They observed:

> Steel's vision of Britain's political future resembled Jenkins' in almost every particular. He was in favour of the welfare state but against detailed state control of the economy, in favour of private enterprise and the free market but against untrammelled capitalism and the ethics of selfishness and greed, in favour of free trade unionism but against the war of all against all that the unions had conducted during the Winter of Discontent. He was, like Jenkins, an enthusiast for Europe, for an incomes policy based on consent and for an end to what he saw as the sterile bickering over the boundaries between the public and private sectors ... Also like Jenkins, Steel was a staunch liberal on social issues and matters of conscience.[95]

An awareness of this common ground led Roy Jenkins to recall ten years later the often-quoted comment, attributed to Grimond, that Steel and he 'got along well because he was a good social democrat and I was an Asquithian liberal (in other words paradoxically complementary and not instinctive rivals) ...'.[96] Yet in spite of the two Leaders' similarity of political outlook, there were many in the Liberal Party, particularly on its radical community politics and local government wing, whose early view of the SDP seemed to chime with Grimond's – that it was likely to be an essentially conservative and consensus-minded political force.

That assessment was either evident or implicit in the writings of a number of prominent Liberals during the course of 1981 – including, notably, those of Michael Meadowcroft. He in particular was concerned with differentiating Liberalism from social democracy, thereby clarifying the Liberal Party's ideological identity. In expressing early doubts about proceeding to an alliance, Meadowcroft had complained of 'the rather patronising attitude of some Social Democrats towards Liberalism', which displayed 'a surprising unwillingness to acknowledge any philosophic integrity for Liberalism'. Did those Social Democrats really think, he asked, 'that so many individual Liberals, anxious for political influence, would commit themselves to long sentences of hard labour in a third party unless they believed firmly in its coherent and distinctive political position?'.[97]

Meadowcroft made his own contribution to the development of that ideological position in his booklet, *Liberal Values for a New Decade*, published as the sequel to Donald Wade's *Our Aim and Purpose*, which had appeared in four successive editions between 1961 and 1967. Meadowcroft's booklet was a response, in his own words, to '… the current need to apply our political principles to the crisis in Western industrialised society with its minimal growth, high inflation and increasing unemployment …'.[98] It was also the first of a series of booklets in which, in the political equivalent of 'apologetics in theological terms', he sought to set out Liberal beliefs in relation to other political creeds.[99]

From a similar perspective, some of the leading Liberal community politicians had already underlined what they considered to be the major shortcomings of British social democracy. In their eyes these lay in its pursuit of economic growth regardless of the environmental consequences, in its bureaucratic and technocratic approach and ethos, and, specifically, in the housing and urban redevelopment policies and programmes implemented by Labour-controlled councils. In the light, therefore, of the emergence of the new Social Democratic Party in 1981, those radical Liberal activists tended to regard such criticisms as still valid. As David Thomson wrote in 1985:

> To many Liberals the strategy of community politics was a direct reaction to the corporatism and ineffectiveness of the old-style social democracy. Was the nature of this new beast any different?[100]

Since the 1960s, and particularly since the early 1970s when the term 'social democracy' was first widely used in British political discourse,[101] it had been viewed by many Liberals as a moderate form of socialism that was centralist, statist, bureaucratic and paternalistic in nature. By the early 1980s, however, the co-founders of the SDP had, as we have seen, become committed at least to the principle of political and economic decentralisation. In David Owen's case, his decentralist convictions were deep-seated, having been been influenced in his youth by, amongst others, G.D.H. Cole's writings.[102] But in spite of the shared commitment of the 'Gang of Four' to decentralisation, Gordon Lishman, for one, was not convinced. Historically, he claimed, that was 'not what social democracy has ever meant, insofar as it has had any coherent identity at all'.[103] In any case, he asked, did 'Dr Owen mean administrative decentralisation, or a real change in the relation between ordinary people and the institutions of the state?'.[104]

As well as these Liberal suspicions about the engrained centralism of British social democracy, further doubts centred on its inherent statist and paternalistic tendencies. Such reservations derived in an important sense from the implications of the distinction which the historian, Peter Clarke, had recently drawn between, on the one hand, the approach of 'moral reformers' epitomised by the Edwardian New Liberals and, on the other, that of 'mechanical reformers' personified by the early Fabian socialists. In the former case, social reform would be brought about, it was believed, primarily through the spontaneous, voluntary activity of individuals and their communities. In the latter case, it would be achieved by organisational methods and through the agency of a benevolent State serviced by skilled political and administrative elites.[105] The Liberal preference for the approach of 'moral reform' was itself rooted in the belief that, in the words of Leonard Hobhouse, 'the heart of Liberalism is the understanding that progress is not a matter of mechanical contrivance, but of the liberation of living spiritual energy'.[106]

With Clarke's distinction in mind, the statist and paternalistic tendencies that appeared to many Liberals to be, along with its centralism, endemic to social democracy could be seen as rooted in a Fabian approach of 'mechanical reform'. The statism of social democracy was thus a reflection of its belief that social reform should spring mainly from the deliberate activity of a benevolent State. But Liberalism had consistently stressed the danger of too much power vested in the central State. Indeed, Liberals recognised that the quest for benevolent government had, all too often, as Ralf Dahrendorf pointed out, led in practice to big government, which was 'always ... liable to encroach on individual liberties'.[107]

The paternalistic tendencies of social democracy also clearly stemmed from this Fabian approach of 'mechanical reform'. In contrast, the Liberal principle of voluntarism which underlay an approach of 'moral reform' gave rise to a style of political activity based on collective enablement rather than state provision. In justification of that approach, Michael Meadowcroft observed that there was 'a vital distinction between doing things for people and enabling them to do them for themselves'.[108] In similar terms, Alan Beith pointed out that:

> Socialist paternalism in its milder, non-revolutionary form is still marked off from Liberalism by an irrepressible determination to give people what their rulers think is good for them.[109]

In the early 1980s, then, it still seemed to many active Liberals, particularly those on the Party's radical community politics and local government wing, that there were significant ideological differences between social democracy and the mainstream of British Liberalism. Tony Greaves, for example, later recalled that initially he felt 'absolutely no ideological affinity with the SDP'.[110] Ian Bradley summed up this sense of estrangement when he wrote in 1985 that some Social Democrats 'retain a vestigial Fabian authoritarianism, an egalitarianism which produces a strong state', and, with reference to Clarke's distinction, 'a preference for mechanical rather than moral reform ...'. But Bradley also recognised 'a powerful cry' in the ranks of the SDP for decentralisation, voluntarism and internationalism.[111] This had been evident, as we have seen, not just in the treatises of the original 'Gang of Three', most clearly in Owen's *Face the Future*, but also in the writings of some social-democratic politicians and thinkers who had joined the SDP at its foundation, most notably Evan Luard and David Marquand. The latter had, after all, called for 'a new-model libertarian, decentralist social democracy', and had decried the process whereby, encumbered by its Fabian legacy, old-style social democracy had 'degenerated, in practice, into a system of social engineering ...'.[112]

Furthermore, as David Sassoon has pointed out, social democracy had always been, in a sense, a 'revisionist' ideological tendency, adapting its doctrine to the endless mutations of capitalism as well as to the periodic shifts in electoral opinion.[113] The latest stage of revision, which Marquand favoured, was the attempt to avoid or curb the neo-Fabian centralist and paternalistic tendencies of social democracy. That might well involve an ideological approach different in kind from the revisionist socialism, or in Marquand's own phrase, 'Keynesian social democracy', espoused by Crosland, Gaitskell and Douglas Jay in the 1950s and early 1960s. But such a process of revision might nonetheless give rise to a form of social democracy compatible with the main strands of British Liberalism.

Indeed, in retrospect Marquand did not consider that there was any wide ideological gulf separating the SDP from the Liberals during the early 1980s. Rather, he regarded the main difference between the two parties as 'one of culture not of ideology'. The SDP thought of itself as 'more businesslike, competent, managerial and efficient' than the Liberals and that, in his judgement, was 'the real dividing-line between the two parties'.[114] Shirley Williams has concurred with that view, recalling that in her eyes 'the big difference' between the parties lay in 'their organizational and managerial styles', with the SDP's more parliamentary focus and the Liberals' more localist approach. This contrast, she believed, was 'more important than the relatively small ideological differences' between the parties.[115]

From the Liberal side of this real or imagined divide, Richard Holme, one of David Steel's closest confidants and advisers during the 1980s, later stated that he was 'quite clear that there weren't fundamental ideological differences' between the two parties.[116] A more sceptical Liberal participant in the debate, Tony Greaves, has conceded, too, that in spite of his early estrangement from the Social Democrats, much of the sense of ideological difference felt by many radical Liberals at that time derived from 'perceptions and engrained attitudes' rather than from clearly developed arguments.[117]

The period immediately following the launch of the SDP in March 1981 was one of steady progress both for that party and for the Liberals. In the May local elections, which the SDP was not ready to contest, the Liberals secured 250 net gains. At the SDP's first electoral test in July, at a parliamentary by-election in the safe Labour seat of Warrington, the new party's candidate, Roy Jenkins, with Liberal support, came within 1,759 votes of overturning a previously comfortable Labour majority of over 10,000. In nearly half of the local government by-elections contested between Warrington and the end of 1981, Liberal and SDP candidates were victorious.[118] The mood of mounting optimism within both parties was evident in the concluding sentence of David Steel's speech at the 1981 Liberal Assembly in September, when he told the delegates:

> ... I have the good fortune to be the first Liberal leader for over half a century who is able to say to you at the end of our annual assembly: go back to your constituencies and prepare for government.[119]

On the eve of that same Assembly in Llandudno, a packed fringe meeting responded enthusiastically to platform speeches by Roy Jenkins, Jo Grimond and Shirley Williams in favour of an alliance between the Liberal Party and the SDP. The next day that cause was formally endorsed and ratified at the Assembly proper by a large majority.[120] A month later the Liberal candidate, Bill Pitt, won the Croydon North-West by-election from the Conservatives. This was the first time since 1945 that the Liberals had won a Conservative/Labour marginal parliamentary seat.[121] In November Shirley Williams won a dramatic victory at Crosby, turning a 18,000 Conservative majority into one of over 5,000 for the SDP. In December a Gallup poll put the two Alliance parties' combined support at 50 per cent, underlining their appeal at a time when the two major parties were suffering from a degree of unpopularity unprecedented in the post-1945 period. Soon afterwards, in February 1982, Simon Hughes won a by-election for the Liberals at Bermondsey, a previously safe Labour seat in the London docklands. In March Roy Jenkins returned to Parliament after an absence of six years when he won the Glasgow Hillhead by-election. But by that time the Alliance surge was beginning to slacken, while the Conservatives started to regain popularity, a development that was furthered by the successful outcome of the Falklands War in June 1982. Moreover, the Alliance parties' subsequent decline in their poll ratings, which was significant but not unduly alarming, was accompanied by tensions caused by the protracted and increasingly difficult process of parliamentary seat-allocation between the two parties for the next general election. The problems created here were about the details, rather than the principle, of allocation, about, that is, as David Dutton has observed, 'deciding precisely which seats would be entrusted to each party in a way that offered any chance of an equality of successful electoral outcomes ...'.[122]

The finalisation, by the time of the 1982 Liberal Assembly, of these arrangements for seat-allocation, widely regarded within the SDP as tilted in favour of the Liberals, was later judged by David Owen to be the decisive turning-point in the SDP's gradual movement towards a merger with the Liberal Party.[123] Owen recorded in his diary in September 1982 that he was opposed for two reasons, ideological and pragmatic, to what he feared was the relentless advance towards a merged party. First, he was 'temperamentally and philosophically a believer in the tradition of social democracy', considering 'that it exists as a separate strand of political thought capable of being mobilized into a political party'. Second, he opposed a merged party on the basis of a hard analysis of 'the electoral consequences of such a merger', believing that it would produce 'insufficient votes to challenge the two-party monopoly of Conservatives and Labour ...'.[124]

By that time, however, other prominent figures within the Alliance recognised a broad area of agreement on both principle and policy – covering, in particular, support for political and economic decentralisation, for a mixed economy and for political and constitutional reform – that was clearly shared by the two parties. Roy Jenkins, who had become the SDP's first elected Leader in July 1982, considered that the policy differences between the Liberals and the SDP were 'much less great than those within either of the two old monopoly parties'. Insofar as such differences did exist between the Alliance parties, there was 'a certain difference of approach on one or two aspects of nuclear weaponry, and on civil use of nuclear power', together with 'certain differences of tradition and outlook and attitude, but not ones which are unbridgeable'. With regard to the SDP's contribution to the Alliance, he believed that it had been possible 'to make the movement more effective by being two rivers flowing in the same direction than if we had just been a single stream'.[125]

In similar vein, Dick Taverne commented a month later that:

> On principles and policies there is a remarkable coincidence. Every word in the Limehouse Declaration might have been penned by David Steel ... On Proportional Representation, support for European unity, the Third World, nationalisation, decentralisation, trade union reform and industrial democracy we agree.

A very similar policy approach was also evident, he pointed out, in such areas as social security, government-industry relations, taxation, freedom of information and citizens' rights. Only on defence policy were there 'serious difficulties', and such disagreements were 'as likely to be found within the parties as between them'. In Taverne's opinion, it would take 'a microscope used by an extreme partisan to spot the differences' over the field of policy as whole.[126] On the Liberal side of the Alliance, Alan Beith agreed with that judgement, and, in view of the broad policy agreement within the Alliance, thought that 'purism of either the SDP or the Liberal variety (and there is probably more of the latter) will only blur the message'.[127] He later set out the electoral case for the Alliance in a book, published for the 1983 General Election, which provided a wide-ranging survey of the Alliance parties' policies and of the principles underlying them.[128]

On the eve of the forthcoming election, to be held on 9 June, Jo Grimond's fourth work of political thought, *A Personal Manifesto*, was published. Grimond had, as we have seen, spoken in support of the formation of the Alliance at the 1981 Liberal Assembly. He had even been described by Roy Jenkins at a London rally as the 'father of the Alliance', an accolade which, as Peter Barberis has commented, 'may have been a seductive gesture to the Liberals, but ... was well merited'.[129] In *A Personal Manifesto*, however, Grimond reiterated some of the doubts which he had expressed earlier about the centrist approach of both the SDP and the Liberal leadership, about the over-cautious nature of the Alliance and its quest for what he had called 'that old political nirvana' of the middle ground. In the preface to the book he stated that he did '... not believe that a centrist group, whether supported by a new "wet" party or by a coalition of compromise, will have much future'. In his view, 'the voter of the floating centre' should therefore 'be offered not conservatism with a socialist tinge but a new radicalism', to the advancement of which he hoped his book would make a contribution.[130]

Grimond argued that if the Alliance was to break the mould of British politics, it had to devise some method of reconciling 'greater fairness in the enjoyment of wealth and opportunities' in society with the stimulation of enterprise. To further those ends, he placed his emphasis not on redistributive measures, which all too often resulted in 'bureaucratic blight and the stifling of the entrepreneur', but rather, as he had urged in his previous work, on the need 'to encourage common outlooks and efforts by building on the local community, by promoting co-operation and joint enterprise among smaller groups'.[131]

Against the prevailing current of orthodox Alliance thinking, Grimond also reaffirmed his belief in the enduring importance of economic liberal ideas. He observed that, whereas books 'by active Liberal politicians about Liberalism' had been 'comparatively rare' in recent years, there had nonetheless been 'a large output of liberal writing'. Yet in his judgement, the Liberal Party had 'not paid sufficient attention to the ideas, not all new but many of them interesting in a new context', which had been 'promulgated by such writers as F.A. Hayek, Ralph Harris, Arthur Seldon and others associated with the Institute of Economic Affairs, Norman Macrae and other contributors to *The Economist*, Robert Oakeshott and others interested in the co-operative movement, the new publicists in America, Alan Peacock, Sam Brittan and the large number of liberal economists'.[132] Grimond regretted that the Liberal leadership in particular had 'not over the last twelve or fifteen years shown much interest in new radical political or economic thought'. He noted, too, that his attempt in *The Common Welfare* 'to develop a theory of community action designed as an alternative to state socialism and as a means of raising the standards of the poor communities' had not been taken up.[133]

Grimond's overall, broad prescription for the Alliance was that it should advocate policy measures 'which will promote liberalism within the community and socialism without the State'.[134] By the latter phrase, which was itself the title of an earlier, interesting and revisionist work of social-democratic thought by Evan Luard, Grimond had in mind policies which would advance the common good by harnessing self-interest through the market – for instance, through producer cooperatives exemplified by the Mondragon system in Spain which he so admired. In the short term, the Alliance, aiming to muster 'the support of all those who seek a modification of recent Tory policies', ought to 'display sensitivity to the reactions of those who see not only their livelihood but also cherished and familiar bulwarks like their communities and their professions sacrificed (as they believe) to a cold economic theory'.[135] But in the longer term the Alliance needed, in his view, to 'propound more radical ideas' designed to offer 'a better life, in a more satisfactory society, than state socialism and the bureaucracies can provide'. Its goal should be to foster 'a more diversified society with more equality of opportunity and more participation'.[136]

Grimond's carefully phrased reservations about the current drift of Alliance policy and about the apparent lack of radicalism offered by 'a coalition of compromise' were to some extent vindicated by the 1983 Alliance general election manifesto, *Working Together for Britain: A Programme for Government*, which had been drafted and produced rapidly by one person, Christopher Smallwood, the SDP's policy coordinator. Ian Bradley later described the manifesto as '... a pallid and uninspiring programme indeed compared with those put forward in the publications of the Tawney Society and the Association of Liberal Councillors, or with [Grimond's] the *Personal Manifesto*'.[137] That judgement needs, however, to be qualified by a recognition of the national political and economic climate – one both of policy and ideological polarisation and of high unemployment – in which the manifesto was prepared and presented to the British electorate.

In its introduction the manifesto declared:

> Two parties, one with a proud history, and one born only two years ago out of a frustration with the old system of politics, have come together to offer an alternative government pledged to bring the country together again.[138]

This emphasis on national unity and reconciliation was really the dominant theme of the Alliance's 1983 election manifesto just as it had been of the Liberal manifesto of February 1974. It was reinforced, again as had been the case nine years earlier, by a reaction against the politics of confrontation and extremism. *Working Together for Britain* thus underlined the desire of the Alliance 'to call a halt to confrontation politics', and to offer the electors 'a new road of partnership and progress' in place of 'dogma and bitterness'.[139]

On the central issues dividing the two major parties in 1983 – issues in the areas of economic and industrial policy – the manifesto appeared to offer the kind of middle-way, Butskellite policies of which Grimond had been so recently sceptical. Its key commitment was to a reduction of unemployment to one million over the coming two years, a goal which would be funded by increased government borrowing of £3 billion. It proposed an immediate programme designed to create jobs both through measures of housing and environmental improvement and in the labour-intensive National Health Service and personal social services.[140] In order to reduce unemployment without an increase in the rate of inflation, the manifesto advocated 'a fair and effective pay and prices policy that will stick'. Although such a policy would seek to be more 'flexible' than the short-term arrangements of previous Conservative and Labour governments, it nonetheless appeared as 'semi-dirigiste' as Grimond had feared. For the Alliance policy would be based on agreed norms and ranges according to which pay settlements should be negotiated, and would involve the establishment of a Pay and Prices Commission to monitor pay awards in large companies, 'with powers to restrict price increases caused by wage settlements which exceed the agreed range'. Furthermore, just as in the Liberal policy advocated by John Pardoe in the mid-1970s, these measures would be backed by a Counter-Inflation Tax imposed on companies paying above the agreed range.[141]

On another key issue, which was emerging in 1983 in the foreground of British politics – namely, the privatisation of nationalised industries – the manifesto again sought to advance a centrist, consensual position. Its aim was to 'get away from the incessant and damaging warfare over the ownership of industry and switch the emphasis to how well it performs'. It opposed plans for the privatisation of British Telecom's main network and of British Airways, aiming instead to 'make the nationalised industries successful and efficient as well as properly responsible to their consumers'.[142] This was an approach far removed from the reappraisal of the existing boundaries of the mixed economy which both Grimond and Pardoe had recommended since the 1970s.

Working Together for Britain did, however, appear more radical in other policy areas. It reaffirmed traditional Liberal support for industrial partnership, proposing 'a major extension' of profit sharing and employee share-ownership, as well as employee councils for all companies employing more than 1,000 people.[143] In addition, the manifesto called for an 'attack on poverty' through 'a major overhaul' of welfare policy, including the eventual integration of the tax and benefit systems.[144]

Marking out, too, distinctive territory compared with that occupied by the two major parties, *Working Together for Britain* emphasised its support for the programme of constitutional and political reform that had been a radical feature of every Liberal manifesto from 1945 to 1979. It advocated devolution to Scotland, with the establishment of a Scottish Parliament, as well as to Wales and the English regions if there was sufficient demand for it, together with a Bill of Rights and legislation providing public access to official information.[145] Above all, as 'the linchpin of our entire programme of radical reform', it proposed the introduction of a voting system based on proportional representation by means of the single transferable vote in multi-member constituencies.[146]

In the fields of defence and foreign policy the manifesto clearly differentiated its approach from Labour's, first, by rejecting unilateral nuclear disarmament and declaring its support for 'the principles of collective security' and hence for active participation in NATO as 'the cornerstone of the country's defence policy'. This involved acceptance of 'the need for a nuclear component in the NATO deterrent whilst the USSR has nuclear weapons'.[147] In addition, the manifesto sharpened differences with Labour by underlining the Alliance's wholehearted support for continuing British membership of the European Community, which had not only increased Britain's political influence but had also been 'unequivocally to our economic advantage'.[148]

The manifesto concluded with the ambitious claim that its 'programme of reform' rivalled 'in scope and imagination that of the Liberal reforming government of 1906–11 or the Attlee government of 1945–51'. It maintained, too, that neither of 'the two old class parties' would 'carry out any of the fundamental reforms – to the system of pay determination, or the structure of industrial relations, or the welfare state, or the political system' – that the Alliance advocated.[149]

The dominant theme, however, of *Working Together for Britain* was not so much the need for radical reform in the Britain of 1983 but rather its initial emphasis on national unity and reconciliation. That theme, together with the related focus on cooperation in place of confrontation and on moderation in place of extremism, had resonated through the speeches of both Roy Jenkins and David Steel over the previous four years, in particular, in the former's 1979 Dimbleby Lecture. But by restating those themes in the changed circumstances of 1983, Jenkins and Steel, as Crewe and King later observed, 'ran the risk of appearing dated and faded, of seeming to be ever so slightly out of touch'.[150] For since the Winter of Discontent of 1978–79 there had been no major strikes and a widespread spirit of national unity had been engendered in 1982 by the Falklands War and its aftermath.

Moreover, the Alliance's election platform, though distinguished by a clear commitment to a far-reaching programme of constitutional and social reform, could be regarded as negative in the sense that 'the Alliance defined itself almost entirely in terms of what it was not'. It was 'not a socialist party, tied to the trade unions and increasingly under the influence of left-wing extremists; and it was not a hard-line monetarist party, tied to big business and increasingly under the influence of right-wing Thatcherism'. It was thus, Crewe and King concluded, 'never made entirely clear what the Alliance was, as distinct from what it was not'.[151] This centrist vagueness inherent in the Alliance's image and character, whilst enhancing its attractiveness to voters disaffected with both the major parties, also indicated a certain lack of positive electoral appeal. As the SDP politician, John Cartwright, often commented during the course of the campaign, the voters 'don't know what tune we're whistling'.[152]

Nevertheless, at the 1983 General Election, held on 9 June, the Liberal/SDP Alliance won a massive popular vote of just over 7.75 million, fewer than three-quarters of a million votes behind Labour, with a national vote-share of 25.4 per cent, only 2.2 per cent less than Labour's. But owing to the vagaries of the first-past-the-post electoral system, the Alliance won only 23 seats – 17 for the Liberals and six for the SDP. In contrast, Labour, in its worst election defeat since 1931, with its lowest vote share since 1918, still won 209 seats, its support being geographically concentrated in its traditional industrial heartlands.

The Alliance had thus failed to replace Labour as the main progressive force in British politics, or even, as David Owen had hoped, to establish a significant bridgehead in the House of Commons. The split in the left-of-centre vote was also one important factor among others that contributed towards the Conservatives' massive overall Commons majority of 144. But the Alliance's electoral performance was still the best third-party result, in terms of national vote-share, since the free trade election of 1923 when the Liberals won 29.6 per cent of the poll. Under a voting system based on proportional representation the level of popular support for the Alliance in 1983 would have been rewarded with about 150 or more seats. In terms, then, of the actual Parliamentary outcome, the 1983 General Election was a disappointment for both the Alliance parties, particularly for those in the SDP who, as David Marquand later recalled, 'wanted to bust the system quickly' rather than engage in 'the long march through the wards'.[153] But the result nonetheless held out to both the Liberal Party and the SDP, in a way that it certainly did not to Labour, the prospect of continued political advance.

Chapter 7
Liberals, Owen and the Social Market Economy: 1983–1988

In the aftermath of the 1983 General Election David Steel, unwell and hurt by criticisms of his leadership from some of his parliamentary colleagues, contemplated resigning as Liberal Leader. Persuaded to reconsider his position, he took a three-month sabbatical, during which the responsibilities of leadership were temporarily transferred to the Party's Chief Whip, Alan Beith.[1] Meanwhile, Roy Jenkins relinquished leadership of the SDP, being succeeded, unopposed, by David Owen in late June 1983. Of the original Gang of Three Bill Rodgers and Shirley Williams had both lost their seats in the June election. In these circumstances David Owen, heading a parliamentary team of only six MPs, was thus in a strong position to shape the character and direction not just of his own Party, but also, potentially, of the Alliance as a whole. As Ivor Crewe and Anthony King have observed:

> For the ensuing four years, between the 1983 and 1987 general elections, David Owen *was* the SDP and the SDP *was* Owen ... He was the party's leader in fact as well as in form. Few challenged his authority.[2]

In the post-1983 situation Owen's central strategic aim was to preserve the SDP's independence as a fourth national political party and to seek to achieve, in cooperation with the Liberals, the ultimate goal of electoral reform and consequently a change in the party political structure. He was, however, strongly opposed to any movement towards merging the SDP's identity with that of the Liberals. In contrast, many others within both the Alliance parties – MPs, candidates, activists and ordinary members alike – favoured closer links between the SDP and the Liberals on the pragmatic ground of the need to use scarce resources – human, organisational and financial – more efficiently.

Some Liberals and Social Democrats at this time argued, too, that there was a firm ideological basis for closer cooperation between the two parties. Early in 1984 Dick Taverne, for example, urged that members of the Alliance parties should 'not pretend to a deep philosophical divide which does not exist'. Many Social Democrats, he noted, who stressed their separate political and ideological identity drew on 'the tradition of Gaitskell and Attlee and the great reforming government of 1945'. But they tended to overlook the fact that Attlee's government 'based its programme on the work of two intellectual giants – Keynes and Beveridge', and that both Gaitskell and Attlee, as social democrats within the Labour Party, 'practised the ideas' of those 'two leading Liberal thinkers of this century'.[3] This point of shared ideological ground had earlier been stressed from the Liberal side of the Alliance by Desmond Banks when he observed that 'the most obvious philosophical link between the Liberals and the Social Democrats is to be found in their common record of support for the ideas associated with the names of Keynes and Beveridge'. That social liberal heritage remained, in his view, a vital contribution to 'the confluence of Liberal thought'.[4]

David Owen, however, in his honeymoon period as the SDP's new Leader was more concerned to reposition his Party ideologically in a distinctive manner, and in doing so, he opened up an area of political debate and controversy both within the SDP and in its relations with its Liberal allies. For instead of pursuing what Jo Grimond had called 'that old political nirvana of the middle ground, Owen favoured a more radical and unorthodox approach. 'If we could simultaneously break right on the market and left on social policy,' he later wrote, then, he believed, his Party 'could find an electorally attractive mix'.[5] In practice, that would involve a combination of market realism and social concern which would differentiate the SDP, and the Alliance, both from the state collectivism of the Labour Party and from the unfettered market individualism of the Conservatives under Margaret Thatcher's leadership.

In order to forge that synthesis, Owen decided to refine the concept of a 'social market economy' which he had first tried to develop in a lecture delivered in 1981. Over the course of the previous years he had gradually become convinced that many of the state collectivist ideas promoted by the Labour Party in the fields of economic and industrial policy – such as state ownership, centralised economic planning, extensive state intervention and over-reliance on Keynesian demand management – had become either discredited or intellectually untenable in the changed climate of the 1980s. He therefore considered it necessary for the SDP 'to break the stranglehold of the 1960s', and to develop instead 'an understanding of the market economy' which he regarded as 'the first essential step towards the radical libertarian force I wanted to create'.[6]

Owen had first expressed his doubts publicly about Labour's collectivist orthodoxies in a Fabian Society lecture delivered in 1978 while he was Foreign Secretary in the Callaghan Government. In Opposition after 1970 he had gained some insight into private-sector management and the workings of the market economy through his involvement in a computer-based consultancy firm.[7] Although politically he remained at that time 'a Croslandite more than anyone', he did not think that even Tony Crosland 'understood the mechanisms of the market economy', and had come to the conclusion, more broadly, that 'the core weakness' in Labour's political thought was its lack of emphasis on wealth-creation within the economy.[8]

Owen's promotion of the idea of a social market economy after 1983 was thus the product of a growing disillusionment with Labour's state collectivist prescriptions. The alternative approach that he was seeking to pursue, crystallised for him in the phrase 'social market', was essentially based on the view that, as Peter Jenkins succinctly put it at the time, 'wealth should be created by market forces but redistributed according to social principles'.[9]

Historically, however, the term, 'social market' had meant something else. It had first been used by German economic liberals in 1946 and taken up by the Christian Democrats, and particularly by Ludwig Erhard, from 1949 onwards. It was understood to mean a market economy in which the State's role was restricted to ensuring that market forces operated without distortions such as abuse of monopoly power. Ideologically, it was designed to provide a third way between state socialism and monopoly capitalism.[10]

'Social market economy' as a term had entered British political discourse in 1975 when it was enthusiastically adopted by Sir Keith Joseph and his recently formed free-market Conservative Centre for Policy Studies. For them the phrase connoted 'a socially responsible market economy' in which '… industry alone creates the wealth which pays for social welfare'.[11] Such an interpretation was broadly similar to that of Erhard and other German economic liberals.

David Owen, however, interpreted the concept in a different way. For him it meant a form of economic organisation that was grounded in a dual commitment to both economic efficiency and social welfare. Shortly after the launch of the SDP, in a lecture delivered at Strathclyde University in May 1981, he had therefore proposed for his new Party a third course distinct from both the monetarist Right and the protectionist Left, a course based on an approach consisting 'of social concern and of market realism'.[12] Such a strategy should be designed, he argued, 'neither to pursue the policies of an inert centre nor to replay the "revisionism" of the Sixties and Seventies'. Rather, it should involve 'a radical reassessment of policy across the board', which was nowhere more important than in 'stimulating a change of attitudes to the market economy'. It would also entail a movement away from 'a continuation of the centralised mixed economy'.[13]

That approach was consistent with Jo Grimond's advocacy, in an article published in June 1981, of 'a new highly decentralised political economy' that would take the place of the mixed economy with its established sectoral boundaries and its '… diluted variety of étatism'.[14] In similar spirit, Owen expressed his growing doubts about the term 'mixed economy', which he had earlier used with unqualified approval, notably in his recently published 1981 treatise, *Face the Future*. For he now considered that it had 'become a portmanteau description to which virtually anyone on the Left or Right can subscribe'. It was a label which even Labour Party Clause IV socialists could use 'without real commitment to the merits of the private sector'.[15]

In his 1981 Strathclyde lecture Owen also stressed, like Grimond, the need to turn away from 'the centralised prices and incomes policies of the past', and, more generally, to revitalise Britain, a country 'ensnared at the centre of government by committees, corporatist attitudes and a web of bureaucracy'.[16] Owen drew on the text of his 1981 lecture both for his article, 'Agenda for Competition and Compassion', published in the journal of the Institute of Economic Affairs in October 1983,[17] and for the opening chapter of his second major political work, *A Future That Will Work*, published in 1984. He had been invited by the IEA to write an article for its *Economic Affairs*, and later recalled that the free market think-tank's journal seemed to him 'the perfect forum' which would provide 'a clear signal' of the SDP's 'change in ... economic outlook' since the IEA had by that time clearly 'established itself as the progenitor of Margaret Thatcher's emphasis on the market'.[18]

Owen's espousal of the social market economy was accompanied by a call for a greater emphasis on micro-economic policy, which meant 'accepting a more restrained view of the role of government and giving more attention to the value of marginal change'.[19] This shift of focus would involve the promotion of industrial democracy, trade union reform, including the introduction of more democratic procedures, and the decentralisation of pay-bargaining structures.

Like David Steel and Roy Jenkins, Owen called, too, for an end to 'the yo-yo polemics about nationalization or privatization', but added significantly that:

> ... we should not freeze the frontier between the public and private sectors. It is best neither to endorse the status quo nor close one's mind to the objective case for privatization but to put the onus of proof on those who wish to change the frontiers.[20]

He recognised the fact that privatisation had 'little value where a state-owned monopoly is merely turned into a privately owned monopoly and where competition in the market is reduced rather than increased'.[21] Yet his cautiously open-minded attitude towards the case for privatisation of nationalised industries was nonetheless a new departure in centre-left thinking at that time. Like Grimond, Owen decried the 'tendency to amalgamate the public and private sectors as part of an amorphous mixed economy rather than to define the frontiers and objectives of the market'. That tendency involved a failure to recognise that one of the necessary differences between the two sectors was that profits were 'the motive force of the private sector' while service was 'the motive force of the public sector'.[22]

In broader ideological terms, Owen depicted his conception of a social market economy as 'a new synthesis, a combination of what are too often wrongly assumed to be incompatible objectives'.[23] He realised that it was 'not an easy balance to achieve', which during the period of his leadership, in his speeches and writings, would be expressed in terms of a series of apparent dichotomies: market realism and social concern, competitiveness and compassion, and, in his most frequently used phrase, an approach that was both 'tough and tender'. Owen thus underlined the need to 'grapple simultaneously with the values inspired by a competitive market economy and the values to be fostered in a society determined to reduce social deprivation and poverty'.[24] 'Without a social conscience to modify commercial realism,' he argued, 'the polarization of British society will continue and the disadvantaged in society will feel increasingly alienated.'[25] Reversing those social trends would require redistribution of the surplus produced by the market – both through fiscal policy and by means of a generous welfare system. Such a stance clearly diverged from that of the early German advocates of the social market, and, to a significant extent, too, from that of its more recent champions in the Conservative Centre for Policy Studies. Owen's more egalitarian interpretation of the social market was also developed further during this period by two of the SDP's policy advisers – by Alex de Mont, who was Owen's economic research assistant for four years, helping to chart the SDP's change of course in economic policy, and by the social policy specialist Nick Bosanquet.[26]

Much of Owen's formulation of the case for a social market economy was in tune with mainstream Liberal thinking, as well as with the tone and language of the 1981 Limehouse Declaration, with its celebration of 'the innovating strength of a competitive economy'. Many of the points he stressed in advancing his case had also been made, as we have seen, by Jo Grimond and John Pardoe in their various writings and speeches during the late 1960s and 1970s. Indeed, in an interview in autumn 1983 Owen drew attention to the fact that both Grimond and Pardoe shared his enthusiasm for the free market.[27] Yet Owen's firm emphasis on the merits of the market economy and its essential elements – profit, competition and enterprise – nonetheless generated controversy, and, in some cases, outright opposition, within both the Alliance parties. Reservations about the new direction in which Owen was taking the SDP politically and ideologically, a change of course which he had clearly signalled at the SDP conference in September 1983, were expressed publicly and privately by the other members of the old Gang of Four.[28]

In May 1985 Bill Rodgers thus argued, in a Tawney Society lecture entitled 'My Party – Wet or Dry?', that the SDP should remain 'unequivocally [on] the centre-left' of British politics and, alluding to Owen's conception of a social market economy, stated his view that:

> The antithesis of 'tough and tender' brilliantly encapsulates the social market approach, but 'tough' is the dominant mood and can elbow

'tender' out of the way. It is time to talk more of our tender dimensions and to make it better known that we are a party of social reform, deeply concerned with the welfare of our people.[29]

Two months later, Roy Jenkins, in another Tawney Society lecture, referred in a coded manner to 'some ludicrous suggestions in the past few months that the SDP is on its way to becoming a junior Thatcherite party'. But 'the whole spirit and outlook of the SDP, its leaders and its members', were, Jenkins insisted, 'profoundly opposed to Thatcherism', which he equated, in terms of domestic policy, not only with a fatalistic acceptance of 'massive unemployment buttressed by deindustrialisation and the run-down of public services', but also with the increasing centralisation of political power in Britain. Specifically, too, in opposition to an important part of Owen's critique of centrist economic orthodoxies, Jenkins reaffirmed what he called 'our original SDP view in favour of a stability of frontier between the nationalised and the private sector ...'. That view, he pointed out, had been based on two premises: first, 'that ownership, provided that it was not constantly changing, was not terribly important; and that kicking industries like footballs up and down the field, as in the classic case of steel, was highly undesirable for effective management'. Moreover, unlike Owen, Jenkins did not welcome the practical implications of a market-driven change in the boundaries of the mixed economy. He was 'not prepared,' he explained, 'to chase off indiscriminately after the fashionable false god of privatization, even when it is bedizened with the paint of proclaiming, mostly falsely, a better service to the consumer'.[30]

These comments, Jenkins later recalled, were a response to what he was 'coming to regard as David Owen's instinctive sympathy for the Thatcherite style and consequent lurch to the right'.[31] This interpretation of Owen's chosen course for the SDP, as an 'apparent flirtation with Thatcherism',[32] lay at the heart of many of the objections levelled, within both of the Alliance parties, at Owen's idea of a social market economy. Such objections seemed to hinge on the contemporary political associations bound up with Owen's free-market rhetoric, as well as on what was widely perceived as the personally abrasive style of presentation underlying it. They centred less on the intellectual content of Owen's actual views on economic policy – views concerning, for instance, such issues as privatisation, prices and incomes policies, trade union reform or the dynamism of the market.

In part, too, the critical reaction of many leading Social Democrats to Owen's emphasis on the social market sprang, in Alan Beith's judgement, from the fact that they 'tended to take a consensus view on where the limits of State power should be'. For they believed, with regard to the economy, that 'somehow we'd got to the optimal relationship with State power, one that shouldn't be pulled in either way – towards, that is, either the Left or Right'. To those Social Democrats, therefore, Owen appeared to be disturbing that relationship by shifting it in a Rightward direction.[33]

In Owen's support, however, his economic adviser, Alex de Mont, argued that the charge of 'Thatcherism with a human face' levelled by some observers, both within and outside the Alliance, at Owen's advocacy of a social market economy was 'wide of the mark'. Instead, de Mont defined the idea as 'a reconstructed version of social democracy for the 1980s and 1990s with a distinctly redistributive and market-based thrust'. In his view, Owen was making the crucial political point that there was 'no necessary incompatibility between striving for competitive efficiency and social equity'. That was 'a chord which Mrs Thatcher has never struck and shows no sign of doing so in the future'.[34] Moreover, de Mont added, the Thatcher governments, by turning state monopolies into private monopolies in the name of privatisation, to date had promoted neither competitive free markets nor better service for the consumer, a point which Owen had also made in his speeches and writings since becoming the SDP's Leader. Seeking to differentiate Owen's conception of the social market further from free-market Conservativism, de Mont argued, too, that:

> The best way to promote a progressive social market economy is to achieve a more widely dispersed ownership of property and assets, in both public and private industry, so that the benefits of capital ownership become widely available – instead of being confined to the privileged few.[35]

Such a view had long formed, of course, an important part of the Liberal case for 'popular ownership', advocated since the Yellow Book of 1928 and embodied in the Liberal Party's *Ownership for All* reports of 1938, 1949 and 1959. More recently, it had been a position advocated in an earlier analysis of Alliance economic policy by Samuel Brittan,[36] who added his own definition of the social market as a form of economic organisation within which there would be 'nothing incompatible in wanting to extend the use of competitive markets and at the same time to support a generous measure of redistribution and provision of public goods'.[37]

In spite of these emphases on the distributist implications of the social market economy, many Liberals at this time were unconvinced by David Owen's espousal of the cause itself. In December 1984 the Liberal Party Council passed a resolution urging the Party's Standing Committee to prepare a statement on the subject. In the autumn of that year the Liberty 2000 Group had also been set up by the Standing Committee in order to redefine Liberal policy and 'to reassess Liberal themes in the light of the need to reverse the intellectual dominance of Thatcherism'.[38] Among other things, that would involve a restatement of the Liberal approach to the market economy. Malcom Bruce, a member of the Liberty 2000 Group, even candidly admitted that this undertaking was partly designed as 'a counter to some of the things David Owen was saying'.[39] Bruce himself took a cautious, pragmatic and somewhat ambivalent view of the 'market' part of

Owen's conception of the social market economy. Liberals, he pointed out, 'have never questioned the role of the market but over the years have had to confront its limitations'.[40] The evolution of British Liberalism had in fact been characterised by 'a recognition ... that the market mechanism will not always allow the most efficient or the fairest distribution of resources', and that 'the market has no inherent morality, no responsibility, no aesthetics'. The 'new enthusiasts for unbridled market forces', tended, he maintained, to forget all that. Furthermore, the New Right had in practice not only failed to tackle monopolies, but had also 'perpetrated even worse abuses – in selling off state assets many of which owe their financial strength to historic public investment and public monopoly'.[41]

Bruce therefore stressed the 'urgent need to reassert a more balanced philosophy'. That presumably, he reflected, explained 'the emergence of Social Market economics', which seemed, however, to him 'no different from the Liberal economic pragmatism that evolved over the past century'. For the need to strike the proper balance between market forces and state intervention in order to improve opportunities for the weak and disadvantaged had been a problem which Liberals had 'spent 100 years confronting and refining'.[53] British Liberalism had thereby 'devised a philosophical approach of pragmatic, balanced economics', which recognised the reality that 'markets must operate', but also 'that they suffer limitations and distortions' which 'from time to time at least require selective intervention'.[42] Bruce's conclusion, then, as a Liberal, was that 'with this philosophy and the distinguished record of its exponents – who needs Social Market Economics – and what the devil's the difference anyway?'.[43]

A few months later, in a Liberty 2000 Group report, *Markets and the Responsible State*, Bruce developed these thoughts further. 'Twentieth Century Liberals,' he maintained, were 'well placed to attack the New Right ... from practical experience which produced a clear expression of the responsibility of Government within a market economy through such as Lloyd George, Keynes and Beveridge'.[44] Bruce did not here restate his view that 'Liberal economic pragmatism' was not significantly different from Owen's idea of a social market economy. However, a developed and detailed Liberal response to Owen's cause did seek to draw a clear and explicit distinction between the two approaches. Following the Liberal Party's commitment to produce a statement on the social market economy, a booklet by Leighton Andrews was published in the autumn of 1985. Entitled, in an adversarial spirit, *Liberals versus the Social Market Economy*, it contained an analysis that was not only generally critical of Owen's advocacy of the social market but also, more broadly, ambivalent at best about various aspects of the market economy itself. Andrews quoted with approval Michael Meadowcroft's view that '... Liberals recognise the faults of capitalism and should seek to minimise rather than maximise the effects of the market', favouring cooperative structures instead of placing an 'emphasis on the market "principle"'.[45] Andrews was also disdainful towards the economic liberal views propounded in 'the vacuous Liberal Party of the 1950s' and still promoted by 'the right-wing Institute of Economic Affairs', as well as 'by right-wing Liberal ideologists such as Roy Douglas and, more recently, Lord Grimond and the Gladstone Club'. Indeed, Andrews noted that David Owen had referred approvingly to Jo Grimond and John Pardoe as 'exponents of market ideas'. Yet while the latter both remained 'Liberal folk-heroes, guaranteed to fill halls, excite the emotions and raise audiences to their feet', it was, in Andrews's view, 'now debatable whether they actually represent the mainstream of Liberal Party thinking'.[46] In 1985, when economic liberal ideas and policies were being so zealously promoted by the Thatcher governments, albeit often in a selective manner, this was a revealing contemporary comment, by an influential Liberal activist[47] on the standing within the Party of those who continued to reaffirm their belief in the merits of a market economy.

Stressing, however, the need to reassert the cause of liberty in a reaction against the forces of statism and corporatism, a reaction which Andrews conceded was 'the positive aspect of Dr Owen's attempt to shake the SDP out of its Jenkinsite conception of the post-war British state as a benevolent place ...'[48], it was argued nonetheless that 'the essential difference in the Liberal and social market responses' was that:

> ... instead of seeking the solution in the abstract form of the market, the Liberals begin with the actual position of individuals in relation to the communities they inhabit and organise within. Rather that extolling particular forms of ownership, public or private, Liberals stress the importance of personal control, and seek ways of strengthening that. The market may enhance that – it may also inhibit it.[49]

That statement reflected the widespread Liberal tendency to be more interested in the distribution and decentralisation of power for the benefit of individuals and their communities than in the question of the relationship between the market and the State. Arguably, it exemplified, too, the general lack of interest in economic policy within the Liberal Party during the 1980s.[50] It was nevertheless consistent, it is true, with the empirical rather than absolutist view of economic organisation that was embedded in 20th-century British Liberal thought. But in its ideologically neutral, or, at best, ambivalent attitude towards the market, Andrews's statement was also far removed from the unequivocal recognition of the benefits of the market economy that had been evident in the writings of the most influential British Liberal thinkers – from Dodds to Grimond – over the previous 40 years.

Andrews restated his view of the market economy in his booklet, *Liberty in Britain*, also published in 1985. This had a semi-official status as a Liberal statement of principles since it was the final report of the Party's Liberty 2000

Group. Seeking to distinguish a Liberal approach based on community and individual liberty both from a socialist approach based on the State and from a Conservative one based on the market as its 'sacred principle', Andrews underlined the various shortcomings of the market which, in his view, had become apparent under the Thatcher governments. He argued that:

> The market approach and the promise to roll back the state have been shown to be chimeras. This will not surprise Liberals. The market is rarely free ... [It] is constantly undermined by large corporations and multi-nationals carving out quasi-monopoly positions. The international market is distorted by cartels, dumping agreements and Government action. [...] The market offers no guarantee of a sane use of scarce resources. Nor does it prevent the despoliation of the natural world ...[51]

In sharp contrast to the contemporary Conservative emphasis on 'the primacy of the market', the 'key organising principle' of British Liberalism over the past 15 years, Andrews pointed out, had been community politics. That had indeed been Liberalism's 'decisive contribution to contemporary political discourse', which in practice had been 'identified with local politics, local neighbourhoods, local communities'.[52] The work of the Liberty 2000 Group since it had been set up in the autumn of 1984 had been 'to re-interpret that view as the kernel of modern Liberalism'[53], presenting it as the alternative both to Labour's discredited statism and to the dominance of a market-obsessed Thatcherite Conservativism.

In *Liberals versus the Social Market Economy*, Andrews had made it clear that, in his view, David Owen was helping to legitimise that Thatcherite ideological tendency. Or at any rate, by espousing the social market, Owen was playing 'the dangerous game' of occupying the Conservatives' ground, thereby running the electoral risk of 'tarring the Alliance with Thatcher's brush'.[54] This fear that Owen's recent redirection of the SDP's course involved a 'lurch to the Right' and a 'flirtation with Thatcherism' was shared by many Liberal activists in the mid-1980s. Tony Greaves has recalled that there was strong resistance to Owen's cause within the Liberal Party at that time. Yet in retrospect it seemed to him that 'we were arguing more about direction than content'.[55]

In the view of Alan Beith, this widespread opposition within the Party to Owen's espousal of the social market economy stemmed, above all, from the fact that the idea itself was tainted in many Liberal eyes with 'guilt by association' with Thatcherism. For in their implementation by the Thatcher governments, economic liberal ideas were 'not informed or humanised by political liberalism at all ... not informed by a recognition of the danger of the centralisation of political power'. Thatcher's regime was, in Beith's judgement, 'blindly applying *some* economic liberal ideas', but in the process 'maximising the power of both the State and private monopolies'. For many Liberals, therefore, all of that 'gave economic liberalism a bad name', and led to a situation in which, in particular, privatisation in any form 'didn't gain much acceptance' in the Liberal Party during the 1980s.[56]

David Owen himself, however, was indifferent to the charge of guilt by political association, later stating that '... the label of "sub-Thatcherite" ... did not worry me ... It was a small price to pay to rid the SDP of being stuck in the 1970s, promising a better yesterday'. To him advocacy of the social market economy was thus a vital part of the SDP's 'attempt, late in the day admittedly, to throw off the centrist "splitting the difference" image with which we had been landed'.[57]

But what appeared to many within both of the Alliance parties to be the abrasive style and manner with which Owen promoted the cause of the social market provided them with another good reason for opposing it. That style had tended, as Bill Rodgers had observed, to emphasise 'toughness' as the dominant mood at the expense of 'tenderness'. As the conservative political commentator, Charles Moore, had noted in 1983:

> Every time David Owen enthuses about bombs and the free market he carries conviction. Every time he talks of welfarism and public services he sounds bored.[58]

More broadly, Owen's critics argued, both at the time and later, that Owen's concept of a social market economy lacked a clear or precise meaning. It was unclear, they maintained, whether the main emphasis lay on the 'social' or the 'market' factor in the formula.[59] The concept could thus be interpreted as meaning a market economy accompanied either by a minimal State that intervened only to ensure competition and curb monopolies, or by an active, enabling State that intervened in order to correct market failures and to promote redistribution and social welfare. It was consequently unclear what the economic and social policy implications of the idea were for the SDP's, and the Alliance's, programme and strategy.

But on another level, that is, 'the level of emotional and political symbolism', the social market could, as David Marquand has contended, be perceived as providing Owen and the SDP with 'a banner, a rallying cry, an assertion of identity'.[60] For the idea proved useful, in terms of both policy and rhetoric, in widening the gap between a more market-oriented SDP and the more collectivist and interventionist approach of social democrats such as Denis Healey, Roy Hattersley and John Smith, who had remained loyal to Labour. The idea of the social market also enabled Owen to differentiate the SDP under his leadership from the centrist interventionism associated not only with his predecessor, Roy Jenkins, but also with David Steel and the Liberal Party establishment.

Moreover, as Steel, Bruce and other leading Liberals had often pointed out, acceptance of the market had long been recognised by the Liberal Party as an economic and political reality. In contrast, Owen and other Social Democrats arguably had to over-emphasise their commitment to the market economy because of their recent Labour past and in the face, too, of the need to distinguish themselves clearly from the anti-market attitudes of the Labour Left. Owen and his supporters also had to demonstrate that social democracy was a flexible and dynamic creed. Otherwise they ran the risk, as Ralf Dahrendorf observed, of being perceived as 'merely survival politicians, essentially about the past rather than about the future'.[61] Yet in stressing their commitment to the market, 'with the zealotry of converts', they appeared, in the eyes of many Liberals, to understate 'the need for checks and balances, to regulate and manage the market'[62], which since Keynes and the Yellow Book had been widely accepted by British Liberals.

Nevertheless, through Owen's assiduous advocacy, the social market economy was one of the few distinctive ideas to emerge from SDP thinking between 1983 and 1987. It also opened up one of the few areas of ideological debate and controversy within a Liberal Party whose leading members' energies were consumed during that period by negotiations with the SDP over both seat allocation and election manifesto policy commitments.

Furthermore, there was a distinctive and valuable aspect of Owen's project that should be underlined. For as one of its detractors, Duncan Brack, has acknowledged, Owen was 'in his own fashion ... attempting to create a new "third way" for the 1980s'.[63] In recognising the need to turn away from the collectivist remedies of the 1960s and 1970s towards a positive acceptance of the market economy, and yet somehow to combine market realism with social concern, competitiveness with compassion, Owen was seeking to transcend not only Labour's discredited state collectivism but also the harsh, unbridled market individualism of the New Right. In grasping, therefore, the importance of achieving that new balance and synthesis in the changed conditions of the 1980s, 'Owen's mind was moving', as Bill Rodgers later conceded. In retrospect, Charles Kennedy, too, the SDP's youngest MP in the 1980s, later considered that Owen in this respect was 'a guy ahead of his time'.[64] In a similar vein, a contemporary observer from the Liberal side of the Alliance, Archy Kirkwood, later commented, with regard to Owen's dedicated pursuit of his chosen 'third way', that: 'We should have realized that there was a wind of change' blowing through British politics at that time, a wind that Owen had discerned.[65]

In spite, then, of its imprecision and lack of clarity, Owen's conception of the social market economy was thus really verbal shorthand for his own version of the benign, progressive synthesis – the combined commitment to the market economy, to the common welfare and to political and constitutional reform – which Jo Grimond had been promoting from *The Liberal Future* in 1959 through to *A Personal Manifesto* in 1983. Owen's attempt to reconcile enterprise with fairness, competitiveness and efficiency with social generosity was, therefore, neither novel nor original. But as Crewe and King have noted, while 'Owen's ideas taken separately were not new ... they were new in combination ...'.[66] Moreover, in the face of the major economic and social changes sweeping through Britain during the 1980s, it was a political approach with relevance and appeal. As Dick Taverne observed in 1985, writing more broadly about the SDP's, and the Alliance's, prescribed remedy for 'the social and economic malaise of our society':

> None of it has not been advocated before. We cannot claim ideological virginity. Indeed we leave ideological passion to the Left and the Right. But in the twilight of the old ideologies a fresh combination of realism and compassion will be a necessary and welcome change.[67]

The ideological debate generated after 1983 within the Liberal Party, the SDP and the Alliance by Owen's espousal of the social market was overshadowed in 1986 by a dispute over defence policy, the one area in which substantial differences of opinion existed between, and to some extent within, the two Alliance parties. In the summer of 1984 a Joint Commission on Defence and Disarmament had been set up to draw up proposals for an agreed Alliance defence policy. This was prompted in particular by the contentious issue of the future of Britain's independent nuclear deterrent, since the existing Polaris nuclear submarines, dating from the 1960s, were scheduled to be replaced by the late 1990s. The Commission was designed to avoid the kind of bitter disagreements that had plagued the Labour Party over defence policy in 1983.

The Commission's report eventually concluded, in June 1986, in favour of Britain's continued membership of NATO, of a continued American military presence in Europe, and of the continuing presence of US bases, including nuclear bases, on British soil. However, it deferred the decision over the future of Britain's independent nuclear deterrent – over the question, that is, of 'whether, and if so, how' the Polaris missile system should be replaced when it became obsolete in the late 1990s. The report maintained that a final decision on the issue did not need to be taken for several years since the Polaris submarines would remain in service 'well beyond the end of the next Parliament'.[68]

The fact that the Commission's report would not commit the Alliance to replacing the Polaris system was indiscreetly leaked to the Press – in the form of two of *The Scotsman* newspaper's lobby correspondents – by David Steel in May 1986 in advance of the report's publication the following month. This admission subsequently resulted in a press report in *The Scotsman* which claimed misleadingly that the Liberal position on non-replacement of Polaris had prevailed in the Commission's conclusions. David Owen's angry reaction led to his reaffirming his conviction, in a speech to the Council for

Social Democracy, that Britain should remain a nuclear weapon State, and that, if the Alliance intended to advocate the cancellation of the Thatcher government's Trident missile programme, then it should also stress the need for a viable replacement.

After the Commission's report was published on 11 June, Owen and Steel attempted to lower the temperature raised by the dispute through exploring the possibility of a European, rather than exclusively British, nuclear deterrent. This hastily conceived proposal was narrowly defeated, however, at the Liberal Assembly at Eastbourne in September, with Simon Hughes and Michael Meadowcroft vehemently opposing the idea of a nuclear element in future European cooperation on defence policy.

A subsequent compromise led to a new Alliance defence statement in mid-December 1986, presented by Owen and Steel, which in effect endorsed Owen's well-established position on the issue. The Alliance, it declared, was committed to a minimum British nuclear deterrent until it could be safely negotiated away in a global, multilateral disarmament agreement. The precise form of any future replacement for Polaris was not specified. The Joint Commission's proposal to defer the decision on the issue had thus been overturned. The Alliance's leaders' proposal for a European deterrent was, however, omitted from their joint statement.[69]

The political price for this very public and acrimonious dispute was a high one: an Alliance opinion poll rating of 35 per cent in January 1986 fell to 23.5 per cent by the year's end.[70] But prospects improved early in 1987 following a successful relaunch rally at the Barbican Centre in London in January and a by-election victory in February at Greenwich, where Rosie Barnes secured a gain for the SDP over Labour with a majority of over 6,600 and a 53 per cent vote-share. This was the SDP's first by-election victory in a Labour-held seat. Soon afterwards, in March, the Liberals, with Matthew Taylor as candidate, comfortably retained their Truro seat at a by-election arising from the tragic death of David Penhaligon in a road accident just before Christmas 1986. The earlier decline in the Alliance's fortunes in the wake of the defence dispute had tended, too, to obscure the reality of two impressive by-election performances in May 1986 – the first at Ryedale where the Liberal candidate, Elizabeth Shields, overturned a 16,000 Conservative majority to secure a 5,000-vote majority; the second, at West Derbyshire where the Liberal candidate came within 100 votes of overturning a 15,000 Tory majority.

This sustained Alliance advance in by-elections was subsequently reflected in national opinion poll findings in March 1987 which showed Alliance support at 31–31.5 per cent – either level with Labour or marginally ahead.[71] Moreover, the SDP/Liberal Alliance's performance in the May 1987 local elections, in which the two parties gained over 450 seats and the equivalent of a national vote share of 27 per cent, provided the highest base of support from which any third party had launched itself into a general election campaign since the 1920s.[72] In spite, then, of the damaging row in 1986, there were high hopes in May-June 1987 of a breakthrough by the Alliance parties at the imminent election, even though there was also widespread expectation of a third successive Conservative victory.

The Barbican Rally in London, in January, had earlier coincided with the publication of *The Time Has Come: Partnership for Progress*, a detailed 128-page joint policy statement published in the names of Owen and Steel, and aiming 'to set out the foundations of agreement on which the Liberal/SDP Alliance will base its platform at the next General Election'.[73] *The Time Has Come* did not mention Owen's idea of a social market economy. Instead, it was guarded in its references, for instance, to the merits of privatisation, and declared, in tune with previous statements made frequently by Steel and Jenkins, that 'the old ideological battle over the ownership of industries between the Conservative and Labour Parties is a diversion'.[74] More broadly, the document stated, too, that 'Social Democrats and Liberals recognize that the operation of markets does not always produce socially desirable results'. The market would not by itself 'reverse the widening gap between the regions, rebuild the inner cities or revive the industrial areas'. Nor could the market ensure sufficient long-term investment in essential infrastructure, or 'guarantee the universal availability of essential services such as health care or education'.[75] In addition, *The Time Has Come* contained firm commitments to a formal incomes strategy and to budgetary expansion – policy positions which Owen had either challenged or repudiated.[76]

Even though *The Time Has Come* contained no explicit references to the 'social market economy', it did, however, endorse its broad, underlying approach, stating that '... the SDP and the Liberal Party bring together ideas which the Conservative and Labour Parties believe to be mutually exclusive: enterprise and welfare, a market economy and social justice ...'.[77] But in other respects, the document appeared to reaffirm Alliance support for the centrist prescriptions of the day in its overall approach to economic strategy.

Nevertheless, in the same month as the Alliance's Barbican Rally, David Owen attempted to elaborate further a progressive interpretation of the social market, placing its significance within a broader historical context. In a Tawney Society lecture entitled, 'Social Market and Social Justice', he observed that 'in the last ten years the "conventional wisdom" that informs politics in Britain has changed', since 'markets are emphasised rather than planning, incentives rather than intervention, the activity of the individual rather than that of the State'.[78] However, 'a dangerous myth', Owen maintained, had arisen about that process of change, a myth that portrayed it as a transformative 'Thatcherite Revolution', thereby maintaining 'that the new "conventional wisdom" is Conservative wisdom'. But that view was 'mistaken, because it accepts that the New Right – deficient in social concern, lacking in basic liberal values, deeply centralist in outlook, and with a tradition that prefers retrenchment to reform – should even claim to be a movement for progressive politics'.[79]

The Conservatives under Margaret Thatcher's leadership, in Owen's judgement, were 'not, therefore, the creators or the owners of the new "conventional wisdom"'. Their victory in 1979 had been 'the effect of change and not its cause', reflecting far-reaching developments that had changed the climate of British politics. Among these Owen identified, first, 'the failure of conventional macro-economic management', whereby successive post-war governments had, for instance, been incapable of controlling inflation through centralised incomes policies, and second, a gradual disillusionment with 'the efficacy of state planning and state ownership' since the use of statist methods by successive post-war governments had failed to bring about improvements in either economic performance or industrial relations. Third, the activities of the trade unions during the 1960s and 1970s – from the failure of the Wilson Government's *In Place of Strife* proposals in 1969 through to the Winter of Discontent of 1978–79 – had 'profoundly affected political thinking and public opinion'. As a consequence, the need both for a reduction in trade union power and for an increase in trade union democracy had become 'crystal clear' and the Conservatives had 'wisely reflected' that view before and after their 1979 election victory.[80]

All of these political developments had in turn generated the perceived need '... to reverse our relative economic decline, to end corporatist policies, to roll back the power of the centralised state'.[81] The SDP's own response had been, in Owen's words, to develop 'a new emphasis and direction which put us within the conventional wisdom but with our own distinctive imprimatur'[82] – an emphasis that for him was crystallised in the idea of the social market. In such a spirit he sought to distance himself from the charge of a 'flirtation with Thatcherism', levelled at him by Jenkins and others, by stating that 'an efficient market economy requires public investment', and hence higher public expenditure on education and training and on housing, which were 'wholly compatible with a market-orientated micro-economic policy'.[83]

Owen was concerned to present this approach in sharp contrast to the Thatcher governments' 'incompetent contribution to the destruction of our manufacturing base', as well as to their indifference to 'the increasing shabbiness of our public services ...'. He pointed, too, to the Conservatives' stance and record on privatisation, which had 'mirrored the dogmatism of Labour's nationalisation', creating private monopolies in place of State monopolies. However, more explicitly than other leading Alliance politicians had done, he also identified the potential benefits of privatisation as the 'undoubted gains in terms of greater management freedom, wider equity ownership, and getting the Treasury off the managers' backs'. These were benefits which to date had been 'offset by the absence of effective competition and consumer pressure from the ability to shop around'.[84]

The social market espoused by Social Democrats was also, Owen claimed, very different in character from Thatcher's vision of 'popular capitalism' since the SDP favoured 'redistribution of assets and not just their sale', as well as greater industrial democracy and more cooperative ventures. In addition, the operation of a social market economy required government action to counteract, through the strengthening of competition policy, the growing concentration of economic power produced by the rising tide of mergers and takeovers in 1980s Britain. Such action should be accompanied, too, he argued, by a stronger system of regulation in the City of London to curb various malpractices and cases of fraud which had arisen since the deregulation of financial markets in 1986. For Social Democrats, Owen declared, would 'never accept unbridled capitalism'.[85]

What, then, Owen had attempted to achieve in this Tawney lecture was to sharpen the distinction between the social market and New Right approaches to the problem of reversing Britain's relative economic decline. In doing so, he had gone at least some of the way to rebutting the charge that the ideological course which he had pursued since 1983 had involved a dalliance with 'Thatcherism', a word which he himself seldom used since, in his view, while it should not be a term of adoration , neither should 'Thatcherism' be a term of abuse.[86] Owen's progressive interpretation of the idea of a social market might thus have been expected to allay the fears of many Liberals. Yet such a stance could still be regarded by some observers as little different from what Malcolm Bruce had called well-established 'Liberal economic pragmatism', which the Party had been refining for 100 years. In his commitment to measures of popular ownership and industrial democracy, Owen could also be seen as reaffirming the value of longstanding Liberal causes.

What, however, was more significant and distinctive about Owen's overall approach was that his emphasis on the need for a balance between market realism and social concern was based on a clear recognition of the fact that the terms of British political debate and the policy agenda of British government had changed decisively in the 1980s. They had been redefined and transformed, as he had perceived, by the emergence of a new 'conventional wisdom' in the face of major political and economic developments. The Thatcher governments, through their policies and legislation, had reinforced the new conventional wisdom instilled by those developments; they had even falsely laid claim to its ownership. In view of that central political reality, the Opposition parties – and the SDP and Alliance, particularly – would, in Owen's judgement, have to adjust and adapt accordingly, whilst retaining their own progressive values and principles. They would therefore, as Chris Huhne noted at the time, 'also have to become enthusiasts for the market ... for more competition, more choice, and a stronger attack on monopolies'.[87] But in doing so, a party of the Centre-Left would also need to imbue the new market-led orthodoxy with what Owen had called its own 'distinctive imprimatur' of social concern.

Moreover, in Owen's interpretation of these changed terms of debate, the SDP's, and the Alliance's, commitment to the beneficial aspects of the market economy needed to be stressed, perhaps even over-emphasised, because state collectivist ideas and policies, and the attitudes they generated, had become so entrenched in British politics and industrial society over the past 40 or more years, and because market economics had consequently been reviled as 'right-wing' in character not just, predictably, on the Left but on the Centre-Left, too. Jo Grimond had made that point back in 1982 when discussing Sir Keith Joseph's promotion of economic liberal ideas within the Conservative Party. Joseph was 'at the moment ... putting stress on the market economy,' Grimond noted, 'because the British have gone too far the other way ...'. In a similar manner, the Institute of Economic Affairs, as a major vehicle for the transmission of economic liberal ideas, was, he observed, 'examining and shaking many cherished establishment beliefs in Britain' and was thus 'one of the forces for change', challenging the post-war collectivist orthodoxy.[88]

In spite of David Owen's attempt to infuse his idea of a social market economy with a progressive interpretation, the term itself did not appear in the 1987 SDP/Liberal Alliance general election manifesto, *Britain United: The Time Has Come*. Although the idea had become closely associated with Owen's leadership of the SDP since 1983 and officially adopted as a central SDP policy stance at the Party's Buxton conference in 1984, it did not, therefore, feature prominently in the Alliance programme during the run-up to the 1987 General Election, to be held on 11 June.

The manifesto itself was the outcome of a 18-month policy-making process, the first year of which had been devoted to producing the preceding joint policy statement. The Alliance parties' two policy committees set up a team of 14 people to prepare the actual manifesto, with principal drafting responsibilities delegated to Alan Beith.[89] As an essentially negotiated document, the manifesto's policy programme consequently reflected the process of compromise which its preparation had entailed. One of the Liberal members of the manifesto team, Richard Holme, later recalled the shortcomings of that process, observing that:

> Negotiated manifestos are not a good idea, whether intra-party, or, as this was, between parties. They tend towards the lowest common denominator rather than the highest common factor.[90]

Whereas Holme was proud, he pointed out, of the part he subsequently played in preparing the 1992 and 1997 Liberal Democrat manifestos, he could not 'say the same of the last Alliance platform', which he considered 'bland and uninspiring'.[91]

In May 1987 that was also the overall view of much of the British media. *The Independent*, for instance, while generally sympathetic to the

Alliance, commented: 'As a rallying cry, moderate dirigisme is not frightfully inspiring'.[92] That seemed a fair assessment of the tone and approach of much of the document. Nevertheless, in their jointly signed foreword, David Owen and David Steel signalled the Alliance's radical intent, maintaining that 'the task of drawing Britain together again can only be achieved through political, economic and social reform on a scale not contemplated in our country for over 40 years'.[93] Yet the most radical part of the manifesto consisted of its proposals for constitutional reform, in a section entitled 'The Great Reform Charter'. These covered electoral reform, for both British elections and elections to the European Parliament; freedom of information legislation; incorporation of the European Convention on Human Rights into British law; devolution to Scotland and Wales; and reform of the House of Lords as well as of House of Commons procedures.[94]

In spite of his disappointment with the blandness of the manifesto as a whole, Richard Holme had already produced a lucid theoretical justification for this programme of constitutional reform in his book, *The People's Kingdom*, published earlier in 1987. Developing a critique of the British State as over-centralised, secretive and poorly governed through a system of elective dictatorship, he had called for a democratic renaissance based on 'a post-paternalist role for government ... with power spread rather than centralised', and with government itself 'more devoted to encouragement than control ... less in charge and more in support'.[95] Underlying his proposals for a radically reformed and decentralised political system, Holme identified a number of fundamental Liberal principles that were 'primarily political, about the way in which power is used and distributed ...'. Among these he stressed the principle of subsidiarity, which, by holding that as much collective decision-making as possible should take place 'close to the person affected', thereby 'turns paternalism on its head, for powers which need to be exercised at a higher level are then generally understood to have been delegated upwards'.[96]

The People's Kingdom also contained an eloquent defence of the classical liberal emphasis on the moral primacy of the individual. 'The satisfactions of common achievement,' Holme observed, were ultimately 'experienced only through the perception of each individual in the group'. Furthermore, he believed, 'a sense of personal uniqueness must precede a sense of shared commonality ... empathy and altruism, let alone combination for mutual advantage, depend on a degree of self-validation and confidence'.[97]

In an earlier essay Holme had addressed in vivid terms the potential problem posed for a reforming movement 'of incremental change' by the advocacy of major constitutional change, which in the past had 'often been the product of great convulsion and revolution'. The means of resolving that apparent dilemma lay, in his view, in the recognition of the fact that:

> The foundations and parts of our constitutional structure are sound. What is needed is to take the old house seriously, to rebuild and extend

it, to redecorate and illuminate it and to make it the living home of a hopeful democracy again.[98]

The 'Great Reform Charter', which Owen and Steel had launched publicly in May 1987, and which was set out in *Britain United*, did put forward clear and radical plans for a constitutional refurbishment of that kind. Elsewhere in the document, however, what *The Independent* had called 'moderate dirigisme' was in evidence. The manifesto's macro-economic proposals thus consisted mainly of an 'incomes strategy' reinforced by a counter-inflation tax on companies that granted inflationary pay increases; higher capital investment in national infrastructure designed both to 'support the framework of services on which industry and society depend, like transport, homes, school, hospitals and drainage', and thereby to provide jobs for the long-term unemployed; and membership of the exchange rate mechanism of the European Monetary System in order to promote currency stability and reduce interest rates.[99] The manifesto also proposed to revive manufacturing industry as 'the driving force at the core of our economy' by such interventionist methods as 'a new Cabinet Industrial Policy Committee responsible for overseeing the development and implementation, in cooperation with industry, of a broad industrial strategy, with long-term priorities'.[100]

Nowhere did *Britain United* explicitly refer to Owen's idea of a social market economy, though some of the central themes associated with it were endorsed. The document thus advocated a strong competition policy with tighter controls over company mergers. While adopting a pragmatic *ad hoc* position on the boundaries of the public and private sectors, viewing them on the basis of 'objective criteria related to competition and efficiency', it also looked favourably at the prospect of the privatisation of British Steel. It supported, too, trade union reform, aimed at 'giving unions back to their members' through the extension of postal ballots and internal elections, and it 'vigorously opposed' pre-entry union closed shops. In addition, the manifesto advanced the traditional Liberal cause of industrial partnership through wider employee participation in decision-making and by means of an extension of schemes for employees' share-ownership and profit-sharing.[101] In spite of commitments in its macro-economic strategy to state-interventionist policies, *Britain United* also declared in its introduction, in a passage entirely consonant with the British Liberal tradition, that:

> Governments should not try to do what can be better done by individuals, by communities, by voluntary organisations or by private enterprise, but should set about enabling people to help themselves ...[102]

Finally, towards the back of the manifesto, a short section contained the formula which had resolved the Alliance dispute over defence policy at the end of 1986. The SDP/Liberal Alliance, it was stated, accepted 'the obligations of NATO, including the presence of Allied bases and nuclear weapons on British soil ...', and pledged to 'maintain, with whatever necessary modernisation, our minimum nuclear deterrent until it can be negotiated away, as part of a global arms negotiation process, in return for worthwhile concessions by the USSR which would enhance British and European security'. The future modernisation of the British deterrent, in terms of its capability, would be 'at a level no greater than that of the Polaris system'.[103]

Shortly after the launch of the Alliance's election campaign, Matthew Simmonds in *The Independent*, noting the lack of a single reference to the 'social market' in the entire document, commented that 'until the Alliance realizes that you do not emphasize the "social" in the social market by diluting the role of the market, it will continue to lack the cutting-edge which it requires'.[104] David Owen later explained that this omission resulted from the fact that he had not sought to ensure the inclusion of the phrase in the manifesto since to Roy Jenkins, the SDP's appointed economics spokesman, the social market was 'a sub-Thatcherite term', and to the Liberals it 'had become an anathema', amounting to 'Owenism'. Instead, therefore, Owen had left it to Ian Wrigglesworth on the manifesto's drafting committee 'to concentrate on establishing market principles and competition rather than forcing the term "social market"'.[105]

More broadly, the overall blandness of the tone and content of the manifesto, about which Richard Holme and others subsequently complained, was the product of the negotiated compromises through which it was prepared. Owen later pointed out that from his perspective it seemed that:

> We could not openly endorse the social market for Liberals felt that positioned us too close to the Conservatives; we could not wholeheartedly support the British nuclear deterrent, for the Liberals were still deeply divided on this issue. Nor could we present Labour as totally unfit to govern because that meant closing the option of being able to form a coalition with them ...[106]

The Alliance election campaign itself, though generally professional in its operations, often seemed confused, uninspired and devoid of a joint strategy or overall theme. The dual leadership at times generated apparent differences of opinion between Owen and Steel about how the Alliance would react were it to hold the balance of power after the election. Such differences arose, or could be inferred, in spite of the two Leaders' expressed desire not to make a preferential choice between the Conservatives or Labour with regard to post-election arrangements.[107]

At the 1987 General Election the Alliance won 22 seats, 17 to the Liberals and five to the SDP. The two parties secured 23 per cent of the total British poll, with 7.3 million votes. The Alliance's vote had remained stable but, in the face of another comfortable Conservative victory with an overall majority of 102, the Liberals and SDP had clearly failed to hold the balance of power, or to replace Labour as the main opposition to the Tories, or even to secure a significant bridgehead in the House of Commons. Significantly, too, there had been no real breakthrough in English urban, Labour-held constituencies, territory in which, back in 1981, it had been hoped that the SDP would make a decisive contribution to the Alliance. Of the 22 Alliance seats, the majority were in the English West Country, rural Wales and Scotland. Furthermore, among the individual Alliance casualties were three of the original 'Gang of Four', Jenkins, Rodgers and Williams, who failed to be elected. Of the 28 SDP MPs who were in the House of Commons in the period between the Party's foundation and the 1983 General Election, only three – Cartwright, Maclennan and Owen – remained.

The Liberals and SDP had nonetheless, it is true, achieved in the 1980s, through their alliance, the best third-party results in two successive general elections since the 1920s. But within the constraints of the existing electoral system, the even geographical spread of the Alliance vote, like that of the Liberals in the past, meant in practice that an impressive 23 per cent vote share in 1987 could not be translated into significant parliamentary representation. The overall result, in effective political terms, for the Alliance, and for the SDP in particular, was thus one of bitter disappointment.

In the weekend in June following the general election, David Steel responded to a statement made by David Owen, in a press conference in Plymouth just hours after the final election results were declared, which had indicated the SDP Leader's opposition to a merger between his Party and the Liberals. In response, in a drafted memorandum, Steel called for a 'democratic fusion' of the two parties.[108] Earlier, in July 1986, on the occasion of the tenth anniversary of his accession to the Liberal leadership, he had already declared that, in his view, an eventual formal union of the two parties was inevitable and desirable.[109]

Owen, however, remained adamantly opposed to such a prospect. His various post-election pronouncements, both at Plymouth and subsequently, on a possible merger of the two Alliance parties underlined the consistency of his stance on the issue. Indeed, Steel later expressed his agreement with David Butler and Dennis Kavanagh's judgement that for Owen:

> ... the Alliance ought never have been a 'partnership of principle', but a plain and simple electoral pact. [...] If the relationship was to be only an electoral pact, his dislike of joint spokesmen, joint policy-making and joint selection, his rejection of a single leader, and his veto over clear organisational links, all can be seen as a perfectly coherent political position. Most Liberals never understood that this was David Owen's basic attitude to the Alliance.[110]

That position was confirmed, therefore, by Owen's firm opposition to Steel's advocacy of a 'democratic fusion', which in turn led to his calling for an internal ballot of SDP members on the question of whether to begin merger negotiations with the Liberal Party. That proposal was eventually endorsed in August 1987 by 57.4 per cent of those SDP members who voted, with 42.6 per cent supporting the continuing independence of the SDP. Since, however, the turnout was 77.7 per cent, this meant that, in effect, less than half the total SDP membership (that is, 44.6 per cent) had actually voted for advancing towards a merger.[111]

In the wake of the result of the ballot, Owen resigned as SDP Leader on 6 August. His apparent defiance of the democratic decision of the SDP membership generated intense resentment both among Liberals and within sections of his own party. Yet his position was, as we have seen, consistent with his longstanding reluctance to surrender the political independence of the SDP. Indeed, in a letter to rank-and-file Social Democrats written in late June 1987 Owen had reaffirmed his belief that 'the fight to maintain the SDP as a separate party' was 'essential for the medium term at least'. In support of that view, he had argued that:

> ... without the SDP, the Alliance would never have been able to maintain the policy stance that we did over the Falklands, over the miners' dispute, over the Right to Buy council house legislation, over the market economy, over the Prevention of Terrorism Act, over deployment of cruise missiles that has led to the imminent INF agreements, over the integration of tax and social security, and over maintaining the minimum nuclear deterrent. There are a host of other policy areas where the SDP voice has been crucial...[112]

As the historians of the SDP later observed, Owen had thus emphasised the policy differences separating the SDP from its allies over the previous six years 'in such a way as to leave the clear impression that the alliance with the Liberals had never been a partnership of principle but only a not-very-happy marriage of convenience'.[113] After resigning as SDP Leader, he soon made clear his intention to work towards the formation of a new fourth party in British politics – in effect a continuing SDP. In the meantime, however, the 1987 Liberal Assembly at Harrogate in September voted overwhelmingly for merger negotiations, which began tentatively at the end of that month and concluded, after nearly four months, in mid-January 1988.

In September 1987, in the same month that the Liberal Assembly approved the start of merger negotiations, Alan Beith, one of the potential leaders of a new merged party, set out his views on the development of Liberal philosophy and strategy in his booklet, *The Fullness of Freedom*.[114] Writing about the same time, the other main aspirant to leadership, Paddy Ashdown, in a pamphlet entitled, *After the Alliance*, also outlined his own political vision.[115] To the supporters, within both the Liberal Party and the SDP, of the future merged party that he and Beith aspired to lead, the problems in the 1987 election campaign that had arisen from the co-existence of two leaders with their different strategic stances had been compounded, too, by difficulties generated by the workings of the Alliance itself during the previous six years – over policy-making, candidate selection, seat allocation, headquarters organisation, and so on. However, the merger negotiations initiated in late September 1987 turned out to be protracted and often acrimonious. They eventually culminated in mid-January 1988 with four of the Liberal team, representing a substantial element of Party activist opinion, resigning either over the question of the new party's name or on the issue of including a commitment to NATO in the preamble to the new party's constitution.[116]

Moreover, a controversial joint policy document, *Voices and Choices for All*, largely written by the new SDP Leader, Robert Maclennan, and two of his researchers, but released as the work of both the party Leaders, included proposals for extending VAT to food, children's clothing and domestic fuel, for ending both universal child benefit and tax relief on mortgage interest, and for retaining the Trident missile system as the British nuclear deterrent. In the ensuing uproar within the Liberal Party, the press conference designed to declare agreement on the foundation of the new party was hastily postponed and the offending policy document withdrawn, being memorably dispatched by Des Wilson as a 'dead parrot'. It was soon replaced by a shorter, less contentious statement, largely based on the 1987 Alliance election manifesto.[117]

At the end of January 1988 special conferences of the Liberal Party and the SDP endorsed the merger, with motions in favour passed overwhelmingly. However, the final ballots, announced on 2 March, of the memberships of the two parties were not entirely convincing in their outcome, and in the case of the SDP, distinctly unenthusiastic. On a low turnout of 52.3 per cent, 87.9 per cent of Liberals voted for merger. But in view of that turnout, 54 per cent of Party members had either abstained or voted against merger. More significantly, in the SDP ballot, on a 55.5 per cent turnout, 65.3 per cent voted for merger, while 34.7 per cent voted against. In those circumstances, therefore, only 36 per cent of the total SDP membership had voted for merger; 64 per cent had either abstained or voted against.[118] David Owen, encouraged by the unconvincing outcome of the SDP ballot, subsequently set up a Council for Social Democracy which soon evolved under his leadership into the continuing SDP.

In view of these differences and divisions, and the disputes and tensions underlying them, it had thus, at its inception, been, in Chris Cook's description, a 'merger most foul'.[119] Yet there were many members of the Social Democratic Party who would nonetheless have concurred with Roy Jenkins's later, vividly expressed judgement that: 'The Missouri is not a pointless river because, after a fertilising and dramatic course, it eventually unites with the Mississippi'.[120]

That confluence did indeed occur when the new merged party, the Social and Liberal Democrats, as it was eventually named, was formally launched on 3 March 1988, with David Steel and Robert Maclennan as its joint interim leaders. At its foundation, it was represented by 19 MPs and about 3,500 local councillors, and had a declared membership of 100,000.[121]

Chapter 8
Recovery after a Painful Infancy: 1988–1997

The infancy of the new party, the Social and Liberal Democrats, was an acutely painful one, reflecting the bitterness of the merger process that had brought it into existence. As David Dutton has observed, the party was 'founded more on the ruins of its predecessors than as the beneficiary of their respective political traditions'.[1] From its formation in March 1988 through to the European Parliament elections of June 1989, the first months of its life were marked by falling opinion-poll ratings, declining membership, low morale at the grass roots and poor local election and parliamentary by-election results. The latter were exemplified by the party's performance at the first parliamentary by-election of the new Parliament at Kensington in July 1988, where the Social and Liberal Democrats, faced by a rival candidate of the continuing SDP (which had been relaunched in March 1988), won a vote share of only 10.7 per cent, finishing in a poor third place. Later that month, following the initial period of the interim joint leadership of David Steel and Robert Maclennan, Paddy Ashdown defeated Alan Beith in the new party's first leadership contest, winning 41,000 votes to Beith's 16,000. Ashdown, aged 47, was duly elected Party Leader on 28 July 1988.

Before his election, there had already been some public expressions of concern about the new party's perceived lack of ideological direction. In the pages of *The Radical Quarterly*, for example, Gordon Lishman lamented what he considered to be the former Liberal leader David Steel's 'lack of interest in political ideas ... and his obsession with the tactics of politics to the apparent exclusion of political content'.[2] It was therefore necessary for the new party's next Leader to 'lead from the front in terms of ideas and policy' and to 'be interested in the content and goals of politics, as well as the strategy and tactics'. For the Liberal Party had conspicuously endured, Lishman argued, 'twenty-two years of leadership without a real interest in policies and ideas'. The task of 'taking the intellectual initiative against Thatcherism' would require a leader 'capable of stimulating ideas and discussion ... in a coherent ideological framework', and, Lishman concluded:

> As everything important in social democratic ideas is contained within modern liberalism and, I hope, social democratic practices which have been least acceptable to Liberals – centralism, paternalism and managerialism – are matters of style and habit rather than of basic belief, that framework must be liberal.[3]

Ashdown, the successful candidate for the leadership, later responded to Lishman's appeal by acknowledging that for Liberals, 'a party founded not on class or interest but on political values, the battleground of ideas is doubly significant'. For him the role of the Leader was thus,

> as Jo Grimond showed so superbly ... to introduce new ideas to the party, to stimulate debate ... and then to communicate the party's values in terms and with a message that the electorate finds it easy to relate to.[4]

Ashdown confessed that he mistrusted 'the notion of a "big idea"' which seemed to him 'seductively simplistic'. Nevertheless, he considered that there was 'a set of ideas emerging from within the Party which gives me great confidence in our ability to capture the political initiative'. Some of the 'most interesting' of those ideas were 'rooted in the notion of the rights, duties and entitlements which attach to the citizen ...'.[5] This focus on the value of citizenship Ashdown was soon to emphasise in his speeches and published writings.

Ashdown's rival for the leadership of the new party, Alan Beith, had argued, in contrasting terms, that Liberals would be 'throwing away a priceless heritage if we do not build on the wholly distinctive identification this party has with one big idea ... that the relationship between the individual and institutional power must be transformed'. Liberals, he maintained, were 'alone in insisting that people should be encouraged to take power in their own communities', and 'alone in challenging the authoritarianism of Tory central government and Labour town hall ...'.[6] In *Leadership for Freedom*, a pamphlet setting out his claims for the Party leadership, Beith argued, too, that the Social and Liberal Democrats were also distinctive in insisting 'that you can have a sense of community and mutual responsibility in a successful and enterprising economy'.[7]

Beith's emphasis on the importance of community, together with Ashdown's focus on the value of citizenship, were themes explored at greater length, and within a broader historical context, by one of the original SDP's leading political thinkers, David Marquand, in a book published the same year, 1988, and entitled *The Unprincipled Society: New Demands and Old Politics*. This,

Marquand's first extended work of political thought and analysis, was actually conceived, as he later pointed out, in the mid-1980s, and 'written in the glare of Thatcherism's high noon'.[8] It examined 'the long hegemony of post-war Keynesian social democracy' and 'the crises which destroyed it'. The book was also 'intended as a contribution to the search for a new governing philosophy' in the wake of the breakdown of the post-war collectivist consensus.[9]

The substance of *The Unprincipled Society* consisted of three main elements: first, an alternative account both of the rise and fall of the post-war consensus and of the relative decline of the British economy; second, a critique of the rival doctrines of economic liberalism, as it had been revived and promoted by the Thatcher governments, and neo-socialism, as it had been propagated by the Bennite Left of the Labour Party; and third, the tentative outline of what Marquand proposed as an alternative, communitarian public philosophy.[10] In his account of national economic decline, Marquand advanced the distinctive and contentious thesis that Britain, unlike more successful mixed economies, had failed to evolve a 'developmental state' capable of harnessing market forces to the long-term national interest. The reason for this shortcoming lay, in his view, in a British political culture which, since the early 19th century, had been suffused with the individualist attitudes of economic liberalism. In his related explanation of the fall of the post-war consensus, Marquand argued that its governing philosophy, what he referred to as 'Keynesian social democracy', had declined because, in the light of economic crises and change, its fundamental weakness had been exposed – namely, that it was 'a philosophy of public intervention without a notion of the public realm or the public good'.[11]

In its place, therefore, Marquand offered a public philosophy rooted in the values of mutual obligation and common purpose. It would seek to 'restore the bonds of community' in an increasingly fragmented society. Moreover, this new public philosophy would be based on the notion of what Marquand called 'politics as mutual education', a process whereby members of a political community, through argument and persuasion, found solutions to their common problems. In his view, such an approach was best practised within small groups, which were more likely 'to develop a sense of community and common purpose'. That in turn implied a wide diffusion of both responsibility and power. From such a climate might then emerge 'a flourishing political community' that would be 'a mosaic of smaller collectivities, which act as nurseries for the feelings of mutual loyalty and trust which hold the wider community together, and where the skills of self-government may be learned and practised'.[12]

What Marquand described as 'the rather inchoate cluster of assertions and aspirations which has gathered around the slogan of the "Social Market"', as promoted by David Owen and his supporters in the 1980s, was unlikely to 'restore the bonds of community' in these ways. For it presupposed 'a market-liberal conception of economic motivation and behaviour' that was 'logically incompatible' with the very notion of community that alone justified the process of redistribution which the social market, in its progressive interpretation, sought to achieve. In Marquand's judgement, the 'social market' idea was thus 'in essence, an attempt to squeeze communitarian conclusions out of individualistic premises', and its political advocates were in reality 'market liberals with tender hearts'.[13]

This criticism had, as we have seen, been firmly rejected by David Owen himself in his insistence that non-market social criteria for redistribution and the provision of public goods could indeed be combined with a realistic view of the market incentives and criteria necessary for effective wealth-creation. Social democrats, Owen had declared in 1987, after all were not supporters of unbridled capitalism.[14]

Irrespective, however, of the degree of validity of Marquand's strictures against the idea of the social market and its underlying rationale, there was clearly much in his notion of a 'communitarian public philosophy' which chimed with the decentralist basis of both mainstream and radical British Liberal thinking, and which could therefore be found congenial within the new Party. Duncan Brack, its new Director of Policy, thus reviewed Marquand's book in favourable terms,[15] while a *Radical Quarterly* editorial declared that Marquand's 'eloquent analysis of the breakdown of the post-war consensus' had 'at last provided the embryonic Social and Liberal Democrats with an analysis which the Labour Party cannot match'.[16]

The potential ideological debate within the new party which Marquand's work had helped to stimulate was, however, overshadowed during the first year of its existence by a prolonged dispute over its appropriate name. That in itself was bound up symbolically with the question of the Party's political and ideological identity. In September 1988 Paddy Ashdown informed the Party's Federal Executive, its main governing and strategic body, that he thought that the Party should be known by the abbreviated name of 'The Democrats'.[17] *The Radical Quarterly*, however, regarded his proposal as symptomatic of the Party's lack of a clear philosophy. It maintained that:

> As well as being long-winded, 'Social and Liberal Democrats' does not identify any coherent group of people – let alone of ideas ... . 'The Democrats' is even worse. If the idea is democracy, it does not refer to anything special or define values differently from those which the Conservatives or Labour ... would claim to uphold.[18]

The Deputy Leader of the Party since July 1988, Alan Beith, had also expressed his profound unease about Ashdown's suggestion of 'The Democrats' as the Party's name, declaring that:

> ... a short title that does not include the word Liberal is simply unacceptable. 'Democrat' I personally deeply and irrevocably oppose ... I am

not just a Democrat. I am a Liberal. It's about the relationship between individuals and society as a whole ...[19]

Beith later recalled that the proposed short name of 'The Democrats' involved, in his view, 'throwing away the identification of the Party as a Liberal party and being subsumed in some vague notion of being "Democrats"'. The nomenclature would thus potentially be 'bad for support and would weaken the power of the philosophy of the Party'.[20] Ashdown's proposal was nonetheless formally endorsed by the Party's autumn conference at Blackpool in late September 1988. The dispute that this decision subsequently generated within the Party was not, however, to be resolved until its fortunes reached their nadir the following year. For by the summer of 1989 the Democrats' deteriorating financial situation, exacerbated by rapidly falling Party membership, became acute, nearing the point of bankruptcy. Furthermore, the new Party's electoral performance continued to decline throughout 1989. There were poor results in the May local elections, with 190 seats lost. In the six parliamentary by-elections held between July 1988 and June 1989 the Party's vote share fluctuated from a peak of 26 per cent to a trough of 1.5 per cent.[21] The most conspicuously disastrous result of all was in the June 1989 European Parliament elections where the Party finished in fourth place nationally behind the Green Party, and achieved an overall vote share of only 6.4 per cent. This was the worst election performance by a British third party since the 1950s.

At the close of the day of the European elections, Paddy Ashdown recorded in his diaries the fact that he was 'plagued by the nightmare that the party that started with Gladstone will end with Ashdown'.[22] Ten days later he wrote despondently that he had endured

[a] very, very black week which may well mark the end of the Party altogether. It's down to me and a few others to try and keep the thing together.[23]

While the new Party was thus struggling for its very survival, its first major statement of principles had nonetheless been published, in January 1989. The production of this document, entitled, *Our Different Vision: Themes and Values for Social and Liberal Democrats*, sprang from the perceived need within the Party to sharpen its image and define its identity at a time when, in the wake of the bitter disputes over the merger in 1988, both of those things seemed to many observers indistinct and unclear. The Federal Policy Committee therefore took the view that the talents and expertise of the many policy specialists within the Party should be harnessed to the task of clarifying its fundamental values and beliefs, which could then be reflected in its policy development and promoted in its publicity and campaigning.[24]

Drafted by a working group that included Alan Beith, Richard Holme, David Marquand and Baroness (Nancy) Seear among its members, *Our Different Vision* declared at the outset that the Party stood for 'three basic values – liberty, equality and community'. Those values, drawn from the new Party's 'overlapping traditions of social liberalism and social democracy', were interrelated. For liberty entailed equality of opportunity since 'if some have greater opportunities than others, then some are less free than others'. Furthermore, liberty and equality without community were 'hollow' since individuals were social creatures not isolated atoms, who could fulfil their potential 'only as members one of another'.[25] The Social and Liberal Democrats also stood, the statement declared, for the related value of 'equal citizenship – the badge of belonging to a political community and the means through which political communities take shape'. For citizenship was 'exercised in and through a political community'.[26]

Reviewing *Our Different Vision* in the journal *New Democrat*, Leighton Andrews considered it to be 'one of the finest short statements of contemporary Liberalism that I have read'. If, he reflected, the Liberal/SDP Alliance had 'possessed a political map of this nature', then its supporters 'would never have been waylaid in the dark alleys of social market theory, let alone chased that bloody parrot up a cul-de-sac'.[27] Andrews was particularly impressed by the document's analysis of 'four key interlocking sets of changes', namely, those 'in the pattern of production, in the world economy, in demography and in political culture'. In addressing them, the document had, in strategic terms, avoided what he called 'the kind of sentimental, wet response which says that things would be so much better if we could only get back to the old consensus, to the days when a social democratic elite thought it ran the country'.[28]

In its depiction of the Party's interrelated core values of liberty, equality and community, the statement which Andrews had praised echoed the words of the Preamble to the new Party Constitution, which had been drafted in January 1988 towards the end of the prolonged and tortuous merger negotiations,[29] and eventually adopted after the two Alliance parties' merger ballots in March 1988. The Preamble stated that the new Party

> ... exists to build and safeguard a fair, free and open society, in which we seek to balance the fundamental values of liberty, equality and community, and in which no-one shall be enslaved by poverty, ignorance or conformity.

The Preamble had proceeded to declare that:

> We champion the freedom, dignity and well-being of individuals; we acknowledge and respect their right to freedom of conscience and their right to develop their talents to the full. We aim to disperse power, to

foster diversity and to nurture creativity. We believe that the role of the state is to enable all citizens to attain these ideals, to contribute fully to their communities and to take part in the decisions which affect their lives.[30]

Some of those words and sentiments also echoed the original 1936 Preamble to the Liberal Party Constitution, which had been very slightly amended in 1969. Yet one commentator later compared the new Preamble unfavourably with its predecessor, originally drafted by Ramsay Muir and Elliot Dodds. Daniel Johnson, writing in *The Radical Quarterly*, thus noted that both the 1988 Preamble and *Our Different Vision* had committed the new Party 'to a philosophy giving equal weight to liberty, equality and community', whereas the old Liberal Party Constitution had proclaimed that Liberals 'put freedom first', meaning 'that it is our most important value – but not our only one'.[31] In contrast to the emphasis on the balance between liberty, equality and community that was so prominent in the two recent documents, a Liberal philosophy that could provide a guide to, and support for, the policies of the Liberal Democrats, Johnson argued, should be

> ... one which gives liberty first priority, puts equality second and places community third ... Liberty takes priority in a logical sense. That is to say that one starts with liberty as a fundamental value. One then rejects all forms of equality which are incompatible with liberty. One then rejects all forms of community which are incompatible with liberty and equality. One is left with a coherent and clearly Liberal theory of value, which solves many of the decision problems presented by the idea of balance.[32]

Later in 1989 Paddy Ashdown set out his own attempt to provide his Party with an ideological compass of that kind in his book *Citizens' Britain*, written during the summer and published for the autumn party conference. Ashdown later recalled that he had decided to write the book 'as a part of my plan to reverse the decline of the Party and start building for the future'. Its aim was 'to mark out a core of ideas which would articulate what we stood for and explain why we still had a role'. More ambitiously, it was designed to appear '... not just as a motley collection of ideas, but as a framework for the new shape of progressive politics in Britain'.[33]

Emphasising the interrelated values of community and citizenship, Ashdown's *Citizens' Britain* looked forward to a more participatory democratic society emerging in the future, in which there would be a widespread popular awareness of 'the importance of an active life as members of a community, and the value of shared resources'.[34] At the heart of such a society Ashdown envisaged the need for a new conception of citizenship which would imply 'a new settlement of the terms of the basic contract which defines the citizen's relationship with government and with each other'.[35] This view of citizenship would embrace three elements: first, rights – of a civil, political and economic nature; second, entitlements, by which Ashdown meant the means of access to the 'opportunities and resources we need to be valued and valuable members of society'; and third, responsibilities, complementing those rights and entitlements, and to be recognised at the level of community.[36]

What would be the wider role of government in this 'citizens' Britain'? The days of the corporate State were over, Ashdown stressed, but it was 'not sufficient to define the role of government as an idle bystander, while the free market is allowed to run rampant, with the powerful winning and the weakest going to the wall'. In line with his central emphasis on citizenship rights and entitlements, he argued that the chief function of government should be 'to enhance, enable and empower the individual'.[37] In the field of social policy the practical implications of this were that government should seek to define and establish the citizens' social entitlements – involving access to health care, education and welfare – without acting as a monopoly provider of public services. In the field of economic policy, too, the primary task of government was 'not to be a participant but to be an enabler and, especially, to be the regulator which ensures that the working of markets is not only free, but also fair, open and honest'.[38]

A month after the publication of *Citizens' Britain,* the Party's protracted name dispute was at last resolved when an all-member ballot resulted in overwhelming support for the nomenclature, 'Liberal Democrats'. Ashdown later admitted:

> I underestimated people's sense of insecurity about losing their old parties, and especially the importance of the 'Liberal' name and tradition. This debate, which on the surface was about the name, was, in reality, about our identity and both dominated and disrupted the first year of the new Party.[39]

That error of judgement had been, he confessed, 'a terrible mistake', the biggest that he had made during the entire period of his leadership. For his original proposal to exclude 'Liberal' from the new Party's name had been tantamount to asking people 'to divorce themselves from a tradition in which their heart was absolutely steeped, this tradition of liberalism ...'[40]. Recalling that mistake nearly 20 years later, he attributed it in part to his being in a sense a Liberal outsider, having come to his Party late, and therefore failing to understand 'the importance of these tribal DNA structures with the Party', which helped to bind it together.[41]

The widely popular restoration of the 'Liberal' name in October 1989 not only rectified Ashdown's early error but also appeared symbolically to mark a turning-point in the Party's fortunes. For gradual recovery at last became evident throughout 1990 and 1991. In the first place, the electoral threat of both the Green Party and the continuing SDP rapidly receded. Indeed, after the latter's disastrous performance at the Bootle by-election in May 1990, David Owen and his colleagues formally announced the following month that their Party was finally being wound up. Furthermore, there were notable victories for the Liberal Democrats in parliamentary by-elections – at Eastbourne in October 1990, in a major breakthrough for the Party, and, the following year, at Ribble Valley and Kincardine and Deeside in March and November 1991 respectively. A good performance was achieved, too, in the May 1991 local elections in which the Party secured 520 net gains and won control of 19 councils. All of this progress was accompanied by improved poll ratings for both the Liberal Democrats and their Leader.

Alongside the Party's revival during 1990 and 1991, the formulation of its policy was evolving in a more market-oriented manner. As chair of the Party's Federal Policy Committee since his election as Leader in July 1988, Paddy Ashdown had set out to steer his Party towards a much greater emphasis on the market economy and its essential elements. He later admitted that he and Alan Beith, the Party's Treasury spokesperson, had 'quite deliberately' sought 'to change the policy of the party away from ... a soggy corporatism to a more liberal policy, more interested in competition, small businesses and enterprise'.[42] The Party, in his view, 'had a collectivist instinct', probably influenced by the process of building up its base in local government. Before the merger, the Liberal Party, too, had, he believed, 'allowed itself to get swallowed up in the lazy collectivist consensus of the '60s and '70s'.[43]

The movement away from those corporatist and collectivist positions consequently became clearly apparent in Liberal Democrat economic policy after 1990. At Ashdown's instigation, there were significant departures from the Alliance past. In place of Keynesian demand management, increased state investment to reduce unemployment and prices and incomes policies to control inflation, the emphasis was shifted on to a more vigorous competition policy, selective private investment in public services and decentralisation of pay bargaining. It was proposed, too, that operational independence should be granted to the Bank of England in order to set interest rates and thereby maintain price stability, and there was a commitment of support, too, for European Economic and Monetary Union.[44]

As well as this shift towards a less state-interventionist and more market-oriented approach to economic policy, there were also significant initiatives during this period in the fields of environmental and education policy. In the case of the former, previous Liberal Party proposals were developed further, including a proposed transfer of the burden of taxation away from income towards pollution and resource depletion. In education policy, Ashdown's original proposal, first flagged in his party conference speech in autumn 1990, for raising income tax by one penny in the pound in order to fund extra necessary investment in education became a distinctive official Party policy.

These three areas of policy development, along with more established Liberal commitments to electoral and constitutional reform and to European cooperation and integration, eventually formed the mnemonic 'five Es' structure around which was composed the Liberal Democrats' 1992 General Election manifesto, *Changing Britain for Good*. This structure had been largely developed by Richard Holme, the manifesto co-ordinator [45] and expressed in detailed terms in the 15,000-word document, prepared for a general election to be held on 9 April.

Underlining the pro-market shift in attitude since Ashdown had become Leader, the manifesto stated that: 'In the economic sphere we know that the free market is the best guarantee of responsiveness to choice and change'. Liberal Democrats aimed 'to encourage a competitive and enterprising economy which is environmentally sustainable, founded on partnership and advanced skills and closely integrated with Europe'. Committed to both the free market and free trade, the Party regarded the role of government as one of 'enabling firms and entrepreneurs to have the best possible chance', which meant 'encouraging competition, investing in skills, involving employees in the success of their companies, nurturing small businesses, playing a positive part in the construction of the new European economy and, above all, bringing greater stability to national economic management'.[46]

Specific policy commitments included a major economic recovery programme, with increased government spending on transport, housing, hospitals and schools and on energy efficiency and conservation projects, all designed to reduce unemployment by at least 600,000 over two years. The manifesto also called for the break-up of monopoly providers of utilities such as British Telecom and British Gas, for private operators to have access to the British Rail track network, and for a tougher competition policy to be achieved by combining the Monopolies and Mergers Commission with the Office of Fair Trading.[47] In addition, *Changing Britain for Good* advocated a counter-inflation strategy based on an operationally independent Bank of England, free to set interest rates, and on the entry of sterling into the exchange rate mechanism of the European Monetary System.[48] Such a strategy thus clearly replaced the reliance on centralised prices and incomes policies that had characterised Liberal and Alliance manifestos during the 1970s and 1980s.

In the second of the '5 Es', education policy, the manifesto committed the Liberal Democrats to increasing public investment in education by £2 billion in the first year, with priorities for preschool education, education and training for 16–19 year olds, and adult education. This programme would be funded by raising the rate of income tax by one penny in every pound,[49] the distinctive policy that Ashdown had first proposed in autumn 1990. In the field of environmental policy, proposals included the creation of a new Department of Natural Resources for the purpose of environmental protection; the adoption of alternative indicators, such as social and personal quality of life and environmental quality, to supplement conventional measures of GDP; and the use of market mechanisms such as energy taxation and tradable emission licenses for industry as means of reducing pollution.[50]

On European policy *Changing Britain for Good* declared Liberal Democrat support for closer European integration and for the movement towards a 'fully integrated, federal and democratic European Community'. In particular, it endorsed acceptance of the Maastricht timetable for Economic and Monetary Union that had been agreed in the Treaty on European Union signed in February 1992, as well as its proposals for increased powers for the European Parliament and for active EC social, environmental, regional and scientific policies.[51]

Finally, the manifesto, proposed 'at the heart' of the Liberal Democrats' election programme a wide-ranging programme of constitutional reform including a voting system based on proportional representation for all national, European and local elections; Home Rule for Scotland and Wales, with the creation of a Scottish Parliament and Welsh Senedd; reform of the House of Lords; a reformed and strengthened system of local government; freedom-of-information legislation; incorporation of the European Convention on Human Rights into British law; and a written constitution for the United Kingdom backed by a Supreme Court.[52]

Although the concept of a 'social market', as developed by David Owen in the 1980s, was not expounded in *Changing Britain for Good*, an underlying approach of combining market realism with social concern, competitiveness with compassion, was implicit in the manifesto's emphasis of the need to promote both private enterprise and public investment. Support for a more competitive market economy was thus supplemented by advocacy of higher public expenditure – notably, on education, training and health care – and increased investment in the country's essential infrastructure.[53]

This was a distinctive synthesis that led *The Independent* to comment that at the 1992 General Election the Liberal Democrats were 'alone in understanding that the market can be a potential ally in serving social ends'. More broadly, it maintained that 'across a spectrum of issues' the Party was 'more in sympathy with the spirit of the times that either of the two big parties', while *The Guardian* considered that *Changing Britain for Good* 'far out-distances its competitors with a fizz of ideas and an absense of fudge'.[54] The manifesto's interrelated central themes certainly helped to give it a greater coherence and a more radical edge than its Alliance predecessors of 1983 and 1987.

As the 1992 campaign developed, it appeared to *The Guardian* that, whereas Labour had 'merely defended the vote it seemed to have when the election was called', the Liberal Democrats, by contrast, had been 'the movers and shakers', producing all of 'the movement and the arguments', with Paddy Ashdown 'the only real winner of the campaign', having 'indefatigably carried so much of the fight on his own shoulders'.[55] Yet as the campaign reached its climax, with opinion polls indicating the possibility of a hung parliament, that prospect placed the Liberal Democrats in a more defensive posture. For they were obliged to address the question of how they would respond to such an outcome, and whether they would be prepared to support a minority Conservative or a minority Labour government.

The eventual election result, after the nation went to the polls on 9 April, reflected the consequence of that factor of indecision in a late swing to the Conservatives. Nationally, the Liberal Democrats nevertheless polled nearly 6 million votes, securing 18.3 per cent of the total poll and 20 seats. These included four gains, all in England, and six losses, among which were the three seats won in the by-elections of the 1987–92 Parliament. The strongest areas of support for the Party in Britain were the South West and South East of England, which provided 31.4 per cent and 23.4 per cent of its vote respectively.

The outcome for the Liberal Democrats, while generally satisfactory, was thus ultimately disappointing, with only 20 MPs and a million fewer votes than the Alliance had won in 1987. The number of second places for the Party had also fallen from 261 to 154. Labour's partial recovery, in spite of the Conservatives' winning overall majority of 21, had also undermined Ashdown's original strategic aim of eventually replacing Labour as the main alternative to the Conservatives. But compared with the bleak and desperate days of 1988–89, the Liberal Democrat performance was nonetheless creditable, particularly in the English West Country. The 1992 election had revealed, too, some clear evidence of tactical voting among the electorate, notably in constituencies where the Liberal Democrats could present themselves as the main challenger to the Conservatives.[56] More broadly, the Party had demonstrated that it had developed, after a painful infancy, into a mature and significant national political force.

Paddy Ashdown, who had fought what was widely regarded as a highly effective campaign, attributed the late swing to the Conservatives to a visceral fear of Labour in the minds of many voters. However, as he recorded in his diary on 10 April, the 1992 General Election had produced 'the result I always said I wanted, with the Tories ahead and Labour going down to a fourth defeat and into an internal battle'.[57] In his judgement, that outcome had thus created the opportunity for moving towards a realignment of the Centre-Left in British politics and for advancing the cause of electoral reform.

In more immediate terms, the result of the 1992 General Election marked the end of a phase of Ashdown's leadership that had achieved, in his own words, 'survival from a point of near extinction'.[58] That achievement owed much to his own drive, energy and charisma, and to the efforts, too, of a few of his closest advisers and confidants, including, notably in his view,

Richard Holme.[59] The Party's survival was also due, as Duncan Brack has recalled, to

> ... the campaigning tenacity of the core of party activists who did not leave in the dark days of 1988–90, and saw off the other competitors for the centre-left ground – the Owenite SDP and the Greens – revealed most obviously in the shock by-election victory of Eastbourne, in October 1990.[60]

In the aftermath of the 1992 General Election, Ashdown signalled a clear strategic shift for his Party in a speech delivered in his constituency, at Chard in Somerset, on 9 May 1992. Whilst reviewing the Liberal Democrats' strategic options in the wake of the Conservatives' fourth successive victory and Labour's fourth successive defeat, he argued that the Liberal Democrats' overriding purpose should be to

> ... create the force powerful enough to remove the Tories; to assemble policies capable of sustaining a different government; and to draw together the forces in Britain which will bring change and reform.

In view of Labour's prolonged electoral failure, the role of the Liberal Democrats should be to act as

> ... the catalyst, the gathering point for a broader movement dedicated to winning the battle of ideas which will give Britain an electable alternative to Conservative government.[61]

Significantly, too, Ashdown argued at Chard, in a manner reminiscent of Grimond, that the Liberal Democrats should 'work with others to assemble the ideas around which a non-socialist alternative to the Conservatives can be constructed'. The Party ought, therefore, to be 'much less exclusive in our approach to politics than we were in the last Parliament, and much more inclusive to others in this one'. What, in his view, was needed was 'a new forum and a debate on a much wider scale – one which is owned by no particular party and encompasses many who take no formal part in politics, but wish to see a viable alternative to Conservatism in Britain'.[62]

In contrast, then, to the careful but somewhat unconvincing stance of neutrality that had been adopted by the Liberal Democrats at the 1992 election – with regard to their possible support for either a minority Conservative or a minority Labour government in the event of a hung Parliament – Ashdown was now offering a different course. His speech implied, though it did not explicitly state, his future commitment to a strategy of realignment of the Centre-Left that Grimond and Steel, in their different ways, had pursued in the past. That was certainly Ashdown's underlying aim since, as he later recalled, the Chard speech was designed 'to launch, as I hoped, the process of realignment of the left through closer co-operation between ourselves and Labour'.[63]

Ashdown had thus in four years moved far from his early view, expressed during the Party leadership campaign in 1988, that his Party's task was to replace rather than ally with the Labour Party as the main non-Conservative party of reform. That strategic goal, arguably always unrealistic in view of Labour's geographically concentrated electoral support, had been rendered even more difficult to attain by the Labour Party's process of modernisation – in organisational, policy and ideological terms – under Neil Kinnock's leadership[64] since 1987, and by its partial electoral recovery in 1992. The Liberal Democrats' position of equidistance in relation to the Conservatives and Labour had been undermined, too, by their evident policy convergence with Labour in recent years – on Europe and public investment and, in particular, over constitutional reform, including, especially, devolution to Scotland. On the other hand, it could at least be said that the stance of equidistance had assisted Ashdown in maintaining a distinctive, independent identity for his Party in the face of that policy convergence, and in thereby preventing its absorption by a reviving Labour Party.

At any rate, the Chard speech sparked a subsequent debate within the Liberal Democrats on the Party's strategic direction. The result was a dual emphasis on the need, on the one hand, for retaining and refining its distinctive approach and character, but, on the other, for exploring, where appropriate, opportunities for inter-party cooperation in advancing towards common goals.[65] The first of those commitments was embodied in another 'themes and values' document, following on from *Our Different Vision* in 1989, which sought to sharpen the image of the Party in terms of its core philosophical values and beliefs, and thereby to convey a clearer idea of its fundamental aims and principles – not only to its own members and supporters but also to the media and the wider electorate. The document in question, *Facing up to the Future*, was largely drafted by Duncan Brack and published in June 1993 as the main successor to *Our Different Vision* as a statement of Party philosophy and principles. Indeed, Brack later pointed out that from the outset the Liberal Democrats had 'made a systematic effort to derive their policy proposals consistently from a core philosophy'. For in sharp contrast to the other main parties, that exercise was considered necessary since the new merged party 'lacked the benefit of an instinctive understanding of what the party stands for amongst the electorate, the media and even their own members and activists (particularly in the immediate post-merger period)'.[66]

Like its predecessor document, *Facing up to the Future* underlined the Party's core value of liberty, stating that Liberal Democrats desired 'a society which gives individual men and women opportunities to pursue their aims, develop their talents and fulfil their potential free from interference'.

In addition, it made clear that the second of the new Party's triad of interrelated core values – equality – derived from its fundamental commitment to liberty, conceived in its positive sense as the presence of opportunity, since 'if some have fewer opportunities than others, then they are less free'. But the form of equality pursued by the Liberal Democrats could not be equality of outcome, which undermined individual freedom in various ways, but rather 'equality of opportunity and choice'. It was stressed, however, that 'gross inequalities of income, wealth and power' were 'not only morally objectionable and destructive of a sense of community', but also generated 'a vicious spiral of multiple deprivation', reinforcing inequality in different areas and thereby creating 'insuperable barriers' to equality of opportunity and choice.[67]

The Party's emphasis on its third core value – community – also derived, it was observed, from its commitment to liberty in two important respects: first, in the sense that individuals lived in communities, 'whether based around locality, workplace, mutual interest or mutual affection', which formed the 'natural frameworks' within which they exercised and expressed their freedoms; and second, because local communities provided the political environment in which power could be decentralised to local and neighbourhood levels, thereby making possible wider citizen participation, another important aspect of freedom.[68] *Facing up to the Future* thus indicated a clear link of continuity in British Liberal ideology, tracing this emphasis back to the theory and strategy of community politics developed and promoted in the 1970s. As in the recent past, therefore, the policy implications of this ideological position would be both the fostering of local political structures and the promotion of local community projects of various kinds in, for instance, such areas as economic development, housing, planning, crime prevention and policing.

In the area of economic policy, *Facing up to the Future* also reaffirmed the Liberal Democrats' firm post-1990 commitment to a market economy, contending that:

> The operation of competitive markets in the economy is essential to generate prosperity, to maximise choice, to decentralise economic power and to stimulate innovation and adaptability.[69]

The document stressed, however, the fact that the market was 'a mechanism, not an end in itself', and that there were 'many instances of market failure', including 'monopoly power ... uncosted externalities such as environmental degradation and the failure to supply public goods'. Those shortcomings therefore clearly justified 'an active role for government' and a rejection of 'the laissez-faire approach'. But since 'bureaucratic failure' inherent in state intervention was also frequent and damaging, the Liberal Democrat preference in response to market failure was to explore 'near-market or regulatory solutions' such as energy taxation or regulation of monopolies, rather than to rely on direct state intervention.[70]

While these ideological and strategic statements were seeking to clarify the Liberal Democrats' purpose and sense of direction, the Party's steady improvement in its performance in both local elections and parliamentary by-elections continued in impressive style. It made net gains of 308 and 341 in the 1992 and 1993 local elections respectively, and in May 1994 gained control of 19 councils with 388 gains.[71] Following the 1995 local elections the Liberal Democrats overtook the Conservatives as the second party of local government, and now had more than 5,000 local councillors throughout the length and breadth of the British Isles. In many urban areas, too, the Party had become the main opposition to Labour. In addition, in 1994 the Liberal Democrats won their first-ever seats in the European Parliament, and in parliamentary by-elections won morale-boosting victories, with commanding majorities, at Newbury in May 1993, at Christchuch in July 1994, with a swing of 35.4 per cent, the biggest in British by-elections since 1945, and at Eastleigh in June 1994.

But just as the Party's fortunes were being favourably affected in the short term by the Major Government's growing unpopularity and by the Conservative Party's internal strife, so were the Liberal Democrats' prospects in the medium and long term rendered uncertain by highly significant developments within the Labour Party. John Smith's sudden death in May 1994 and Tony Blair's subsequent accession to the Labour leadership in July of that year accelerated the process of modernisation that had been initiated by Neil Kinnock after the 1987 General Election. Blair's resolute direction of Labour further into the centre ground of British politics was dramatically underlined by the rewriting, in 1995, of Clause IV of the Party's Constitution, since 1918 the symbol of its traditional socialist commitment and hence its ideological totem. This was accompanied by an unequivocal endorsement of the market economy and by an overt desire to transform Labour into a modernised European social democratic party.

These developments could be interpreted from one viewpoint as endangering the Liberal Democrats' position by appearing to occupy part of their political ground. But from another perspective they could be regarded as offering once more the prospect, by which both Grimond and Steel had been lured, of a realignment of the Centre-Left in British politics. Certainly Ashdown became preoccupied both with the dangers posed by the former possibility and with the major opportunities that might arise from the latter. In August 1994 he recorded in his diaries:

> ... I seem to have completely lost direction. I have been building the Party to fill a certain gap in politics, which I know is there and which would give us real electoral appeal. But then along comes Blair with all the power of Labour behind him, and fills exactly the space I have been aiming at for the last seven years.[72]

Ashdown later admitted, too, that Blair's election as Labour Party Leader the previous month had marked 'the deepest and most desperate point of depression in my whole leadership of the party'. For he knew that Blair's arrival on the political scene was a mixed blessing. How, then, he wondered at the time, were the Liberal Democrats going to respond to, and survive, the advent of Blair and 'New' Labour? How were they to 'ride that wave rather than have it swamp us?'[73] Certainly it seemed to him that Blair in 1994 was 'articulating very powerfully all the things I'd been writing, saying, doing and wanting to achieve'. The political ground thus appeared to have been 'cut massively from under our feet'.[74]

Later in 1994 Ashdown set out his thoughts on the future course that the Liberal Democrats should be pursuing in these changed circumstances in *Making Change Our Ally*, a pamphlet concerned, in his words, with 'the challenges facing Britain in the run-up to the end of the century',[75] including in particular the overriding need for the country 'to change old practices and structures in order to create a flexible, competitive, enterprise economy, capable of earning a living in the world, whilst maintaining a civilised society at home'.[76] Ashdown acknowledged here the fact that some of what the post-1979 Conservative governments had achieved 'needed to be done and should not be undone', including trade union reform, 'the raising of standards of service and efficiency in our economy including in the public sector, the stripping down of the old structures of the corporate state and the liberalisation of our market system'. Yet alongside those improvements 'terrible damage', he stressed, had been inflicted through the undermining of the 'pluralist nature of our democratic institutions', the neglect of basic infrastructure, the withering of the country's industrial base, high unemployment, the widened gap between rich and poor, and the undervaluation of education and training.[77]

As well, therefore, as pursuing the goal of a more competitive market economy, it was essential, too, Ashdown argued, 'to recreate a society based on the concept of responsible citizenship'. For both the free-market Conservative approach of aiming 'to get from the market what we can for ourselves' and the antithetical state socialist approach of 'encouraging the view that there is no need for individual responsibility, since the State will take care of everything', had been manifest failures. What was needed in their place was 'a new balance between rights and duties and a new context in which this balance can be understood by the ordinary citizen'. In addition, Ashdown emphasised 'the importance of community' as a means of developing 'a new civic order'. That meant 'supporting "intermediate" institutions – the voluntary sector, housing co-operatives and tenant management groups; and encouraging participation and responsibility in the community of work'. In short, it should be the aim of the Liberal Democrats in facing those challenges to nurture 'a society of self-reliant individuals and strong communities'.[78]

These were themes that Ashdown had already explored in his book, *Citizens' Britain*. Grafted on to an unequivocal support for a competitive market economy, and combined with a commitment to political and constitutional reform, his emphasis on the interrelated ideas of active citizenship and community provided, from his perspective, the essential elements of a progressive synthesis for the 1990s, an updated expression of what Jo Grimond had sought in the past to offer as a radical alternative to both Conservatism and state socialism. As an important strategic step towards the practical realisation of such ideas, Ashdown had decided privately by 1994 to abandon his and his Party's stance of equidistance, that is, the Liberal Democrats' official policy of maintaining an equal distance between themselves and both the Conservatives and Labour, and of not favouring either of those parties. The Liberal Democrats should thus, he was now convinced, 'accept publicly that we can't support a Tory Government after the next election', and should 'then set some very tough conditions for our relationship with Labour'.[79]

The rationale for that relationship had already been set out in Ashdown's 1992 Chard speech. In addition, the Scottish Constitutional Convention, which involved, with his approval, meetings since 1989 between leading Labour and Liberal Democrat politicians over the details of future devolution to Scotland, had already established the pattern that cooperation between the two parties might assume. Indeed, in his view, the Convention had provided 'the model that Blair and I tried to replicate' from July 1994 up to the ensuing 1997 General Election.[80] Ashdown had also reached the conclusion that he and Blair shared a great deal of political common ground. There was 'very little difference between his thinking and mine', he had recorded in his diaries in December 1993, and they had 'come to the same analysis from different directions'.[81]

Ashdown's aim of achieving clear cooperation with the Blair-led Labour Party was furthered when the Liberal Democrats' Federal Executive received and endorsed, on 25 May 1995, a statement from him which formally ended the Party's established stance of equidistance. The decision was subsequently approved with little dissent by the Party's federal conference in September.[82] In view of the changing climate of British politics that Blair's new leadership was rapidly bringing about, that seemed a sensible political decision in many ways. For in that climate, as Alan Leaman later recalled, the Liberal Democrats had appeared by the beginning of 1995 to be 'confused and fragile ... with an uncertain message'. That internal condition had in no way been alleviated by policy reverses for the leadership at the 1994 autumn party conference in Brighton, setbacks which had produced, in Leaman's view, 'a palpable lack of self-confidence around the upper reaches of the party'.[83]

With the abandonment of equidistance in May 1995, came, too, the rejection of the notion, fostered both by the Alliance during the 1980s and by

Ashdown at the beginning of his leadership, that Labour could be replaced as the main progressive force in British politics. In its place became embedded his belief that the Liberal Democrats could position themselves alongside Blair's 'New' Labour as a distinctive, independent party, yet as a significant part, too, of the Centre-Left, eager to pursue cooperation with the Labour Party in order to defeat the Conservatives at the next general election.

As early as April 1994 Ashdown was convinced that this strategic goal, 'the Project' as he had come to refer to it, could even be directed, in spite of his Party's comparative weakness in terms of resources and parliamentary strength, in a Liberal direction. As he wrote in his diaries, he believed that 'one of the historic roles of the Liberal Democrats, and of my leadership of the Party, is to use this opportunity and my relationship with Blair to start the process of creating a completely new shape for our politics ...'. Furthermore, he reflected,

> ... if, as it appears, I have more in common with Blair than he has with his left wing, surely the logical thing is for us to create a new, powerful alternative force which would be united around a broadly liberal agenda.[84]

By June 1985, however, with the fortunes of John Major's Conservative government declining further, Ashdown was expressing his concern that '... Labour has stolen our ground comprehensively'.[85] Over a year later, his gloomy reflection on Blair's 1996 Labour Party Conference speech was:

> Same words, same notions, same sentiments, same policies as I have been trying to get on to the agenda now for eight years. And he comes along and takes it off me in one![86]

Nevertheless, in the period following the abandonment of equidistance in May 1995 largely clandestine negotiations had been set in train between small teams from both the Liberal Democrats and the Labour Party with the common aim of moving towards agreement in certain policy areas. The most significant aspect of this process was the undertaking, at the request of Blair and Ashdown, by two senior parliamentary figures, namely, Robin Cook, Labour's Shadow Foreign Secretary, and Robert Maclennan, the Liberal Democrat constitutional affairs spokesman, to initiate talks in October 1996 about the possibility of future cooperation between the two parties on constitutional reform. The outcome of these talks was the Cook-Maclennan Agreement of March 1997, which specified the form that such cooperation might take in the next Parliament.

The ideological basis for this process had been indicated not only by Ashdown's admission in December 1993 that he and Blair appeared to share a common political vision; it had also been explicitly underlined by Blair himself, who, in a 1995 speech, had contended that Labour should 'welcome the radical left-of-centre tradition outside of our own party, as well as celebrating the achievements of that tradition within it'.[87] In that same speech Blair had pointed out that historically democratic socialism in Britain was 'the political heir of the radical Liberal tradition'.[88] One of his closest aides and advisers, Philip Gould, also argued that Labour's break with the Liberal Party after 1918 had meant that it had severed its links with Britain's 'other great radical movement', thereby precluding 'the possibility of building one united progressive party'. The ideological consequence, he noted, had been one of 'divided intellectual traditions, separating Liberalism, with its emphasis on individualism and tolerance, from Labourism, which stressed solidarity and social justice'.[89] Ashdown noted in September 1996 that Blair, too, had expressed to him his regret that 'our parties weren't able to stay together in the early part of the [20th] century', and that Lloyd George, who had been 'incomparably the most radical figure of the second and third decade of the twentieth century', had ultimately not been 'in a party that could deliver'. It was necessary, therefore, in Blair's view, 'to bring these two streams back together again'.[90]

Since Ashdown had commenced his private discussions with Blair, back in December 1993, about possible cooperation between Labour and the Liberal Democrats, it had become evident that the most contentious issue was likely to be electoral reform. Blair had conceded in November 1995 that the major advantage of proportional representation was that it would allow 'a reshaping of politics along more rational lines'. Yet he had also told Ashdown that in general he was 'not persuaded' of the merits of proportional representation, even though Ashdown made it very clear that for Liberal Democrats such uncertainty would create a 'road block to progress'.[91] Nevertheless, over a year later, in February 1997, a month before the Cook-Maclennan Agreement was forged, a decision was taken by the two parties that after the next general election an independent commission would be established to investigate the whole question of electoral reform and even to advance the case for a referendum on the issue.[92]

The abandonment of equidistance in 1995 that had made possible cooperation between the Liberal Democrats and the Labour Party had thus created the conditions in which the most contentious issue at the heart of that process could at least be clearly addressed. But Ashdown's repositioning decision also had beneficial internal consequences for his Party. For as Alan Leaman later recalled, that crucial strategic shift was soon turned into 'a springboard for a policy-led campaign' over the next two years which gave the Liberal Democrats a much-needed sense of relevance and purpose.[93]

The eventual culmination of these developments was the Liberal Democrat manifesto for the 1997 General Election. Entitled *Make the Difference*, its preparation had been coordinated by William Wallace and its content largely drafted by Neil Stockley, the Party's Director of Policy since 1995. Like its predecessor of 1992, it was a radical and coherent document which again placed a firm emphasis on the themes of constitutional reform, environmental protection and internationalism. It also contained a sharper focus on the need for increased investment in public services, including the 1992 commitment to fund higher expenditure on education through a small increase in the standard rate of income tax.

In the field of economic policy the Liberal Democrats were committed to restoring stability after the preceding cycles of boom and bust by giving the Bank of England operational independence in order to achieve lower inflation, and by keeping to the 'golden rule' of public finance: that over the economic cycle total borrowing should not exceed total investment. The best framework, moreover, for securing lower inflation and greater exchange rate stability was considered to be that of the single European currency. It was 'in Britain's interest to take part in this', the manifesto declared, provided that three conditions were met: first, that the single currency should be 'firmly founded on the Maastricht criteria'; second, that Britain should meet those criteria; and third, that British participation in the single currency should be approved by a national referendum.[94]

The Party would also seek to promote small businesses, enterprise and self-employment which were 'the engine of a modern dynamic economy and a vital source of new jobs and growth'. Another priority would be to begin to shift taxation away from jobs, wealth and goods to pollution and the depletion of natural resources as part of a strategy for building a sustainable economy.[95] In addition, on environmental policy, the Party's priorities included setting tougher targets for the reduction of traffic pollution and energy waste and for cutting carbon dioxide emissions, perceived as the main cause of climate change. In general, there was a pledge to build environmental protection 'into every economic decision and every area of government policy'.[96]

Of the other key themes which had pervaded the manifesto's 1992 predecessor, internationalism was again given a strongly European emphasis. The Liberal Democrats' central commitment in foreign policy, it was stated, was to 'ensure that Britain plays a leading role in shaping Europe, democratising its institutions and strengthening its role as a framework for prosperity, peace and security'. In addition to its conditional support for British membership of the single European currency, the manifesto maintained, more broadly, that Britain's interests could 'best be pursued through constructive participation in an enlarged European Union' that was 'decentralised, democratic and diverse'.[97]

Finally, with regard to political and constitutional reform, the Liberal Democrat commitment was to 'modernise Britain's outdated institutions, rebuild trust, renew democracy and give Britain's nations, regions, and local communities a greater say over their own affairs'. For those purposes the Party's policy priorities, as in the past, were to create a fair voting system and to decentralise political power by creating a Scottish Parliament, a Welsh

Senedd and a strategic authority for London. To safeguard individual liberties, a Bill of Rights would be established, with the European Convention
on Human Rights incorporated into British law. To break open the excessive secrecy of British government a Freedom of Information Act should
be passed, making the system more open and accountable and thereby
helping to rebuild public trust in the political process. British democracy
would be renewed not just by introducing a fair voting system but also, it
was proposed, by reforming the structure and procedures, and strengthening the influence, of the House of Commons and by reforming the House
of Lords.[98]

During an election campaign sharply focused on the manifesto's key
themes, the Liberal Democrats and their Leader concentrated their efforts on
their 75 most winnable seats. The consequent outcome of the 1997 General
Election, held on 1 May, was the largest third-party contingent in the House
of Commons since 1929, with 46 Liberal Democrat MPs elected. The Party's
share of the total national poll fell, however, from 18.3 per cent in 1992 to
16.8 per cent, and its total popular vote also declined, from just under 6 million to just over 5.2 million. Ten Liberal Democrats were elected in Scotland
and the Party captured a large part of the English West Country, particularly Cornwall, Devon and Somerset.[99] Tactical voting to the benefit of the
Party was also widely evident in constituencies where Liberal Democrat
candidates drew support in order to defeat a sitting Conservative.[100] Such
tactical voting was reinforced by victories in constituencies in which Liberal
Democrats had built up a strong local government base, thereby enhancing
their electoral credibility.

The widespread popular reaction against the Major Government, from
which the Liberal Democrats had thus derived much benefit, also swept
Tony Blair and the Labour Party to a landslide victory with 419 seats and
a huge, record-breaking Commons majority of 179. Many of those seats
were gained in what previously were solidly Conservative constituencies.
But Ashdown's view that the rise of Blair and 'New' Labour presented an
opportunity as well as a threat appeared to have been electorally vindicated.
For his determination, as he later put it, to 'ride that wave rather than have
it swamp us'[101], and his leadership skills in facing that surging tide, had
been contributory factors in securing a Liberal Democrat parliamentary
breakthrough. The declared aim of his leadership's second phase, from 1992
to 1997, namely, in his words, 'to build a political force with the strength,
policy and positions to matter again in British politics'[102], was thus at least
half way to being achieved.

The strategy underlying that aim had amounted, as we have seen, to a third
version of the one pursued, in different ways and different circumstances,
by Jo Grimond and David Steel – that of a realignment of the Centre-Left in
British politics. The ideological basis for the Liberal Democrats' role in such
a realignment had been elaborated, Ashdown later pointed out, in his 1989

book *Citizens' Britain*, which had 'acted as a signpost' for him and his Party, mapping out 'the ground on which I hoped we would stand'.[103] In terms of practical policy commitments, his strategy had given rise, through the Cook-Maclennan Agreement of March 1997, to detailed proposals for future cooperation between the Liberal Democrats and the Labour Party over constitutional reform. The scale of Labour's victory in May 1997, together with the Liberal Democrats' significant parliamentary presence, had now formed the conditions that would determine how much of that detail would be translated into government legislation and, more broadly, how much of Ashdown's project of realignment would become a firmly established political reality.

Chapter 9
Ashdown's Unfinished Project: 1997–1999

In the aftermath of Labour's 1997 landslide victory, the likelihood of Liberal Democrat participation in a Centre-Left coalition seemed remote. For the clear transformation that had occurred within the British political climate was, as David Dutton has observed, the fact 'that the electorate had undermined the assumption with which the Project itself had begun, that Labour could not on its own unseat the Conservative government'.[1] Moreover, within a triumphant and resurgent Labour Party there was widespread opposition to closer links with the Liberal Democrats.

Nevertheless, in the immediate aftermath of the election Tony Blair made it clear to Paddy Ashdown that he still favoured what he called 'a framework for co-operation'[2] between the two parties. This he envisaged would take the form of one or more Cabinet Committees, thereby building on the Cook-Maclennan Agreement of March 1997. Referring to this proposed innovation, Blair at the time asked rhetorically:

> Who knows what the ultimate destination for all this might be? It could be merger some way down the track. Or maybe not.[3]

The short-term outcome of this initiative was the appointment in July 1997 of five leading Liberal Democrats – namely, Ashdown himself, Alan Beith, Menzies Campbell, Richard Holme and Robert Maclennan – to a Joint Consultative Committee established to examine government proposals for constitutional reform. There was thus formal Liberal representation within the structures of British government for the first time since 1945 and in a form, essentially that of a Cabinet sub-committee, that went beyond that of the Lib-Lab Agreement of 1977–78.

Ashdown, however, informed Blair in mid-May 1997 that he rejected the idea that this significant political innovation would lead to a formal merger of the two parties within the foreseeable future.[4] But he nonetheless clung to the view, expressed two years earlier, that he and Blair 'should try to mend the schism that split apart the progressive forces in British politics in the early years of this century, giving the Tories more chances to govern than they deserved'.[5]

Meanwhile, Tony Blair continued to express his own belief that the two parties shared common ideological ground, telling the post-election Labour Party Conference in autumn 1997 that:

> My heroes aren't just Ernie Bevin, Nye Bevan and Attlee. They are also Keynes, Beveridge, Lloyd George.[6]

Blair's 'framework for co-operation' between 'New' Labour and the Liberal Democrats was reinforced by the appointment of Lord (Roy) Jenkins in December 1997 to head the independent commission that would examine the issue of electoral reform, including the possible introduction of proportional representation.

In spite of these developments, Liberal Democrat criticisms of Labour government policy – particularly on civil libertarian, environmental and public investment issues – were by this time steadily increasing. Furthermore, the Party's spring conference in March 1998 at Southport approved a proposal, moved by Gordon Lishman, for a 'triple lock' on any further moves that might threaten the political independence of the Liberal Democrats.[7] In effect, that meant that closer formal cooperation with Labour would require the support of either three-quarters of Liberal Democrat MPs and of the Party's Federal Executive, or of a two-thirds majority of a special conference, or, failing either of those outcomes, of a majority in an all-member ballot.

It remained, however, Ashdown's view that 'the Project' should be sustained, at least until the Jenkins Commission on Electoral Reform had reported later in 1998. In January of that year he recorded his belief that the Liberal Democrats could be 'the focal point at which a new liberal consensus can gather to form the predominant political force for our time'. Yet at the same time he was despondent at the thought of 'reassembling policy for the next General Election and fighting it once more through the Party Conferences, especially with such a strong pull in the party to revert to the policies of the 1970s'. In the face of such a prospect, he even expressed a strong desire to resign the leadership, believing that it was 'time for someone else to take over'.[8] By July 1998 Ashdown was feeling similarly despondent about the ultimate purpose of 'the Project'. He had 'hoped we could mend the near century-long schism between the two parties on the basis of a liberal agenda', but now feared that such an achievement was 'probably off for another generation'. Faced with that prospect, he was now, he confessed, 'absolutely clear in my mind that I cannot continue any longer'.[9]

During this period, however, a significant development was occurring within the climate of British ideological debate. In September 1998 a Fabian pamphlet by Tony Blair was published, entitled *The Third Way: New Politics for the New Century*. In this, Blair restated in an extended form his belief in the ideological common ground shared by 'New' Labour and the Liberal Democrats. He also sought to demonstrate that his 'New' Labour government was one firmly based on social-democratic values, albeit reformulated to suit changed conditions.

'The Third Way,' Blair maintained at the outset, was, in his view, 'the best label for the new politics which the progressive centre-left is forging in Britain and beyond'. Its essential concern was nothing less than 'a serious reappraisal of social democracy, reaching deep into the values of the Left to develop radically new approaches'.[10] Moreover, this 'Third Way', he insisted, was 'not an attempt to split the difference between Right and Left'. Rather, it drew its vitality 'from uniting the two great streams of left-of-centre thought – democratic socialism and liberalism – whose divorce this century did so much to weaken progressive politics across the West'. Blair considered that there was 'no necessary conflict' between the traditional liberal assertion of 'the primacy of individual liberty in the market economy' and the social-democratic promotion of 'social justice with the state as its main agent', since there was now an awareness of the fact that 'state power is one of the means to achieve our goals, but not the only one and emphatically not an end in itself'.[11] Such views echoed Blair's earlier portrayal, in his 1995 Fabian speech, of democratic socialism and radical Liberalism as ideological cousins.[12] By 1998 his advocacy of the Third Way as 'a modernised social democracy' was his own contribution to a wider debate on the Centre-Left in the late 1990s, one that had been ignited in particular by the publication in autumn 1998 of the highly influential book, *The Third Way: The Renewal of Social Democracy*, by the sociologist Anthony Giddens.[13]

Blair argued that pursuit of this Third Way – a course distinct both from the state collectivism of the Old Left and from the market individualism of the New Right – was a necessary response to the major changes – economic, political and social – sweeping through the West at the end of the 20th century. Among these he highlighted 'the growth of increasingly global markets and global culture; ... technological advance and the rise of skills and information as key drivers of employment and new industries; ... a transformation in the role of women ... offering half the population the chance ... to fulfil their full potential according to their own choices; ... and radical changes in the nature of politics itself', with governments responding to pressures both 'from localities and regions wanting more control of their own affairs, and from a globalised world in which a growing number of problems depend on international co-operation'.[14]

For Blair, the Third Way response to such major changes and challenges ought to 'meet four broad policy objectives' – the development of, first, 'a dynamic knowledge-based economy founded on individual empowerment and opportunity, where governments enable, not command, and the power of the market is harnessed to serve the public interest'; second, a 'strong civil society enshrining rights and responsibilities, where the government is partner to strong communities'; third, 'a modern government based on partnership and decentralisation, where democracy is deepened to suit the modern age'; and fourth, 'a foreign policy based on international co-operation'.[15] Blair developed these points further in a 1999 statement issued jointly with the recently elected German Social Democratic Chancellor, Gerhard Schroeder, entitled, *Europe: The Third Way/Die Neue Mitte*.[16]

Before the publication of Blair's Fabian pamphlet, there had already been a few Liberal Democrat responses to Third Way thinking of this kind. In May 1998, in an open letter to the Prime Minister in the *New Statesman*, Ralf Dahrendorf argued that the very notion of a Third Way, which Blair had begun to advocate as a political model, appeared inconsistent with the pluralist nature of an open society. For 'the whole point about open societies in an open world,' Dahrendorf contended, was 'that they do not have to follow text-book models'. There were, for instance, 'dozens of variants' even of 'capitalism in a globalised environment'. Italian capitalism differed significantly from British or German or Swedish capitalism, and they would all 'remain different to the benefit of us all'.[17] Dahrendorf nonetheless welcomed as 'a worthwhile effort' Blair's emphasis on 'the need to thrive in global markets', whilst 'not ignoring social and cultural needs'. But, in his view, the title of the 1995 report of the commission that he had chaired at Paddy Ashdown's instigation, namely, *Wealth Creation and Social Cohesion in a Free Society*, while admittedly 'a little elaborate and in need of explanation', already provided a satisfactory description of Blair's project.[18]

Dahrendorf later elaborated these points in 1999 when, with reference to the Blair/Schroeder joint statement, he observed that 'some of the Third Way ideas are not at all dissimilar to the thrust of the report' of that independent commission. Both the joint statement and the 1995 report were, in their different ways, addressing the question that all countries were trying to answer at that time, namely, 'how can we create sustainable conditions of economic improvement in global markets without sacrificing the basic solidarity or cohesion of our societies or the institutions of the constitution of liberty'.[19]

Dahrendorf underlined, however, what he considered to be two major shortcomings inherent in the Third Way approach. First, the term itself indicated 'an unfortunate need to have a unified or at any rate uniquely labelled ideology'. For whereas 'the great liberation of the revolution of 1989' had in many eyes 'ended the dominance of ideological thought systems', the Third Way, by contrast, presupposed 'a more Hegelian view of the world', something Dahrendorf added, that was 'disconcerting' indeed for an 'inveterate Popperian'. The Third Way model thus forced its adherents 'to define themselves in relation to others, rather than by their own peculiar combination of ideas'; and in the process those other, opposing ideas often had 'to be invented, even caricatured for the purpose'.[20]

The second major shortcoming of the Third Way approach, in Dahrendorf's view, and this, he stressed, was his 'most serious comment on the present political debate', was that in all the speeches, pamphlets and books on the subject 'one word hardly ever appears and never in a central place. That word is liberty'. That, he believed, was 'no accident' since the Third Way was 'not about either open societies or liberty'. Indeed, there was, he noted, 'a curious authoritarian streak in it', evident, for instance, in Anthony Giddens' reference to a 'second wave of democratisation', involving the deconstruction of democratic institutions, with the possible replacement of parliaments by referendums and focus groups. That authoritarian tendency was implicit, too, he noted, in the Blair-Schroeder document's 'curious statement: "The state should not row but steer"'. In other words, the document was implying, Dahrendorf suggested, that the State 'should not provide the wherewithal, but determine the direction [...] It will no longer pay for things, but tell people what to do'.[21]

While noting this 'curious silence' of the practitioners and theorists of the Third Way 'about the fundamental value of a decent life, liberty – old, very old liberty if you wish', Dahrendorf pointed out that in setting up the Commission on Wealth Creation and Social Cohesion a few years earlier, he had insisted, in adding the words, 'in a free society' to describe its area of concern. In doing so, he had 'thought of Beveridge (*Full Employment in a Free Society*) but also of Singapore'. In 1999 it seemed to him 'more important than even a few years ago to begin a new political project with the insistence on liberty before we turn to social inclusion and cohesion'.[22]

In an earlier contribution to the debate on the Third Way, the political philosopher Alan Ryan had made a similar criticism to Dahrendorf's, but with a more explicit historical focus. The Third Way, Ryan maintained, was 'neither New Labour, as its admirers say, nor warmed-over Thatcherism, as its detractors say'. Rather it was 'a reversion to a very old idea' embedded in the ideology of the New Liberalism that had animated the reforming Liberal governments of 1906–14. The New Liberal Third Way had been 'concerned to find productive ways of expanding the state's role while preserving liberalism's devotion to individual freedom'. To the extent, therefore, he concluded, that 'New' Labour's Third Way was 'a coherent or acceptable approach to government it resembles the New Liberalism of the beginning of the century'. But 'to the extent that it does not resemble it' as, in his view, in the Blair governments' illiberal tendencies or proposals on certain issues, then its project was 'neither coherent nor attractive'.[23]

During this period there were a few other notable Liberal Democrat contributions, besides Dahrendorf's, to the debate sparked by Tony Blair's favoured political model. Bill Rodgers, for example, delivered a lecture entitled, 'Whose Third Way to Where?', at the autumn party conference in September 1998. In this, he raised the question of whether 'New' Labour's main concern in advancing the cause of the Third Way was with 'remaining competitive in the global market to maximise wealth creation', or whether it also had 'a purpose beyond that which involves social justice and the prospect of the redistribution of wealth'. Rodgers maintained, too, that Giddens, the Third Way's most influential theorist, had overlooked the past contribution of the Liberal Party in developing distinctive ideas of citizenship and community.[24] Shirley Williams, too, considered some of the main themes in the developing debate in an article in *The Reformer*, the journal of Liberal Democrat policy and strategy.[25]

A more extended discussion, however, of those themes, and the issues they raised, appeared in *Liberal Democrats and the Third Way*, a booklet published in December 1998 by the Centre for Reform, the recently created Liberal Democrat-inclined public policy think-tank. Concerned with developing and promoting long-term thinking and policy formation among Liberal Democrats, the Centre for Reform had been established in the autumn of 1997, with the encouragement of Paddy Ashdown and the financial support of the former Liberal MP, Richard Wainwright. It was formally launched at the spring 1998 party conference.[26]

In *Liberal Democrats and the Third Way*, edited by the new think-tank's first director, Richard Grayson, Neil Stockley commented on the Party's limited role to date in advancing discussion and analysis of the Third Way. Why, he asked, 'have we not actively engaged in the debate and why have we done so little to make an overt contribution ... and present a distinctive vision of our own?'.[27] In tune with that observation, William Wallace considered that Liberal Democrats had 'no choice but to respond' to the language of the Third Way, with all its 'buzz words of progressive social science', since the Blair government was using it 'to define the agenda of political debate'.[28] Wallace noted, too, the broader ideological implications of the Third Way for the Liberal Democrats. It represented, in his view, 'a search for a presentable set of ideas for the Blairite project and for the allies it is looking for in social democratic (or post-social democratic?) governments in West Europe and North America'. The Third Way thus 'encapsulated the Blair project – which seeks to build a broad centre/centre left coalition which will dominate British politics for the next generation'. Furthermore, Wallace warned, the explicit aim of that project was 'to capture our political ground, *and* to absorb our party'. It was thus an attempt 'to establish an intellectual hegemony over progressive politics'. In the face of that reality, Liberal Democrats needed, therefore, to 'redefine their terms and relate them to contemporary dilemmas'.[29]

Wallace nonetheless recognised the common ground shared by social liberals and social democrats: the search for 'ways of reconciling liberty and equality, social justice and freedom of opportunity, private enterprise and public services'. He noted, too, that the Third Way's 'focus on the symbiotic relationship between a strong civil society and an active state' echoed the New Liberalism of Green and Hobhouse, 'though Third Way theorists, who seem to have read nobody published before the 1960s, don't acknowledge such roots'.[30] In similar vein, Neil Stockley pointed out, too, that all four of Blair's broad policy objectives, as set out in his Fabian pamphlet – namely, a dynamic knowledge-based economy, a strong civil society, active government rooted in partnership and decentralisation, and a foreign policy based on international cooperation – 'sound very familiar because they are all themes of dozens of Liberal, SDP and Liberal Democrat policy statements and pamphlets over the past three decades'.[31]

In view of this common ground, in terms of both ideology and policy, it was necessary, Wallace argued, for Liberal Democrats to respond in a distinctive and constructive manner to 'New' Labour's Third Way thinking, first of all by emphasising 'democracy and diversity' since, for all its 'rhetoric about renewing democracy and strengthening communities, Blairism remains confused about democracy – and about local democracy most of all'. In sharp contrast, Liberal Democrats recognised that:

> A healthy democratic community needs dissent: argument, open discussion, dialogue. For that you need many parties, not one; councils, not just elected mayors; participation, not presentation to passive voters.[32]

Blairites, however, were 'caught in the contradictions between central control and devolution, determined to impose discipline over the proper diversity of democratic politics'.[33] Or, as Richard Grayson put it, Third Way politicians appeared to be 'favouring a limited pluralism within what would effectively be a one-party state, rather than a genuinely diverse pluralism within a multi-party state'.[34]

Liberal Democrats should also respond to Third Way thinking, Wallace maintained, by addressing the question of 'the boundary between the public and the private, which the Thatcher period shifted radically and which the Third Way slides across'. That meant both ensuring 'that the state is not captured by private interests' and restating the New Liberal view of 100 years ago 'that there is a public interest, which is more than the sum of private interests'. It meant, too, reaffirming 'the importance of public service, denigrated by the last government, towards which the Blair government appears ambivalent ...'. Restoring that lost emphasis required a recognition of the role that those who worked in the public services and in local government played 'in underpinning civil society'. Finally, and more broadly, a reappraisal of 'the boundary between the public and the private' involved underlining what Ralf Dahrendorf had referred to as 'the importance of public space: the places in which active citizens meet and interact, the fora which bring individuals out of their cars and living rooms to interact as members of democratic communities ...'.[35]

Wallace concluded by suggesting that Liberal Democrats should use the challenge of the Third Way 'to redefine Liberalism and social democracy ourselves' and 'to provide a more deeply rooted alternative' to the Third Way thinkers' 'rather shallow and rootless reconceptualization'.[36] In similarly confident terms, Neil Stockley concluded his own reflections by suggesting that, instead of viewing the Third Way as an attempt by 'New' Labour 'to steal some of our clothes, or at least, our place in the political marketplace', Liberal Democrats should regard Blair's chosen ideological stance as 'an opportunity, to redefine where we stand, to develop our ideas, particularly on social citizenship and the regeneration of civil society and to "get out in front" during a dynamic and exciting phase of UK politics'.[37]

Liberal Democrats and the Third Way amounted, then, to the first extended and coherent response by Liberal Democrat thinkers to Third Way ideas. It offered at least the outline of an alternative to what Wallace had called 'the thin frame of Third Way concepts',[38] an alternative that would draw on core Liberal values of liberty, democratic pluralism, decentralisation and internationalism. It would be rooted, too, in social liberal concerns with social citizenship rights and with the interrelationship between a vibrant civil society and an enabling State; and it would be informed by a post-1960s Liberal emphasis on environmental protection and sustainability. But in outlining that Liberal alternative, Wallace and, before him, Dahrendorf had also emerged as among the most incisive critics of 'New' Labour's Third Way, exposing its shortcomings. The shared common ground, but also the clear differences of principle and outlook, that they had identified in the two ideological approaches consequently led Wallace to 'strongly suspect' that Liberal Democrats would 'want to accompany' followers of the Blairite project 'some of the way, but that our final destinations remain separate'.[39]

In terms of policy and strategy, however, Paddy Ashdown still wanted to proceed along what Wallace had called 'the same broad road as the Blairites',[40] and, as we have seen, favoured its ideological foundation. It had been characterised, after all, by Ralf Dahrendorf in terms of the phrase *Wealth Creation and Social Cohesion in a Free Society*, the title of the report of the commission set up at Ashdown's initiative. For Ashdown himself had 'always believed that there did not have to be a sharp, dichotic differentiation between economic success and social justice (very much the issue taken up by Blair)', and Dahrendorf, 'a great influence' as a respected liberal thinker, could help to articulate that belief.[41]

Moreover, in order in translate such conviction into the practical forms of policy and strategy, Ashdown in October 1998 had drafted a minute which he sent to Jonathan Powell, Tony Blair's Chief of Staff, to be shown to the Prime Minister. Entitled, *What Happens Next?*, it restated his view that his overriding strategic aim as Liberal Democrat Leader was 'to use this parliament, the current strength of our party and the opportunity presented by Blair, to bring about the reshaping of the left in British politics with the same vision as Grimond and Steel'. That would be 'the first step in a more general reshaping of politics in Britain', which would in turn also affect the Right.[42]

In addition, Ashdown pointed out that he had always believed that this Project would take place in three phases. In the first of these, 'the climate of tribalism and hostility' between Labour and the Liberal Democrats would be altered and replaced at the national level with one of 'goodwill and the presumption of co-operation'. In Phase II the two parties would 'move to full co-operation, in government'. In Phase III the two parties 'would consider whether their close identity of interest might best be served by institutionalizing their relationship to reflect the fact that they are now a cohesive unit representing a united political force in the country'. At that particular time, October 1998, Ashdown considered that the two parties had 'essentially been in Phase I since around the time of the Cook/Maclennan agreement' of March 1997.[43]

Later that month, however, he recorded his concern that the Joint Consultative Committee, such an important feature of development in Phase I, was 'becoming more ceremonial than functional'.[44] That unease was reinforced by the government's reaction to the publication of the Jenkins Commission Report on Electoral Reform on 29 October 1998. The report proposed a voting system which became known as 'AV Plus'. Under this, 80–85 per cent of MPs would be directly elected by constituencies by means of the alternative vote (AV) system. The remainder (about 100–120 additional, top-up MPs) would be elected under a list system based on geographical areas so as to produce a broadly proportional overall outcome.

Although the Commission's proposed option was a compromise as far as the Liberal Democrats were concerned, Ashdown nonetheless welcomed the Report as an 'historic step forward', which offered the electorate an opportunity 'to break out of the prison of the first-past-the-post system'.[45] Blair had earlier made promises to Ashdown that, upon publication of the Jenkins Report, he would publicly support its recommendations and initiate a referendum on electoral reform before the next general election.[46] But in the event, Blair adopted a formally neutral stance on the Report's proposals. On the issue of a referendum, he delayed taking an immediate decision on the basis of his calculation that there was insufficient support within either the Cabinet or the Labour Party as a whole for electoral reform.[47]

In the face of Downing Street's immediate, lukewarm response to the Jenkins Report's proposals, Ashdown had felt, in his own words, 'badly let down', 'very angry and very depressed', and resolved then to resign the Party leadership.[48] But even though the Prime Minister maintained that in principle he still wanted to proceed towards a referendum on the issue,[49] the hard political reality was, as Steven Fielding has commented, that:

> ... Blair could live without [electoral] reform: if he privately considered it ultimately desirable it was not of immediate importance. Blair would push for change only when it was absolutely necessary to sustain his party in power.[50]

In spite, however, of Blair's prevarication, in November 1998 a joint statement by himself and Ashdown announced that the remit of the Joint

Consultative Committee was to be extended beyond constitutional matters, and portrayed that decision as 'an important step in challenging the destructive tribalism that can afflict British politics even where parties find themselves in agreement'. It would thereby, they maintained, 'deepen co-operation and result in widening support for the kind of progressive change which we wish to see and to which we believe the British people are strongly committed'.[51]

There was strong Liberal Democrat opposition, within both the Party's Federal Executive and its Federal Policy Committee, to that joint statement, which, it was feared, would further erode the Party's political independence. The JCC's field of responsibility was nonetheless widened in January 1999 to cover foreign affairs and defence policy. But with the government's shelving of the Jenkins Report, Ashdown had already realised that his hopes of moving significantly beyond Phase I of 'the Project' had been dashed, and that with them had receded the prospect of an imminent realignment of the Centre-Left in British politics. In the light of that realisation, and, in the face, too, of sustained hostility within much of his Party towards closer links with the Blair government, Ashdown announced his resignation as Party Leader on 20 January 1999. This was to take effect following that year's set of local, Scottish and Welsh and European Parliamentary elections.[52]

In an assessment of Ashdown's leadership, Duncan Brack has concluded that he was 'the most significant Liberal leader since Jo Grimond'. It is a favourable judgement that many would endorse, for as Brack has recalled, Ashdown 'created out of the wreckage of the Liberal/SDP Alliance a professional, modernised and effective Liberal party'. Moreover, from the nadir of the Party's fortunes in June 1989 when its standing in national opinion polls was within the statistical margin of error of zero, he subsequently took it to 'stunning local election and by-election victories ... and a higher number of Commons seats than at any time since 1929'.[53]

Yet the central aims of the third phase of Ashdown's leadership, the period from 1997 to 1999, appeared to have been ultimately unfulfilled. That was a period in which he resolved, in his own words, that his Party should 'get on to the field and play in what I believed would become a very fluid period of politics'. For he had 'never been at all attracted to the notion that it was sufficient for us to be the unpaid think-tank for new ideas in British politics; or the repository for community politics without a purpose'. It was his conviction that 'Liberalism is too important for that'.[54]

In strategic terms, Ashdown had grasped, as Andrew Rawnsley commented at the time of his resignation announcement, 'that there was more to be gained by treating New Labour as an opportunity rather than a threat'. He had, after all, recognised in Tony Blair 'a similar impatience with the ancient and often artificial divides of British politics', and 'detected a shared desire not to give another century to the Conservatives by splitting the Centre-Left'.[55] The practical expression of those attitudes was the fulfilment of a programme of constitutional reform desired by the Liberal Democrats since 1988, and cherished before them by the Liberal Party and the SDP. That programme embraced devolution to Scotland and Wales, first-stage reform of the House of Lords, mild forms of proportional representation for Scottish, Welsh and European elections, and the incorporation of the European Convention on Human Rights into British law.

But in spite of that considerable achievement, Ashdown and a large part of his Party gradually grew apart. The increasing estrangement of Liberal Democrat activists had been evident in the decision by the spring 1998 conference to place a 'triple lock' on any moves that might jeopardise the Party's political independence. It was even more starkly apparent in November 1998 in the reaction to Blair and Ashdown's statement extending the remit of the Joint Consultative Committee.

This deep-seated scepticism within much of the Party about closer links with Labour in government stemmed in part from a collective awareness of the danger of guilt by association, as experienced by the Liberal Party in 1977–78, if the Blair government became, as governments invariably do, widely unpopular. More acutely, it sprang from a fear that the Party might eventually become absorbed by its larger, more powerful potential partner. There were, of course, a number of precedents for this in British political history. Yet as David Dutton has pointed out:

> Despite an abiding sense of history and a belief that the twentieth century might end as it had begun with a Progressive Alliance of the centre-left, Ashdown seemed curiously unaware of the historical fate of the junior partners of peacetime coalitions.[56]

Earlier groups of Liberals, notably, the Liberal Unionists and, in the more recent past, the National Liberals, had in time been 'absorbed within the embrace of their more powerful ally', thereafter disappearing 'without trace from the political stage'.[57] Ashdown was aware, however, of the need for electoral reform before proceeding towards inter-party cooperation in government. He realised that there was a potential trade-off between, on the one hand, some loss both of support and of distinctive definition by going into a coalition government as a junior partner, and, on the other, the gains that would accrue to his Party through achieving a fairer electoral system.[58]

The internal political reality that accompanied Ashdown's 'audacious but fundamentally flawed' efforts to forge a much closer relationship with Blair's 'New' Labour was, as Tony Greaves has recalled, 'that Liberal Democrats loved their leader but insofar as they sensed his strategy, most wanted none of it'.[59] But above all, 'the Project' was undermined by the sheer size of Labour's parliamentary majority after 1997, by widespread opposition within its ranks both to closer links with the Liberal Democrats and to electoral reform, evident in the response to the Jenkins Commission Report in October 1998, and by Blair's inability or unwillingness to overcome that opposition. As Andrew Rawnsley noted when Ashdown announced his decision to stand down, 'Mr Blair wrote him a cheque for electoral reform, but has still not got round to signing it'. For that very reason, Ashdown could claim that, in the area of constitutional reform, he had 'conquered every mountain ... except ... the most important one', without which 'a fundamental recasting of the political landscape could not be achieved'.[60]

Nevertheless, with regard to his qualities as leader, few within the Party, parliamentarians, activists and rank-and-file members alike, would dissent from Duncan Brack's overall judgement that Ashdown

> ... was an excellent communicator ... and until his last two years was an excellent party manager. He retained his energy, drive and enthusiasm, and his love for the party and what it stood for, in the most trying circumstances. And above all, having saved his party from extinction and built it into an effective political force, he did something with it. He left it with a distinctive and rigorous policy programme and, through the Cook-Maclennan constitutional reforms, he changed for good the structure of government within the UK ...[61]

Chapter 10
Advance and Debate: 1999–2005

The period between Paddy Ashdown's sudden resignation announcement in January 1999 and his eventual departure from the Leadership in June of that year was marked by a series of significant electoral tests for the Liberal Democrats. In addition to the annual local elections, these consisted of elections in May for the new Scottish Parliament and National Assembly for Wales, both to be conducted under an additional member system of proportional representation, and of elections in June for the European Parliament, the first of their kind in Britain to be held under a form of PR, in this case one based on a closed regional list system. The Party's overall performance in the three contests was uneven and unexceptional, but ultimately satisfactory in at least two respects. In the Scottish Parliament elections, where the main battle-lines were drawn between Labour and the Scottish National Party, the Liberal Democrats won 17 seats out of a total 129 members. Although they were narrowly beaten into fourth place in the total poll by the Conservatives, the eventual outcome was nonetheless a Labour-Liberal Democrat coalition, with Jim Wallace serving as Deputy First Minister. In the Welsh Assembly elections the Liberal Democrats won six out of 60 seats, again, as in Scotland, coming fourth in the overall poll. Finally, in the June European Parliament elections, Liberal Democrat representation increased from two to ten MEPs with 12.7 per cent of the total vote.[1] In spite of the fact, then, that the Party's advance in these three sets of elections was modest and limited, the satisfactory aspects of the contests lay, first, in the emergence of coalition politics in Scotland and, later, Wales, and second, in an increase in the Party's representation in the European Parliament. Moreover, the Scottish and Welsh elections in themselves, together with the new electoral system under which the European elections were held, were in part, at least, the beneficial practical consequences of Ashdown's 'Project'.

After Ashdown stood down as Leader on 11 June, two months later Charles Kennedy, aged 39, and first elected as SDP MP for Ross, Skye and Inverness West in 1983, was declared successor to Ashdown on 9 August, having been the victor in a contest with four other MPs, with Simon Hughes as his main challenger. Upon assuming the leadership, Kennedy's Party in August 1999 was a considerably stronger force than in its early years. It now had 46 MPs, 10 MEPs, 17 MSPs in Edinburgh, 6 AMs in Cardiff, and about 4,800 local councillors throughout Britain.

Apart from his more relaxed and informal political style, Kennedy also differed from his predecessor in his strategic emphasis. He had been ambivalent or uneasy in the recent past about Ashdown's stance of 'constructive opposition' to the Blair government, believing that it was causing the Liberal Democrats, in Kennedy's words, 'to pull our punches'.[2] At the Party's spring 1998 conference which had approved the 'triple lock' on closer links with Labour, he had stated that:

> The members ... favour, as I do, co-operation with the Labour party and Labour government over constitutional reform, [but] they don't want the process to blunt our distinctive identity. We are an independent political party out to win votes and secure influence and power.[3]

Philosophical support for Kennedy's scepticism about sustaining 'the Project', and for his concern about eroding the Liberal Democrats' distinctive identity, was provided by the publication in 1999 of a book by Conrad Russell, the distinguished historian who was also a Liberal Democrat peer and member of the Party's Federal Policy Committee. Entitled *An Intelligent Person's Guide to Liberalism*, it consisted, in its author's words, of 'a work of political philosophy, not of short-term political polemic ...'. It was an 'attempt to answer the question ... "what is the creed for which it [a Liberal party] stands, the essence by which one Liberal may recognise another across the centuries?"'.[4] In seeking out that essence, Russell used as his 'touchstone' 'the ideas which have given continuity to the Liberal Party in its various forms since 1679'.[5] For Liberalism, as 'one of the world's major political philosophies',[6] drew its inspirational strength, in his view, from a long line of philosophical and, indeed, organisational continuity stretching back in Britain to the 17th century.

Russell was thus writing from the perspective offered by a particular vision of the Liberal Democrats as a party 'committed to a deep Liberal philosophy'.[7] His book was therefore 'an attempt to identify, not just the present creed of a party, but the continuity over the centuries in the basic principles of Liberalism'.[8] He recognised, however, that there was a rival vision of the Party as 'part of a larger force called the centre-left'. The assumption reinforcing that vision was '... that "progressive" forces must be moving roughly in the same direction, and that, somewhere in the area of commitment to social justice, there is a broad common ground which holds them together'.[9]

In Russell's view, that description of the Liberal Democrats as placed firmly within the progressive forces of the Centre-Left had provided, of course, though he did not explicitly make the point, the historical and philosophical rationale for Ashdown's private development of 'the Project' since Blair had become Labour Leader in 1994. It was itself a vision firmly based, Russell contended, on a 'two-sides, left-right analysis' which carried with it 'something of the class-based thinking which has been the hallmark of the twentieth century'.[10]

Russell conceded that these two rival visions of the Party were 'not mutually exclusive', and that previously the Liberal Party had 'lived through the past century by the creative tension between them', and that, 'unless or until it becomes clear that Labour is no longer a party of the centre-left' Liberals would 'no doubt continue to do so'.[11] But he himself had been 'turned into a passionate adherent' of the particular vision of the Liberal Democrats as a party committed to a distinctive and deep-rooted Liberal philosophy. He had been converted to that view, he explained, by his experience of entering Parliament and thereby realising the extent of 'the arrogance of power shown by government'.[12] But Russell went further than that observation, stating, without, surprisingly, citing any supporting historical evidence or argument, that the vision of the Party to which he adhered 'rejects any notion of a thing called the centre-left', and instead judged Labour 'by how far it measures up to Liberal principles'.[13]

At any rate, Russell's realisation of the extent of the 'arrogance' of governmental power led him in his book to explore the historical development of a set of fundamental Liberal themes and principles. The oldest of these, deriving from the Whig opposition to political absolutism in the 17th century, and upon which he placed primary emphasis, was a concern with the control and accountability of power, particularly executive power. In British politics there was no other party besides the Liberal Democrats, Russell maintained, 'which will collectively give the need to control power quite as high a priority as we do'. That concern was 'our starting point, our bedrock and our unifying principle'.[14]

More broadly, the distinctive political creed that Russell was seeking to identify and define at the end of the 20th century was recognisably a social-liberal one that espoused both a positive view of liberty and consequently an active role for government. A 'purely negative definition of liberty' as the absence of coercion or restraint led, he argued, 'to Thatcherism, not Liberalism ... to an identification of liberty with minimum government action'. In contrast, the Liberal Party, he pointed out, 'at all stages of its existence' had been 'dedicated to defending the powerless against privilege'. It had therefore advanced a positive view of liberty as 'opportunities to exercise choices, to be won by legislative action and defended by the State against the intolerance of those who would deny them', Throughout its history the Liberal Party had thus come to conceive of liberty 'not as minimum government, but as minimum oppression', and commitment to that latter cause had been placed firmly 'in the party's bedrock'.[15]

The new Liberal Democrat Leader also appeared to embrace a social liberal creed of this kind. In his book, *The Future of Politics*, published the following year, in time for the Party's autumn 2000 conference, Charles Kennedy set out in its pages to explain the nature of his political beliefs and convictions. It contained 'one person's reflections on the United Kingdom', and attempted to answer such questions as: 'What makes this Kennedy fellow tick? ... What fires his passion? ... Why is he a Liberal Democrat, and who are these Liberal Democrats anyway?'.[16] The book, which thus combined autobiography with political reflection, began with an acknowledgement of the influence of Roy Jenkins' 1979 Dimbleby Lecture, which offered, in Kennedy's words, 'a vision of a radical, decentralist and internationalist party, combining the best of the progressive Liberal and social democratic traditions'. That, in his view, 'was a vision of the party that the Liberal Democrats have become'.[17]

The Future of Politics was structured around the centrality of freedom – in its personal, social, economic and political aspects. Describing himself as 'a Highland liberal', Kennedy distinguished a liberal agenda from the kind of anti-statist, libertarian agenda promoted by many British Conservatives during the 1980s. The latter, he observed, 'rightly wanted a market economy, but they wrongly wanted a market society, in which the cash bottom line counted above all else'.[18] In contrast to their libertarian agenda, Kennedy advocated a liberal agenda in which 'government refuses to interfere in the lives of individuals, but plays a very active role wherever it can advance liberty for everyone'.[19] A liberal agenda of that kind should, in his view, rest on four key principles: namely, the belief, first, that 'Government cannot solve all problems, and sometimes does more harm than good'; second, that 'some problems are best left to government', particularly those concerning the delivery of public services such as health care and education; third, that 'where government does act, it needs to do so differently', in many cases at local or regional, rather than national, levels of government; and fourth, that 'central authority should be used to stamp out inequality rather than enforce conformity'.[20]

These points were lucidly conveyed and were clearly in line with the post-1906 British Liberal tradition. Yet Kennedy's biographer, Greg Hurst, could later express the view that the book nevertheless revealed 'a startling lack of original thinking on policy or a strand of political thought that was identifiably his own' and 'firmly entrenched' Kennedy's 'image as a man for mood and strategy rather than policy'.[21] Against that view, however, Conrad Russell, a few months after the publication of *The Future of Politics*, maintained that Kennedy, in setting out his liberal agenda, had actually 'offered a bigger challenge to Liberal thinking than we have yet shown any sign of rising to' since he had 'asked us to work out afresh, and for new circumstances, what are and what are not the purposes of the state'.[22] In other words, Kennedy had reopened the Liberal debate on the distinction between what Keynes, drawing upon Bentham, had called the Agenda and Non-Agenda of the State.[23]

With regard to the Party's more immediate political strategy, Kennedy's scepticism about his predecessor's stance of 'constructive opposition' to the Blair government became evident in his attitude towards the Joint Consultative Committee, originally established in July 1997. The first meeting of the Committee under Kennedy's leadership was held in December 1999. Its remit was to discuss House of Lords reform, freedom of information legislation and enlargement of the European Union. The Committee's second, and final, meeting under his leadership was held seven months later in July 2000. It agreed a common position for the Labour government and the Liberal Democrats on reforms to the United Nations' peacekeeping and humanitarian capabilities in advance of a UN summit in New York.[24] Kennedy was reluctant, however, to extend the remit of the JCC, as Tony Blair wished, from constitutional issues and foreign affairs into domestic policy areas – such as health care, education and pensions – where the two parties held broadly similar positions. For, as his biographer has observed, Kennedy 'had no real interest in maintaining, and certainly not in extending, a controversial mechanism inherited from his predecessor that had little scope to influence government policy yet risked contaminating the Lib Dems' independence'.[25]

Morale within the Party, meanwhile, had been boosted by the Romsey by-election result in May 2000 when the Liberal Democrat candidate, Sandra Gidley, captured a safe Tory seat on a 12.5 per cent swing, aided by tactical voting which cut Labour support to only 4 per cent of the poll. This impressive victory increased the number of Liberal Democrat MPs to 47. A few months later, the autumn 2000 conference endorsed the latest of the Party's 'pre-manifesto' documents, *Freedom in a Liberal Society*, which emphasised, as Charles Kennedy's contemporaneous book had done, the centrality of the idea and value of freedom within the Party's political philosophy and programme, whilst insisting that the promotion of freedom went hand-in-hand with the pursuit of fairness and social justice, the decentralisation of political power and the protection of the environment.[26] The subsequent 20,000-word 2001 Liberal Democrat general election manifesto, co-drafted by Richard Grayson and Matthew Taylor, and entitled *Freedom, Justice, Honesty*, was launched in May 2001, with the election date having been set for 7 June. The manifesto's key policy priorities were proposals for higher public investment in schools, hospitals and policing, for an increase in the basic state pension, and for free personal care for the elderly. It was stressed, too, that all of the Liberal Democrats' policies had 'a green dimension'. There was therefore, 'an environmental section in every chapter, a green thread binding together all our thinking'.[27]

In order to fund its proposals for increased public expenditure on education – so as to cut school class sizes, increase funding on books and equipment and abolish university tuition fees – the manifesto restated the distinctive Liberal Democrat proposal, advanced since 1992, of an extra penny on the basic rate of income tax. Its other main public spending pledges would be funded by an increase in the top rate of income tax to 50 per cent and by closing loopholes in capital gains tax.

On economic policy, the manifesto adopted an unequivocally pro-market stance. The Liberal Democrats, it declared, were 'committed to a free market economy in which enterprise thrives'; they recognised that 'competition and open markets are by far the best guarantee of wealth creation'. It was government's role, therefore, 'to ensure the conditions under which innovation and competition can flourish and benefit the greatest number of people'. It was stressed, too, that 'Liberal Democrats' social objectives cannot be achieved without the creation of wealth and the promotion of enterprise'.[28]

On constitutional issues, the manifesto stated that Britain's political system had 'changed for the better since 1997'. In particular, the Liberal Democrats, as inheritors of the more-than-a-century-old Liberal tradition of support for devolution, had 'welcomed the opportunity to play our part in the creation of the Scottish Parliament, the National Assembly for Wales and the Northern Ireland Assembly'.[29] But the manifesto proposed, too, to strengthen the powers of the Scottish Parliament and to allow the Welsh Assembly to pass primary legislation and to vary taxes. With regard to electoral reform, support was pledged, as a first step, for the system of AV+, as proposed by the Jenkins Commission in 1998. Ultimately, however, it was proposed that the Single Transferable Vote system should be used for Westminster elections and, in the immediate future, for local government and European elections.[30]

On European policy, the Party's priorities were enlargement of the European Union to include the emerging democracies of central and eastern Europe; reform of the EU's institutions to make them more open, democratic and effective; and British entry into the euro, subject to a decision by the British people in a referendum. But in spite of that last commitment, the manifesto made it clear that, while the Liberal Democrats were 'firm supporters of the European Union', nonetheless 'as critical members of the European family', they were also 'firm on its failings'. For Europe needed 'a new agenda for reform', with Britain playing a leading role in that process.[31]

Among the main items on that agenda, it was argued that the liberal principle of subsidiarity, established in the Maastricht Treaty of 1992, should be 'fully respected'. While the EU should 'have the resources and powers to act in areas where problems cannot be solved at a national level', it should therefore 'stay clear when European action is not necessary'. The European Commission should also be made 'more democratically accountable', with its legislative proposals 'individually justified and explained'. Indeed, all of the EU institutions should be opened up, with the Council of Ministers, in particular, being required to meet in public whenever it discussed legislation and to publish a record of its proceedings. The national veto in the Council of Ministers should be retained 'in areas of vital national interest to the UK' – that is, on constitutional issues, on defence, national resources, budgetary and tax matters, and on regulations on pay and social security. At home, Westminster's scrutiny both of European legislation and of the activities of British ministers attending the Council of Ministers should be improved.[32] These proposals amounted to a radical and coherent programme of EU reform, far removed from the common depiction, not always without some justification, of the Liberal Democrats as hitherto a party of uncritical Europhiles. The proposed measures contributed to an overall party programme in *Freedom, Fairness, Honesty* that was both wide-ranging and radical in tone and content.

In the ensuing general election campaign, co-organised by Lord (Chris) Rennard, who had directed the Romsey by-election campaign, and Lord (Tim) Razzall, a prior agreement was made between the Labour and Liberal Democrat leaderships, in spite of Charles Kennedy's strategic stance of 'effective opposition' to the Blair Government, to coordinate their parties' national campaigns so as the maximise the electoral damage that could be inflicted on the Conservatives.[33] As Rennard later recalled, this planned coordination was based on 'the realisation at the time that most of the Liberal Democrat themes were consistent with some of the Labour themes and inconsistent with Conservative themes'.[34]

In spite of financial constraints imposed by a reduced budget in comparison with 1997, the Party and its Leader fought an effective campaign, leading to a highly satisfactory outcome on 7 June.[35] The Liberal Democrats won 52 seats, the largest number won by a British third party since 1929, when the Liberals were reunited under Lloyd George's leadership. The Party lost two seats but gained eight new ones, seven of them from the Conservatives. Many of the seats narrowly won in 1997 were held with commanding majorities. For the first time, the Liberal Democrats won a seat in every region in England, achieving this by targeting and winning Chesterfield in the East Midlands. With 4.8 million votes, the Party also increased its national vote share by 1.5 per cent to 18.3 per cent. The favourable outcome vindicated the Party's constituency targeting strategy, designed by Chris Rennard, since 1989 the Liberal Democrats' Director of Campaigns and Elections. It underlined, too, the political strengths of Charles Kennedy, on whom the national campaign had been centred, demonstrating, in his biographer's words, 'the electoral appeal of this unusually self-deprecating politician'.[36]

Only five months, however, before the 2001 General Election, there had been some literary expressions of discontent with what was perceived as the Liberal Democrats' intellectual inertia. In the pages of *Liberator*, Simon Titley had complained of a lack of fresh political thinking and a paucity of ideological debate within the Party. 'One senses,' he wrote, 'no real intellectual life, and no contribution from the top to creating one.'[37] Contrasting the situation in 2001 sharply with the intellectually vibrant climate of the Grimond era, Titley even questioned the ultimate political purpose of the Liberal Democrats in the light of this apparent lack of intellectual vitality. 'Are we nothing more,' he asked, 'than a repository for the demands of special interests, or a group of political geeks?' Perhaps, he speculated, the Party's focus on grass-roots activism and its success in local elections had 'taken its toll', in the sense of diverting its attention from political thought and ideological debate.[38]

At a formal level, however, and in a developed manner, Titley's concerns were addressed by the publication in June 2002 of a new 'themes and values' document, entitled *It's About Freedom*. In this, the first major revision of the 1989 document, *Our Different Vision*, Alan Beith pointed out in its foreword that in British party politics Liberal Democrats had 'a distinct advantage which we do too little to advertise or exploit'. For the Party was 'based on a clear set of beliefs' which could be traced back not only to the 19th century, when they were clearly articulated by John Stuart Mill, but even, as Conrad Russell had observed earlier, to the 17th century conflict between Crown and Parliament. 'Fundamental to Liberalism,' Beith explained, was 'a belief in the freedom of the individual', and that freedom was 'threatened from many directions: by over-mighty states, by private concentrations of power, by the actions of other individuals, or by circumstances which leave the individual without access to power or opportunity'. As a consequence, Liberalism had been concerned with 'the creation of a democratic system of government which can protect individual liberty and whose institutions are themselves restrained from usurping the freedom of the individual'.[39]

The document itself began by stating that: 'The core of the Liberal Democrat intellectual inheritance is Liberalism.' The Party's ideological starting-point was thus a belief in 'the autonomy and worth of the individual', and hence a conviction that 'any interference with the freedom to live as he or she chooses requires to be justified, if it can be, by reference to a system of values drawn from that primary recognition of individual freedom'. But while reaffirming that classical liberal view of freedom, *It's About Freedom* also acknowledged, in social liberal terms, that: 'The freedom of the individual is, however, limited if he or she is prevented by economic deprivation, lack of education, disadvantage or discrimination from exercising choices about how to live or from participating in the democratic process.'[40]

In the economic sphere, the existence of free markets was recognised as 'a part of liberalism because they represent the extension of the concept of freedom into trade'. Yet the caveat was added that 'freedom in the market place is neither self-sustained nor sufficient to provide for all those things which a liberal society should have'. There was consequently a need both for 'institutions ... which keep markets free and prevent monopoly' and for 'other mechanisms ... to ensure that individuals have access to the things which markets are unable to provide'.[41]

With a significant difference of emphasis from that of *Our Different Vision*, the Liberal Democrats' first major statement of principles, which had given equal weight to the three core values of liberty, equality and community, *It's About Freedom* pointed out that, while Liberal Democrats were 'strong campaigners for social justice', it was also

> ... important to recognise that we place the principle of freedom above the principle of equality. Equality can be of importance to us in so far as it promotes freedom. We do not believe that it can be pursued as an end in itself, and believe that when equality is pursued as a political goal, it is invariably a failure, and the result is to limit liberty and reduce the potential for diversity. When equality is pursued as a goal, it also tends to lead to the belief that the central state has the power to achieve it and must be trusted to do so, whatever the cost to liberty.[42]

In place of that kind of lumpen egalitarianism, Liberal Democrats focused on 'the extent to which poverty and lack of opportunity restrict freedom'. From that standpoint they could 'justify the use of public expenditure, redistributive taxation, social insurance and active community provision'. Such methods were designed 'to make people free, not to constrain them into economic equality, which is unachievable in practice'. Moreover, even if a crudely egalitarian goal were achievable, 'it would require a static economy in which no-one could become unequally prosperous by successful enterprise'.[43]

It's About Freedom concluded by reaffirming the principle of freedom as 'the clarion call for Liberal Democrats'. In its final paragraph there were even echoes of the Preamble to the old Liberal Party Constitution of 1936 in the assertion that Liberal Democrats aimed to restore a vision and sense of idealism to British politics 'by putting freedom first, and creating new opportunities for every citizen in a liberal society'.[44] Indeed, even though there were some confusing or ambiguous references to 'Liberal Democracy' scattered throughout the document, as if that phrase denoted a political doctrine rather than, in reality, a particular type of political regime, *It's About Freedom* had nevertheless gone further than previous Liberal Democrat 'themes and values' documents or election manifestos in declaring that Liberalism was both 'the core of the Liberal Democrat intellectual inheritance' and the Party's enduring political creed.

Meanwhile, in the period after the 2001 General Election the shift in the Liberal Democrats' overall political strategy under Charles Kennedy's leadership had become steadily more apparent. His approach of 'effective opposition' to the Blair Government, in place of Paddy Ashdown's stance of 'constructive opposition', eventually led to the suspension of the Joint

Consultative Committee in September 2001. This was formally announced in a joint statement by Tony Blair and Kennedy which stressed the fact that the JCC had 'done useful work' and remained 'available to resume its work if further constitutional items became ready for discussion'. Both party leaders declared, too, that they were still 'committed to constructive parliamentary dialogue' and would 'continue to undertake joint work on specific issues where appropriate'.[45]

In spite of this diplomatic form of words, the suspension of the Joint Consultative Committee in effect signalled the severance of formal links between the Liberal Democrats and the Blair Government. More broadly, Kennedy's stance of 'effective opposition' appeared to involve moving away from the strategy of a realignment of the Centre-Left which Grimond, Steel and Ashdown had, in their different ways, pursued in the past. Kennedy sought instead to chart the different, and less elevated, course of building the Liberal Democrats into a stronger, independent party of opposition.

A year later the Party's policy and ideological position on the issue, increasingly central to British politics, of public service reform was clarified in a major document, entitled, *Quality, Innovation, Choice*. Published in August 2002, this was the report of a policy commission on public services chaired by Chris Huhne,[46] who in its introduction identified four challenges posed by the perceived shortcomings of public services as they currently operated in Britain. These were: to guarantee long-term funding for schools and hospitals, and for all public services; to improve choice, quality and access to public services; to ensure collective decision-making at the lowest effective level, closest to the people who actually used public services; and finally, to stop Whitehall interfering with decisions taken by public service professionals, such as doctors, nurses and teachers.[47]

The report recommended that guaranteed funding for hospitals and schools should be achieved by earmarking National Insurance to the National Health Service in the form of a ring-fenced, renamed NHS Contribution, and by replacing Council Tax with a fair system of local income taxation for the funding of local services such as schools. The second objective – improving choice and access – should be pursued in health care, for example, through the provision of greater patient choice by allowing access to any beneficial and cost-effective treatment within the UK. The third challenge – to ensure decentralisation and local accountability of public services – required, in the report's view, the promotion of a diversity of providers – traditional public sector, private, voluntary and mutual – of public services. Finally, central government's role in relation to public services should be limited to information-gathering and other related activities instead of interference with day-to-day decisions.[48]

Underpinning those policy recommendations, which had been based on extensive research into Continental European methods of public service delivery, certain distinctive and firmly established Liberal principles on public services were identified. Since the Liberal Democrats, the document declared, were 'the natural champions of high quality public services, standing in the tradition of Lloyd George and Beveridge', that in turn entailed a recognition of the need for 'adequate levels of funding, which must be decided by political representatives'.[49] But in addition, *Quality, Innovation, Choice* placed particular emphasis on the principles of choice and decentralisation; people 'should be able to choose who will deliver their services wherever practicable, and be able to make meaningful choices over where and when they receive a service'. That process 'might involve a choice of providers within the public sector, or of co-operative ventures, volunteering and mutualism, as well as the classical choice of public versus private'.[50]

This combination of wider choice through diversity of provision and decentralisation of decision-making was commended as the means both of ensuring democratic accountability and the delivery of public services 'on a more sensitive, human scale', and of promoting experimentation and innovation.[51] In broader ideological terms, the report, with its emphasis on a greater role for mutual/voluntary and other non-profit-distributing providers, allied to its declared commitment to 'working with private sector companies providing public services, as one of the possible ways of driving up standards',[52] marked out a distinctive space for the Liberal Democrats in the contemporary debate on public service reform. For with its attention to the role of mutual/voluntary providers, the report offered an alternative approach to polarised ideological positions based on either an elevation of the private sector and demotion of the public sector or vice versa. Furthermore, with its consistently decentralist and localist thrust, *Quality, Innovation, Choice* provided an approach to public service reform that not only differentiated the Liberal Democrats from its two major rivals but also transcended, or at any rate channelled, a growing internal debate within the Party over the increased role of the private sector in public service delivery.

Policy and ideological debate of this kind was, however, overshadowed in 2003 by more dramatic developments in foreign affairs. Throughout 2002 it had become increasingly clear that US President George W. Bush favoured military intervention in Iraq in order to remove Saddam Hussein and his brutal regime. In line with the motion passed at the Liberal Democrats' autumn conference in late September 2002, Charles Kennedy's own nuanced position on the prospect of war in Iraq was that he would support American and British military action against Saddam Hussein's regime if such action were approved by the United Nations and if there existed firm evidence of illegal weapons capability and of Saddam's intent to use it.[53]

Early in 2003 Kennedy agreed to speak at a rally in Hyde Park following the massive Stop the War demonstration in London on Saturday 15 February.[54] He and his Party remained insistent that a second UN resolution, supplementing Resolution 1441 (which had been passed by the UN Security Council in November 2002, calling on Iraq to comply with weapons inspections), was needed to authorise and endorse military action in Iraq. That second resolution failed, however, to materialise, in effect being blocked by President Chirac of France. On 18 March, in a final House of Commons debate before the War, all 53 Liberal Democrat MPs,[55] along with 139 rebel Labour MPs and 15 Conservatives, voted for a cross-party amendment stating that the case for war had not been made. Liberal Democrats had thereby opposed the Blair Government's decision to support American military action in Iraq. Blair nonetheless secured Parliamentary approval of military action, by a majority of 179, with the aid of Conservative support. The war began two days later, culminating in the toppling of Saddam Hussein's statue in Baghdad on 9 April.

In Britain the electoral impact of the Iraq War became evident amidst its bloody, insurgency-ridden aftermath. A by-election was held in September 2003 in Brent East in north London, a constituency with large British Asian, both Hindu and Muslim, communities. In what had previously been a safe Labour seat, the Liberal Democrat candidate, Sarah Teather, overturned a Labour majority of over 13,000 to win the election by 1,158 votes. The result, which in large part was caused by widespread revulsion at the decision by Blair and his government to engage in the military invasion of Iraq, appeared both to vindicate Kennedy's stance on the war and to underline the fact that his own, and his Party's, political profile had been significantly raised by that stance. Indeed, Sir Menzies Campbell, the Liberal Democrats' foreign affairs spokesman during this period, later observed that the Iraq War 'did give Charles a platform', and, more widely, 'gave the party definition and distinctiveness'.[56]

The repercussions of the Iraq War dominated British political debate throughout 2003 and during much of 2004. A succession of events – the discrediting of the Blair Government's two pre-war intelligence dossiers, a long-running conflict between Downing Street and the BBC, the suicide of the Ministry of Defence weapons specialist, Dr David Kelly, and the subsequent Hutton Inquiry into the circumstances surrounding his death – kept the war and its aftermath at the top of the political agenda.

Within the Liberal Democrats, however, ideological and domestic policy debate was reignited in 2004 by the publication in September of *The Orange Book: Reclaiming Liberalism*. Published in time for the Party's autumn conference in Bournemouth and co-edited by David Laws and Paul Marshall,[57] this collection of individual policy essays by eight, mostly Parliamentary, contributors, sought, in Marshall's words, 'to examine how the principles of Liberalism can be applied to a range of problems facing Britain at the beginning of the 21st Century'.[58] Charles Kennedy wrote a brief foreword to *The Orange Book* in which he noted that the contributors had produced 'a challenging set of policy ideas, which are hard-headed in their economic liberalism but equally committed to the vision of a fairer society and greater opportunity for all...', a vision that lay at the heart of his Party. 'Not all of the ideas in *The Orange Book*,' he continued, 'are existing party policy, but all are compatible with our Liberal heritage.'[59]

In *The Orange Book's* opening essay, *Reclaiming Liberalism*, David Laws defined the foundations of British Liberalism as 'a belief in personal, political, economic and social liberalism, combined with a strongly internationalist approach to extending these self-same freedoms across the world'.[60] By 'personal liberalism' Laws meant 'the freedom of the individual from all kinds of oppression', while 'political liberalism' connoted for him 'the belief that power should be exercised through accountable and democratic structures, as close to the people affected as possible, and therefore with the maximum possible decentralisation of power and decision making'.[61] The third strand of liberal thought, 'economic liberalism', consisted in 'the belief in the value of free trade, open competition, market mechanisms, consumer power, and the effectiveness of the private sector'. Such convictions were 'combined with opposition to monopolies and instinctive suspicion of state control and interference, particularly in relation to the ownership and control of business'.[62] The final 'essential element', 'social liberalism', had emerged towards the end of the 19th century, and had clearly played, Laws noted, 'a central role in the policy agenda of the great Liberal administration of 1906–11', bringing to Liberalism 'an acceptance and understanding of the insight that personal, political and economic liberalism are not by themselves an adequate basis for securing for each individual a deeper and more meaningful sense of freedom'. For those who were 'without a job, without enough food on the table, without education, and without access to adequate housing and healthcare', could not be said 'to enjoy freedom in any sense that most people would understand'.[63]

Turning to assess Liberal Democrat policies and attitudes in relation to these four strands of the British Liberal tradition, Laws considered that in the cause of personal liberalism the Party had 'continued to speak up for freedom of the individual and against oppression by the state and by majorities',[64] even though there were times, in his view, when some Liberal Democrats espoused what he called a 'nanny state liberalism ... a "liberalism à la carte", in which different liberals embrace different policies, not on the basis of whether these policies are truly liberal, but on the basis of whether or not their objective seems to be "worthy" or well-intentioned'.[65]

In the cause of political liberalism, Liberal Democrats and their predecessor, the Liberal Party, Laws observed, had also 'consistently been at the forefront of steps to liberalise the political system in the UK' – in terms of greater democratic accountability, freedom of information, transparency and decentralisation of political power. Nonetheless, in European policy, he added, 'two great liberal principles – a commitment to internationalism and to decentralisation – could at times come into collision.' [66]

It was while examining the third strand of liberal thought – economic liberalism – that Laws' views could, however, be regarded by some Liberal

Democrats as ideologically more contentious. 'Over the decades from the 1930s to the 1980s,' he maintained, the Liberal commitment to free market principles, and hence to economic liberalism in general, had been 'slowly watered down'; those beliefs had been 'progressively eroded by forms of soggy socialism and corporatism, which have too often been falsely perceived as a necessary corollary of social liberalism'.[67] Historically, there were, in his view, three main reasons for this development. First, in the early 20th century 'the common aspiration of both the Labour Party and the Liberal Party for broadly social liberal objectives' had bred a confusion between ends and means, which in turn had generated both a commitment to various forms of state intervention and 'a progressive dilution of the traditional liberal beliefs in the benefits of markets, choice, the private sector and competition'.[68] Second, the period of mass unemployment in the 1930s had created a climate of opinion in which the main challenge was conceived to be 'how Government could intervene to deal with market failure, rather than how Government could prevent market mechanisms from being interfered with by monopolies and tariffs'. Finally, during the 1940s, '... perhaps the highest point of state management and control of the economy in the history of Britain', it had been 'the state and not the market that seemed to provide the necessary solutions to our social and economic problems, and free trade and free competition seemed like nineteenth-century relics in a brave new world of "scientific" policy and benign political management'.[69]

As a consequence, over the past 50 years there had arisen 'a tension in the Liberal Party and the Liberal Democrats between the heritage of economic liberalism and the tendency to reach for statist solutions to economic problems'.[70] Furthermore, during the 1980s the confusion between ends and means in economic strategy had been increased, Laws noted, by the Conservative Party's decision 'to embrace the language, and some of the substance, of economic liberalism in their economic policies – which put competition, choice, the private sector and the market mechanism back on centre-stage'. Yet in view of the political and ideological complexion of the Thatcher governments, some Liberals had 'wrongly concluded ... that economic liberalism must be intrinsically part of a right-wing Conservative agenda, rather than a traditional Liberal commitment'. In the 1980s, therefore, 'only a few voices on the margins of the party' had been 'left to warn about the relative neglect of so much of the economic liberal legacy'.[71] Such voices, as we have seen, included, notably, those of Jo Grimond and John Pardoe and, within the SDP, that of David Owen. Meanwhile, Laws noted, 'Liberals and Social Democrats were merely left arguing lamely that the boundary between the public and private sectors should be left undisturbed, wherever it happened to be at the time'.[72]

Twenty or more years later, Laws considered that in the field of social policy a key question for Liberal Democrats was 'to what extent we can draw on our heritage of economic liberalism to address some of the current problems in public service delivery'. That, he insisted, 'categorically' did not mean rejecting the social liberal agenda, 'as some Liberal Democrats seem wrongly to fear'. Rather, it involved asking 'to what extent we can utilise choice, competition, consumer power and the private sector to deliver a better deal for those on low incomes, as well as for those who can already fend for themselves'.[73] More broadly, the Liberal Democrats, in order 'to achieve power, and to exercise it effectively', needed to have a sharpened policy agenda based on 'a synthesis of the personal, political, economic and social liberalism, which is our bequest from earlier generations of liberals'. They needed, in particular, 'to continue to embrace our social liberal agenda, while demonstrating that it is not incompatible with our economic liberal heritage'.[74]

Laws' overall approach was shared by his parliamentary colleague and fellow economist, Vince Cable.[75] In an *Orange Book* essay entitled 'Liberal Economics and Social Justice', Cable maintained that in Britain there was 'now a reasonably settled consensus that the task of modern government is to manage an open market economy, providing macro-economic stability allied to micro-economic flexibility and, alongside this, to try to achieve a sense of equity across social classes and generations'. Yet within that 'broad consensual framework', and hence within a climate of diminished ideological conflict, Liberal Democrats could still, Cable pointed out, occupy a distinctive political space by reaffirming the value of their liberal traditions, within which there were certain 'consistent threads: a commitment to a liberal and open economy, interwoven with a concern for social justice'.[76]

In considering, as David Laws had done, the application of economic liberal ideas to the field of social policy, Cable observed that 'one of the defining characteristics of economic liberalism is a belief that a system with many individual consumers and competing providers will provide a more satisfactory outcome than one based on monopoly, either of the private sector or the state'. 'A major challenge to economic liberals', therefore, in his view, was 'how to achieve greater individual, consumer, choice and greater diversity and competition amongst producers in the field of public services, where the state provides a (near) universal service (usually) free at the point of use'. 'The key public services – health, education and policing' already, he pointed out, in practice involved 'a complex mixed economy of private and public sector provision and consumption'. The issue here was thus 'rarely one of absolute ideological clarity, but of where the shifting boundaries are and should be'.[77]

In the light of those realities, Liberal Democrats, Cable argued, should 'be instinctively drawn to arrangements that try to obtain the best synthesis of public service ethics and the entrepreneurship, financial discipline and professional management of the private sector'. They should therefore 'reject the dogmatism of right and left who oppose one or the other on ideological grounds', including those who believed 'that a public service involves a monopoly of public service provision'. The overarching vision for Liberal Democrats should consequently be 'one in which a mixture of public sector, private and mutually owned enterprises compete to provide mainstream services'. Provided that the State performed 'its central function of ensuring that there is a regime for standard-setting and testing', then there was 'no overriding reason why the state itself should provide the service'.[78]

That approach to public service reform should be accompanied and strengthened, Cable stressed, as the 2002 Huhne Commission report had also made clear, by 'a system of governance that is both democratic and decentralised'. Instead of the Blair Government's insistence that decision-making with regard to public services should be 'driven centrally, at ministerial level, through operational targets', he favoured as 'a more satisfactory model ... one in which the strategic framework for commissioning services is set by a democratically elected authority, as local as possible ... and the "providers" (schools, universities, GP practices, hospitals) are independently managed at an operational level'.[79]

There were other perceptive and sometimes challenging contributions to Liberal Democrat thought and policy in *The Orange Book*, though none was as unequivocal as the essays by Cable and Laws in advancing the case, in general, for reclaiming economic liberalism for the Party and, in particular, for applying economic liberal ideas to the cause of public service reform. In an essay on the European Union, Nick Clegg sought to define for the Liberal Democrats in the debate on Europe a position of critical pro-Europeanism, which to some extent had been anticipated in the Party's 2001 General Election manifesto.[80] That would involve, in his words, 'adopting a clear stance that addresses the need for EU reform whilst promoting the simple and overwhelming case for EU integration'. Clegg favoured 'the evolution of the European Union in a more open, decentralised, accountable direction', pointing out that such a course was 'exactly what Liberal Democrats have always advocated'.[81] In promoting the case for European integration, he supported greater international cooperation within the EU on cross-border issues such as international commerce, environmental protection, aspects of foreign policy and international crime prevention. 'Supranational EU governance' of that kind represented 'the most fitting response to the modern challenges of globalisation'.[82] But he also called for the repatriation of responsibilities for many policy areas – such as social, agricultural and regional policy – to the national governments of EU member states.[83]

In advancing the case for 'a Liberal Europe', Clegg also stressed the importance of pursuing '... a Liberal approach to the exercise of power in the EU', which involved an insistence 'on checks and balances, on diffused centres of power and on the greatest degree of parliamentary accountability'.[84] Specifically, he called for greater transparency in the activities of ministers and officials within the Council of Ministers and for a more sceptical and scrutinising attitude towards the European Commission.[85]

Such a process was, however, hampered, in Clegg's view, by the political reality 'that there is no cohesive pan-European "demos"', no fully engaged community, that is, of European voters able 'to exert effective pressure on those wielding authority', thereby holding them to account. 'In the absence of a European "demos",' he concluded, '... the primary source of meaningful political legitimacy in the EU remains the nation state, at least for the foreseeable future.' For that reason, improving transparency and accountability within EU institutions was 'all the more important', as was the need for national parliaments 'to improve their own scrutiny of EU affairs and of the way in which their own governments act within the EU'.[86] Moreover, since the normal channels of accountability would 'remain imperfect as long as there is no European "demos"', then, Clegg argued, 'the allocation of authority at EU level must only be countenanced if there is an overwhelming and compelling reason to do so'.[87] The application of the liberal principle of subsidiarity, requiring the decentralisation of decision-making, therefore meant in practice 'that the EU must only act if there is a clear cross-border issue at stake, or when collective EU action brings obvious benefits to all member states that they would not be able to secure on their own'.[88]

It was not difficult to see why such views might ruffle some Liberal Democrat feathers, and why they were even subsequently misrepresented in some quarters as Eurosceptical. In truth, Clegg's essay constituted a reflective, measured and refreshingly open-minded development of Liberal Democrat thinking on Europe. His application of the principles of political liberalism to the European sphere was reinforced in *The Orange Book* by two essays that attempted to do the same at global and local levels. Chris Huhne, in a sharply analytical essay entitled 'Global Governance, Legitimacy and Renewal', thus underlined the need for reinforcing the existing framework of global governance – embracing the UN, the EU, the IMF and other international organisations – which had proved its inadequacy, particularly in the fields of human rights, security, world poverty and environmental protection.[89] Concerned, too, with interpreting the principles of political liberalism from a local perspective, Ed Davey pointed out that during the 20th century 'Britain became one of the most centralised democracies in the western world, as both socialist thinkers and conservative forces saw central state power as the best way to impose their own order'.[90] But just as the 20th century had been for Britain 'the century of centralism', so 'the challenge for the New Liberals of the [new] century' was to advance again the liberal case for political decentralisation. To 'win the case for a Liberal localism', Davey maintained, the Party had to demonstrate both 'that social justice will not be harmed, but actually enhanced' through decentralised decision-making, and that stronger local government could be a mechanism for checking state power and for promoting quality and choice in public services for the individual.[91] By effecting that shift in the balance of political power away from the central State, the Liberal Democrats would thereby, Davey observed, be meeting 'the J.A. Hobson measure' – namely, that:

> Liberalism will probably retain its distinction from socialism, in taking for its chief test of policy the freedom of the individual citizen, rather than the strength of the State ...[92]

That quotation from the Edwardian Liberal thinker was an apposite one since *The Orange Book* was in part, as David Laws later recalled, 'an attempt to disentangle, and to make clear the distinction between, a Labour philosophy and set of aspirations and a Liberal one'. For there existed, in his view, 'a strong default instinct' among many in the Party to align themselves on economic issues 'almost with a moderate Labour position'.[93] There had also been, as Laws later maintained, 'a lack of a clear narrative distinguishing the liberal role and expectation of the state from that of an historically more statist Labour party'.[94]

Reaction among Liberal Democrats to the publication of *The Orange Book* in September 2004 was, however, distinctly lukewarm and in some cases hostile or even, in the view of one of its essayists, 'vitriolic'.[95] A fringe meeting to launch the book at the party conference in Bournemouth was cancelled amid concern that the controversy surrounding, in particular, David Laws' proposal for a continental-style health insurance scheme, set out in another of the book's essays, might overshadow the conference itself and the Liberal Democrats' future electoral strategy.[96] Indeed, the hostile reaction to *The Orange Book* among some Liberal Democrat MPs and activists did stem to a large extent from that controversial policy proposal,[97] which had already been rejected by the Party's public services policy commission in 2001–2, and which, more broadly, was perceived as striking at a popular, core national institution with a long history of Liberal support stretching back to the Beveridge Report. Moreover, in Charles Kennedy's view, Laws and other supporters of that proposal had failed to foresee the strategic dangers arising from its advocacy in the run-up to the next general election. These were, first, that 'the media would leap on that proposal as a totemic one – that is, as clearly signalling a lurch to the Right', and second, that in every target seat in which the Liberal Democrats would be trying to win over Labour voters in order to defeat the Tories, Labour would be putting out leaflets saying 'Lib Dems want to privatise the Health Service'. Laws' proposal would thus, Kennedy believed, 'have sent a very confusing message'.[98]

A broader, ideological reason for the unfavourable response to *The Orange Book* among some Liberal Democrats lay in the attempt by David Laws and Vince Cable to reclaim economic liberalism for the Party. Such a response sprang, in Laws' view, from a 'residual collectivism' which could be traced back in the recent past to the 1970s and 1980s, and which reflected 'a confused and ambiguous attitude towards economic liberalism' within the Liberal Party and the Alliance during those decades. This in turn had led to 'a muddled compromise which largely left the public/private divide where it was, rather than taking a particular position for or against privatisation or nationalisation'. The upshot was that by the beginning of the 21st century 'ideas about markets had already been hijacked by the Tories and sounded therefore as if they were a compromise with Conservatism'. To talk of choice, competition and markets among some Liberal Democrats, it seemed to him, was consequently to run the risk of being labelled 'a surrogate Tory'.[99]

Reviewing *The Orange Book* in *Liberator* in September 2004, Simon Titley expressed no surprise at the controversy that *The Orange Book* had generated since, in his judgement, 'an ideological row within the Liberal Democrats was inevitable'. The Party encompassed, he maintained, 'essentially three competing strands of thought – left libertarians, social democrats and economic liberals'. Yet 'the intellectual contradictions of the 1988 merger were never,' he continued, 'satisfactorily resolved – indeed, debate was actively discouraged, leaving an ideological vacuum'.[100] Titley noted that one of the main reasons why *The Orange Book* had attracted interest was that 'controversially, it advocated a return to "economic liberalism"'. But its economic focus was for him the chief source of its inadequacy. 'The lack of human spirit,' he argued, 'is the biggest failure of *The Orange Book*', for 'its (mostly male) authors see people as primarily economic actors, approaching life in terms of dessicated financial calculations'. The book's 'basic fault' was thus that it was 'suffused with spiritual poverty and a grim economistic approach to life'.[101]

Such a line of criticism seemed like a residual expression of the tendency within the Liberal Party during the 1970s and 1980s to be more concerned with the distribution and decentralisation of power than with the relationship between the market and the State, and arguably, too, echoed its consequent lack of interest during that period in either economic theory or economic policy. Certainly it was the case that most of the *Orange Book* contributors had previously been professional economists, or else had extensive experience of business and finance. Their accession to the Liberal Democrats, as MPs or MEPs, had undoubtedly increased the Party's economic expertise without noticeably imbuing it with 'a grim economistic approach …'.

Nonetheless, *Liberator* itself was prepared to congratulate the *Orange Book*'s contributors 'for producing the thing at all' since it had been 'a long time since any [Liberal Democrat] MPs have addressed the party's whole intellectual direction, rather than comment on individual policies'. Indeed, *Liberator* had 'long argued that the lack of debate about ideas in the party has been a serious failing, and the technical aspects of campaigning – the "how" of politics – have superseded the "why" of politics in importance, and not to the party's long-term advantage'.[102]

Over two years later, in a comparison of *The Orange Book* with its distinguished 1928 yellow predecessor, *Britain's Industrial Future*, Ed Randall questioned not so much the former's dominant economic tone but rather the fact that, in his view, *The Orange Book* 'simply lacked the ambition, intellectual penetration and shared analysis needed to write a political programme ...'.[103] In contrast, the 1928 *Yellow Book* had been at once 'a brilliant analysis of Britain's most deep-seated problems, an eminently sensible and practical prescription for public policy-makers and the key to reinvigorating British liberalism'. Randall conceded, however, that the authors of the 2004 *Orange Book* 'could not claim – nor did they – that their contributions had been scrupulously researched or that they had been able to distil the insights and wisdom of the country's most eminent economists ... [or] that their approach represented a great challenge to economic orthodoxy ...'.[104]

The aims of *The Orange Book* had indeed, as Randall noted, been more modest than that. At the time of its publication in September 2004, David Laws had stressed the fact that, consisting as it did of ten individual essays, it was 'not a joint manifesto',[105] even though, as Paul Marshall maintained in his introduction to the book, those essays, 'taken together', did represent 'a hard-headed, coherent whole which illuminates the practical relevance of Liberalism, classical and "New", to contemporary problems'.[106] The chief motivation underlying the preparation of *The Orange Book*, Marshall later recalled, was to produce 'a work of reclamation', re-emphasising the importance of the Liberal Democrats' economic liberal heritage, which, in the editors' view, had been lost sight of in recent years. An additional motive was to provide 'a shop-window of the talent of the Party'.[107]

That central aim of *The Orange Book* – reclaiming economic liberalism – had formed, too, as we have seen, part of an attempt, most lucidly set out in Laws' opening essay, to present and promote a synthesis of personal, political, economic and social liberalism. Such an endeavour was conceived both as a means of distinguishing the Liberal Democrats ideologically from their Conservative and Labour opponents and as a guide to the Party's policy programme with regard to contemporary problems and issues. But while reclaiming economic liberalism for the Party, it was also necessary, as Laws stressed, to apply some of the essential ideas drawn from that tradition – competition, choice, enterprise – to a social liberal agenda focused on the widening of the individual's opportunities, notably in the field of social policy.

For those reasons, therefore, Laws and Cable maintained that there was no incompatibility between economic and social liberalism. Indeed, the tendency of some Liberal Democrats to depict the debate generated by *The Orange Book* as a polarised left/right ideological dispute was in reality both historically uninformed and politically misleading. Furthermore, the very process, reinforced at the time by sections of the media, of identifying divisions within the Party in terms of 'economic liberals' and 'social liberals', though not without some justification, ran counter to its internal political reality. For the Liberal Democrats had never been factionalised in the way that the Labour Party had so manifestly been throughout its history.

Setting his face against such factionalism, Charles Kennedy shared the view of Laws, Cable and others that social liberalism and economic liberalism were reconcilable ideological tendencies. As Party Leader he dealt with those policy and ideological differences that did arise between social and economic liberals by 'segmenting' them in different areas of social and economic policy,[108] preferring, on his own admission, to have as spokespersons in those areas 'round pegs in round holes'.[109] Furthermore, those differences for Kennedy were a source of creative tension since, in his view, within the Party 'that spectrum gives rise to the combustion that, you hope, produces innovative policies'.[110]

In the meantime, the months preceding the forthcoming 2005 General Election had been generally encouraging in electoral terms for the Liberal Democrats. In the elections for the European Parliament in June 2004 the Party had increased its number of seats from ten to 12, including one gained for the first time in the North-East of England, and had raised its vote share by 2.3 per cent compared with 1999. In the simultaneous local elections, the Liberal Democrats beat Labour into third place in terms of share of total votes cast, gaining 137 council seats and winning control of the city council in Newcastle-upon-Tyne. A month later, in a fiercely contested parliamentary by-election in Leicester South, the Liberal Democrat candidate, Parmjit Singh Gill, won what had previously been a safe Labour seat, adding to the gain at Brent East in September 2003. Chris Rennard, who had masterminded the Party's by-election campaigns since Eastbourne in 1990, commented that: 'In real elections we are now overtaking the Conservatives, and in many, many seats we are now the true challengers to Labour'.[111]

After the autumn 2004 party conference in Bournemouth, in which Charles Kennedy presented the Liberal Democrats as the alternative at the next general election to 'two essentially conservative parties', his Party faced a Labour government and Prime Minister whose popularity, in the wake of the Iraq War, were clearly in decline, with a Conservative opposition failing to gain substantial sympathy or support. When, therefore, the 2005 General Election campaign began unofficially in January, although officially in April, it seemed to many, as Sir Menzies Campbell later observed, that the Liberal Democrats' 'moment had come', with the prospect of defecting voters from either Labour or the Conservatives turning to the third party 'for refuge'.[112] In the light of that opportunity, the climate seemed favourable for the ensuing campaign. Indeed, since the late autumn of 2004 national opinion poll ratings for the Liberal Democrats had ranged from 18 to 25 per cent, averaging about 20 per cent.

The Liberal Democrat manifesto for the 2005 General Election, to be held on 5 May, was formally launched by Charles Kennedy at the beginning of the campaign in mid-April.[113] In his written introduction to the manifesto, Kennedy had stated his belief 'that the 2001–2005 parliament will be remembered as the period during which the Liberal Democrats came of age, ushering in a new era of truly three-party politics'. They had, he claimed, during that period 'again and again ... been the real opposition to Tony Blair's discredited Government – over Council Tax, student top-up and tuition fees, and ID cards'.[114]

The manifesto itself, entitled *The Real Alternative*, and drafted by Matthew Taylor, declared at the outset that the 'guiding principles' underlying the Liberal Democrat programme were 'freedom, fairness and trust'. 'Freedom' was valued both in its negative sense as the absence of 'unnecessary interference by government or society' and in its positive sense as the presence of opportunities for individuals 'to pursue their aims, develop their talents and shape their successes'. 'Fairness' was emphasised 'because ill-health, disability, poverty, environmental pollution and the fear of crime curtail freedom, just as much as discriminatory laws or arrest without trial'. Finally, 'trust' was stressed 'because to deliver freedom and fairness, we need to give citizens the power to hold government to account', which meant bringing government 'closer to the people it is meant to serve ...'.[115]

The key Liberal Democrat policy commitments included free personal care for elderly and disabled people and the abolition of university student tuition and top-up fees. Both of those spending pledges were to be funded out of a new 50 per cent tax rate on the portion of individual earnings exceeding £100,000 a year. That measure, the sole net tax increase in the manifesto, would affect only one per cent of taxpayers. In addition, there was a commitment to increasing the number of police officers on the streets by 10,000, to be funded by abandoning Labour's 'expensive, illiberal and ineffective ID card scheme'.[116]

On international affairs, the manifesto restated the Party's opposition to the Iraq War, declaring that: 'We should not have gone to war in Iraq. There were no weapons of mass destruction, there was no serious and current threat, and inspectors were denied the time needed to finish their job. Thousands of soldiers and civilians have been killed and it has cost the UK over £3.5 billion'. Sir Menzies Campbell added that '... Britain was taken to war against Iraq without express UN authority and on a flawed prospectus', and that the Blair Government 'built its case on unreliable intelligence, in circumstances of doubtful legality'.[117]

With regard to Europe, the manifesto stressed the need for reform of the EU, in the light of its recent enlargement, in order to make it 'more efficient and more accountable'. It maintained that the proposed new constitution would help to achieve that aim 'by improving EU coherence, strengthening the powers of the elected European Parliament compared with the Council of Ministers and enhancing the role of national parliaments'. The constitution also, it was claimed, 'more clearly defines and limits the powers of the EU, reflecting diversity and preventing over-centralisation'. For all those reasons, therefore, Liberal Democrats were 'clear in our support of the constitution, which we believe is in Britain's interest – but ratification must be subject to a referendum of the British people'.[118]

On UK constitutional issues, in a section headed 'Better Government', *The Real Alternative* highlighted the tendency in recent decades for British Prime Ministers to exercise 'a growing domination over the political system, insufficiently accountable to Parliament or the people'. Liberal Democrats would therefore seek to 'curb this excessive concentration of power', by cutting back the powers of patronage through plans for a predominantly elected second chamber, by preventing the politicisation of the Civil Service, and by strengthening the powers of Parliament to scrutinise the executive by means of an enhanced Select Committee system. In addition, the manifesto advocated the implementation of the single transferable vote (STV) system for all British local elections as well as for elections to the House of Commons, Scottish Parliament and National Assembly for Wales.[119]

As in 2001, the manifesto displayed 'a green thread of environmental awareness' running through every area of its policy commitments, thereby seeking to vindicate Charles Kennedy's claim that the Liberal Democrats were 'by far the greenest of the three main UK political parties'.[120] Its specific environmental policies were focused on three principal goals: tackling climate change; reducing pollution and waste; and producing cleaner power. In pursuit of those aims, the manifesto stressed the need for Britain to achieve its targets from the Kyoto Protocol well before the deadline. It also placed an emphasis on the reduction of overall energy use by ensuring that at least 20 per cent of the UK's electricity derived from renewable sources by the year 2020.[121]

The Liberal Democrats' election campaign, beginning in mid-April, was co-organised, as in 2001, by Chris Rennard, since 2003 the Party's Chief Executive, and its leading election strategist since 1989, and Tim Razzall, the campaign chairman. The policy emphasis of the campaign shifted in its second half from domestic issues to Iraq, a move which ignited Kennedy's personal contribution. However, in the final week Liberal Democrat candidates often found themselves undermined by the appeal to wavering Labour voters in marginal constituencies of Tony Blair's claim that a vote there for the Liberal Democrats might pave the way for an overall Conservative victory.[122]

In the event, the Liberal Democrats nonetheless polled just under 6 million votes, nearly 1.2 million more than in 2001. They won 62 seats, 11 gained from Labour and three from the Conservatives, and secured a 22 per cent vote share, up from 18.3 per cent in 2001. In a memorandum written a few months later to Charles Kennedy, which served both as a 'post-mortem' on the 2005 General Election and as a guide to strategy for the ensuing Parliament, Tim Razzall noted as 'the biggest achievement' of the Liberal Democrat campaign the fact that the Party had managed 'to persuade the media that this was a three party election' for the first time since the Alliance campaign in 1983. Another 'massive achievement', Razzall pointed out, was that during the 2005 campaign the Liberal Democrats had been able to advance policy positions – on abolition of Council Tax and student tuition fees, opposition to the Iraq War, provision of free long-term personal care for the elderly, and an increase in the top rate of income tax – that were not only popular but also clearly associated in the minds of voters with the Party.[123] But above all, of course, the outcome of the 2005 General Election was that the Liberal Democrats had won 62 seats, amounting to the largest third-party force in the House of Commons since 1923, when the Liberal Party was reunited under the leadership of Herbert Asquith.

Chapter 11
Crisis, Consolidation and Reaffirmation: 2005–2007

In spite of an electoral outcome in 2005 that had produced the largest parliamentary Liberal party representation since 1923, there were nonetheless misgivings among some Liberal Democrats that their Party had failed to exploit even more emphatically a uniquely favourable conjunction of political circumstances – namely, an increasingly unpopular Labour government, a Conservative opposition that showed few signs of significant recovery, and the bitter aftermath of a war which, alone among the three main parties, the Liberal Democrats had consistently opposed. Sir Menzies Campbell later referred to 'a gnawing feeling of disappointment'[1] which he shared with his colleagues in the weeks following the election as they wondered whether it might be a generation or more before such favourable circumstances might reappear at a British general election.

In his memorandum to Charles Kennedy in the summer of 2005, Tim Razzall, however, noted that, in spite of the achievement of winning 62 seats, the Party had 'allowed certain sections of the media – encouraged by over optimism from some of our colleagues – to turn this into failure'. But there was, in his view, 'no factual evidence that this election was a missed opportunity for us'. For during the six months leading up to the election campaign in April 2005, Liberal Democrat opinion poll ratings, he pointed out, had ranged from 18 to 25 per cent, with an average rating of about 20 per cent. Under the first-past-the-post voting system that range of poll ratings would be translated into a range of parliamentary seats stretching from 55 to 70, 'depending on our ground war targeting'. The total of 62 seats actually won was therefore 'bang in the middle of the 55 to 70 range'.[2]

Nevertheless, it was also Razzall's view that during the forthcoming Parliament the Liberal Democrats had to 'agree a narrative', as distinct from a theme or a slogan, a narrative, that is, such as the 'Set Britain Free' message conveyed by the Conservatives in 1951 and 1979, or the 'get rid of Tory sleaze' message conveyed by Labour in 1997. Razzall stressed, too, his view that 'we must not get drawn into the sterile debate as to whether the party is moving to the right or is to the left of Labour'. For while polling data indicated that 'we are positioned marginally to the left of centre in people's minds', it was nonetheless also 'clear that few modern voters define their position in left/right terms'. The Liberal Democrats' objective should therefore be 'not to get deflected in the futile left/right debate, but to maximise the small "l" liberal vote which comes from both sides and is enough to give us a majority'.[3]

Partly as a contribution to developing the kind of coherent narrative that Razzall had in mind, and partly as an audit on existing Party policy, a new policy review was set up after the 2005 General Election at the instigation of a group of Party officials and members of the Federal Policy Committee. The first stage of this exercise was a consultation paper, *Meeting the Challenge*, drawn up by a FPC working group and published in August 2005. Its emphasis on developing a political narrative involved explaining what the Party was *for*, in terms of its core liberal values and beliefs, embodied in its policies, rather than merely what it was *against*. It was thus concerned with establishing the philosophical linkage between the Liberal Democrats' major policy positions. As Duncan Brack later commented, this emphasis reflected the criticism that the Party's 2005 manifesto had been 'a comprehensive listing of things the party was against, but with no underlying narrative tying it all together and giving voters a sense of what the party was for'.[4]

A convincing narrative, as developed by political parties, was defined in the consultation paper as 'a storyline that voters can relate to, explaining [a party's] basic purpose and providing the context for [its] specific policies'. Margaret Thatcher's 1979 narrative was cited as an example, one based on 'promising to roll back the frontiers of the state, curb the power of the unions and better reward personal endeavour and hard work'.[5] In addition to this task of developing a Liberal Democrat narrative, the other main aim of the policy review exercise was to examine existing Party policy in the light of the challenges – economic, environmental, social and international – facing any British government after the next general election, and to identify the areas in which policy needed to be developed and modified.[6]

While, however, these developments were under way, there was growing post-election unease within the Party on other levels. Many of the 20-strong group of new Liberal Democrat MPs were increasingly disturbed by what they perceived as poor internal organisation within the parliamentary party and lack of communication with the Leader's office.[7] That unease was combined with increasing dissatisfaction with an apparent lack of strategic direction from the leadership.[8] Nevertheless, the Party's electoral fortunes remained buoyant when in July 2005 it successfully defended a Liberal Democrat-held seat at a parliamentary by-election in Cheadle.[9] But the following autumn party conference in Blackpool turned out badly for the leadership. There were platform setbacks for motions calling for a cap of 1 per cent on the EU's budget and for partial privatisation of the Royal Mail, proposals which were either defeated or referred back. The response to the latter motion, which had been tabled by Norman Lamb and supported by Charles Kennedy,[10] was, at least in part, a reflection of the growing ideological debate within the Party since 2001.

That debate was further stimulated by a pamphlet on public service reform by Vince Cable. published in the same month as the autumn conference. Entitled *Public Services: Reform with a Purpose*, it was an elaboration by Cable of some of the key themes, notably those of choice, public accountability and decentralisation, which had been developed in the Party's 2002 report, *Quality, Innovation, Choice*, together with a refinement of some of the ideas presented in his own *Orange Book* essay, 'Liberal Economics and Social Justice'. 'Doctrinal opposition to competition, choice and private provision' in the field of public services, Cable wrote, was 'as misplaced as naïve enthusiasm for markets and privatisation'. There was 'much to learn from the financial disciplines and management skills of private companies' as there was also 'from examples of poor value for money and poor service delivery by the private sector'.[11] Moreover, the political debate in Britain on public service reform, he pointed out, 'often confuses ends and means' since:

> Being for or against 'markets' or 'targets' or 'choice' defines the protagonist in some kind of ideological identity parade, yet these are different – though not exclusive – means to achieve the ends of public services: productivity improvement or consumer welfare.[12]

The currently favoured method of attaining those ends, the Blair Governments' setting of 'numerous centralised targets for schools, hospitals, police forces and local government', was in practice 'doing considerable harm since targets are often contradictory, have unintended consequences and undermine local decision making and professional confidence, and competence'.[13] But at the same time, the depiction of 'markets in public services ... as some kind of litmus test of commitment to reform', was, Cable argued, 'foolish since the conditions for efficiently functioning markets exist in some contexts but not others'.[14]

As the 2002 Huhne Commission report had also maintained, decentralisation was, in Cable's judgement, 'the key to public service reform'. For it would 'motivate staff, meet the particular preferences of local communities and encourage diversity and experiment'. Decentralisation ought to be accompanied by 'effective local accountability', at the heart of which should exist 'stronger and better local government'. That in turn would open up 'a wider debate on decentralisation of revenue raising, devolution of powers within the larger local authorities and electoral reform'.[15]

At the ill-fated autumn 2005 party conference in Blackpool, which coincided with the publication of Cable's reflections, Richard Grayson, the Party's former Director of Policy and the Leader's former adviser, expressed his view, in a radio interview, that Charles Kennedy's 'style was more chairman than leader' and that the Party 'wants to be led rather than necessarily being chaired'.[16] Grayson thereby, as Sir Menzies Campbell later recalled, 'provided a spark that turned the mix combustible', putting into words 'what so many Liberal Democrats felt but until then had been unable to express so succinctly or tellingly'.[17] Moreover, with regard to that Blackpool conference, Campbell reflected, too, that 'with the benefit of hindsight', he could 'see its significance in the chronology of events that led to Charles's resignation', even though he 'had little sense of its potential at the time'.[18]

From mid-November 2005 onwards this undercurrent of unease became apparent within the parliamentary party in the form of rapidly spreading discontent with the perceived lack of direction supplied by Kennedy's leadership. As this mood gathered momentum, events culminated in a press statement by Kennedy in early January 2006, in which he admitted that for the past 18 months he had 'been coming to terms with and seeking to cope with a drink problem'. He concluded, however, by announcing that he would be calling a leadership election in which he would be a candidate and invited any colleagues who believed 'that they can better represent the longer-term interests of the party' to stand against him.[19] But in the face of the threat of mass resignations from the front bench of the parliamentary party, Kennedy eventually made the decision, two days later, to resign as Leader, announcing this in a statement at the Party's London headquarters in Cowley Street on 7 January.[20]

In his resignation statement, Kennedy also referred to 'some serious internal political issues' which the new Party Leader and the Party itself would need to address and resolve. There was, he acknowledged, 'a genuine debate' with the Party, which was 'somewhat crudely caricatured at times as being in rather redundant terms between left and right; in rather simplistic terms as between social liberals and economic liberals; in rather misleading terms as between traditionalists and modernisers'. He himself had 'never accepted that these are irreconcilable instincts – indeed, quite the opposite', and he believed that unity remained 'fundamental to our further advance and success'.[21]

In terms of the number of Liberal Democrat MPs elected in 2005, Charles Kennedy had been the most successful Liberal leader since 1923. It is certainly debatable, however, whether he or his predecessor, Paddy Ashdown, was in practice the more effective third-party leader in the post-1945 period. Ashdown, after all, was operating in more difficult political circumstances, acutely so in the first phase of his leadership, and in a potentially perilous climate for his Party after Blair's accession to the Labour leadership in 1994. Yet under Ashdown's leadership the number of Liberal Democrat MPs more than doubled in the breakthrough of 1997.[22]

In a sharply critical assessment, Duncan Brack has argued that Kennedy lacked not only a clear or coherent policy agenda (a vacuum which was filled after 2003 by his stance on Iraq) but also the ability to manage the Party, providing it with a clear strategic direction.[23] Brack has conceded, however, that at certain pivotal moments and on certain critical issues Kennedy displayed good judgement – for example, in taking on the Conservatives on the issues of immigration and asylum at the Romsey by-election in 2000, in gradually disentangling his Party from the Joint Consultative Committee, and in refusing to participate in the 2004 Butler Inquiry into pre-war intelligence concerning Iraqi weapons of mass destruction.[24]

On Iraq, too, it can be argued that Kennedy demonstrated sound judgement on the need for a second UN resolution and provided firm leadership in a stressful and febrile political climate. Until the period following the 2005 General Election and leading up to his eventual resignation, he was also, to a large extent, a unifying party leader. As Paddy Ashdown later commented:

> ... the party was far more united, contented – I don't mean that in any sense pejoratively – under Charles's leadership than it was under mine. And so I think he was the right leader for the time'[25]

Finally, and of course very significantly, Kennedy remained a popular national political figure, with an enduring electoral appeal. This was evident even in the midst of his recurrent personal problems. In the summer of 2005, for instance, one journalist referred to 'a Charles Kennedy mystery', whereby, in the face of what she described as 'a ferocious whispering campaign' against him, the Liberal Democrats continued to poll strongly with a rating consistently above 20 per cent, while a Populus poll showed Kennedy's own trust rating at +16 against –13 for Tony Blair.[26] As Kennedy's biographer pointed out:

> ... People liked him. His style was different and unconventional for a politician. He was approachable, proportionate in his language, softly spoken, very witty, but modest and self-deprecating, too.[27]

Following his resignation in January 2006, Charles Kennedy nonetheless campaigned the following month in the by-election at Dunfermline and West Fife – the Scottish constituency next to the seat of Gordon Brown, then widely expected to be Tony Blair's successor as Labour Leader. The result was a remarkable victory for the Liberal Democrats and their candidate, Willie Rennie, who overturned a Labour majority of 11,562 to win by a margin of 1,800. The outcome was all the more impressive in view of the adverse media coverage that had dogged the Party for the previous two months.[28]

In the ensuing leadership election, Sir Menzies Campbell, the Party's Deputy Leader since 2003, emerged as the victor, beating the rival candidates, Chris Huhne and Simon Hughes. Campbell was duly announced as the third Liberal Democrat Leader on 2 March 2006.[29] At the outset his three main leadership objectives, as he later recalled, were, first, 'to restore stability and purpose' in the Party following Kennedy's resignation; second, 'to make the internal operations of the party more professional'; and third, to prepare the Party for the next general election.[30]

Each of those objectives was essentially organisational. The need to give the Liberal Democrats, in addition, a clearer policy and ideological focus and direction – which Kennedy's critics claimed that as Leader he had failed to provide – had been, as we have seen, one of the overriding aims of the *Meeting the Challenge* policy review exercise initiated in the summer of 2005. Following a wide consultation process, the culmination of the policy review was the publication in July 2006 of the policy document, *Trust in People: Make Britain Free, Fair and Green*. Drafted by Duncan Brack, it re-emphasised the fact that the primary task of the policy review exercise had been:

> Starting from the Liberal Democrat principles (as set out in the 2002 policy paper, *It's About Freedom*), to build up a coherent overview that helps people understand instinctively what Liberal Democracy [sic] is about ... in all areas, not just over a few eye-catching headline policies.[31]

In terms of the core liberal values underlying the Party's political narrative, explaining what it stood for, *Trust in People* set out the Liberal Democrat vision of 'a free Britain' as one in which 'people have the greatest possible control over their own lives'. The Liberal Democrats also wanted, it was stressed, 'to create a much fairer society, which means a much less unequal one', a goal that was depicted 'not as an end in itself, but as a precondition of freedom ...', since 'inequality limits freedom'. Moreover a fairer society was to be equated with greater social cohesion, since a more divided and unequal society, by contrast, not only undermined community involvement and political engagement, but also fostered crime and anti-social behaviour. 'The pursuit of a more equal society ... as a precondition of freedom' would therefore, it was stated, be 'a major political goal for the Liberal Democrats in the approach to the next election and a major plank of our campaign'.[32]

The egalitarian tone and focus of this section of the document involved a distinct and deliberate change of emphasis from the Party's 2002 'themes and values' paper, *It's About Freedom*, which *Trust in People* had taken as its initial point of reference.[33] For the earlier statement of principles had stressed the fact that Liberal Democrats 'place the principle of freedom above the principle of equality'. The pursuit of equality 'as a political goal' would in practice, it had warned, not only 'limit liberty and reduce the potential for diversity', but also tend to foster 'the belief that the central state has the power to achieve it [greater equality] and must be trusted to do so whatever the cost in liberty'[34]. Duncan Brack, as the principal author of *Trust in People*, had been influenced by the work of the social epidemiologist, Richard Wilkinson,[35] who had examined the impact of inequality upon health and social relations. Brack had recognised that the document's sharply egalitarian emphasis, implying a change from the principle of equality of opportunity to that of greater equality of outcome, would appear ideologically contentious to some in the Party. But he believed that such a shift in political thinking would help to stimulate internal party debate on the issues that it raised.[36]

The subsequent endorsement of *Trust in People* by the autumn 2006 Party conference was nonetheless accompanied by a major policy change, namely, the abandonment, at Sir Menzies Campbell's instigation, of the Party's commitment to the 50p top rate of income tax, which he believed was 'against aspiration ... discouraged ambition – and ... didn't produce huge sums of money'.[37] This policy shift was to be supplemented, however, by a commitment to broader tax plans that were fiscally neutral yet designed to be redistributive in effect by raising the threshold for income tax and cutting the basic rate, whilst removing tax reliefs for the well-off and increasing environmental taxes.[38]

The strong emphasis on the need for egalitarian redistribution in parts of *Trust in People* was evident again in a collection of essays that was commissioned by the centre-left think-tank, the Institute for Public Policy Research, and published in time for the Party's spring 2007 conference. Entitled *Beyond Liberty: Is the Future of Liberalism Progressive?*, the book contained contributions from both academics and Liberal Democrat MPs, peers and activists.[39]

Referring to tensions in the Party's recent past between social and economic liberals, Richard Grayson noted in his own contribution that some of the 2004 *Orange Book* essayists had stressed in a later volume 'the extent to which economic liberalism is compatible with social liberalism' and had reformulated their arguments 'from a more progressive perspective'.[40] In Grayson's view, this development, combined with the Liberal Democrats' adoption of the new tax policy, suggested 'that a period of political strife within the party over the role of economic liberalism may be coming to an end', and that there was a growing realisation among the advocates of both social and economic liberalism that it was 'possible to construct a message in which both are interdependent'.[41]

As an illustration of Grayson's point, David Laws observed in *Beyond Liberty* that:

> The balance of emphasis between economic and social liberalism has changed over the years, in the Liberal Party and in its successors – the SDP/Liberal 'Alliance' of the 1980s and the Liberal Democrats. Or perhaps, more accurately, the extent to which social liberal goals are to be delivered through statist or economically liberal means has changed over time.[42]

Such changes, Laws noted, had 'reflected the economic and social circumstances of the time, the climate of political debate, and the views of the leading personalities in Liberal/Liberal Democrat politics'. Furthermore, he pointed out that his argument in *The Orange Book* that the Liberal Democrats should 'reclaim our economic liberal heritage' had been 'misunderstood, or even misrepresented, as implying a downgraded commitment to the party's social liberal roots'. Yet *The Orange Book* had really 'argued for a synthesis of economic and social liberalism and for a clearer distinction between social liberalism and socialism'. His own central argument, he explained, was 'that social liberal goals should be pursued with economically liberal means – that social liberalism does not inevitably mean "big government" solutions'.[43]

Laws developed this point further by distinguishing 'the liberal role and expectation of the state from that of an historically more statist Labour Party',[44] maintaining that:

> The liberal state encourages personal responsibility and freedom; [...] seeks to secure a stable environment for wealth creation, but does not interfere in this process itself. [Indeed] ... on economic management, the role of the state in business, and in micro-economic interventionism, the liberal view of the state's role is a strictly limited one.[45] [The liberal state also] ... ensures that basic services are available to every citizen, but does not need to provide all of these itself, and devolves as much power to the local level as possible.[46]

Laws' conception of the liberal State thus revealed a mistrust of the use of statist methods and solutions in pursuit of social liberal goals. Such an approach seemed consistent with the way in which leading Liberal Democrats distinguished themselves ideologically from British social democracy after nearly 10 years of the Blair Governments. In an article published earlier in 2007, Richard Grayson made such a distinction explicitly in terms of a distrust of the central State. As a party, the Liberal Democrats, he maintained, were 'more accurately described as a social liberal party because of its wariness of the state, which is so often lacking in social democracy ...'.[47] 'On the key issue of the state,' Grayson pointed out, 'the Liberal Democrats and social democrats start from very different perspectives.' For whereas Liberals were suspicious of the State, there was 'little evidence of social democrats fearing it at all'. Even when social democrats focused on the need to decentralise government and political power, their reasoning was 'based on a concern with improving the effectiveness of government, rather than with fears over the power of the state'.[48] Such an approach was in sharp contrast with the Liberal Democrats' 'different conception of the state' illustrated both by their emphasis on constitutional reform and, more recently, in the 2002 report of the Huhne commission on public services, by their focus on the need for democratic local accountability.[49]

Elsewhere, however, in the *Beyond Liberty* collection of essays an overtly egalitarian view of the State's role in reducing inequality was evident in an advancement of the case for 'a renewal of progressive liberalism'.[50] Steve Webb, in particular, argued that 'a "full-blooded" understanding of liberalism as being about people's positive freedom to actively achieve things, rather than simply the freedom from constraints, must imply taking fairness seriously', viewing that ideal not 'as some reluctant and unwelcome travelling partner', but as 'an indispensable partner'.[51]

At the Liberal Democrats' spring 2007 conference in Harrogate, at which the *Beyond Liberty* collection of essays had been launched, Sir Menzies Campbell made a political decision that conspicuously put his leadership on the line. In the debate on the future of the Trident nuclear missile system, he spoke from the floor in favour of cutting Trident's nuclear capacity in half, while postponing the decision to replace it until that became necessary in 2014. He thereby swayed the debate against an amendment calling for a decision to be made there and then to scrap Trident when it became obsolete.[52]

Two months later, in the face of a Tory revival that had been growing since David Cameron's election as new Conservative Party Leader in December 2005, the Liberal Democrats lost 246 seats, and overall control of four councils, in the May 2007 English local council elections. The seat losses were, however, lower than the Party's internal prediction of about 600 likely losses, and its overall vote share of 26 per cent was only one point lower than in 2006, and more or less equal to Labour's. Nevertheless, the results were for many Liberal Democrats a source of concern, and fuelled press speculation, too, about Campbell's continuing leadership. A week after the May elections Tony Blair announced that he would be resigning as Prime Minister on 27 June. As widely expected, Gordon Brown succeeded him as Prime Minister and Labour Leader.

Later in 2007 a further significant contribution to ideological and policy debate within the Liberal Democrats appeared on the eve of the autumn party conference. Entitled *Reinventing the State: Social Liberalism for the 21st Century*, this substantial collection of essays by 21 Liberal Democrat contributors stated that its overriding concern was with 'reinventing the British state so that it delivers social justice and environmental sustainability through a decentralised and participatory democracy'.[53] The book's 'central idea' was 'that the state has a major role in ensuring liberty, equality and prosperity'. But 'to play that role in a way that does not itself become threatening of liberal values', it was stressed, 'the state must itself be radically reinvented in the direction of the local and the democratic'. That would mean 'a state in which power is radically devolved, so that state action becomes about creative and powerful local government being the first place in which people come together to tackle their shared problems'.[54]

'Reinventing' the State in such a way was justified, it was argued, by the recent changes in the political and economic environment. For throughout much of the 1980s and 1990s political debate had largely 'focused on the values of the market in economic, social and environmental policy'. But the limitations of the market were now 'becoming increasingly obvious'. It was clear, for example, that the 'ever more serious threat of uncontrolled climate change' could not be met by market mechanisms alone, and that the introduction of markets into public services had achieved 'at best mixed results'. Moreover, while both Conservative and Labour governments had been 'obsessed with market-based solutions', Britain had demonstrably become 'a divided and unfair society'.[55]

The egalitarian thrust of the kind of social liberalism expounded in *Reinventing the State* was most clearly developed in the essays by David Howarth and Duncan Brack. In 'What is Social Liberalism?', Howarth observed that since the late 19th century social liberals had believed that, alongside classical liberal beliefs in civil and political liberties and in international free trade, liberalism also 'required a commitment to a fair distribution of wealth and power, which in turn led to support for redistributive taxation and public services as ways of fairly distributing wealth and for democracy as a way of fairly distributing power'.[56]

More recently, the notion expressed in British political debate that there was a fundamental difference between 'social liberals' and 'economic liberals' was really, Howarth maintained, 'a confused view, which comes about through not understanding the difference between means and ends'. To illustrate this point, he considered David Laws, widely regarded as an 'economic liberal', to be nonetheless 'an advocate of a very social-liberal view of redistribution'.[57] The use of market mechanisms that Laws and others favoured, Howarth recognised, would 'always have attractions for liberals, because they decentralise decision-making and encourage innovation – both important liberal enthusiasms'. But they would 'never be more than means rather than ends in themselves'.[58] Moreover, he stressed, 'for all social liberals, whenever the use of the market might undermine the central aim of social liberalism – namely a society that protects effective freedom for all and which thus can generate and recognise a legitimate form of government – the market has to give way'.[59]

For Howarth, the more significant difference in British liberal debate was between what he called 'maximalist' social liberals and 'minimalist' social liberals. The former recognised the need for supplementary principles of fairness to guide the redistribution of wealth. The latter recognised 'only the principle that there should be redistribution to the extent that maintains the conditions for political freedom'.[60]

In an essay with a more explicitly egalitarian focus, and which developed points made in the 2006 policy review paper, *Trust in People*, Duncan Brack began with the reminder that the 2002 statement of principles, *It's About Freedom*, the initial reference-point for the policy review, had relegated the principle of equality 'to at best second place'[61] in the Party's set of core values. But although Brack had served on the working group that produced the 2002 document and thereby shared collective responsibility for it, he now believed that it 'drastically understates the importance of the pursuit of equality as the essential underpinning of our ultimate aim of individual freedom'. For, in his view, the promotion of the values of both freedom and community would be 'compromised by a lack of attention to equality'.[62]

Furthermore, Brack explained, by the principle of equality he did not just mean equality of *opportunity*, 'the Liberal get-out for most of the past century'; he also meant 'equality of *outcome* – or to be more accurate, a significant reduction in inequality of outcome'. He was therefore concerned to advance the case 'for promoting (or restoring) equality to the place where the party put it in its founding constitution, as a "fundamental value" balanced against – rather than subordinate to – the other two [i.e., liberty and community]'.[63]

Brack rested his case on two main arguments – first, 'that the extent of income and wealth inequality in modern-day Britain is seriously undermining the fabric of society and needs urgently to be tackled by government, not just for the sake of those at the bottom of the income and wealth pile, but for all of us'; and second, that '... a commitment to reduce levels of income and wealth inequality fits naturally into our Liberal philosophy';[64] Observing that Britain over the past 30 years or so had become a more unequal society, in terms of both income and wealth inequality and falling rates of social mobility, Brack, drawing on the work of Richard Wilkinson and others, then examined the negative impact of inequality in terms of rates of crime and anti-social behaviour and levels of social cohesion, community involvement and political participation. His conclusion was that there was 'a pervasive relationship between inequality and social outcomes'.[65]

Seeking to reduce the social effects of inequality – such as poverty, unemployment and ill-health – derived, moreover, from the Liberal commitment to freedom in its positive sense as the individual's exercise of choice and realisation of opportunity. The record of the post-1906 Liberal governments and the ideas of the New Liberal political thinkers clearly underlined that practical and philosophical linkage. But in taking action to reduce inequality at the present time, it was important, Brack stressed, that Liberal Democrats did not simply recreate 'the centralised and directive state' that Labour had built in the past.[66] Instead, there was a need for 'a more decentralised, responsive and participatory structure and style of government'. Furthermore, the kind of inequality that Liberal Democrats should be concerned to reduce, in his view, was the inequality 'which stems from the unequal distribution of endowments',[67] and hence which derived from inherited disadvantage rather than from individual choice or preference.

In another essay in *Reinventing the State*, Chris Huhne advanced the case for localism as a central part of 'the Liberal narrative'. For him localism entailed 'the decentralisation not just of management decisions but of political responsibility to a human scale where voters can once again identify – and complain to, or praise, or boot out – decision-makers in their community'. Such a process was entirely consistent with liberal philosophy which was concerned, *inter alia*, with curbing 'the undue exercise of power over individuals'.[68] Huhne further argued that 'those who distrust localism for fear that it will lead to greater inequality are mistaken', and cited international evidence demonstrating 'that there is no relationship between the degree of decentralisation of political power in a society and income inequality'.[69]

Moreover, it was Huhne's belief 'that the roots of much disillusionment and disenchantment with our political system lie in the destruction of the powers of local government and local governance', which had occurred under both Labour and Conservative governments, thereby destroying 'the vital first rungs on the ladder of electoral participation'. The 'exercise of power and discretion at local level' was therefore, in his view, 'probably the single most important change that we could introduce to ensure that people reconnect with the political system'.[70] In terms of social policy, too, as the commission which he chaired had concluded in 2002, the decentralisation of political power was, Huhne maintained, 'crucial if local decision-makers are to be held to account by those who use public services, which in turn is necessary for their long-term improvement'.[71]

Reinventing the State, with this localist focus, together with its redistributive and interventionist thrust, had been conceived to a large extent as a response to *The Orange Book* of 2004 and to the economic liberal direction that some of its contributors had clearly been recommending for the Liberal Democrats.[72] Or perhaps more accurately, the book was designed to counter the media interpretation of *The Orange Book* as indicating a shift to the Right for the Party.[73] Certainly it was an attempt to present a social liberal agenda as an alternative line of approach, and to influence the Liberal Democrats' future policy programme and election manifesto from an avowedly social liberal perspective. *Reinventing the State* was also thereby seeking to remedy one of the Liberal Democrats' perceived shortcomings – namely, that, as one of the book's contributors later put it, the Party had 'been generally hopeless at communicating its values and policies to the wider world'.[74]

In all these respects, then, as Michael Meadowcroft, while favourably reviewing *Reinventing the State*, acknowledged, *The Orange Book* had 'clearly been a great catalyst'. Indeed, in his view, the Liberal Democrats, alone amongst the major parties, had consequently 'reinvented internal political debate without, apparently, being overly put off by inevitable accusations of party disunity'.[75] The main focus of that debate had been, as we have seen, on the different perspectives offered to the Party by 'social liberals' and 'economic liberals'. Yet much of the tension between those positions rested on a confusion between ends and means. The real debate was thus not between incompatible ideological viewpoints, but rather about whether the social liberal goals of promoting effective freedom and a wider distribution of wealth and power were to be achieved by collectivist or economically liberal methods. Indeed, tracing the debate to its deeper historical roots, David Howarth had pointed out that 'one should not ... exaggerate the differences between classical and social liberalism' since they both began with 'the view that a state that fails to secure political freedom is not legitimate'.[76] That, together with the belief that concentrations of either state or private power – whether political or economic – posed a threat to the individual's personal and political liberty,[77] therefore provided British Liberalism with 'a very substantial shared base'.[78]

David Laws' contribution to the debate in his earlier essays had involved pointing out that much of the opposition to economic liberalism within the Liberal Democrats, and earlier within the Liberal Party and the Alliance, stemmed from a residual collectivism that was a product, first, of the postwar settlement in British government from the 1940s to the 1970s, and second, of the experience of the Thatcher governments of the 1980s. It might be added, too, that since 1988 the deep-seated collectivist attitudes widely apparent within the Liberal Democrats had been nurtured by the political reality that a disproportionately high percentage of the new Party's activists were local councillors, who held a firm belief in the efficacy of local government.[79]

At the time of the publication of *Reinventing the State*, it was widely expected that Gordon Brown would call an autumn 2007 general election in order to take advantage of his political honeymoon as new Prime Minister and Labour Leader. That was the climate of opinion in which the Liberal Democrats held their autumn party conference in Brighton, which Sir Menzies Campbell had aimed to make 'as strong an election launch pad as possible'. After making a highly effective and well-received Leader's speech, he believed that he had at last 'laid the leadership questions to rest'.[80] But with opinion polls revealing that the Conservatives were rapidly closing Labour's lead, Gordon Brown announced on 6 October that there would not, after all, be an autumn general election.

Faced with the prospect of two years or more of 'the media's obsession' with his age, which in his view was obscuring both the Party's radical policy agenda and the progress made under his leadership,[81] and in the face, too, of anonymous briefings of the press by Liberal Democrat MPs and peers, which fuelled speculation about the future of his leadership, Sir Menzies Campbell formally announced his resignation as third Liberal Democrat Leader on 15 October 2007, after a tenure of only 19 months.[82] Rather than regret or relief at the time, his 'principal emotions were frustration and irritation'. For he considered that the three principal objectives that he had set for the Party when he became Leader in March 2006 – namely, to restore its stability, to improve the professionalism of its internal operations, and to prepare it for a general election – had 'all been achieved'. Yet the postponement of the election had robbed him of 'the chance to show just how far I had taken the party'.[83]

But in spite of those achievements, together with Campbell's improved Commons performances and his widely praised final Leader's conference speech, it appeared that all of that, as Duncan Brack later wrote, 'came too late', for 'in today's media-intensive world, initial images are set very quickly and are very difficult to dislodge once formed'.[84] Moreover, in explaining the background to Campbell's sudden resignation, another significant point to be stressed was that the Party's gradual decline in its opinion poll ratings throughout 2007 'began to trigger panic amongst those unfamiliar with hard times, the party having been on a fairly consistent upward trend since about 1995 ...'.[85]

In the ensuing leadership election, the two candidates were Nick Clegg, MP for Sheffield Hallam since 2005, and Chris Huhne, MP for Eastleigh since 2005. Both had previously been MEPs. Huhne had stood against Campbell in 2006 and had been runner-up. After that contest it had been widely expected that he and Clegg would be the leading candidates to succeed Campbell following, it had been assumed, the next general election. After Clegg and Huhne had announced their intention to stand for the leadership, Paddy Ashdown declared his support for Clegg, and David Steel for Huhne. Both Sir Menzies Campbell and Charles Kennedy remained silent on that question.

In their manifestos and speeches during the campaign itself, which, like the 2006 contest, turned out to be a protracted one, both Clegg and Huhne stressed the centrality of liberal values within their vision of what the Party stood for. In a questionnaire in *Liberator* they thus both espoused the cause of a principled Liberal politics in place of what Clegg described as a 'sort of "sat-nav" politics' based on turning 'this way to shore up the core vote, that way for the floating vote ... the politics of cynics for whom tactical "positioning" is all – a hollow, gutless politics stripped of all meaning'. Clegg declared that he would seek instead to base his Party's appeal to the electorate on liberal values rather than on 'the popular mood of the day' in a Britain which was, he maintained, 'by instinct and by tradition a liberal nation' with 'a golden thread of liberal thought' running through the course of its history. Huhne, too, pointed out that he had 'left business for politics to promote liberal policies, not to be a slick salesman for whatever product the pollsters say is in vogue'.[86]

Huhne considered, however, that in spite of the Liberal Democrats' campaigning strength, which was 'a huge practical asset in our armoury', the Party had 'failed to deploy successfully, at a national level, the biggest potential weapon of all ... a sense of what liberal values actually are', thereby ensuring that 'voters know instinctively what our party's about, in the same way they understand Labour and the Tories' gut instincts'. From a similar perspective, Clegg regarded the Liberal Democrats' greatest asset as the fact that they were 'the only truly liberal party in British politics', and 'the politics of the 21st century', he believed, would 'increasingly be played out on liberal territory'. The Liberal Democrats had 'home advantage' since their liberalism was 'instinctive' and authentic, and because, too, they had been espousing for years liberal causes, which now had to be championed in new ways.[87] Whilst declaring this shared commitment to a principled, even ideologically driven, political approach rooted in liberal values, Clegg was anxious to avoid the trap of lurching into 'the old politics of left and right'. 'Trying to split the party into "left" or "right", "economic" or "social" liberal,' he pointed out, made 'no sense' to him. That was 'divisive language' which the Party's opponents wished to impose on it.[88]

In a speech delivered a few days after announcing his intention to stand for the leadership, Clegg had identified five major challenges that, in his view, would dominate political debate in his lifetime. These he described as the challenges concerned with 'empowering individuals, extending opportunity, balancing security and liberty, protecting the environment, and engaging with the world'. Liberalism, he maintained, which was 'a vital and compelling alternative to the old politics of left and right', and one that was both 'intellectually coherent and politically relevant', was the only political philosophy capable of meeting those five challenges.[89] In addressing, for instance, the challenge of 'engaging with the world', it was 'the only creed that can make sense of globalisation', a process which had 'the potential to make us all richer, financially and culturally', but also 'the power to unsettle and destabilise'. Moreover, the 'great external threats we face – from climate change to terrorism to cross-border crime' – were all, he pointed out, 'linked by one fact: that power has been globalised, but our methods for controlling it have not'. The challenge was therefore 'to construct a system of global governance capable of controlling global power'. Only liberalism, Clegg observed tellingly, 'with its easy accommodation both with the market economics that drive globalisation and the international politics needed to regulate it', was 'capable of guiding us in this process'.[90]

Nearly two months after Clegg's October speech, he was formally elected, on 18 December 2007, as the fourth Leader of the Liberal Democrats, having narrowly beaten the rival candidate, Huhne, by a few hundred votes. The leadership campaign itself was later described by Clegg's predecessor, Sir Menzies Campbell, as 'tetchy', one that had 'made the news only when the candidates were engaged in a clash of personalities rather than an exchange of ideas'.[91] Yet in that October speech, delivered amid the Victorian elegance of the National Liberal Club in London, Clegg had sought to underline the continuing force and relevance of Liberal ideas in the face of the dominant political issues of the early 21st century. Fifty-one years, then, after Jo Grimond had been elected Leader of the Liberal Party in November 1956, in the midst of the Suez crisis, Clegg had thus reaffirmed the enduring value of his Party's Liberal creed and inheritance, which Grimond, through his own leadership and influence, had done so much to revitalise.

Conclusion

The revival of British Liberalism since Jo Grimond became Leader of the Liberal Party in November 1956 has in itself revealed a broad continuity of Liberal values, ideas and principles stretching back not just to the 19th century but even, as Conrad Russell pointed out, to the 17th-century conflict between Crown and Parliament. That continuity could still be detected in the dark days of 1945–55 that preceded the revival. As we have seen, the dominant Liberal issues of that period – free trade and co-ownership in industry – were not only based on the view of Liberalism as a third way free of the pitfalls and defects of both state socialism and monopoly capitalism; they were also issues that were supplemented by the Liberal Party's consistent stances on civil liberties, on political and constitutional reform, and on international cooperation. The Liberal third way would thus be committed to the promotion of the personal, economic and political freedoms of the individual, and would involve the decentralisation of political and economic power, and hence, in Elliot Dodds' words, '...the spreading of property, power, responsibility and control'.[1]

Those ideas and themes were even more clearly apparent in the subsequent Liberal revival that was first discernible in the winter of 1955–56, but more clearly demonstrated following Jo Grimond's election as Party Leader. In the late 1950s a greater emphasis was placed on the themes of constitutional reform and internationalism, the latter acquiring an increasingly European focus. Under Grimond's leadership greater priority, too, was given to new policy formulation and to the clearer communication of Liberal ideas and policies in relation to both established and emerging policy issues. That development underlined the continuing importance which Liberals attached to political ideas and ideological conviction. In large part that in turn was due to the fact that, as Malcolm Baines has observed, they 'did not have a firm base in either class or interest around which they could unite' and therefore 'had to rely on a shared ideological heritage to hold the party together'.[2]

In the Grimond era political ideas also had more than just that unifying significance. For he himself, as Peter Barberis has pointed out, was, in terms of ideas and published output, the most fertile and prolific Liberal parliamentarian since Lloyd George.[3] Grimond thus sought to reinvigorate British Liberalism during the late 1950s and early 1960s, giving it a fresh impetus and direction. That was evident in his books, *The Liberal Future* in 1959 and *The Liberal Challenge* in 1963, as well as in his pamphlets, articles and speeches. His personal endeavour was sustained, too, after his resignation as Leader in 1967 right through to his last major political work, *A Personal Manifesto* in 1983. The recurrent themes in his political thought which have been identified in this study included a positive as well as a negative view of liberty; an empirical approach towards Liberalism, conceived as 'a philosophy based on the individual and his experience'[4]; a pragmatic and ambivalent attitude towards, and even mistrust of, the State; and a commitment to the ideal of active citizenship, through wider participation, within a decentralised political system, within civil society, and within a restructured market economy strengthened by the benefits of popular ownership.

With regard to that last point, Grimond, as has been noted, held an empirical rather than an absolutist view of the appropriate form of economic organisation. The market economy, he realised, was 'an artificial system ... subject to control and alteration'. But he nonetheless did not doubt that 'the Free Enterprise system' was 'the best instrument to hand' for increasing 'the prosperity and freedom of choice of individuals, leaving a margin over for the support of communal activity'.[5] That qualified approval of the market had long characterised Liberal economic thinking and was to do so in the years following Grimond's resignation. Yet the benefits of the market economy, which he clearly acknowledged, were later to be questioned or even overlooked by some Liberals during the 1970s and 1980s.

After Grimond stood down as Leader in January 1967, and following the Liberal Party's disastrous performance at the 1970 General Election, his emphasis on the value of wider citizen participation was reinforced by the Party's endorsement of the theory and strategy of community politics. The principal aim of that development was the creation of a participatory society in which people in local communities could gain greater control over their living and working environments, thereby achieving a greater sense of involvement in decisions affecting their lives. Community politics was thus in harmony with the distributist strand of British Liberalism, articulated most clearly in the writings of Elliot Dodds, which stressed the importance of the wider diffusion of power and responsibility. But in its more radical post-1970 form that aim was promoted and valued not just so that individual citizens might more easily influence the structures of government, but also so that they might exercise power themselves through voluntary bodies and community groups and organisations.

Throughout the 1970s, and into the early 1980s, the theory of community politics became the dominant ideological strand within British Liberalism. It provided, in Leighton Andrews' words, its 'key organising principle' and 'its decisive contribution to contemporary political discourse'.[6] The practice of community politics also pervaded the ethos of the Liberal Party and constituted its major strategy for local government campaigning, although not its central national strategy.

The 'market revolution' of the 1980s posed, however, an ideological dilemma for the Liberal Party and, indeed, for the SDP/Liberal Alliance. For the selective appropriation of economic liberal ideas and policies by the Thatcher Governments after 1979 was widely perceived by Liberals as having socially divisive consequences, in terms of the resultant mass unemployment, deindustrialisation and run-down of public services during that period. This is turn generated a widespread suspicion about, or even hostility towards, economic liberalism in the minds of many Liberals and Social Democrats.

Instead, however, of pursuing what Grimond called 'that old political nirvana, the middle ground' with its 'semi-dirigiste policies',[7] David Owen, as Leader of the SDP after 1983, chose to promote the concept of a social market economy that would combine market realism with social concern. That project was stigmatised by many Liberals, and by some within his own Party, too, as 'a flirtation with Thatcherism' or as 'Thatcherism with a human face'. In truth, as Owen later explained, it was his attempt to respond to the newly established, market-oriented 'conventional wisdom' of the 1980s with what he called the SDP's 'distinctive imprimatur'[8] of a concern with questions of social justice and social inclusion. As this study has maintained, Owen's promotion of the idea of a social market economy could thus also be viewed as a further attempt to devise the kind of progressive synthesis – combining a commitment to a competitive market economy, to the common welfare and to political and constitutional reform – that Jo Grimond had been advocating since the late 1950s, and which had been endorsed, too, during the late 1960s and the 1970s by John Pardoe in his writings and speeches.

During the 1980s, however, that kind of approach remained unorthodox within the SDP/Liberal Alliance, and although it was implicit in some of the Alliance's policy commitments, it appeared to be overshadowed by, in Grimond's words, a 'reformed and diluted variety of étatism'.[9] Many Liberals during that period seemed more concerned, too, ideologically with the distribution and decentralisation of power than with the relationship between the market and the State, or with debates about the most desirable form of economic organisation.

But after the formation of the Social and Liberal Democrats in 1988, economic liberal ideas were revived and propounded within the new party, from the early 1990s onwards, under the leadership of Paddy Ashdown. In his book, *Citizens' Britain*, and in his speeches and other writings, Ashdown sought to design and promote his own version of a progressive synthesis, combining support for a competitive market economy with a commitment to the related ideals of community and active citizenship as well as to political and constitutional reform. In doing so, he drew directly from the Liberal tradition in presenting that synthesis as an alternative both to state socialism and to free-market Conservatism.

After Ashdown's resignation as Party Leader in 1999, and following the 2001 General Election, in particular, there was a growing feeling among some Liberal Democrat politicians and thinkers that the Party's economic liberal heritage was being neglected or sidelined during that period, and therefore needed to be re-emphasised. That was a major motivation underlying the publication of *The Orange Book* in 2004. In its opening essay, 'Reclaiming Liberalism', David Laws made a renewed attempt to reformulate and represent the Liberal progressive synthesis which Grimond and Ashdown, with their different emphases, had sought to develop. In Laws' case, that undertaking involved an assertion of his belief that his Party's social liberal agenda was demonstrably compatible with its economic liberal heritage.

The subsequent response to *The Orange Book* among many Liberal Democrats was, at least in part, an indication of their ambivalence about market economics, an attitude shaped by historical experience, most recently by that of the Thatcher era. Their response was influenced, too, politically by a perceived association of economic liberalism with a 'right-wing' agenda, a view which, while understandable in the light of the recent past, was from a longer-term perspective historically uninformed.

Nevertheless, one of the editors of *The Orange Book* later expressed his regret that it had not contained an essay on the nature of market failure.[11] Such an inclusion might have led to a more balanced debate in sections of the Party. However, the publication in 2007 of another significant collection of essays, *Reinventing the State,* offered an alternative, overtly social liberal, approach – both more interventionist and more egalitarian – for the Liberal Democrats in the light of the limitations of the market. But inherent in its emphasis on an enabling State operating at a local and accountable level could be detected, in some eyes, along with the opportunities provided by decentralisation, the danger of new forms of state or bureaucratic failure to match the aspects of market failure that *Reinventing the State* had identified in its overall analysis.

Writing in 1998, Conrad Russell had observed that the Liberal Democrats' first Leader, Paddy Ashdown, had inherited a 'mixture of traditions' – one of which was a distrust of the State, 'in which we can hear the voices of Gladstone and Grimond'. The other was rooted in a willingness to use the power of the State to widen opportunities and to disperse wealth and power, a political approach personified by Lloyd George. Those two Liberal traditions, Russell noted, were 'not incompatible, but, like a team of high-spirited horses they are not easy to drive together'. 'Technically and ideologically,' he concluded, such a blend was 'extremely difficult to mix in the right proportions'.[12] That process might, however, be facilitated, it could be argued, by a broad agreement among British Liberals that, in the words of the 1987

Alliance election manifesto: Governments should not try to do what can be better done by individuals, by communities, by voluntary organisations or by private enterprise ...'.[13]

Because it raised important and contentious issues of that kind, the ideological debate generated by *The Orange Book* and *Reinventing the State* appeared to be a healthy development for the future course of British Liberalism. Moreover, as Charles Kennedy had contended in his resignation statement of January 2006, there was a strong case for regarding social and economic liberalism as complementary, rather than antithetical, ideological tendencies.[14] For, in addition to the fact that, as David Howarth and David Laws both pointed out, much of the debate rested on a confusion between ends and means, there was much common ground shared by the two schools of thought – consisting, in particular, of a mistrust of the central State; a preference for decentralist and voluntarist methods of promoting personal opportunity and social welfare; an antipathy towards concentrations of either state or private power – whether political or economic; and a firm commitment, maintained by all British Liberals, to the defence of personal and political liberty.

What could also be widely agreed by Liberal Democrats was the need, stressed in the policy review of 2005–06, to develop a clear and coherent political narrative that would both explain the Party's values and purpose and provide the context for its specific policies. That need was all the more urgent in the face of the continuing, unresolved problems facing the Party in the early 21st century – notably, those of establishing a distinctive political identity, and of risking the potential appropriation, as in the past, of its ideas and policies by its rivals. As John Stevenson has noted, the Liberal Party, possessing no copyright on political ideas, was at times in its history 'more important as a source of ideas which have entered the mainstream of political debate than as a vehicle for carrying them out'.[15] But as Paddy Ashdown observed in his diaries, Liberalism was 'too important' for the Liberal Democrats to act merely as 'the unpaid think-tank for new ideas in British politics; or the repository for community politics without a purpose'.[16]

The Liberal Democrat 'themes and values' documents since 1988 – most notably, *Our Different Vision, Facing up to the Future, It's About Freedom* and *Trust in People* – had been prepared on the basis of this agreed need to clarify and define the Party's political identity and philosophical purpose. They were literary responses, too, to other continuing problems facing the Party, namely, those surrounding its third-party status, and the dilemmas arising from it – in particular, that of how to preserve its independent identity whilst being prepared to engage in inter-party cooperation. As we have seen, that particular dilemma emerged in the case of each of the three strategies of a realignment of the Centre-Left, developed by Grimond, Steel and Ashdown, from the late 1950s to the late 1990s. In addition, the need for a clearly defined political identity and purpose has been underlined by the historic electoral problem of the volatility of the Liberal vote, illustrated, for instance, by the fact that in the general elections between 1959 and 1979 only about 50 per cent of Liberal voters remained loyal at the following election.

Since the 1970s a number of important developments in British politics have nonetheless created for the Liberal Democrats a clearer and wider space on the political landscape. Among these changes may be identified: the decline of class politics, and the consequent phenomenon of class dealignment in voting behaviour; more broadly, the erosion since the late 1980s of the capitalist/socialist divide in European politics, which had been since 1918 its major ideological fault-line; and, related to both those factors, the electoral reality that far fewer British voters than in the past define their position in left/right terms. In addition may be cited the fact that in recent decades Britain has become in certain important respects a more liberal society – notably, in attitudes towards ethnicity, gender, sexuality and sexual orientation. All these developments, then, have created greater opportunities for the Liberal Democrats, but have also reinforced the need for the Party to define its ideas, values and policies more clearly, and to communicate them, along with its overriding purpose, more effectively to the wider public.

It has been a central contention of this historical study that the kind of benign, progressive synthesis forged and promoted by Jo Grimond from the late 1950s onwards provided the original basis for a political narrative defining and conveying the fundamental purpose of a reformulated Liberalism. That progressive synthesis was later developed, as has been noted, in their different ways and in different circumstances, by other leading Liberals and Liberal Democrats. Although the times have changed radically, the essential elements of that synthesis, drawn from the Liberal tradition, remain constant and highly relevant to the transformed political and economic climate that has emerged over 50 years later. It can be argued, too, that such a synthesis is not incompatible with the kind of social-liberal agenda favoured by many Liberal Democrats in recent years. Admittedly, there are clearly legitimate differences of opinion about the appropriate use of market-driven policy measures. But the social liberal emphasis on effective freedom and on a relocated, decentralised State can serve to strengthen and enhance the kind of ideological approach refined by Grimond and by those who came after him.

Moreover, if, as Nick Clegg has maintained, 'the politics of the 21st century will increasingly be played out on liberal territory', with Liberalism the political creed most capable of meeting the new challenges – among them, the need to defend liberty whilst ensuring security, and the need to secure international cooperation so as to benefit from, yet regulate, the effects of globalisation – then in that case the Liberal Democrats, as 'the only truly liberal party in British politics', may well have 'home advantage'.[17] It may fairly be concluded, therefore, as the 2002 policy document, *It's About Freedom*, clearly stated, that 'the core of the Liberal Democrat intellectual inheritance is Liberalism', and yet also, as Alan Beith argued in its Foreword, that the Party, as the inheritor of that rich political tradition, had 'a distinct advantage which we do too little to advertise or exploit'.[18] The task facing the Liberal Democrats in the early 21st century will be to attain greater power and influence in British politics whilst respecting and reaffirming that Liberal tradition, with its various strands and its enduring values and beliefs, a tradition which had been revived and restored a half-century earlier.

Chronology

(Linking influential political writings, by Liberal, SDP and Liberal Democrat politicians/thinkers, and major Party statements with key events in British Liberal and Liberal Democrat history since 1956).

1956	September	Clement Davies announces his intention to resign Liberal Party leadership.
	November	Jo Grimond elected new Liberal Party Leader.
1957		George Watson (ed.), *The Unservile State: Essays in Liberty and Welfare.*
1958	March	Liberals win Torrington by-election. First Liberal by-election gain since 1929. (For a complete list of Liberal, SDP and Liberal Democrat by-election victories from 1958 to May 2000, see Cook, *A Short History of the Liberal Party,* Appendix III, p.271.)
1959		Jo Grimond, *The Liberal Future.*
		Roger Fulford, *The Liberal Case.*
		Report of Ownership for All Committee published.
		Liberal Party General Election Manifesto 1959, *People Count.*
	8 October	1959 General Election: Liberals win 6 seats, with 1.6 million votes and 5.9 per cent vote share.
1962	March	Liberals win Orpington by-election. (Most dramatic British by-election result since 1933.)

1963		Jo Grimond, *The Liberal Challenge*. George Watson (ed.), *Radical Alternative: Studies in Liberalism by the Oxford Liberal Group*. Liberal Party membership peaks at 350,000.
1964		Liberal Party General Election Manifesto 1964, *Think for Yourself – Vote Liberal*.
1964	15 October	1964 General Election: Liberals win 9 seats, with 3 million votes and 11.2 per cent vote share.
1965	March	David Steel wins Roxburgh, Selkirk and Peebles by-election for Liberals.
1966		Liberal Party General Election Manifesto 1966, *For All the People*.
	31 March	1966 General Election: Liberals win 12 seats, with 2.3 million votes and 8.5 per cent vote share.
1967	January	Jo Grimond resigns as Liberal Party Leader. Jeremy Thorpe elected new Liberal Party Leader. Donald Wade, *Our Aim and Purpose* (4th edn)
1969		*Liberals Look Ahead* (Report of the Liberal Commission)
1970		Liberal Party General Election Manifesto 1970, *What a Life! Show 'Em You Care*.
	18 June	1970 General Election: Liberals win 6 seats, with 2.1 million votes and 7.5 per cent vote share.
	September	Adoption of Community Politics resolution by Liberal Assembly.
1972	October	Liberals win Rochdale by-election.
	December	Liberals win Sutton and Cheam by-election.
1973	May	900 Liberal gains in local elections. (Party's best performance since 1945.) Liberals win control of Liverpool City Council.
	July	Liberals win Isle of Ely and Ripon by-elections.
	November	Liberals win Berwick-upon-Tweed by-election.
1974		Liberal Party General Election Manifesto February 1974, *Change the Face of Britain – Take Power – Vote Liberal*.

	28 February	February 1974 General Election: Liberals win 14 seats, with over 6 million votes (largest Liberal vote in 20th century) and 19.3 per cent vote share.
		Liberal Party General Election Manifesto October 1974, *Why Britain Needs Liberal Government*.
	10 October	October 1974 General Election: Liberals win 13 seats, with 5.3 million votes and 18.3 per cent vote share.
1976	May	Jeremy Thorpe resigns as Liberal Party Leader; Jo Grimond becomes caretaker leader.
	July	David Steel elected as new Liberal Party Leader.
1977	March	Lib-Lab parliamentary pact formed.
1978		Jo Grimond, *The Common Welfare*.
	January	Special Liberal Assembly endorses renewal of Lib-Lab pact.
	May	David Steel announces imminent termination of Lib-Lab pact.
1979	March	Labour government falls after being defeated on vote of no confidence (first such occasion since 1924).
		Liberal Party General Manifesto 1979, *The Real Fight Is for Britain*.
	3 May	1979 General Election: Liberals win 11 seats, with 4.3 million votes and 13.8 per cent vote share.
	November	Roy Jenkins' Dimbleby Lecture, 'Home Thoughts from Abroad'.
1980		Bernard Greaves and Gordon Lishman, *The Theory and Practice of Community Politics*.
1981		David Owen, *Face the Future*.
	January	Limehouse Declaration by the 'Gang of Four' (Roy Jenkins, David Owen, Bill Rodgers and Shirley Williams) launches Council for Social Democracy.
	March	Social Democratic Party formally established.

	June	*A Fresh Start for Britain* (joint statement of agreed principles issued by the Liberal Party and the SDP).
1982	July	Roy Jenkins elected first SDP Leader.

1983		Alan Beith, *The Case for the Liberal Party and the Alliance*.
		Jo Grimond, *A Personal Manifesto*.
	February	SDP/Liberal Alliance General Election Manifesto 1983, *Working Together for Britain*.

	9 June	1983 General Election: SDP/Liberal Alliance wins 23 seats (17 to Liberals, 6 to SDP), with over 7.75 million votes and 25.4 per cent vote share.
		David Owen elected new SDP Leader.

1985		David Steel and Richard Holme (eds), *Partners in One Nation: A New Vision of Britain 2000*.
		Roy Jenkins, *Partnership of Principle: Writings and Speeches on the Making of the Alliance*.

1986		David Steel, *The Decade of Realignment: The Leadership Speeches of David Steel*.
	June	Report of SDP/Liberal Joint Commission on Defence and Disarmament.
	September	Liberal Assembly votes against nuclear element in future European defence policy.

1987		*The Time Has Come: Partnership for Progress* (Alliance joint policy statement).
		Richard Holme, *The People's Kingdom*.

	May	SDP/Liberal Alliance gains over 450 seats and equivalent of 27 per cent vote share at local elections.
		SDP/Liberal Alliance General Election Manifesto 1987; *Britain United: The Time Has Come*.
	11 June	1987 General Election: SDP/Liberal Alliance wins 22 seats (17 to Liberals, 5 to SDP), with 7.3 million votes and 23 per cent vote share.
		David Steel calls for a 'democratic fusion' of the Liberal Party and the SDP.
	August	SDP members vote to begin merger negotiations with the Liberal Party.
		David Owen resigns as SDP Leader.

	September	Liberal Assembly votes overwhelmingly for merger negotiations with SDP. Merger negotiations begin.
1988		David Marquand, *The Unprincipled Society: New Demands and Old Politics.*
1988	January	Merger negotiations are concluded. Special conferences of Liberal Party and SDP endorse merger.
	March	In Liberal all-member ballot, 87.9 per cent of Liberal members vote for merger (on turnout of 52.3 per cent). In SDP all-member ballot, 65.3 per cent of SDP members vote for merger (on turnout of 55.5 per cent). Foundation of the Social and Liberal Democrats (with David Steel and Robert Maclennan as joint interim leaders).
	July	Paddy Ashdown elected first Leader of the Social and Liberal Democrats.
	September	Short name of 'The Democrats' endorsed by new party's autumn conference.
1989		Paddy Ashdown, *Citizen's Britain.*
	January	*Our Different Vision: Themes and Values for Social and Liberal Democrats* (new party's first broad statement of principles).
	June	The Democrats finish in fourth place, behind the Green Party, with only 6.4 per cent vote share in European Parliament elections.
	October	All-member party ballot results in support for nomenclature, 'Liberal Democrats'.
1990	October	Liberal Democrats win Eastbourne by-election.
1992		Liberal Democrat General Election Manifesto 1992, *Changing Britain for Good.*
	9 April	1992 General Election: Liberal Democrats win 20 seats, with just under 6 million votes and 18.3 per cent vote share.
	May	Paddy Ashdown's Chard speech.

1993	June	*Facing up to the Future* (Liberal Democrat statement of principles).
	July	Liberal Democrats win Christchurch by-election (on biggest swing – 35.4 per cent – in British parliamentary by-elections since 1945).
1995	May	Ending of Liberal Democrats' position of equidistance between the Conservative and Labour parties. Liberal Democrats overtake Conservatives as second party of local government.
	July	Report on *Wealth Creation and Social Cohesion in a Free Society*.
1997	March	Cook-Maclennan Agreement on future cooperation between Labour and Liberal Democrats over constitutional reform. Liberal Democrat General Election Manifesto 1997, *Make the Difference*.
	1 May	1997 General Election: Liberal Democrats win 46 seats (biggest parliamentary Liberal party since 1929), with 5.2 million votes and 16.8 per cent vote share.
	July	Establishment of Joint Consultative Committee to examine Labour government proposals for constitutional reform.
1998	October	Report of Jenkins Commission on Electoral Reform.
	November	Joint statement by Blair and Ashdown announcing extension of remit of JCC beyond constitutional matters.
1999		Conrad Russell, *An Intelligent Person's Guide to Liberalism*.
	January	Paddy Ashdown announces his resignation as Liberal Democrat Leader (to take effect in June).
	May	Liberal Democrats win 17 seats in elections for new Scottish Parliament and 6 seats in elections for new National Assembly for Wales.
	June	Liberal Democrats win 10 seats in elections for European Parliament. Ashdown steps down as Liberal Democrat Leader.
	August	Charles Kennedy elected new Liberal Democrat Leader.

2000		Charles Kennedy, *The Future of Politics*.
	July	Final meeting of Joint Consultative Committee.

2001		Liberal Democrat General Election Manifesto 2001, *Freedom, Justice, Honesty*.
	7 June	2001 General Election: Liberal Democrats win 52 seats, with 4.8 million votes and 18.3 per cent vote share.
	September	Suspension of Joint Consultative Committee.

2002	January	*It's About Freedom* (Liberal Democrat statement of principles).
	August	*Quality, Innovation, Choice* (Report of Liberal Democrat Policy Commission on Public Services).

2003	February	Charles Kennedy speaks at rally following 'Stop the [Iraq] War' demonstration in London.
	March	53 Liberal Democrat MPs vote (along with 139 Labour MPs and 15 Conservative MPs) for House of Commons cross-party amendment stating that the case for war in Iraq had not been made.
	September	Liberal Democrats win Brent East by-election.

2004		Paul Marshall and David Laws (eds), *The Orange Book: Reclaiming Liberalism*.
	June	Liberal Democrats win 12 seats in elections to European Parliament.

2005		Liberal Democrat General Election Manifesto 2005, *The Real Alternative*.
	5 May	2005 General Election: Liberal Democrats win 62 seats (largest parliamentary Liberal party since 1923), with nearly 6 million votes and 22 per cent vote share.

2006	January	Charles Kennedy resigns as Liberal Democrat Leader.
	March	Sir Menzies Campbell elected new Liberal Democrat Leader.
	July	*Trust in People: Make Britain Free, Fair and Green* (report of Party's 2005–2006 policy review).

2007		Duncan Brack, Richard S. Grayson and David Howarth (eds), *Reinventing the State: Social Liberalism for the 21st Century*.
	October	Sir Menzies Campbell resigns as Liberal Democrat Leader.
	December	Nick Clegg elected new Liberal Democrat Leader.

Notes

Preface

1. Duncan Brack, Introduction to Iain Dale (ed.), *Liberal Party General Election Manifestos, 1900–1997* (London: Routledge Politico's, 2000), p. 16.
2. ibid.
3. See Ivor Crewe and Anthony King, *SDP: The Birth, Life and Death of the Social Democratic Party* (Oxford: Oxford University Press, 1995).

Chapter 1

1. See Conrad Russell, *An Intelligent Person's Guide to Liberalism* (London: Duckworth, 1999), p. 13
2. Chris Cook, *A Short History of the Liberal Party, 1900–2001*, 6th edn (Basingstoke: Palgrave Macmillan, 2002), p. 130
3. Philip Fothergill was Chairman of the Liberal Party Organisation, 1946–49, and again in 1952, and President of the Party, 1950–52.
4. Frank Byers was Liberal MP for North Dorset, 1945–50, and in 1946 succeeded Tom Horabin as Liberal Chief Whip in the House of Commons.
5. On Martell's contribution to party reorganisation during this period, see Mark Egan and Roy Douglas, 'Edward Martell', in Duncan Brack et al. (eds) *Dictionary of Liberal Biography* (London: Politico's, 1998), pp. 249–52.
6. See Cook, op. cit., p. 131.
7. J. Graham Jones, 'Grimond's Rival', *Journal of Liberal Democrat History*, 34/35, Spring/Summer 2002, p. 27.
8. J. Graham Jones, 'Churchill, Clement Davies and the Ministry of Education', *Journal of Liberal Democrat History*, 27, Summer 2000, p. 7
9. See Cook, op. cit., p133.
10. Roy Douglas, 'The Liberal Predicament, 1945–64', *Journal of Liberal History*, 50, Spring 2006, p. 15.
11. Clement Davies, letter to Gilbert Murray, 11 May 1950, Clement Davies Papers, J/3/26, National Library of Wales, quoted in Alun Wyburn-Powell, *Clement Davies: Liberal Leader* (London: Politico's, 2003). p. 189.
12. *Yorkshire Evening Post*, 30 September 1950; quoted in J. Graham Jones, 'Churchill, Clement Davies and the Ministry of Education', p. 10.
13. Cook, op. cit., p. 133
14. Davies consulted Lady Violet Bonham Carter, Frank Byers, Jo Grimond, Lady Megan Lloyd George and Lord Samuel, of whom only Violet Bonham Carter at that time urged Davies to accept Churchill's offer. See J. Graham Jones, 'Churchill, Clement Davies and the Ministry of Education', p. 14.
15. *The Times*, 22 November 1951; quoted in Geoffrey Sell, 'A Sad Business: the Resignation of Clement Davies', *Journal of Liberal Democrat History*, 24, Autumn 1999, p. 14. On Churchill's varied motives, partly sentimental and generous and partly expedient, underlying his offer to Davies, see: Douglas, 'The Liberal

Predicament, 1945–64', p. 16; Cook, op. cit., p. 134; J. Graham Jones, 'Churchill, Clement Davies and the Ministry of Education', pp. 7, 13.

16. This agreement, formed between Lord Woolton, Chairman of the Conservative Party, and Lord Teviot of the Liberal Nationals (renamed the National Liberals in 1948), led to the establishment of joint Conservative-National Liberal associations in those constituencies in which both parties were already in existence. See David Dutton, *A History of the Liberal Party in the Twentieth Century* (Basingstoke: Palgrave Macmillan, 2004), pp. 160–1.

17. Dutton, op. cit., p. 177

18. Wyburn-Powell, op. cit., p. 209.

19. Roy Douglas, *A History of the Liberal Party, 1895–1970* (London: Sidgwick & Jackson, 1971), p. 265.

20. See John Stevenson, *Third Party Politics since 1945: Liberals, Alliance and Liberal Democrats* (Oxford: Blackwell, 1993), p. 37.

21. See Matt Cole, 'An Analysis of Voting Records of Liberal MPs, 1951–59', unpublished paper, University of Birmingham; cited in Wyburn-Powell, op. cit., p. 217.

22. Douglas, *A History of the Liberal Party, 1895–1970*, p. 267.

23. ibid., pp. 277, 255

24. Sell, 'A Sad Business', p. 17.

25. Roy Douglas, 'Philip Fothergill', in Brack et al. (eds), op. cit., p. 117.

26. Dutton, op. cit., p. 138

27. See Stevenson, op. cit., pp. 40–2; Dutton, op. cit., pp. 182–3

28. Dutton, op. cit., p. 179.

29. See Stevenson, op. cit., p. 41; Sell, 'A Sad Business', p. 15.

30. Stevenson, op. cit., p. 41.

31. ibid.

32. Dutton, op. cit., p. 182.

33. Michael Steed, 'The Liberal Tradition', in Don MacIver (ed.), *The Liberal Democrats* (Hemel Hempstead: Prentice Hall/Harvester Wheatsheaf, 1996), p. 42.

34. Malcolm Baines, 'The Survival of the British Liberal Party, 1932–1958', DPhil thesis, University of Oxford, 1989, p. 122.

35. See Jorgen Rasmussen, *The Liberal Party: A Study of Retrenchment and Revival* (London: Constable, 1965), pp. 204–6.

36. Baines, op. cit., p. 122.

37. This process was assisted by the formation at Oxford in 1953 of the Unservile State Group. Chaired by Elliot Dodds, the Group was designed to provide a forum for the development and dissemination of liberal ideas, but was not committed to any particular school or variety of liberalism. See Chapter 2 below, and Peter Barberis, 'The Unservile State Group', in Duncan Brack and Ed Randall (eds), *Dictionary of Liberal Thought* (London: Politico's, 2007), pp. 406–7. On Elliot Dodds' broader contribution to Liberal thought, see Donald Wade and Desmond Banks, *The Political Insight of Elliot Dodds* (Leeds: Elliot Dodds Trust, 1977); Robert Ingham, 'Elliot Dodds', in Brack and Randall (eds), op. cit., pp. 93–6.

38. On the free trade issue within the Liberal Party between 1945 and 1955, and the activities of the Liberal free traders, see Richard Cockett, *Thinking the Unthinkable: Think-Tanks and the Economic Counter-Revolution, 1931–1983* (London: HarperCollins, 1994), pp. 107–8, 126–30, 135–6; and John Meadowcroft and Jamie Reynolds, 'Liberals and the New Right', *Journal of Liberal History*, 47, Summer 2005, pp. 45–51.

Chapter 2

1. See Alan Watkins, *The Liberal Dilemma* (London: MacGibbon and Kee, 1966), pp. 75–6.
2. See Geoffrey Sell, 'A Sad Business: The Resignation of Clement Davies', *Journal of Liberal Democrat History*, 24, Autumn 1999, p. 16.
3. Clement Davies, speech at Liberal Assembly, Folkestone, 29 September 1956, *Manchester Guardian*, 1 October 1956; quoted in Michael McManus, *Jo Grimond: Towards the Sound of Gunfire* (Edinburgh: Birlinn, 2001), pp. 112–13.
4. *Manchester Guardian*, 27 September 1956; quoted in Sell, 'A Sad Business', p. 16.
5. McManus, op. cit., p. 112.
6. See David Dutton, *A History of the Liberal Party in the Twentieth Century* (Basingstoke: Palgrave Macmillan, 2004), p. 192.
7. ibid., p. 188
8. See Ruth Fox and Robert Ingham, 'National League of Young Liberals', in D. Brack and E. Randall (eds), *Dictionary of Liberal Thought* (London: Politico's, 2007), pp. 294–5.
9. See Wallace, 'Survival and Revival', in Vernon Bogdanor (ed.), *Liberal Party Politics* (Oxford: Oxford University Press, 1983), p. 50.
10. Major-General Grey, letter to Frank Byers, 10 March 1958: CD Papers C/1/107; quoted in Geoffrey Sell, 'Liberal Revival: Jo Grimond and the Politics of British Liberalism, 1956–67', PhD thesis (University of London, 1996), p. 68. The Liberal Party Research Department, headed by Harry Cowie, was established in September 1959.
11. See Wallace, in Bogdanor (ed.), op. cit., p. 49.
12. Sell, 'Liberal Revival', pp. 196–7.
13. ibid., p. 51
14. See Jorgen Rasmussen, *The Liberal Party: A Study of Retrenchment and Revival* (London: Constable, 1965), p. 137.
15. Nathaniel Micklem, *Aspects of Liberal Policy* (London: Liberal Publication Department, 1958), p. 10.
16. Roger Fulford, *The Liberal Case* (Harmondsworth; Penguin, 1959), p. 100. See also Sir Andrew McFadyean, *The Liberal Case* (London: Allan Wingate, 1950).
17. George Watson (ed.), *The Unservile State: Essays in Liberty and Welfare* (London: Allen and Unwin, 1957), p. 7.
18. As stated in *Liberal News*, 16 December 1955.
19. See Nancy Seear, 'Relations in Industry', in Watson (ed.) op. cit., p. 189. (Seear was at that time Lecturer in Social Science and Administration at the London School of Economics.)
20. ibid.
21. Nathaniel Micklem, 'The Challenge of Liberalism', in Watson (ed.), op. cit., p. 312. (Micklem was at that time President of the Liberal Party and sometime Principal of Mansfield College, Oxford).
22. Seear, 'Relations in Industry', in Watson (ed.), op. cit., p. 188.
23. See C. A. R. Crosland, *The Future of Socialism* [1956] rev. edn (London: Cape, 1964), Ch.1; see also Tudor Jones, *Remaking the Labour Party: From Gaitskell to Blair* (London: Routledge, 1996), pp. 29–33
24. Peter Wiles, 'Property and Equality', in Watson (ed.), op. cit., pp. 89–90. (Wiles was at that time Fellow in Economics at New College, Oxford.)
25. ibid., p. 90

26. See George Watson, 'Remembering Beveridge', *Liberal Democrat History Newsletter*, 14, March 1997.
27. Elliot Dodds, 'Liberty and Welfare', in Watson (ed.), op. cit., p. 19.
28. William Beveridge, *Full Employment in a Free Society: A Report* (London: Allen & Unwin, 1944), p. 36; quoted in Dodds, 'Liberty and Welfare', in Watson (ed.), op. cit., p. 19.
29. Seear, 'Relations in Industry', in Watson (ed.), op. cit., p. 187.
30. 'Where Liberals Stand 13: Nationalisation', *Liberal News*, 26 April 1957.
31. Wiles, 'Property and Equality', in Watson (ed.), op. cit., p. 104.
32. ibid., p. 106.
33. ibid., p. 108.
34. ibid.
35. Seear, 'Relations in Industry', in Watson (ed.), op. cit., p. 192.
36. Wiles, 'Property and Equality', in Watson (ed.), op. cit., p. 109.
37. Alan Peacock, 'Welfare in the Liberal State', in Watson (ed.), op. cit., p. 113. (Peacock was at that time Professor of Economic Science at the University of Edinburgh.)
38. ibid., p. 117, 118.
39. ibid., p. 130.
40. ibid., p. 125.
41. Richard Cockett, *Thinking the Unthinkable, Think-Tanks and the Economic Counter-Revolution, 1931–1983* (London: HarperCollins, 1994), p. 128
42. Donald Wade, *Towards a Nation of Owners* (London: Liberal Publication Department, 1958), p. 1.
43. ibid., pp. 4, 9.
44. *Industry and Society* was widely regarded within the Labour Party at that time as a revisionist socialist document; see Jones, *Remaking the Labour Party*, pp. 30, 33.
45. Wade, op. cit., p. 9.
46. ibid., p. 10.
47. ibid., pp. 6, 3.
48. ibid., pp. 6, 7.
49. ibid., pp. 39–40.
50. *Ownership for All: Report of the Liberal Party Ownership for All Committee* (London: Liberal Publication Department, 1959), p. 8. On the original 1938 *Ownership for All* Report, see John Meadowcroft and Jaime Reynolds, 'Liberals and the New Right', *Journal of Liberal History*, 47, Summer 2005, pp. 45–51.
51. *Ownership for All* (1959), p. 5.
52. ibid.
53. ibid., p. 6
54. *Britain's Industrial Future: the Report of the Liberal Industrial Inquiry* (London: Ernest Benn, 1928; reprinted 1977), p. 243; quoted in *Ownership for All* (1959), p. 7.
55. *Ownership for All* (1959), p. 10.
56. See Charles Taylor, Stuart Hall, Raphael Samuel and Peter Sedgwick, 'The Insiders', *Universities and Left Review*, 3 (Winter 1958).
57. Minutes of a meeting of the Liberal Party Organization Council, 9 May 1959; Liberal Party Papers, 2/1/37, British Library of Political and Economic Science, London.
58. *Liberal News*, 1 February 1957, p. 1
59. ibid.

60. See Rasmussen, op. cit., pp. 138–9.
61. Roy Douglas, *Liberals: A History of the Liberal and Liberal Democrat Parties* (London: Hambledon and London, 2000), p. 264.
62. Malcolm Baines, 'The Survival of the Liberal Party', DPhil thesis, University of Oxford, 1989, p. 117.
63. See *Liberal News*, 12 February, 26 February 1959; cited in Rasmussen, op. cit., p. 139.
64. Steed, 'The Liberal Tradition', in Don MacIver (ed.), *The Liberal Democrats* (Hemel Hempstead: Prentice Hall/Harvester Wheatsheaf, 1996), p. 55.
65. See Wallace, 'Survival and Revival', in Bogdanor (ed.), op. cit., pp. 46–7.
66. Grimond, speech at Liberal Rally, Albert Hall, London, 10 November 1958; quoted in Watkins, op. cit., p. 93.
67. See Jo Grimond, *Memoirs* (London: Heinemann, 1979), p. 218.
68. On these disputes, see: Jones, *Remaking the Labour Party*, Chapter 3; Eric Shaw, *The Labour Party since 1945* (Oxford: Blackwell, 1996), Chapter 3; and Andrew Thorpe, *A History of the Labour Party*, 3rd edn (Basingstoke: Palgrave Macmillan, 2008), Chapter 7.
69. Dutton, op. cit., p. 189.
70. Peter Barberis, *Liberal Lion: Jo Grimond: A Political Life* (London: I.B. Tauris, 2005), p. 105.
71. See Dutton, op. cit., p. 189.
72. Jo Grimond, *The New Liberalism* (London: Liberal Publication Department, 1957), p. 8.
73. Peter Barberis, 'Grimond', in Brack and Randall (eds.), op. cit., p. 149. On this and other recurrent themes in Grimond's political thought and writings, see ibid. pp. 147–50; and Barberis, *Liberal Lion*, pp. 207–9.
74. Grimond, *The New Liberalism*, p. 10.
75. ibid. On these points, see also Jo Grimond, 'The Reform of Parliament,' in Watson (ed.), op. cit., pp. 27–53.
76. Jo Grimond, *The New Liberal Democracy* (London: Liberal Publication Department, 1958), p. 6.
77. ibid., pp. 9,16.
78. Barberis, *Liberal Lion*, p. 77.
79. Jo Grimond, 'The Principles of Liberalism', *The Political Quarterly*, Vol. XXIV, No.3, July–September 1953, p. 236.
80. ibid. The quotation is from A. E. Housman, *Last Poems*, IX (London: Grant Richards, 1922). Grimond quoted the same couplet from Housman's poem 25 years later in the Preface to his book, *The Common Welfare* (London: Maurice Temple Smith, 1978).
81. See Jo Grimond, *The Liberal Future* (London: Faber & Faber, 1959), Chapter 3.
82. ibid., p. 15.
83. ibid., pp. 15–16.
84. ibid., p. 16.
85. ibid., p. 17.
86. ibid., p. 29.
87. ibid., p. 31.
88. ibid.
89. ibid., p. 60.
90. ibid., p. 72.
91. ibid., p. 62.

92. ibid., p. 79.
93. ibid.
94. Geoffrey Foote, *The Republican Transformation of Modern British Politics* (Basingstoke: Palgrave Macmillan, 2006), p. 89.
95. Grimond, *The Liberal Future*, p85.
96. ibid., p. 80.
97. ibid., p. 81.
98. ibid.
99. ibid.
100. ibid., p. 90.
101. ibid., pp. 180–1.
102. ibid., p. 181.
103. Fulford, op. cit., p. 52.
104. Grimond, *The Liberal Future*, p. 181.
105. Foote, op. cit., p113.
106. Liberal Party General Election Manifesto 1959, *People Count*, in Iain Dale (ed.), *Liberal Party General Election Manifestos 1900–1997* (London: Routledge/Politico's, 2000), p. 99.
107. ibid.
108. ibid., p. 101.
109. ibid., p. 100.
110. ibid.
111. See D. E. Butler and Richard Rose, *The British General Election of 1959* (London: Macmillan, 1960), p. 65.
112. *People Count*, in Dale (ed.), op. cit., pp. 100–1.
113. ibid., p. 100.
114. Wallace, 'Survival and Revival', in Bogdanor (ed.), op. cit., p. 48.
115. Butler and Rose, op. cit., p. 51.
116. Sell, 'Liberal Revival', p. 13.

Chapter 3

1. Jo Grimond, interview in *The Observer*, 11 October 1959; quoted in Michael McManus, *Jo Grimond: Towards the Sound of Gunfire* (Edinburgh: Birlinn, 2001), pp. 145–6.
2. Grimond, speech at Cambridge, *The Daily Telegraph*, 30 November 1959; quoted in McManus, op. cit., p. 148. On Hugh Gaitskell's 1959 Labour Party Conference speech, see Tudor Jones, *Remaking the Labour Party: From Gaitskell to Blair* (London: Routledge, 1996), pp. 45–51.
3. Grimond, speech at Southport, 19 March 1960; quoted in McManus, op. cit., p. 154. On Labour's 'New Testament', see Jones, op. cit., pp. 51–4.
4. Jo Grimond, 'Liberalism and Nationalisation', *New Statesman*, 24 October 1959, p. 530
5. ibid.
6. Jo Grimond, *The Liberal Future* (London: Faber & Faber, 1959), p. 58.
7. Grimond, *The Times*, 17 March 1962; quoted in David Dutton, *A History of the Liberal Party in the Twentieth Century* (Basingstoke: Palgrave Macmillan, 2004), p. 195.
8. See McManus, op. cit., p. 147.
9. See Jones, op. cit., pp. 41–3.

10. See Adrian Slade, interview with Roy Jenkins, *Journal of Liberal Democrat History*, 38, Spring 2003, p. 7.
11. See, for instance, 'Liberal Revival?', *New Statesman*, 17 October 1959, p. 494.
12. William Wallace, 'Survival and Revival', in Vernon Bogdanor (ed.) (Oxford: Oxford University Press, 1983), pp. 54–5.
13. Jo Grimond, *Memoirs* (London: Heinemann, 1979), p. 208
14. Jo Grimond, *Growth not Grandeur*, New Directions no. 3 (London: Liberal Publication Department, April 1961), p. 12.
15. See Andrew Gamble, 'Liberals and the Economy', in Bogdanor (ed.), op. cit., pp. 202–3.
16. Grimond, *Growth not Grandeur*, p. 3.
17. Roy Douglas, 'The Liberal Predicament, 1945–64', *Journal of Liberal History*, 50, Spring 2006, p. 18.
18. Mark Bonham Carter, 'Liberals and the Political Future', in George Watson (ed.), *Radical Alternative: Studies in Liberalism by the Oxford Liberal Group* (London: Eyre & Spottiswoode, 1962), pp. 18–19.
19. ibid., pp. 19, 20–1.
20. ibid., p. 19.
21. ibid.
22. ibid., p. 22.
23. ibid.
24. ibid., p. 23.
25. See in particular, Anthony Crosland, *The Future of Socialism* (London: Cape, 1956, rev. edn. 1964); Anthony Crosland, *The Conservative Enemy* (London: Cape, 1962); Douglas Jay, *Socialism in the New Society* (London: Longman, 1962).
26. Desmond Banks, *Liberals and Economic Planning*, Unservile State Papers no. 8 (London: Liberal Publication Department, August 1963), p. 3. (Banks was at that time a member of the Liberal Party Executive, Liberal spokesman on social security policy, and Liberal prospective parliamentary candidate for Harrow West.)
27. ibid.
28. ibid., pp. 13–14.
29. ibid., p. 15.
30. ibid., pp. 15–16.
31. ibid., p. 16.
32. ibid., p. 18.
33. ibid., p. 20.
34. ibid.
35. Alan Peacock, *The Welfare Society*, Unservile State Papers no. 2 (London: Liberal Publication Department, 1961), p. 11.
36. ibid, p. 12.
37. ibid.
38. Jo Grimond, *The Liberal Challenge* (London: Hollis & Carter, 1963), p. 13.
39. ibid., p. 7.
40. ibid., pp. 20, 21
41. ibid., p. 23.
42. ibid.
43. ibid., p. 33
44. ibid., p. 10.
45. ibid., p. 142.
46. ibid., pp. 142–3.

47. ibid., p. 140.
48. ibid., pp. 301–2
49. ibid., pp. 144, 155.
50. ibid., pp. 156–7
51. ibid., p. 116.
52. ibid., p. 59.
53. ibid., p. 116.
54. ibid., p. 117
55. ibid., p. 125.
56. ibid.
57. ibid., pp. 297–8
58. ibid., p. 299.
59. ibid.
60. ibid., p. 300.
61. ibid., p. 309
62. ibid.
63. ibid., pp. 316–7.
64. McManus, op. cit., p. 418.
65. Chris Cook, *A Short History of the Liberal Party, 1900–2001*, 6th edn (Basingstoke: Palgrave Macmillan, 2002), p. 141.
66. Dutton, op. cit., p. 199.
67. Wallace, 'Survival and Revival', in Bogdanor (ed.), op. cit., p. 55.
68. Grimond, speech at Liberal Assembly, Brighton, September 1963; reprinted in Duncan Brack and Tony Little (eds), *Great Liberal Speeches* (London: Politico's, 2001), pp. 349, 341–2.
69. Grimond, speech at Carlisle, 20 June 1964; quoted in Peter Barberis, *Liberal Lion: Jo Grimond: A Political Life* (London: I.B.Tauris, 2005), p. 121.
70. Grimond, speech at the National Liberal Club, London, 31 October 1964; quoted in Peter Joyce, *Realignment of the Left? A History of the Relationship between the Liberal Democrat and Labour Parties* (Basingstoke: Macmillan, 1999), p. 135.
71. Grimond, speech at Beckenham, 20 March 1964; quoted in Joyce, op. cit., p. 131.
72. Harry Cowie, *Why Liberal?* (Harmondsworth: Penguin, 1964), p. 11.
73. ibid, p. 43.
74. Liberal Party General Election Manifesto 1964, *Think for Yourself – Vote Liberal*, in Iain Dale (ed.), *Liberal Party General Election Manifestos 1900–1997* (London: Routledge/Politico's, 2000), pp. 107–8.
75. ibid., p. 108.
76. ibid.
77. Cowie, op. cit., p. 38.
78. In an article by Shirley Williams in *The Guardian*, published on the opening day of the Liberal Assembly in late September 1965. See Alastair Hetherington, *The Guardian Years* (London: Chatto & Windus, 1981), p. 326. (Shirley Williams was at that time Labour MP for Hitchin.)
79. *Think for Yourself – Vote Liberal*, in Dale (ed.), op. cit., p. 108
80. ibid., p. 109.
81. Grimond, *Memoirs*, p. 218.
82. ibid., p. 216.
83. Dutton, op. cit., p. 202.
84. See *The Observer*, 18 October 1964; cited in Wallace, 'Survival and Revival', in Bogdanor (ed.), op. cit., p. 57.

85. *The Times*, 8 March 1965; quoted in D. E. Butler and Anthony King, *The British General Election of 1966* (London: Macmillan, 1966), p. 77.
86. See Hetherington, op. cit., p. 324.
87. Grimond, speech at the 1965 Liberal Assembly; quoted in Barberis, op. cit., p. 134.
88. Watkins, *The Liberal Dilemma*, p. 147.
89. Emlyn Hooson, *The Guardian*, 28 June 1965; quoted in Butler and King, op. cit., p. 79. (Emlyn Hooson was at that time Liberal MP for Montgomeryshire.)
90. Nancy Seear, Presidential address at 1965 Liberal Assembly; quoted in Barberis, op. cit., p. 134.
91. *Think for Yourself – Vote Liberal*, in Dale (ed.), op. cit., p. 110.
92. Grimond, *Memoirs*, p. 217.
93. ibid.
94. Liberal Party General Election Manifesto 1966, *For All the People*, in Dale (ed.), op. cit., p. 119.
95. ibid., p. 120.
96. ibid., pp. 120–2.
97. ibid., pp. 120, 121.
98. ibid., p. 132.
99. Wallace, 'Survival and Revival', in Bogdanor (ed.), op. cit., p. 59.
100. ibid., p. 58.
101. Butler and King *The British General Election of 1966*, p. 269.
102. Geoffrey Sell, 'Liberal Revival; Jo Grimond and the Politics of British Liberalism, 1956–67', PhD thesis (University of London, 1996), p. 225.
103. Michael Steed, 'The Electoral Strategy of the Liberal Party', in Bogdanor (ed.), op. cit., p. 84.
104. Sell, op. cit., p. 236.
105. ibid., p. 229.
106. John Campbell, *Roy Jenkins: A Biography* (London: Weidenfeld & Nicholson, 1983), p. 69.
107. See, for instance, Ivor Crewe and Bo Sarlvik, *Decade of Dealignment: The Conservative Victory of 1979 and Electoral Trends in the 1970s* (Cambridge: Cambridge University Press, 1983); Ivor Crewe and David Denver (eds), *Electoral Change in Western Democracies: Patterns and Sources of Electoral Volatility* (London: Croom Helm, 1985).
108. Peter Jenkins, *Mrs Thatcher's Revolution: The Ending of the Socialist Era* (London: Jonathan Cape, 1987), p. 132.
109. Wallace, 'Survival and Revival', in Bogdanor (ed.), op. cit., p. 52.
110. Sell, op. cit., p. 241.
111. Steed, 'The Electoral Strategy of the Liberal Party', in Bogdanor (ed.), op. cit., p. 84.
112. David Steel, *Liberal News*, 23 November 1982.
113. Sell, op. cit., p. 2.
114. See Roy Douglas, *Liberals: A History of the Liberal and Liberal Democrat Parties* (London and Hambledon: Continuum, 2000), p. 271.
115. Michael Steed, 'What Difference Did He Make?' (review of Michael McManus, *Jo Grimond: Towards the Sound of Gunfire*), *Journal of Liberal History*, 40, Autumn 2003, p. 35.
116. Lord Beaumont of Whitley, 'Was Grimond a "Great Man"?', *Journal of Liberal History*, 22, Spring 1999, p. 28.
117. Barberis, op. cit., p. 105.
118. Sell, op. cit., p. 26.

119. ibid., p. 11.
120. Jeremy Thorpe, interview in *The Observer*, September 1973; cited in Dutton, op. cit., p. 208. See, too, Jeremy Thorpe, *In My Own Time: Reminiscences of a Liberal Leader* (London: Politico's, 1999), p. 99.

Chapter 4

1. Chris Cook, *A Short History of the Liberal Party, 1900–2001* (Basingstoke: Palgrave Macmillan, 2002), p. 147.
2. Tony Greaves, 'The Year Things Began to Change', *Liberator*, December 2000, p. 12.
3. David Dutton, *A History of the Liberal Party in the Twentieth Century* (Basingstoke: Palgrave Macmillan, 2004), p. 210.
4. See Ruth Fox and Robert Ingham, 'National League of Young Liberals', in Duncan Brack and Ed Randall (eds), *Dictionary of Liberal Thought* (London: Politico's, 2007), pp. 294–6.
5. ibid., p. 296. On the ideological basis of the Young Liberal movement in the late-1960s, see Simon Hebditch, 'Ideology of Grass Roots Action', in Peter Hain (ed.), *Community Politics* (London: John Calder, 1976), pp. 52–64.
6. See Peter Hellyer, 'Young Liberals: The "Red Guard" Era', *Journal of Liberal Democrat History*, 17, Winter, 1997–98, p. 15.
7. Minutes of Liberal Party National Executive Committee, 31 January 1970, Liberal Party Papers 1/6.
8. Michael Fogarty, 'Liberal Welfare Policy', *New Outlook*, No. 61, February 1967, pp. 16, 18.
9. Arthur Seldon, 'The Case for Vouchers', *New Outlook*, No. 62, March 1967, p. 33
10. Arthur Seldon, 'Liberal Controversy Simplified', *New Outlook*, No. 63, April 1967, p. 33.
11. John Pardoe, 'The Case for Selective Welfare', *New Outlook*, No. 66, September 1967, p. 16.
12. Author's conversation with John Pardoe, 11 June 2008.
13. Richard Lamb, 'Liberal Frustration', *New Outlook*, No. 65, July 1967, pp. 3–4.
14. See Richard Lamb, 'Thorpe and Economic Policy', *New Outlook*, No. 62, March 1967, pp. 3–4.
15. Lamb, 'Liberal Frustration', p. 5.
16. Richard Holme, 'Jeremy's Task', *New Outlook*, No. 65, July 1967, p. 6. (Holme was at that time chairman of the Liberal Campaign Committee.)
17. Minutes of Liberal Party Council, 25 May 1968; cited in Peter Joyce, *Realignment of the Left?* (Basingstoke: Macmillan, 1999), p. 178; see *Liberals Look Ahead* (The Report of the Liberal Commission) (London: Liberal Publication Department, 1969).
18. Donald Wade, *Our Aim and Purpose*, 4th edn (London: Liberal Publication Department, 1967), Foreword.
19. ibid., p. 4.
20. ibid., p. 8.
21. ibid., p. 20.
22. ibid., pp. 21, 22, 23.
23. ibid., p. 23.
24. ibid., p. 28.
25. ibid., pp. 11–13.

26. Samuel Brittan, *Left or Right: The Bogus Dilemma* (London: Secker & Warburg, 1968), p. 11.
27. ibid., p. 137.
28. ibid., pp. 136, 138.
29. Liberal Party General Election Manifesto 1970, *What a Life! Show 'Em You Care*, in Iain Dale (ed.), *Liberal Party General Election Manifestos, 1900–1997* (London: Routledge/Politico's, 2000), pp. 138–9.
30. William Wallace, 'Survival and Revival', in Vernon Bogdanor (ed.), *Liberal Party Politics* (Oxford: Oxford University Press, 1983), p. 65.
31. David Steel, *Against Goliath: David Steel's Story* (London: Weidenfeld & Nicolson, 1989), p. 66.
32. Cook, op. cit., p. 151.
33. Emlyn Hooson, 'What's Left for the Liberals?', *New Outlook*, No. 85, September–October 1970, pp. 3–4.
34. ibid., p. 5.
35. Amendment to resolution on Party Strategy and Tactics, Liberal Assembly, September 1970.
36. Wallace, 'Survival and Revival', in Bogdanor (ed.), op. cit., p. 62.
37. Ruth Fox, 'Young Liberal Influence and Its Effects, 1970–74', *Liberal Democrat History Group Newsletter*, 14, March 1997, p. 18.
38. ibid.
39. Tony Greaves, 'Problems of Self-Government in Pendle', in Hain (ed.), op. cit., pp. 151–2.
40. Author's interview with Gordon Lishman, CBE, London, 3 January 2007.
41. Stuart Mole, 'The Liberal Party and Community Politics', in Bogdanor (ed.), op. cit., p. 259. For expressions of views influencing the development of Liberal community politics, see Tony Greaves and Malcolm MacCallum (eds), *The Blackpool Essays* (London: Gunfire for the National League of Young Liberals, 1967); and Bernard Greaves (ed.), *Scarborough Perspectives* (London: National League of Young Liberals, September 1971).
42. Jo Grimond, *Liberal News*, May 1961; quoted in Alan Watkins, *The Liberal Dilemma* (London: MacGibbon & Kee, 1966), p. 108.
43. Jo Grimond, 'The Nature of Politics', Herbert Samuel Lecture, 13 November 1967 (London: Friends of the Hebrew University of Jerusalem, 1967), p. 3.
44. Joseph Chamberlain, 'A New Political Organisation', *Fortnightly Review*, XXII (1877), p. 126; quoted in Mole, 'The Liberal Party and Community Politics', in Bogdanor (ed.), op. cit., p. 259.
45. Bernard Greaves and Gordon Lishman, *The Theory and Practice of Community Politics* (Hebden Bridge: Association of Liberal Councillors, 1980), reprinted in *Community Politics Today* (Hebden Bridge: Association of Liberal Democrat Councillors, 2006), p. 37.
46. ibid., pp. 10, 11–12. On the broader intellectual and cultural influences shaping community politics, see John Meadowcroft, 'The Origins of Community Politics: New Liberalism, Grimond and the Counter-Culture', *Journal of Liberal Democrat History*, 28, Autumn 2000.
47. Tony Greaves, 'The Year Things Began to Change', p. 13.
48. Fox, 'Young Liberal Influence and Its Effects, 1970–74', p. 17.
49. Dutton, op. cit., p. 218.
50. David Butler and Dennis Kavanagh, *The British General Election of February 1974* (London: Macmillan, 1974), p. 26.

51. Mole, 'The Liberal Party and Community Politics', in Bogdanor (ed.), op. cit., p. 260. See ibid., pp. 260–5 for an account of the Liberals' record in Liverpool.
52. Cook, op. cit., p. 153.
53. Michael Meadowcroft, 'Philosophy behind Strategy' (review of Peter Hain, *Radical Liberalism and Youth Politics*), *Liberal News*, 15 November 1973.
54. Liberal Party General Election Manifesto, February 1974, *Change the Face of Britain: Take Power – Vote Liberal*, in Dale (ed.), op. cit., pp. 147–8.
55. ibid., p. 150.
56. ibid.
57. ibid., p. 154.
58. ibid., p. 155.
59. ibid., p. 156.
60. ibid., pp. 156–7.
61. ibid., pp. 159, 155, 160.
62. ibid., pp. 162–3.
63. Quoted in Dutton, op. cit., p. 220.
64. Butler and Kavanagh, *The British General Election of February 1974*, p. 270.
65. David Butler and Dennis Kavanagh, *The British General Election of October 1974* (London: Macmillan, 1975), p. 47.
66. Butler and Kavanagh, *The British General Election of February 1974*, p. 259.
67. Jeremy Thorpe, *In My Own Time, Reminiscences of a Liberal Leader* (London: Politico's, 1999), p. 99. (Thorpe was referring here, of course, to the increase in Liberal parliamentary representation compared with the situation immediately prior to the February 1974 General Election.)
68. Thorpe had first used this phrase in his letter to Edward Heath following the breakdown of the Downing Street talks. See Butler and Kavanagh, *The British General Election of October 1974*, p. 43n.
69. Quoted in Cook, op. cit., p. 157.
70. Liberal Party General Election Manifesto, October 1974, *Why Britain Needs Liberal Government*, in Dale (ed.), op. cit., p. 171
71. ibid., p. 173.
72. See John Pardoe, *We Must Conquer Inflation* (London: Liberal Publication Department, 1974) for a detailed advocacy of that policy.
73. Duncan Brack, Introduction to Dale (ed.), op. cit., p. 8.
74. See J. Alt, I. Crewe and B. Sarlvik, 'Angels in Plastic: The Liberal Surge in 1974', *Political Studies*, XXV, September 1977.
75. See Butler and Kavanagh, *The British General Election of October 1974*, p. 285.
76. See Chris Cook, 'The Challengers to the Two-Party System', in Chris Cook and John Ramsden (eds), *Trends in British Politics* (London: Macmillan, 1978), p. 132; Ivor Crewe and Bo Sarlvik, *Decade of Dealignment: The Conservative Victory of 1979 and Electoral Trends in the 1970s* (Cambridge: Cambridge University Press, 1983).
77. Dutton, op. cit., p. 219.
78. John Pardoe, 'Towards a Post-Capitalist Society', *Liberal News*, 18 March 1975.
79. ibid.
80. ibid.
81. ibid.
82. John Pardoe, 'What Strategy for Liberals?', *New Outlook*, Vol. 15, Nos 8&9, August–September 1975, p. 16.
83. ibid., pp. 16–17.

84. *Liberalism Today* (London: Liberal Party Organisation, September 1975); Gordon Lishman, 'Searching out the Liberal Soul', *New Outlook*, Vol. 15, Nos 8 & 9, August–September 1975, p. 41.
85. Lishman, op. cit., p. 41.
86. ibid.
87. John Stuart Mill, *On Liberty* [1859] (Harmondsworth: Penguin, 1974), p. 187.
88. Lishman, op. cit., pp. 42–3.
89. Peter Hain, Introduction: 'The Future of Community Politics', in Hain (ed.), op. cit., p. 10.
90. ibid., pp. 21, 24, 25.
91. ibid., pp. 24, 23 On this point, see, too, Hebditch, 'Ideology of Grass Roots Action', in Hain (ed.), op. cit., pp. 52–64.
92. B. Greaves and Lishman, *The Theory and Practice of Community Politics*, in *Community Politics Today* (ALDC, 2006), p. 6.
93. Bernard Greaves, 'The Past and Future of Community Politics', in Greaves and Lishman (eds), *Community Politics Today*, p. 79.
94. For accounts of the Scott affair, see Steel, *Against Goliath*, Chapter 5, pp. 89–110; Simon Freeman and Barrie Penrose, *Rinkagate: The Rise and Fall of Jeremy Thorpe* (London: Bloomsbury, 1996).
95. Steel, op. cit., pp. 108, 107.
96. Dutton, op. cit., p. 208.
97. ibid.
98. Steel, op. cit., p. 109.
99. Wallace, 'Survival and Revival', in Bogdanor (ed.), op. cit., p. 60.
100. Author's conversation with John Pardoe, 11 June 2008.
101. Author's interview with Tony Richards, London, 29 April 2008.
102. Author's interview with Lord Phillips of Sudbury, London, 9 May 2007.
103. Author's interview with Tony Richards, London, 29 April 2008.
104. Richard Lamb, Foreword to Thorpe, *In My Own Time*, p. xviii.
105. Julian Glover, 'Jeremy Thorpe', in Duncan Brack et al. (eds), *Dictionary of Liberal Biography* (London: Politico's, 1998), p. 356.

Chapter 5

1. David Steel, *Liberal News*, July 1970; quoted in David Steel, *Against Goliath, David Steel's Story* (London: Weidenfeld & Nicolson, 1989), p. 70.
2. Steel, *Against Goliath*, p. 86.
3. David Steel, *The Liberal Way Forward*, Strategy 2000, No. 6 (London: Liberal Publication Department, September 1975), p. 14.
4. David Steel, *A House Divided: The Lib-Lab Pact and the Future of British Politics* (London: Weidenfeld & Nicolson, 1980), p. 2.
5. David Dutton, *A History of the Liberal Party in the Twentieth Century* (Basingstoke: Palgrave Macmillan, 2004), p. 227.
6. Steel, *A House Divided*, p. 22.
7. Quoted in Dutton, op. cit., p. 228.
8. Quoted in Steel, *Against Goliath*, p. 120.
9. ibid.
10. ibid., p. 119.
11. ibid., p. 120.

12. For Steel's own account of the formation and development of the Lib-Lab Pact, see Steel, *A House Divided*, passim; and Steel, *Against Goliath*, pp. 127–46.
13. Dutton, op. cit., p. 230.
14. Alastair Michie and Simon Hoggart, *The Pact: The Inside Story of the Lib-Lab Government, 1977–8* (London: Quartet, 1978), p. 183.
15. See Michael Steed, 'The Electoral Strategy of the Liberal Party', in Vernon Bogdanor (ed.), *Liberal Party Politics* (Oxford: Oxford University Press, 1983), p. 94 n27.
16. Jo Grimond, *Memoirs* (London: Heinemann, 1979), p. 250.
17. ibid., p. 251.
18. Steel, *A House Divided*, p. 153.
19. See Dutton, op. cit., p. 231.
20. Grimond, *Memoirs*, p. 255.
21. Jo Grimond, 'Liberal Economics and Democracy' (based on a lecture at the University of Texas in Austin), *New Outlook*, Vol. 16, Nos. 8 & 9, September 1976, pp. 16–19.
22. Grimond, *Memoirs*, p. 257.
23. Jo Grimond, *The Bureaucratic Blight*, Unservile State Papers 22 (London: Liberal Publication Department, 1976), p. 4.
24. ibid., pp. 4, 5.
25. ibid., pp. 9, 10.
26. Robert Bacon and Walter Eltis, *Britain's Economic Problem: Too Few Producers* (London: Macmillan, 1976).
27. Peter Barberis, *Liberal Lion: Jo Grimond: A Political Life* (London: I.B. Tauris, 2005), p. 174.
28. Grimond, *Memoirs*, p. 261.
29. Jo Grimond, *The Common Welfare* (London: Maurice Temple Smith, 1978), pp. 14–15.
30. ibid., pp. 17, 18.
31. ibid., pp. 17–18.
32. ibid, p. 57.
33. ibid., p. 60.
34. ibid., p. 61.
35. ibid., p. 62.
36. ibid., p. 63.
37. ibid.
38. ibid., p. 261. See Robert Oakeshott, *The Case for Workers' Co-ops* (London: Routledge and Kegan Paul, 1978).
39. Grimond, *The Common Welfare*, p. 72
40. See ibid., pp. 72–8.
41. ibid., p. 76.
42. ibid., p. 78.
43. ibid., pp. 200–1. See, too, Stuart Mole, 'The Liberal Party and Community Politics', in Bogdanor (ed.), op. cit., pp. 262–4.
44. Grimond, *The Common Welfare*, p. 213.
45. ibid.
46. ibid., p. 241. On the ideas and projects of Ebenezer Howard, 'the father of the New Towns', see Grimond, *The Common Welfare*, pp. 142–5.
47. Grimond, *Memoirs*, p. 257.
48. Author's interview with John Pardoe, London, 10 May 2007.

49. Gordon Lishman, 'Manifesto for a Magazine', *New Outlook*, Vol. 17, Nos. 8 & 9, September 1977, pp. 9, 13.
50. Author's interview with Gordon Lishman, London, 3 January 2007.
51. Author's interview with Lord Greaves, London, 23 January 2007.
52. Author's interview with John Pardoe, London, 10 May 2007.
53. Author's interview with Gordon Lishman, CBE, London, 3 January 2007.
54. Gordon Lishman, 'Towards a Liberal Society ... Whatever That May Be', *New Outlook*, Vol. 18, No. 2, March 1978, p. 5.
55. ibid., pp. 5–6.
56. ibid., p. 6.
57. ibid.
58. Introduction to Liberal Party General Election Manifesto 1979, *The Real Fight Is for Britain*, by the Rt. Hon. David Steel, MP, in Iain Dale (ed.), *Liberal Party General Election Manifestos, 1900–1997* (London: Routledge/Politico's, 2000), pp. 186–7.
59. See *The Real Fight is for Britain*, in Dale (ed.), op. cit., pp. 189–91.
60. ibid., p. 193.
61. ibid., pp. 193–4.
62. Author's conversation with John Pardoe, 11 June 2008.
63. *The Real Fight is for Britain*, in Dale (ed.), op. cit., p. 194.
64. ibid., p. 195.
65. ibid., p. 197.
66. ibid., p. 199.
67. See William Wallace, 'Survival and Revival', in Bogdanor (ed.), op. cit., p. 71.
68. See Ivor Crewe, 'Is Britain's Two-Party System Really About to Crumble?', *Electoral Studies*, Vol. 1, No. 3 (1982), pp. 280–1; cited in John Curtice, 'Liberal Voters and the Alliance; Realignment or Protest?', in Bogdanor (ed.), op. cit., p. 102.
69. Steel, *A House Divided*, p. 158.

Chapter 6

1. Michael Meadowcroft was at that time chair of the Liberal Party's Assembly Committee.
2. William Wallace, on 'Economics and the Role of the State', in 1979 Liberal Assembly Philosophy Debate, Liberal Party Papers 23/1. (Wallace was at that time a member of the Liberal Party's Standing Committee.)
3. ibid.
4. Ian Bradley, 1979 Liberal Assembly Philosophy Debate, LPP 23/1.
5. Roy Jenkins, 'Home Thoughts from Abroad', Dimbleby Lecture, London, 22 November 1979; reprinted in Roy Jenkins, *Partnership of Principle: Writings and Speeches on the Making of the Alliance* (ed. Clive Lindley) (London: The Radical Centre/Secker & Warburg, 1985), pp. 9, 15.
6. ibid., pp. 20, 21.
7. ibid., p. 20.
8. ibid., pp. 20–1.
9. ibid., pp. 21–2.
10. David Steel, *Against Goliath: David Steel's Story* (London: Weidenfeld and Nicolson, 1989), p. 217.
11. ibid., p. 216. See, too, Roy Jenkins, *A Life at the Centre* (London: Macmillan, 1991), p. 514.

12. See Tudor Jones, *Remaking the Labour Party: From Gaitskell to Blair* (London: Routledge, 1996), Chapter 5.
13. See Evan Luard, *Socialism without the State* (London: Macmillan, 1979) and *Socialism at the Grass Roots*, Fabian Tract 468 (London: Fabian Society, April 1980); David Marquand (ed.), *John P. Mackintosh on Parliament and Social Democracy* (London: Longman, 1982).
14. See David Marquand, 'Inquest on a Movement', *Encounter*, July 1979, p. 9.
15. ibid., p. 18.
16. *Liberal News*, editorial: 'An Eye on the Future', 11 December, 1979, p. 4. (The editor at that time was Terence Wynn.)
17. Jo Grimond, speech at Watford in support of Dane Clouston, Liberal parliamentary candidate at the S.W. Herts by-election; quoted in *Liberal News*, 4 December, 1979.
18. David Steel, *A House Divided: The Lib-Lab Pact and the Future of British Politics* (London: Weidenfeld and Nicolson, 1980), p. 163.
19. David Steel, *Against Goliath*, p. 216.
20. David Steel, *Labour at 80: Time to Retire* (London: Liberal Publication Department, April 1980), p. 2.
21. ibid., p. 8.
22. ibid., pp. 9, 10.
23. ibid., p. 12.
24. Quoted in David Owen, *Time to Declare* (London: Michael Joseph, 1991), p. 439.
25. ibid.
26. ibid., p. 441.
27. ibid., p. 428.
28. Roy Jenkins, Speech to the Parliamentary Press Gallery, London, 9 June 1980; reprinted in Jenkins, *Partnership of Principle*, pp. 24–5.
29. ibid., pp. 25,26.
30. Owen, op. cit., p. 439.
31. David Owen, Bill Rodgers and Shirley Williams, Open Letter to *The Guardian*, 1 August 1980; quoted in Owen, op. cit., p. 447.
32. See Owen, op. cit., pp. 452ff.
33. Roy Jenkins, *European Diary* (London: Collins, 1989), p. 645.
34. On the political manoeuvres behind this decision, see Owen, op. cit., pp. 479–80.
35. Desmond Banks, 'But Just What Is a Social Democrat?', *Liberal News*, 2 September, 1980, p. 8.
36. Ralf Dahrendorf, *After Social Democracy*, Unservile State Paper 25 (London: Liberal Publication Department, 1980), p. 1.
37. ibid., p. 2.
38. ibid., p. 2–3, 4.
39. ibid., p. 20.
40. ibid., p. 2.
41. Jo Grimond, Inaugural 80 Club Lecture to the Association of Liberal Lawyers, National Liberal Club, London, 29 October 1980; reprinted in Duncan Brack and Tony Little (eds), *Great Liberal Speeches* (London: Politico's, 2001), p. 351.
42. ibid., p. 355.
43. ibid.
44. ibid., p. 359.
45. ibid., p. 360.

46. Bernard Greaves, 'The Past and Future of Community Politics', in *Community Politics Today* (Hebden Bridge: Association of Liberal Democrat Councillors, 2006), p. 79.
47. Bernard Greaves and Gordon Lishman, *The Theory and Practice of Community Politics* (Hebden Bridge: Association of Liberal Councillors, 1980); reprinted in *Community Politics Today*, p. 8.
48. ibid.
49. ibid., pp. 8–9.
50. Gordon Lishman, 'Community Politics', *New Outlook*, Vol. 21, No. 1 (1981), p. 22.
51. Author's interview with Lord Greaves, London, 23 January 2007.
52. Lishman, 'Community Politics', p. 22.
53. Greaves and Lishman, op. cit., p. 9.
54. Author's interview with Gordon Lishman, London, 3 January 2007.
55. Bernard Greaves, 'The Past and Future of Community Politics', p. 79.
56. Jo Grimond, *A Personal Manifesto* (London: Martin Robertson, 1983), p. 25.
57. Jo Grimond, 'Liberalism, the Free Market and Original Sin', *The Daily Telegraph*, 17 September 1985, p. 14.
58. Desmond Banks, 'Community Politics', *Liberal News*, 9 August, 1973.
59. Author's interview with Lord Greaves, London, 23 January 2007.
60. Michael McManus, *Jo Grimond: Towards the Sound of Gunfire* (Edinburgh: Birlinn, 2001), p. 397.
61. 'David Steel talks to Christopher Layton', *New Democrat*, November/December 1983, pp. 16–17.
62. David Thomson, *The Shocktroops of Pavement Politics? An Assessment of the Influence of Community Politics in the Liberal Party* (Hebden Bridge: Hebden Royd, September 1985), pp. 28–9.
63. ibid., p. 37.
64. ibid., p. 29.
65. Michael Meadowcroft, interviewed in *Marxism Today*, February 1984; quoted in Thomson, op. cit., p. 29.
66. Author's conversation with Michael Meadowcroft, 14 August 2008.
67. Michael Steed, 'The Electoral Strategy of the Liberal Party', in Vernon Bogdanor (ed.), *Liberal Party Politics* (Oxford: Oxford University Press, 1983), p. 91.
68. ibid.
69. Author's interview with Lord Greaves, London, 23 January 2007.
70. Simon Hughes, 'The Aims Remain the Same', in Association of Liberal Democrat Councillors, *Community Politics Today*, p. 40.
71. Thomson, op. cit., p. 37.
72. See David Marquand, 'Taming Leviathan: Social Democracy and Decentralisation', Rita Hinden Memorial Lecture, London, 23 February 1980 (London: Socialist Commentary Publications, 1980).
73. The Limehouse Declaration, 25 January 1981 ('The Declaration for Social Democracy'), reprinted in Jenkins, *Partnership of Principle*, p. 28.
74. ibid.
75. ibid.
76. Jenkins, *A Life at the Centre*, p. 535.
77. Owen, *Time to Declare*, p. 519.
78. See ibid., pp. 497–8.
79. Jenkins, *A Life at the Centre*, p. 535.

80. Steel, *Against Goliath*, p. 223.
81. Owen, *Time to Declare*, pp. 484–5.
82. ibid., p. 499.
83. David Marquand, *The Progressive Dilemma: From Lloyd George to Blair*, 2nd edn (London: Phoenix, 1999), p. 196.
84. See Chapter 1 ('Social Democratic Values') and Chapter 4 ('The Social Democratic Tradition') of the abridged and revised edition of David Owen, *Face the Future* (Oxford: Oxford University Press, 1981). For Owen's comment on these amendments, see Owen, *Time to Declare*, p. 499.
85. Owen, *Time to Declare*, p. 483.
86. Owen, *Face the Future* (abridged and revised edn), p. 55.
87. Author's interview with David Marquand, Oxford, 7 March 2007.
88. Alan Beith, 'The Gang and its Valuables', *Alliance*, November 1982, p. 30.
89. Jo Grimond, 'Is There a Middle Ground?', *The Spectator*, 31 January 1981, p. 11.
90. Jo Grimond, 'An Alliance of Principle', *The Spectator*, 11 April 1981, p. 9.
91. ibid.
92. Ivor Crewe and Anthony King, *SDP: The Birth, Life and Death of the Social Democratic Party* (Oxford: Oxford University Press, 1995), p. 177.
93. Jo Grimond, 'Widening the Agenda', *The Spectator*, 27 June 1981, p. 12; 'An Alliance of Principle', p. 9.
94. Grimond, 'Widening the Agenda', p. 12.
95. Crewe and King, op. cit., p. 60.
96. Jenkins, *A Life at the Centre*, p. 527. For Grimond's original comment, see McManus, op. cit., p. 350.
97. Michael Meadowcroft, 'An Alliance with Social Democrats Must Be Considered – Very Carefully', *Liberal News*, 17 March 1981.
98. Michael Meadowcroft, *Liberal Values for a New Decade*, 2nd edn (Manchester: North West Community Newspapers, September 1981), p. 1. (First edition published September 1980.) See, too, Michael Meadowcroft, *Social Democracy – Barrier or Bridge?* (London: Liberator Publications, August 1981).
99. Author's conversation with Michael Meadowcroft, 14 August 2008.
100. Thomson, op. cit., p. 22.
101. For significant examples of the use of the terms 'social democratic' and 'social democracy' in British political literature during the early 1970s, see Anthony Crosland, *A Social Democratic Britain*, Fabian Tract 404 (London: Fabian Society, January 1971); and J. P. Mackintosh, 'Socialism or Social Democracy? The Choice for the Labour Party', *The Political Quarterly*, Vol. 43, No. 4, October–December 1972.
102. Author's interview with the Rt. Hon. Lord Owen of the City of Plymouth, London, 29 November 2006.
103. Gordon Lishman, 'Alliance, but What Next?', *New Outlook*, September 1981, p. 2.
104. ibid., p. 3.
105. See Peter Clarke, *Liberals and Social Democrats* (Cambridge: Cambridge University Press, 1978), pp. 5, 65.
106. L. T. Hobhouse, *Liberalism* [first published 1911] (New York: Oxford University Press, 1964), p. 73.
107. Dahrendorf, op. cit., p. 19.
108. Michael Meadowcroft, *Liberalism and the Left* (London: Liberator Publications, 1982), p. 26.

109. Alan Beith, *The Case for the Liberal Party and the Alliance* (London: Longman, 1983), p. 25.
110. Author's interview with Lord Greaves, London, 23 January 2007.
111. Ian Bradley, *The Strange Rebirth of Liberal Britain* (London: Chatto & Windus/ The Hogarth Press, 1985), p. 171.
112. David Marquand, *The Progressive Dilemma: From Lloyd George to Kinnock* (London: Phoenix, 1991), p. 212.
113. See David Sassoon, *One Hundred Years of Socialism: The West European Left in the Twentieth Century* (London: I.B. Tauris, 1996), esp. Chapter 24.
114. Author's interview with David Marquand, Oxford, 7 March 2007.
115. Author's interview with the Rt. Hon. Baroness Williams of Crosby, London, 16 January 2007.
116. Author's interview with Lord Holme of Cheltenham, London, 22 November 2006.
117. Author's interview with Lord Greaves, London, 23 January 2007.
118. See Dutton, *A History of the Liberal Party in the Twentieth Century* (Basingstoke: Palgrave Macmillan, 2004), p. 246.
119. David Steel, 1981 Liberal Assembly speech; reprinted in Brack and Little (eds), op. cit., p. 402.
120. On these developments, see Crewe and King, op. cit., p. 140; Steel, *Against Goliath*, pp. 225–6; Jenkins, *A Life at the Centre*, pp. 546–7; Owen, *Time to Declare*, p. 525; McManus, op. cit., pp. 350–1; and Barberis, *Liberal Lion: Jo Grimond: A Political Life* (London: I.B. Tauris, 2005), p. 186.
121. Chris Cook, *A Short History of the Liberal Party* (Basingstoke: Palgrave Macmillan, 2002), p. 169.
122. Dutton, op. cit., pp. 249–50.
123. See Owen, *Time to Declare*, p. 559. For a contrasting view of the 1982 seats deal, see Crewe and King, op. cit., pp. 189–90.
124. Owen, *Time to Declare*, p. 560.
125. 'Roy Jenkins: The Future of the Partnership', an interview with Christopher Layton, *Alliance*, No. 1, June 1982, p. 19. (The journal *Alliance* was launched in June 1982.)
126. Dick Taverne, 'One Party or Two?', *Alliance*, No. 2, July 1982, p. 10.
127. Beith, 'The Gang and Its Valuables', p. 30.
128. Beith, *The Case for the Liberal Party and the Alliance* (London: Longman, 1983).
129. Barberis, op. cit., p. 186.
130. Grimond, *A Personal Manifesto*, p. viii.
131. ibid., p. 2.
132. ibid., p. 24.
133. ibid., p. 25.
134. ibid., p. 160.
135. ibid., p. 168.
136. ibid., pp. 168, 160.
137. Bradley, op. cit., p. 174. On the Tawney Society, the SDP's think-tank, see Tudor Jones, 'The Tawney Society', in Brack and Randall (eds), *Dictionary of Liberal Thought* (London: Politico's, 2007), pp. 394–5.
138. SDP/Liberal Alliance General Election Manifesto 1983, *Working Together for Britain*, in Iain Dale (ed.), *Liberal Party General Election Manifestos, 1900–1997* (London: Routledge/Politico's, 2000), p. 205.
139. ibid., pp. 206, 205.

140. ibid., p. 209.
141. ibid., p. 210.
142. ibid., p. 214.
143. ibid., pp. 211–12.
144. ibid., pp. 217–18.
145. ibid., pp. 225–8.
146. ibid., pp. 224–5.
147. ibid., pp. 229–30.
148. ibid., p. 231.
149. ibid., p. 233.
150. Crewe and King, op. cit., p. 214.
151. ibid.
152. Quoted in ibid., p. 214.
153. Author's interview with David Marquand, Oxford, 7 March 2007.

Chapter 7

1. See David Steel, *Against Goliath David Steel's Story* (London: Weidenfeld and Nicolson, 1989), pp. 249–53.
2. Ivor Crewe and Anthony King, *SDP: The Birth, Life and Death of the Social Democratic Party* (Oxford: Oxford University Press, 1995), p. 303.
3. Dick Taverne, 'Taverne Calls for a Federal Union', *Liberal News*, 24 January 1984.
4. Desmond Banks, 'Individualism Does Not Ensure Liberty', *Liberal News*, 1 February 1983.
5. David Owen, *Time to Declare* (London: Michael Joseph, 1991), p. 599.
6. ibid., p. 598.
7. See ibid., pp. 599, 165–6.
8. Author's interview with the Rt. Hon. Lord Owen of the City of Plymouth, London, 27 November 2006.
9. Peter Jenkins, 'Whoever Is To Wrest Power from Mrs Thatcher Must Fight Her on Her Own Ground', *The Guardian*, 14 September 1983.
10. See Duncan Brack, 'Social Market', in Duncan Brack and Ed Randall (eds), *Dictionary of Liberal Thought* (London: Politico's, 2007), pp. 386–9.
11. See *Why Britain Needs a Social Market Economy* (London: Centre for Policy Studies, 1975).
12. David Owen, 'The Social Market', Fourth Hoover Address, University of Strathclyde, May 1981, p. 3.
13. ibid., pp. 3–4
14. Jo Grimond, 'Widening the Agenda', *The Spectator*, 27 June 1981.
15. Owen, 'The Social Market', p. 4.
16. ibid., pp. 8, 18.
17. David Owen, 'Agenda for Competition and Compassion', *Economic Affairs*, 4 (October 1983), pp. 26–33.
18. Owen, *Time to Declare*, p. 598.
19. David Owen, *A Future That Will Work: Competitiveness and Compassion* (Harmondsworth: Penguin, 1984), p. 10.
20. ibid., p. 27.
21. ibid., p. 10.
22. ibid., p. 8.
23. Quotation on the cover of paperback edition of *A Future That Will Work*.

24. Owen, *A Future That Will Work*, p. 28
25. ibid., p. 29.
26. See Alex de Mont, *A Theory of the Social Market* (London: Tawney Society, 1984); Nick Bosanquet, 'The Social Market: Principles behind the Policies?', *The Political Quarterly*, Vol. 55, No. 3, July–September 1984.
27. 'No to Fusion: David Owen talks to Richard Lamb', *New Democrat*, September/October 1983, p. 14.
28. See Ivor Crewe and Anthony King, *SDP: The Birth, Life and Death of the Social Democratic Party* (Oxford: Oxford University Press, 1995), p. 335; Roy Jenkins, *A Life at the Centre* (London: Macmillan, 1991), p. 585.
29. William Rodgers, 'My Party – Wet or Dry?', Tawney Society Lecture, 16 May 1985 (London: Tawney Society, 1985), pp. 6, 12; quoted in Crewe and King, op. cit., p. 335.
30. Roy Jenkins, 'A Junior Thatcherite Party? Not While I'm Alive', report of Roy Jenkins, 'Three Years from Warrington: Retrospect and Prospect', Tawney Society Lecture, July 1984; quoted in *Liberal News*, 17 July 1984.
31. Jenkins, *A Life at the Centre*, p. 585.
32. ibid.
33. Author's interview with the Rt. Hon. Sir Alan Beith, MP, London, 13 December 2006.
34. Alex de Mont, 'The Social Market Revisited', *New Democrat*, April/May 1985, p. 7.
35. ibid.
36. See Sam Brittan, 'Home Truths from the Marketplace', *Alliance*, November 1982, p. 12.
37. Sam Brittan, Foreword to Nick Bosanquet, *After the New Right* (London Heinemann, 1983), p. vii.
38. Quoted in Leighton Andrews, *Liberalism after Thatcher* (Hebden Bridge: Hebden Royd, 1985), p. 3.
39. 'Interview with Malcolm Bruce', *Liberal News*, 26 February 1985.
40. Malcolm Bruce, 'The Politics of Economics', *New Democrat*, April/May 1985, p. 9.
41. ibid.
42. ibid., pp. 9–10.
43. ibid., p. 10.
44. Malcolm Bruce, *Markets and the Responsible State* (Hebden Bridge: Liberal Party Publications, September 1985), p. 3.
45. Michael Meadowcroft, LINk Bulletin, March 1984; quoted in Leighton Andrews, *Liberals versus the Social Market Economy* (Hebden Bridge: Hebden Royd, September 1985), p. 15.
46. Andrews, op. cit., pp. 16, 4, 19.
47. Personal communication to the author from Michael Meadowcroft, 5 November 2008.
48. Andrews, op. cit., p. 18.
49. ibid., p. 17.
50. Author's interview with Michael Meadowcroft, London, 8 October 2008.
51. Leighton Andrews, *Liberty in Britain* (Hebden Bridge: Hebden Royd, 1985), pp. 4, 7.
52. ibid., pp. 4, 8.
53. ibid., p. 4.

54. Andrews, *Liberals versus the Social Market Economy*, pp. 21, 22.
55. Author's interview with Lord Greaves, London, 23 January 2007.
56. Author's interview with the Rt. Hon. Sir Alan Beith, MP, London, 13 December 2006.
57. Owen, *Time to Declare*, p. 599.
58. Charles Moore, 'Dr Owen's Model', *The Spectator*, 17 September 1983; quoted in Andrews, *Liberals Versus the Social Market Economy*, p. 11.
59. See Duncan Brack, *The Myth of the Social Market Economy: A Critique of Owenite Economics* (London: LINk Publications, 1989); 'David Owen and the Social Market Economy', *Journal of Liberal History*, 47, Summer 2005.
60. David Marquand, *The Progressive Dilemma: From Lloyd George to Blair*, 2nd edn (London: Phoenix, 1999), p. 201.
61. Ralf Dahrendorf, 'The New Social State: a Liberal Perspective', in David Steel and Richard Holme (eds), *Partners in One Nation: a New Vision for Britain 2000* (London: Bodley Head, 1985), p. 73.
62. Author's interview with Lord Greaves, London, 23 January 2007.
63. Brack, 'David Owen and the Social Market Economy', p. 55.
64. Author's interview with the Rt. Hon. Lord Rodgers of Quarry Bank, London, 1 November 2006; author's interview with the Rt. Hon. Charles Kennedy, MP, Oxford, 30 January 2008.
65. Author's interview with Lord Kirkwood of Kirkhope, London, 5 July 2007.
66. Crewe and King, op. cit., p. 334.
67. Dick Taverne, 'What's New from the SDP?', *New Democrat*, Vol. III, No. 5, 1985, p. 10.
68. *Defence and Disarmament*, Report of the Joint SDP/Liberal Alliance Commission (Hebden Bridge: Hebden Royd, 1986).
69. On the 1986 Alliance defence dispute, see in particular Crewe and King, op. cit., pp. 341–56. For accounts of the dispute from the different viewpoints of some of the key participants, see Jenkins, *A Life at the Centre*, pp. 588–92; Michael Meadowcroft, 'Eastbourne Revisited', *The Radical Quarterly*, No. 5, Autumn 1987, pp. 21–30; Owen, *Time to Declare*, pp. 642–57; William Rodgers, *Fourth among Equals* (London: Politico's, 2000), pp. 249–54; Steel, *Against Goliath*, pp. 263–6.
70. Crewe and King, op. cit., p. 355.
71. Chris Cook, *A Short History of the Liberal Party 1900–2001*, 6th edn (Basingstoke: Palgrave Macmillan, 2002), p. 183.
72. Crewe and King, op. cit., p. 367.
73. David Steel, foreword to David Owen and David Steel, *The Time Has Come* (London: Weidenfeld and Nicolson, 1987), p. 11.
74. Owen and Steel, *The Time Has Come*, p. 56.
75. ibid., p. 38, 39.
76. See ibid., pp. 43–6, 40–42.
77. ibid., pp. 22–3.
78. David Owen, *Social Market and Social Justice*, Tawney Society 5th Anniversary Lecture, 25 January 1987 (London: Tawney Society, 1987), p. 1.
79. ibid.
80. ibid., pp. 1, 2.
81. ibid., p. 3.
82. ibid.
83. ibid.

84. ibid., pp. 3–4.
85. ibid., p. 4.
86. See Brack, *The Myth of the Social Market Economy*, pp. 35–6; Crewe and King, op. cit., p. 423.
87. Chris Huhne, 'In the Social Market the Consumer is King', *The Guardian*, 8 July 1987; quoted in Brack, ibid., p. 57. See, too, Peter Kellner, 'Owen's Ideas Deserve to Survive the SDP Battle', *The Independent*, 6 July 1987.
88. Interview with Jo Grimond in F. Bolkestein (ed.), *Modern Liberalism: Conversations with Liberal Politicians* (New York: Elsevier, 1982), pp. 93, 94.
89. Duncan Brack, 'Introduction' to Iain Dale (ed.), *Liberal Party General Election Manifestos, 1900–1997* (London: Routledge/Politico's, 2000), p. 12.
90. Richard Holme, 'Alliance Days', *Journal of Liberal Democrat History*, 18, Spring 1998, p. 12.
91. ibid.
92. Quoted in Crewe and King, op. cit., p. 374
93. Foreword to SDP/Liberal Alliance General Election Manifesto 1987, *Britain United: The Time Has Come*, in Dale (ed.), op. cit., p. 237
94. ibid., pp. 242–3.
95. Richard Holme, *The People's Kingdom* (Hebden Bridge: Liberal Party Publications, 1987), p. 10.
96. ibid., p. 22.
97. ibid., pp. 27–8.
98. Richard Holme, 'Political Accountability and the Exercise of Power', in Steel and Holme (eds), op. cit., p. 84.
99. *Britain United*, in Dale (ed.), op. cit., pp. 248–9.
100. ibid., p. 249.
101. ibid., pp. 250–1.
102. ibid., p. 239.
103. ibid., pp. 273–4.
104. Quoted in Owen, *Time to Declare*, p. 692.
105. ibid.
106. ibid., p. 682.
107. On the 1987 Alliance General Election campaign, see Crewe and King, op. cit., pp. 374–82; Owen, *Time to Declare*, Chapter 34 (pp. 681–706); John Pardoe, 'The Alliance Campaign', in Ivor Crewe and Martin Harrop (eds), *Political Communications: The General Election Campaign of 1987* (Cambridge: Cambridge University Press, 1989), pp. 55–9; Steel, *Against Goliath*, pp. 277–82; Des Wilson, *Battle for Power* (London: Sphere Books, 1987).
108. See Crewe and King, op. cit., pp. 385–6; Owen, *Time to Declare*, pp. 707–8; Steel, *Against Goliath*, pp. 282–4.
109. See Steel, *Against Goliath*, p. 267
110. David Butler and Dennis Kavanagh, *The British General Election of 1987* (London: Macmillan, 1988), p. 76; quoted in Steel, ibid., p. 283.
111. See Crewe and King, op. cit., pp. 401–2.
112. Quoted in Owen, *Time to Declare*, p. 722.
113. Crewe and King, op. cit., p. 396.
114. See Alan Beith, *The Fullness of Freedom: Policy Priorities for Achieving a Liberal Society*, Liberal Challenge No. 9 (Hebden Bridge: Hebden Royd, 1987).
115. See Paddy Ashdown, *After the Alliance: Setting the New Political Agenda* (Hebden Bridge: Hebden Royd, 1987).

116. On the merger negotiations, see: Crewe and King, op. cit., Chapter 21 (pp. 411–40);
Cook, op. cit., Chapter 16 (pp. 188–201); Dutton, *A History of the Liberal Party in
the Twentieth Century* (Basingstoke: Palgrave Macmillan, 2004), pp. 264–9; Tony
Greaves and Rachael Pitchford, *Merger – The Inside Story* (Colne: Liberal Renewal,
1989), passim; Jenkins, *A Life at the Centre*, pp. 596–600; Owen, *Time to Declare*,
pp. 707–42; Rodgers, *Fourth Among Equals*, pp. 258–62; Steel, *Against Goliath*,
pp. 282–93.
117. This was an allusion to the 1969 Monty Python television comedy sketch in
which a pet-shop customer has been sold a dead parrot. On the 'dead parrot'
episode, see Crewe and King, op. cit., pp. 425–37.
118. Cook, op. cit., p. 200.
119. ibid., p. 188.
120. Jenkins, *A Life at the Centre*, p. 535.
121. Cook, op. cit., p. 201.

Chapter 8

1. David Dutton, *A History of the Liberal Party in the Twentieth Century* (Basingstoke:
Palgrave Macmillan, 2004), p. 269.
2. Gordon Lishman, 'Issues for Radicals', *The Radical Quarterly*, No. 7, Spring 1988,
p. 45. (*The Radical Quarterly* was launched in autumn 1986, under the joint editor-
ship of Tony Greaves and Hannan Rose, as a successor to *New Outlook*.)
3. ibid., p. 47.
4. Paddy Ashdown, 'Building the Future Together', *The Radical Quarterly*, No. 8,
Summer 1988, p. 14.
5. ibid., p. 16.
6. Alan Beith, 'Leading the Team', *The Radical Quarterly*, No. 8, Summer 1988,
p. 21.
7. Alan Beith, *Leadership for Freedom* (Hebden Bridge: Hebden Royd, 1988), p. 6.
8. David Marquand, *The New Reckoning: Capitalism, States and Markets* (Cambridge:
Polity Press, 1997), p. 25.
9. David Marquand, *The Unprincipled Society: New Demands and Old Politics* (London:
Jonathan Cape/Fontana Press, 1988), pp. 12–13.
10. Marquand, *The New Reckoning*, p. 26.
11. ibid.
12. Marquand, *The Unprincipled Society*, p. 239.
13. ibid., pp. 226, 224–5.
14. See Chapter 7 above, n85.
15. See *The Radical Quarterly*, No. 8, Summer 1988, pp. 68–70.
16. *The Radical Quarterly*, Editorial, No. 9, Autumn 1988, p. 10.
17. See Paddy Ashdown, *The Ashdown Diaries Volume 1: 1988–1997* (London: Allen
Lane/The Penguin Press, 2000), p. 12; entry for 24 September 1988.
18. *The Radical Quarterly*, No. 8, Summer 1988, p. 4.
19. Alan Beith, quoted in Tony Greaves and Rachael Pitchford, *Merger: The Inside Story*
(Colne: Liberal Renewal, 1989), p. 89.
20. Author's interview with the Rt. Hon. Sir Alan Beith, MP, London, 13 December
2006.
21. Chris Cook, *A Short History of the Liberal Party*, 6th edn (Basingstoke: Palgrave
Macmillan, 2002), p. 204.
22. Ashdown, *The Ashdown Diaries Volume 1*, p. 50; entry for 15 June 1989.

23. ibid., p. 56; entry for 25 June 1989.
24. See Don MacIver, 'Political Strategy', in Don MacIver (ed.), *The Liberal Democrats* (Hemel Hempstead: Prentice Hall/Harvester Wheatsheaf, 1996), p. 183.
25. *Our Different Vision: Themes and Values for Social and Liberal Democrats* (Hebden Bridge: Hebden Royd, January 1989), pp. 8–9.
26. ibid., p. 10.
27. Leighton Andrews, 'Manifesto for Realignment' (review of *Our Different Vision*), *New Democrat*, Vol. VII, No. 1, 1989, p. 13. (*New Democrat* was launched in April 1983 as, in its own description, 'an independent magazine of the radical centre'.)
28. ibid.
29. See Greaves and Pitchford, op. cit., p. 128.
30. Preamble to the Constitution of the Liberal Democrats, quoted in MacIver (ed.), op. cit., p. 245.
31. David Johnson, 'The Primacy of Liberty', *The Radical Quarterly*, No. 15, Spring 1990, p. 38.
32. ibid., p. 40.
33. Ashdown, *The Ashdown Diaries Volume 1*, p. 44; entry for 14 May 1989.
34. Paddy Ashdown, *Citizens' Britain: A Radical Agenda for the 1990s* (London: Fourth Estate, 1989), p. 22.
35. ibid., p. 32.
36. ibid., p. 36.
37. ibid., p. 43.
38. ibid. On this point, see, too: *Our Different Vision*, p. 17.
39. Ashdown, *The Ashdown Diaries Volume 1*, p. 11 n1; on Ashdown's admission of error, see too: Paddy Ashdown, *The Ashdown Diaries Volume 2: 1997–1999* (London: Allen Lane/The Penguin Press, 2001), p. 494.
40. 'Ashdown as Leader', interviews with Paddy Ashdown by Duncan Brack, Andrew Rawnsley and Harriet Smith, *Journal of Liberal Democrat History*, Spring 2001, p. 12.
41. Author's interview with the Rt. Hon. Lord Ashdown of Norton-sub-Hampton, London, 20 February 2007.
42. 'Ashdown as Leader', op. cit., p. 5.
43. Author's interview with the Rt. Hon. Lord Ashdown of Norton-sub-Hampton, London, 20 February 2007.
44. On this overall policy shift, see, for instance, *Economics for the Future*, Liberal Democrat Federal White Paper 4, 1991.
45. See Duncan Brack, 'Liberal Democrat Policy', in MacIver (ed.), op. cit., p. 107 n15.
46. Liberal Democrat General Election Manifesto 1992, *Changing Britain for Good*, in Iain Dale (ed.), *Liberal Party General Election Manifestos 1900–1997* (London: Routledge/Politico's, 2000), p. 282.
47. ibid., pp. 289–90.
48. ibid., p. 292.
49. ibid., p. 299.
50. ibid., pp. 295, 297.
51. ibid., pp. 310, 311.
52. ibid., pp. 315–18.
53. ibid., p. 288.
54. *The Independent*, 'The Case for the Liberal Democrats', 8 April 1992; Editorial, *The Guardian*, 19 March 1992, quoted in Brack, 'Liberal Democrat Policy', pp. 93, 89.
55. *The Guardian*, 6 April 1992; quoted in Cook, op. cit., p. 209.
56. See Dutton, op. cit., pp. 275–6.

57. Ashdown, *The Ashdown Diaries Volume 1*, p. 159; entry for 10 April 1992.
58. Ashdown, *The Ashdown Diaries Volume 2*, p. 493.
59. See Ashdown's obituary of Lord Holme of Cheltenham, *The Independent*, 17 May 2008, p. 32.
60. Duncan Brack, 'Liberal Democrat Leadership: The Cases of Ashdown and Kennedy', *The Political Quarterly*, Vol. 78, No. 1, January–March 2007, p. 81.
61. Paddy Ashdown, speech at Chard, Somerset, 9 May 1992; republished in Duncan Brack and Tony Little (eds), *Great Liberal Speeches* (London: Politico's, 2001), p. 426.
62. ibid., p. 427.
63. Ashdown, *The Ashdown Diaries Volume 1*, p. 163 n2. On the unpopularity of the Chard speech among much of the Liberal Democrat parliamentary party, see ibid., pp. 164–6.
64. See Tudor Jones, *Remaking the Labour Party* (London: Routledge, 1996), Chapter 6.
65. See MacIver, 'Political Strategy', in MacIver (ed.), op. cit., p. 185.
66. Brack, 'Liberal Democrat Policy', in MacIver (ed.), op. cit., p. 90.
67. *Facing up to the Future: Enduring Values in a Changing World* (Dorchester: Liberal Democrat Publications, June 1993), p. 11.
68. ibid., pp. 11, 16–18.
69. ibid., p. 13.
70. ibid.
71. Dutton, op. cit., p. 278.
72. Ashdown, *The Ashdown Diaries Volume 1*, p. 273; entry for 8 August 1994.
73. 'Ashdown as Leader', op. cit., p. 7.
74. Author's interview with the Rt. Hon. Lord Ashdown of Norton-sub-Hampton, London, 20 February 2007.
75. Ashdown, *The Ashdown Diaries Volume 1*, p. 77 n1.
76. Paddy Ashdown, *Making Change Our Ally* (Dorchester: Liberal Democrat Publications, 1994), p. 2.
77. ibid., p. 4.
78. ibid., p. 16–17.
79. Ashdown, *The Ashdown Diaries Volume 1*, p. 258; entry for 21 April 1994.
80. 'Ashdown as Leader', op. cit., p. 11.
81. Ashdown, *The Ashdown Diaries Volume 1*, p. 244; entry for 1 December 1993.
82. On the background to the decision, see Alan Leaman, 'Ending Equidistance', *The Political Quarterly*, Vol. 69, 1998, pp. 160–9.
83. Alan Leaman, 'The End of Equidistance', *The Reformer*, Summer 1997, p. 4. (*The Reformer* had been launched in autumn 1993 as a periodical dedicated to the discussion and debate of Liberal Democrat policy and strategy.) On these policy reverses, see Ashdown, *The Ashdown Diaries Volume 1*, pp. 281–2; entry for 19 September 1994.
84. Ashdown, op. cit., p. 419; entry for 9 April 1996.
85. ibid., p. 324; entry for 11 June 1995.
86. ibid., p. 463; entry for 1 October 1996.
87. Tony Blair, speech at the Fabian Society commemoration of the 50th anniversary of the 1945 General Election, 5 July 1995; published in Tony Blair, *New Britain: My Vision of a Young Country* (London: Fourth Estate, 1996), p. 7.
88. ibid., p. 12. On Blair's recognition of the historical and ideological links between 'New' Labour and radical Liberalism, see Steven Fielding, 'New Labour and

the Past', in D. Tanner, P. Thane and N. Tiratsoo (eds), *Labour's First Century* (Cambridge: Cambridge University Press, 2000), pp. 367–92; and Steven Fielding, *The Labour Party: Continuity and Change in the Making of New Labour* (Basingstoke: Palgrave Macmillan, 2003), Chapter 2.

89. Philip Gould, *The Unfinished Revolution: How the Modernisers Saved the Labour Party* (London: Abacus, 1999), pp. 27, 397.
90. Ashdown, *The Ashdown Diaries Volume 1*, p. 456; entry for 5 September 1996.
91. ibid., p. 357: entry for 12 November 1995; p. 276: entry for 4 September 1994.
92. See ibid., pp. 520–1.
93. Leaman, 'The End of Equidistance', p. 5.
94. Liberal Democrat General Election Manifesto 1997, *Make the Difference*, in Iain Dale (ed.), *Liberal Party General Election Manifestos, 1990–1997* (London: Routledge/Politico's, 2000), pp. 328–9.
95. ibid., p. 329.
96. ibid., p. 332.
97. ibid., p. 352.
98. ibid., pp. 344–5.
99. For details of the Liberal Democrats' 1997 General Election performance, see Cook, op. cit., pp. 235–9.
100. But on the limits to tactical voting favouring the Liberal Democrats, see Cook, op. cit., pp. 238.
101. 'Ashdown as Leader', p. 7.
102. Ashdown, *The Ashdown Diaries Volume 2*, p. 493.
103. ibid., p. 494.

Chapter 9

1. David Dutton, *A History of the Liberal Party in the Twentieth Century* (Basingstoke: Palgrave Macmillan, 2004), p. 285.
2. Paddy Ashdown, *The Ashdown Diaries Volume 1* (London: Allen Lane/The Penguin Press, 2000), p. 559; entry for 2 May 1997.
3. ibid., p. 560.
4. Paddy Ashdown, *The Ashdown Diaries Volume 2* (London: Allen Lane/The Penguin Press, 2001), p. 15; entry for 15 May 1997. This point was confirmed in the author's interview with the Rt. Hon. Lord Ashdown of Norton-sub-Hampton, London, 20 February 2007.
5. Ashdown, *The Ashdown Diaries Volume 2*, p. 15; entry for 15 May 1997.
6. Tony Blair, speech at Annual Labour Party Conference, September 1997.
7. Author's interview with Gordon Lishman, CBE, London, 3 January 2007.
8. Ashdown, *The Ashdown Diaries Volume 2*, p. 153; entry for 13 January 1998.
9. ibid., p. 238; entry for 26 July 1998.
10. Tony Blair, *The Third Way: New Politics for the New Century*, Fabian Pamphlet 588 (London: Fabian Society, September 1998), p. 1.
11. ibid.
12. See Chapter 8 above, n87.
13. Anthony Giddens, *The Third Way: The Renewal of Social Democracy* (Cambridge: Polity Press, 1998); see, too, Giddens' earlier work, *Beyond Left and Right: The Future of Radical Politics* (Cambridge: Polity Press, 1994), and his later work, *The Third Way and Its Critics* (Cambridge: Polity Press, 2000).
14. Blair, *The Third Way*, p. 6.

15. ibid., p. 7.
16. Reprinted in Bodo Hombach, *The Politics of the New Centre* (Cambridge: Policy Press, 2000), Appendix (pp. 159–77).
17. Ralf Dahrendorf, 'Open Letter to the Prime Minister: Ditch the Third Way, Try the 101st', *New Statesman*, 29 May 1998, p. 21.
18. ibid., p. 22. See *Report on Wealth Creation and Social Cohesion in a Free Society* (London: The Commission on Wealth Creation and Social Cohesion, July 1995).
19. Ralf Dahrendorf, 'Whatever Happened to Liberty?', *New Statesman*, 6 September 1999, p. 25 (based on a lecture delivered at a symposium in Vienna in June 1999).
20. ibid., p. 26.
21. ibid., p. 27.
22. ibid.
23. Alan Ryan, 'Britain: Recycling the Third Way', *Dissent*, Spring 1999, pp. 77, 80.
24. William Rodgers, 'Whose Third Way to Where?', 5th Annual *Reformer* Lecture, Brighton, 20 September 1998.
25. See Shirley Williams, 'The Third Way?', *The Reformer*, Autumn 1998, pp. 6–8.
26. See William Wallace, 'Centre Forum (previously Centre for Reform)', in Duncan Brack and Ed Randall (eds), *Dictionary of Liberal Thought* (London: Politico's, 2007), pp. 56–7.
27. Neil Stockley, 'The Third Way: Where Do Liberal Democrats Stand?', in William Wallace and Neil Stockley, *Liberal Democrats and the Third Way* (ed. Richard Grayson) (London: Centre for Reform, December 1998), p. 25.
28. William Wallace, 'The Third Way and the Fourth ...', in Wallace and Stockley, *Liberal Democrats and the Third Way*, p. 16.
29. ibid., p. 15, 17.
30. ibid., p. 18.
31. Stockley, op. cit., p. 25.
32. Wallace, op. cit., p. 18.
33. ibid., p. 19.
34. Richard Grayson, 'Conclusion: a Liberal Democrat Agenda', in *Liberal Democrats and the Third Way*, p. 38.
35. Wallace, op. cit., p. 21.
36. ibid., p. 24.
37. Stockley, op. cit., p. 33.
38. Wallace, op. cit., p. 24.
39. ibid.
40. ibid., p. 18.
41. Personal correspondence to the author from the Rt. Hon. Lord Ashdown of Norton-sub-Hampton, 24 March 2007.
42. Ashdown, *The Ashdown Diaries Volume 2*, p. 296; entry for 4 October 1998.
43. ibid., p. 297.
44. ibid., pp. 302–03; entry for 22 October 1998.
45. *The Guardian*, 30 October 1998; quoted in Cook, *A Short History of the Liberal Party*, 6th edn (Basingstoke: Palgrave Macmillan, 2002), p. 245.
46. See Ashdown, *The Ashdown Diaries Volume 2*, pp. 266–74.
47. See ibid., p. 322; entry for 3 November 1998.
48. ibid., pp. 316–17; entry for 29 October 1998.
49. See ibid., p. 324; entry for 5 November 1998.
50. Steven Fielding, *The Labour Party: Continuity and Change in the Making of New Labour* (Basingstoke: Palgrave Macmillan, 2003), p. 53.

51. Ashdown, *The Ashdown Diaries Volume 2*, p. 333; entry for 11 November 1998.
52. See Cook, op. cit., pp. 247–51 for an analysis of the results of those elections.
53. Duncan Brack, 'Liberal Democrat Leadership: The Cases of Ashdown and Kennedy', *The Political Quarterly*, Vol. 78, No. 1, January–March 2007, pp. 79–80.
54. Ashdown, *The Ashdown Diaries Volume 2*, p. 493.
55. Andrew Rawnsley, 'Captain Ashdown Quits the Field with an Honourable Discharge. But the Biggest Battle Is Not Yet Won', *The Observer*, 24 January 1999.
56. Dutton, op. cit., p. 291.
57. ibid.
58. Author's interview with Lord Rennard, London, 25 June 2009.
59. Tony Greaves, 'Audacious – but Fundamentally Flawed', review of *The Ashdown Diaries Volume 1*, *Journal of Liberal Democrat History*, 30, Spring 2001, p. 28.
60. Rawnsley, op. cit.
61. Brack, 'Liberal Democrat Leadership', p. 83

Chapter 10

1. For an analysis of the May/June 1999 elections, see Chris Cook, *A Short History of the Liberal Party*, 6th edn (Basingstoke: Palgrave, 2002), pp. 247–51.
2. See Paddy Ashdown, *The Ashdown Diaries, Volume 2* (London: Allen Lane/The Penguin Press, 2001), pp. 191–2, 193: entries for 22 and 24 April 1998.
3. Charles Kennedy, quoted in Peter Lynch, 'Charles Kennedy', in Duncan Brack et al. (eds), *Dictionary of Liberal Biography* (London: Politico's, 1998), p. 212.
4. Conrad Russell, *An Intelligent Person's Guide to Liberalism* (London: Duckworth, 1999), p. 7.
5. ibid., p. 10.
6. ibid., p. 14.
7. ibid., p. 18.
8. ibid., p. 19.
9. ibid., p. 17.
10. ibid.
11. ibid., p. 18.
12. ibid., p. 19.
13. ibid., p. 18. On Conrad Russell's earlier hostility towards both Tony Blair and his government, and hence his opposition in 1997–98 to Paddy Ashdown's 'Project', see Ashdown, *The Ashdown Diaries, Volume 2*, pp. 89 (entry for 11 September 1997) and 339 (entry for 17 November 1998).
14. Russell, op. cit., p. 35.
15. ibid., pp. 67, 68.
16. Charles Kennedy, *The Future of Politics* (London: HarperCollins, 2001), p. xiii (first published in hardback edition by HarperCollins, 2000).
17. ibid., p. xv.
18. ibid., pp. 89, 93.
19. ibid.
20. ibid., pp. 93–4.
21. Greg Hurst, *Charles Kennedy: A Tragic Flaw* (London: Politico's, 2006), p. 119.
22. Conrad Russell, 'What is the State For?', *Liberator*, 272, January 2001, p. 8.
23. See John Maynard Keynes, *The End of Laissez-Faire* (London: Hogarth Press, 1926), pp. 40–47. (Keynes was alluding to Bentham's *Manual of Political Economy*, published posthumously in 1843).

24. Hurst, op. cit., p. 127.
25. ibid., pp. 128–9.
26. See *Freedom in a Liberal Society* (London: Liberal Democrats, September 2000).
27. Liberal Democrat General Election Manifesto 2001, *Freedom, Justice, Honesty*, p. 1.
28. ibid., p. 12.
29. ibid., p. 14.
30. ibid.
31. ibid., p. 18.
32. ibid.
33. See Hurst, op. cit., pp. 133–4.
34. Author's interview with Lord Rennard, London, 25 June 2009. Lord Rennard had been the Liberal Democrats' Director of Campaigns and Elections since 1989, directing the successful by-election campaigns at Eastbourne, Kincardine and Deeside, Newbury, Christchurch, Eastleigh, and Littleborough and Saddleworth. He became the Party's Chief Executive in 2003.
35. On the Liberal Democrats' 2001 General Election campaign, see Hurst, op. cit, pp. 132–9; Cook, op. cit., pp. 259–62.
36. Hurst, op. cit., p. 139.
37. Simon Titley, 'Why Don't Liberals Think Any More?', *Liberator*, 272, January 2001, p. 4.
38. ibid., pp. 3, 4.
39. *It's About Freedom*, Liberal Democrat Policy Paper 50 (London: Liberal Democrats, June 2002), p. 5.
40. ibid., p. 7.
41. ibid.
42. ibid., p. 8.
43. ibid.
44. ibid., pp. 32, 33.
45. Downing Street press statement, 20 September 2001; quoted in Hurst, op. cit., p. 141.
46. Chris Huhne had been Liberal Democrat MEP for South East England since 1999.
47. *Quality, Innovation, Choice*, The Report of the Public Services Commission (London: Liberal Democrats, August 2002), pp. 5, 6–7.
48. ibid., pp. 8–9.
49. ibid., p. 12.
50. ibid.
51. ibid., p. 6.
52. ibid., pp. 31–6, 37.
53. See Hurst, op. cit., pp. 153–6.
54. ibid., pp. 159–62.
55. Liberal Democrat parliamentary representation in the House of Commons had been increased to 53 MPs in autumn 2001 by the defection to the Party of Paul Marsden. Labour MP for Shrewsbury and Atcham. See Hurst, op. cit., pp. 151–2.
56. 'Campbell as Leader', interview by Duncan Brack with Sir Menzies Campbell, *Journal of Liberal History*, 60, Autumn 2008, p. 42. On the Brent East by-election, see Hurst, op. cit., pp. 166–9.
57. David Laws had been Paddy Ashdown's successor as Liberal Democrat MP for Yeovil since 2001. Paul Marshall was co-founder of a leading hedge fund

institution, Marshall Wace Asset Management, and Chairman of the Liberal Democrat Business Forum.

58. Introduction by Paul Marshall in Paul Marshall and David Laws (eds), *The Orange Book: Reclaiming Liberalism* (London: Profile Books, 2004), p. 3.
59. Foreword by Charles Kennedy in Marshall and Laws (eds), op. cit., p. xii.
60. David Laws, 'Reclaiming Liberalism', in Marshall and Laws (eds), op. cit., p. 19.
61. ibid., pp. 19–20.
62. ibid., p. 20.
63. ibid.
64. ibid., p. 22.
65. ibid., p. 24.
66. ibid., pp. 26, 27.
67. ibid., pp. 28, 29.
68. ibid., pp. 29–30.
69. ibid., p. 30–1.
70. ibid., p. 31.
71. ibid., pp. 32–3.
72. ibid., p. 33.
73. ibid., p. 36.
74. ibid., pp. 40, 42.
75. Vince Cable, formerly Chief Economist at Shell International, had been Liberal Democrat MP for Twickenham since 1997.
76. Vince Cable, 'Liberal Economics and Social Justice', in Marshall and Laws (eds), op. cit., pp. 132, 133.
77. ibid., pp. 154, 155, 157.
78. ibid., pp. 160–1.
79. ibid., p. 162.
80. See *Freedom, Justice, Honesty*, p. 18.
81. Nick Clegg, 'Europe: a Liberal Future', in Marshall and Laws (eds), op. cit., p. 72. (Clegg had been Liberal Democrat MEP for the East Midlands since 1999).
82. ibid., p. 73.
83. ibid., p. 98. On this point, see, too, Laws, op. cit., p. 28.
84. ibid., p. 86.
85. ibid., pp. 86–8.
86. ibid., pp. 88, 90.
87. ibid., p. 90.
88. ibid., p. 94.
89. See Christopher Huhne, 'Global Governance, Legitimacy and Renewal', in Marshall and Laws (eds), op. cit., pp. 104–31.
90. Ed Davey, 'Liberalism and Localism', in Marshall and Laws (eds), op. cit., p. 43. (Davey had been Liberal Democrat MP for Kingston and Surbiton since 1997).
91. ibid., pp. 44–5.
92. ibid., p. 45. The quotation is from J. A. Hobson, *The Crisis of Liberalism* (London: PS King & Son, 1909), p. 93.
93. Author's interview with the Rt. Hon. David Laws, MP, London, 20 February 2007.
94. David Laws, 'Size Isn't Everything: Debating the State', in Julia Margo (ed.), *Beyond Liberty: Is the Future of Liberalism Progressive?* (London: Institute for Public Policy Research, 2007), p. 146.
95. Author's interview with the Rt. Hon. Vince Cable, MP, London, 14 December 2006.

96. Author's interview with the Rt. Hon. Charles Kennedy, MP, Oxford, 6 February 2008.
97. Author's interviews with the Rt. Hon. Chris Huhne, MP, London, 3 November 2006, and Lord Rennard, London, 25 June 2009. On David Laws' policy proposal, see his essay, 'UK Health Services: A Liberal Agenda for Reform and Renewal', in Marshall and Laws (eds) op. cit., pp. 191–210. On the reaction to his proposal among Liberal Democrat MPs and activists, see Hurst, op. cit., pp. 204–5. For a critique of the proposal, see Chris Huhne, 'Insurance Fraud', *Liberator*, 298, September 2004, p. 13; for more favourable responses, in reviews of *The Orange Book*, see Jonathan Calder, 'Orange Blossom', *Liberator*, 298, p. 10, and Simon Titley, 'Young Turks or Young Berks?', ibid., p. 9.
98. Author's interview with the Rt. Hon. Charles Kennedy, MP, Oxford, 6 February 2008.
99. Author's interview with the Rt. Hon. David Laws, MP, London, 20 February 2007.
100. Simon Titley, 'Young Turks or Young Berks?', *Liberator*, 298, September 2004, p. 8.
101. ibid., pp. 8, 9.
102. Commentary, *Liberator*, 298, September 2004, p. 3.
103. Ed Randall, 'Yellow versus Orange – Never a Fair Fight: An Assessment of Two Contributions to Liberal Politics Separated by Three-Quarters of a Century', *The Political Quarterly*, Vol. 78, No. 1, January–March 2007, p. 44.
104. ibid., p. 42.
105. David Laws, 'No Need to Fear Liberalism', *Liberator*, 298, September 2004, p. 6.
106. Paul Marshall, 'Introduction', *The Orange Book*, p. 3.
107. Author's interview with Paul Marshall, London, 25 August 2009.
108. Author's interview with the Rt. Hon. Vince Cable, MP, London 14 December 2006.
109. Author's interview with the Rt. Hon. Charles Kennedy, MP, Oxford, 6 February 2008.
110. ibid.
111. Quoted in Menzies Campbell, *Menzies Campbell: My Autobiography* (London: Hodder & Stoughton, 2008), p. 218.
112. ibid., p. 222.
113. On Kennedy's uncertain launch of the manifesto, see Hurst, op. cit., pp. 210–12; Campbell, op. cit., pp. 223–4.
114. Liberal Democrat General Election Manifesto 2005, *The Real Alternative*, p. 2.
115. ibid., p. 9.
116. ibid., p. 9.
117. ibid., p. 14.
118. ibid.
119. ibid.
120. ibid., p. 2.
121. ibid., p. 19.
122. On the 2005 General Election campaign, see Hurst, op. cit., pp. 210–17; Dennis Kavanagh and David Butler, *The British General Election of 2005* (Basingstoke: Palgrave Macmillian, 2005), passim. On the effectiveness of Blair's campaigning tactic, see the memo from Tim Razzall to Charles Kennedy, summer 2005; cited in Hurst, op. cit., p. 264.
123. Memo from Tim Razzall to Charles Kennedy; cited in Hurst, op. cit., p. 264.

Chapter 11

1. Menzies Campbell, *Menzies Campbell: My Autobiography* (London: Hodder & Stoughton, 2008), p. 227.
2. Lord (Tim) Razzall, memo to Charles Kennedy after the 2005 General Election, in Greg Hurst, *Charles Kennedy: A Tragic Flaw* (London: Politico's, 2006), Appendix D, p. 263. (Razzall's assessment was, and is, shared by Chris Rennard: author's interview with Lord Rennard, London, 25 June 2009).
3. Razzall in Hurst, op. cit., p. 266.
4. Duncan Brack, 'The Reluctant Leader' (review of Greg Hurst, *Charles Kennedy: A Tragic Flaw*), *Journal of Liberal History*, 53, Winter 2006–7.
5. *Meeting the Challenge*, Liberal Democrat consultation paper no.77 (London: Liberal Democrats, August 2005), p. 23. For a detailed account and analysis of the Liberal Democrats' 2005–6 policy review, see Peter Dorey and Andrew Denham, 'Meeting the Challenge? The Liberal Democrats' Policy Review of 2005–2006', *The Political Quarterly*, Vol. 78, No. 1, January–March 2007, pp. 68–77.
6. *Meeting the Challenge*, p. 3.
7. See Hurst, *Charles Kennedy: A Tragic Flaw*, pp. 220–1, 225–7; Campbell, op. cit., pp. 227–8.
8. See Hurst, op. cit., pp. 222, 225, 229–30.
9. See Hurst, op. cit., pp. 228–9; Campbell, p. 228
10. In an interview in *The Guardian*, 9 September 2005; cited in Hurst, op. cit., p. 232.
11. Vincent Cable, *Public Services: Reform with a Purpose* (London: Centre for Reform, September 2005), p. 9. (The Centre for Reform evolved into a renamed think-tank which, with the financial support of Paul Marshall, was relaunched in November 2005 as CentreForum. See William Wallace, 'CentreForum (previously Centre for Reform)', in Duncan Brack and Ed Randall (eds), *Dictionary of Liberal Thought* (London: Politico's, 2007), pp. 56–7.
12. Cable, *Public Services: Reform with a Purpose*, p. 21.
13. ibid., p. 52.
14. ibid., p. 53.
15. ibid., p. 10.
16. 'The World at One', BBC Radio 4, 20 September 2005; quoted in Hurst, op. cit., p. 233; and in Campbell, op. cit., p. 231.
17. Campbell, op. cit., p. 231.
18. ibid., p. 230.
19. Charles Kennedy, press statement, 5 January 2006; in Hurst, op. cit., Appendix G, pp. 270–1.
20. See Kennedy, resignation statement, 7 January 2006; in Hurst, op. cit., Appendix 1, pp. 273–5. On the course of the developing leadership crisis, from mid-November 2005 to January 2006, see Hurst, op. cit., pp. 1–23, 234–9; Campbell, op. cit., pp. 232–41.
21. Kennedy, resignation statement, 7 January 2006, in Hurst, op. cit., p. 274.
22. For a comparative assessment of Ashdown and Kennedy as Liberal Democrat Leaders, see Duncan Brack, 'Liberal Democrat Leadership: The Cases of Ashdown and Kennedy', *The Political Quarterly*, Vol. 78, No. 1, January–March 2007, pp. 78–88.
23. See ibid., pp. 83–8.
24. ibid., p. 85. On Kennedy and the Butler Inquiry, see Hurst, op. cit., pp. 186–7; Campbell, op. cit., pp. 213–14.

25. Paddy Ashdown, quoted in Hurst, op. cit., p. 246.
26. Jackie Ashley, in *The Guardian*, mid-July 2005; quoted in Campbell, op. cit., pp. 208–9.
27. Hurst, op. cit., p. 248.
28. On the Dunfermline and Fife by-election, see Hurst, op. cit., pp. 241–2.
29. For Campbell's own account of the 2006 leadership contest, see Campbell, op. cit., Chapter 14 (pp. 243–52).
30. As stated in Campbell's resignation letter, 15 October 2007; quoted in Campbell, op. cit., p. 306.
31. *Trust in People: Make Britain Free, Fair and Green*, Liberal Democrat policy paper 76 (London: Liberal Democrats, July 2006), p. 50.
32. ibid., pp. 8, 16.
33. Author's conversation with Duncan Brack, 27 July 2009.
34. *It's About Freedom*, Liberal Democrat Policy Paper 50 (London: Liberal Democrats, June 2002), p. 8. See Chapter 10 above, n43.
35. See, in particular, Richard Wilkinson, *Unhealthy Societies: The Afflictions of Inequality* (London: Routledge, 1996); and *The Impact of Inequality* (London: Routledge, 2005). See, too, the later work, Richard Wilkinson and Kate Pickett, *The Spirit Level: Why More Equal Societies Almost Always Do Better* (London: Allen Lane, 2009).
36. Author's conversation with Duncan Brack, 27 July 2009.
37. 'Campbell as Leader', interview with Sir Menzies Campbell by Duncan Brack, *Journal of Liberal History*, 60, Autumn 2008, p. 43; see, too, Campbell, op. cit., pp. 264–5.
38. See *Trust in People*, p. 17.
39. Julia Margo (ed.), *Beyond Liberty: Is the Future of Liberalism Progressive?* (London: Institute for Public Policy Research, 2007). (Among its contributors were the Liberal Democrat MPs Vince Cable, Nick Clegg, Chris Huhne, David Laws and Steve Webb.)
40. Richard S. Grayson, 'From Ideology to Politics: Liberal Democrat Values and Policies', in Margo (ed.), op. cit., p. 126. The collection of essays to which Grayson was referring was: Julian Astle, David Laws, Paul Marshall and Alasdair Murray (eds), *Britain after Blair: a Liberal Agenda* (London: Profile Books, 2006).
41. Grayson in Margo (ed.), op. cit., p. 126.
42. David Laws, 'Size Isn't Everything: Debating the State', in Margo (ed.), op. cit., p. 145.
43. ibid., pp. 145, 146.
44. ibid., p. 146.
45. ibid., pp. 154, 149.
46. ibid., p. 154.
47. Richard S. Grayson, 'Analysing the Liberal Democrats', *The Political Quarterly*, Vol. 78, No. 1, 2007, p. 6.
48. Richard S. Grayson, 'Social Democracy or Social Liberalism? Ideological Sources of Liberal Democrat Policy', *The Political Quarterly*, Vol. 78, No. 1, 2007, pp. 39, 37.
49. ibid., p. 37.
50. Julia Margo, 'Introduction: Beyond Liberty?', in Margo (ed.), op. cit., p. 3.
51. Steve Webb, 'Free to be Fair or Fair to be Free: Liberalism and Social Justice', in Margo (ed.), op. cit, pp. 134, 135.
52. See Campbell, op. cit., pp. 273–5.
53. Introduction to Duncan Brack, Richard S. Grayson and David Howarth (eds), *Reinventing the State: Social Liberalism for the 21st Century* (reprinted edn, London: Politico's, 2009; first published 2007), p. ix.

54. Brack, Grayson and Howarth, 'Foreword 2009', in ibid., p. vii.
55. Introduction to Brack, Grayson and Howarth (eds), op. cit., pp. ix–x.
56. David Howarth, 'What is Social Liberalism?', in Brack, Grayson and Howarth (eds), op. cit., p. 1.
57. ibid., p. 2.
58. ibid., p. 3.
59. ibid.
60. ibid., p. 7.
61. Duncan Brack, 'Equality Matters', in Brack, Grayson and Howarth (eds), op. cit., p. 17.
62. ibid., p. 17, 18.
63. ibid., p. 18.
64. ibid.
65. ibid., p. 24.
66. ibid., pp. 26–7.
67. ibid., p. 28.
68. Chris Huhne, 'The Case of Localism: the Liberal Narrative', in Brack, Grayson and Howarth (eds), op. cit., pp. 241, 242.
69. ibid., p. 241. For international evidence indicating the lack of a causal relationship between localism and inequality, see ibid., pp. 251–2.
70. ibid., p. 253.
71. ibid., p. 254.
72. Author's conversations with Richard Grayson, 11 August 2009, and with Duncan Brack, 19 August 2009.
73. Author's conversation with Duncan Brack, 19 August 2009.
74. Simon Titley, 'Dead Centre', *Liberator*, 322, November 2007, p. 8.
75. Michael Meadowcroft, 'Texts for the New Century' (review of *Reinventing the State*), *Liberator*, 321, September 2007, p. 8.
76. Howarth, 'What is Social Liberalism?', op. cit., p. 4.
77. On this point, see, too, Huhne, 'The Case for Localism', in Brack, Grayson and Howarth (eds), op. cit., p. 242.
78. Howarth, 'What is Social Liberalism?', p. 13.
79. In 2009 out of a total Liberal Democrat membership of about 60,000, approximately 5,000 members served as local councillors. On the basis of the assumption that of that total membership roughly 10,000 could be considered activists, Liberal Democrat councillors thus comprised about half of their number. Author's conversation with Duncan Brack, 7 September 2009.
80. Campbell, op. cit., pp. 292, 296.
81. ibid., p. 299.
82. On events leading up to Campbell's resignation, see Campbell, op. cit., pp. 299–308.
83. ibid., p. 306.
84. Duncan Brack, 'Leader Out of Time' (review of Menzies Campbell, *Menzies Campbell: My Autobiography*), *Journal of Liberal History*, 60, Autumn 2008, p. 47. (Brack's review, ibid., pp. 45–8, also contains an overall assessment of Campbell's leadership).
85. ibid., p. 48.
86. 'Strictly Come Voting', *Liberator*, 322, November 2007, p. 11.
87. ibid., pp. 12, 13.
88. ibid., p. 12.

89. Nick Clegg, 'Breaking the Deadlock, Building a Liberal Britain', speech at the National Liberal Club, London, 23 October 2007.
90. ibid.
91. Campbell, op. cit., p. 309.

Conclusion

1. Elliot Dodds, 'The Third Way', 1951; quoted in Donald Wade and Desmond Banks, *The Political Insight of Elliot Dodds* (Leeds: Elliot Dodds Trust, 1977), p. 38.
2. Malcolm Baines, 'The Survival of the Liberal Party, 1932–1958', DPhil thesis (University of Oxford, 1989), p. 122.
3. Barberis, *Liberal Lion: Jo Grimond: A Political Life*, (London: I.B. Tauris, 2005), p. 105.
4. Jo Grimond, 'The Principles of Liberalism', *The Political Quarterly*, Vol. xxiv, no. 3, July–September 1953, p. 236.
5. Jo Grimond, *The Liberal Future* (London: Faber & Faber, 1959), pp. 60, 72.
6. Leighton Andrews, *Liberty in Britain* (Hebden Bridge: Hebden Royd, 1985), p. 4.
7. Jo Grimond, 'Is There a Middle Ground?', *The Spectator*, 31 January 1981, p. 11.
8. David Owen, *Social Market and Social Justice* (London: Tawney Society, 1987), p. 3.
9. Grimond 'Widening the Agenda', *The Spectator*, 27 June 1981, p. 12.
11. Author's interview with Paul Marshall, London, 25 August 2009.
12. Conrad Russell, 'Liberalism and Liberty from Gladstone to Ashdown: Continuous Thread or Winding Stair?', *Journal of Liberal Democrat History*, 20, Autumn 1998, p. 10.
13. *Britain United: The Time Has Come*, in Iain Dale (ed.), *Liberal Party General Election Manifestos 1900–1997* (London: Routledge/Politico's, 2000), p. 239.
14. See Charles Kennedy, resignation statement, 7 January 2006; quoted in Greg Hurst, *Charles Kennedy: A Tragic Flaw* (London: Politico's, 2006), Appendix 1, pp. 274–5.
15. John Stevenson, *Third Party Politics since 1945* (Oxford: Blackwell, 1993), p. 135.
16. Paddy Ashdown, *The Ashdown Diaries Volume 2* (London: Allen Lane/The Penguin Press, 2001), p. 493.
17. Nick Clegg, 'Breaking the Deadlock, Building a Liberal Britain', speech at the National Liberal Club, London, 23 October 2007.
18. *It's About Freedom*, Liberal Democrat Policy Paper 50 (London: Liberal Democrats, June 2002), pp. 7, 5.

Select Bibliography

(For journal/periodical/newspaper articles, and other publications not listed below, see the endnotes.)

Ashdown, Paddy, *After the Alliance: Setting the New Political Agenda* (Hebden Bridge: Hebden Royd, 1987).

Ashdown, Paddy, *Citizen's Britain: A Radical Agenda for the 1990s* (London: Fourth Estate, 1989).

Ashdown, Paddy, *The Ashdown Diaries Volume 1: 1988–1997* (London: Allen Lane/The Penguin Press, 2000).

Ashdown, Paddy, *The Ashdown Diaries Volume 2: 1997–1999* (London: Allen Lane/The Penguin Press, 2001).

Association of Liberal Democrat Councillors, *Community Politics Today* (Hebden Bridge: ALDC, 2006).

Astle, Julian, Laws, David, Marshall, Paul and Murray, Alasdair (eds), *Britain after Blair: A Liberal Agenda* (London: Profile Books, 2006).

Baines, Malcolm, 'The Survival of the British Liberal Party, 1932–1959', DPhil thesis (University of Oxford, 1989).

Banks, Desmond, *Liberals and Economic Planning* (London: Liberal Publication Department, August 1963).

Barberis, Peter, *Liberal Lion: Jo Grimond: A Political Life* (London: I.B. Tauris, 2005).

Barberis, Peter, 'Grimond', in Duncan Brack and Ed Randall (eds), *Dictionary of Liberal Thought* (London: Politico's, 2007).

Beith, Alan, *The Case for the Liberal Party and the Alliance* (London: Longman, 1983).

Beith, Alan, *The Fullness of Freedom: Policy Priorities for Achieving a Liberal Society* (Hebden Bridge: Hebden Royd, 1987).

Blair, Tony, *The Third Way: New Politics for the New Century* (London: Fabian Society, September 1998).

Bogdanor, Vernon (ed.), *Liberal Party Politics* (Oxford: Oxford University Press, 1983).

Brack, Duncan, *The Myth of the Social Market Economy: A Critique of Owenite Economics* (London: LINk Publications, 1989).

Brack, Duncan, 'Liberal Democrat Policy', in Don MacIver (ed.), *The Liberal Democrats* (Hemel Hempstead: Prentice Hall/Harvester Wheatsheaf, 1996).

Brack, Duncan, 'Introduction', in Iain Dale (ed.), *Liberal Party General Election Manifestos 1900–1997* (London: Routledge/Politico's, 2000).

Brack, Duncan, 'Social Market'; 'Social Liberalism'; both in Brack and Randall (eds), *Dictionary of Liberal Thought*.

Brack, Duncan, 'Equality Matters', in Duncan Brack, Richard S. Grayson and David Howarth (eds), *Reinventing the State: Social Liberalism for the 21st Century* (reprinted edn, London: Politico's, 2009; first published 2007).

Brack, Duncan et al. (eds), *Dictionary of Liberal Biography* (London: Politico's, 1998).

Brack, Duncan and Little, Tony (eds), *Great Liberal Speeches* (London: Politico's, 2001).

Brack, Duncan and Randall, Ed (eds), *Dictionary of Liberal Thought* (London: Politico's, 2007).

Brack, Duncan, Grayson, Richard S. and Howarth, David (eds), *Reinventing the State: Social Liberalism for the 21st Century* (reprinted edn, London: Politico's, 2009; first published 2007).

Bradley, Ian, *The Strange Rebirth of Liberal Britain* (London: Chatto & Windus/The Hogarth Press, 1985).

Brittan, Samuel, *Left or Right? The Bogus Dilemma* (London: Secker and Warburg, 1968).

Bruce, Malcolm, *Markets and the Responsible State* (Hebden Bridge: Liberal Party Publications, September 1985).

Butler, D.E. and Rose, Richard, *The British General Election of 1959* (London: Macmillan, 1960).

Butler, D.E. and King, Anthony, *The British General Election of 1966* (London: Macmillan, 1966).

Butler, David and Kavanagh, Dennis, *The British General Election of February 1974* (London: Macmillan, 1974).

Butler, David and Kavanagh, Dennis, *The British General Election of October 1974* (London: Macmillan, 1975).

Butler, David and Kavanagh, Dennis, *The British General Election of 1987* (London: Macmillan, 1988).

Cable, Vincent, *Public Services: Reform with a Purpose* (London: Centre for Reform, September 2005).

Cable, Vincent, 'Liberal Economics and Social Justice', in Paul Marshall and David Laws (eds), *The Orange Book: Reclaiming Liberalism* (London: Profile Books, 2004).

Campbell, Menzies, *Menzies Campbell: My Autobiography* (London: Hodder & Stoughton, 2008).

Clarke, Peter, *Liberals and Social Democrats* (Cambridge: Cambridge University Press, 1978).

Clarke, Peter, 'Liberals and Social Democrats in Historical Perspective', in Bogdanor (ed.), *Liberal Party Politics*.

Clegg, Nick, 'Europe: a Liberal Future', in Marshall and Laws (eds), *The Orange Book*.

Cockett, Richard, *Thinking the Unthinkable: Think-Tanks and the Economic Counter-Revolution, 1931–1983* (London: HarperCollins, 1994).

Commission on Wealth Creation and Social Cohesion, *Report on Wealth Creation and Social Cohesion in a Free Society* (July 1995).

Cook, Chris, *A Short History of the Liberal Party, 1900–2001*, 6th edn (Basingstoke: Palgrave Macmillan, 2002).

Cowie, Harry, *Why Liberal?* (Harmonsworth: Penguin, 1964).

Curtice, John, 'Liberal Voters and the Alliance: Realignment or Protest?', in Bogdanor (ed.), *Liberal Party Politics*.

Crewe, Ivor and King, Anthony, *SDP: The Birth, Life and Death of the Social Democratic Party* (Oxford: Oxford University Press, 1995).

Crewe, Ivor and Sarlvik, Bo, *Decade of Dealignment: The Conservative Victory of 1979 and Electoral Trends in the 1970s* (Cambridge: Cambridge University Press, 1983).

Crosland, Anthony, *The Future of Socialism* [1956] (revised edn, London: Jonathan Cape, 1964).

Dahrendorf, Ralf, *After Social Democracy* (London: Liberal Publication Department, 1980).

Dahrendorf, Ralf, 'The New Social State: A Liberal Perspective', in David Steel and Richard Holme (eds), *Partners in One Nation: A New Vision for Britain 2000* (London: Bodley Head, 1985).

Dale, Iain (ed.), *Liberal Party General Election Manifestos, 1900–1997* (London: Routledge/Politico's, 2000).

Davey, Ed, 'Liberalism and Localism', in Marshall and Laws (eds), *The Orange Book*.

de Mont, Alex, *A Theory of the Social Market* (London: Tawney Society, 1984).

Douglas, Roy, *A History of the Liberal Party, 1895–1970* (London: Sidgwick & Jackson, 1971).

Douglas, Roy, *Liberals: A History of the Liberal and Liberal Democrat Parties* (London: Hambledon Continuum, 2000).

Dutton, David, *A History of the Liberal Party in the Twentieth Century* (Basingstoke: Palgrave Macmillan, 2004).

Fielding, Steven, *The Labour Party: Continuity and Change in the Making of New Labour* (Basingstoke: Palgrave Macmillan, 2003).

Fulford, Roger, *The Liberal Case* (Harmondsworth: Penguin, 1959).

Gamble, Andrew, 'Liberals and the Economy', in Bogdanor (ed.), *Liberal Party Politics*.

Giddens, Anthony, *The Third Way: The Renewal of Social Democracy* (Cambridge: Polity Press, 1998).

Grayson, Richard S. (ed.), *Liberal Democrats and the Third Way* (London: Centre for Reform, December 1998).

Grayson, Richard S., 'From Ideology to Politics: Liberal Democrat Values and Policies', in Julia Margo (ed.), *Beyond Liberty: Is the Future of Liberalism Progressive?* (London: Institute for Public Policy Research, 2007).

Greaves, Bernard (ed.), *Scarborough Perspectives* (London: National League of Young Liberals, September 1971).

Greaves, Bernard and Lishman, Gordon, *The Theory and Practice of Community Politics* (Hebden Bridge: Association of Liberal Councillors, 1980).

Greaves, Bernard, 'The Past and Future of Community Politics', in Association of Liberal Democrat Councillors, *Community Politics Today* (ALDC, 2006).

Greaves, Tony and MacCallum, Malcolm (eds), *The Blackpool Essays* (London: Gunfire for the National League of Young Liberals, September 1971).

Greaves, Tony and Pitchford, Rachael, *Merger: The Inside Story* (Colne: Liberal Renewal, 1989).

Grimond, Jo, *The Liberal Future* (London: Faber & Faber, 1959).

Grimond, Jo, *The Liberal Challenge* (London: Hollis & Carter, 1963).

Grimond, Jo, *The Bureaucratic Blight* (London: Liberal Publication Department, 1976).

Grimond, Jo, *The Common Welfare* (London: Maurice Temple Smith, 1978).

Grimond, Jo, *Memoirs* (London: Heinemann, 1979).

Grimond, Jo, *A Personal Manifesto* (London: Martin Robertson, 1983).

Hain, Peter (ed.), *Community Politics* (London: John Calder, 1976).

Hobhouse, L.T., *Liberalism* [1911] (New York: Oxford University Press, 1964).

Hobson, J.A., *The Crisis of Liberalism* (London: P.S. King & Son, 1909).

Holme, Richard, *The People's Kingdom* (Hebden Bridge: Liberal Party Publications, 1987).

Howarth, David, 'What is Social Liberalism?', in Brack, Grayson and Howarth (eds), *Reinventing the State*.

Huhne, Chris, 'Global Governance, Legitimacy and Renewal', in Marshall and Laws (eds), *The Orange Book*.

Huhne, Chris, 'The Case for Localism: The Liberal Narrative', in Brack, Grayson and Howarth (eds), *Reinventing the State*.

Hurst, Greg, *Charles Kennedy: A Tragic Flaw* (London: Politico's, 2006).

Jenkins, Roy, 'Home Thoughts from Abroad' (November 1979), reprinted in *Partnership of Principle: Writings and Speeches on the Making of the Alliance*.

Jenkins, Roy, *Partnership of Principle: Writings and Speeches on the Making of the Alliance* (ed. Clive Lindley) (London: The Radical Centre/Secker & Warburg, 1985).

Jenkins, Roy, *A Life at the Centre* (London: Macmillan, 1991).

Johnston, Russell, *To Be a Liberal* (Scottish Liberal Party, 1972).

Jones, Tudor, *Remaking the Labour Party: From Gaitskell to Blair* (London: Routledge, 1996).

Jones, Tudor, 'Liberal Democrat Thought', in MacIver (ed.), *The Liberal Democrats*.

Joyce, Peter, *Realignment of the Left? A History of the Relationship between the Liberal Democrat and Labour Parties* (Basingstoke: Macmillan, 1999).

Kavanagh, Dennis and Butler, David, *The British General Election of 2005* (Basingstoke: Palgrave Macmillan, 2005).

Keynes, John Maynard, *The End of Laissez-Faire* (London: Hogarth Press, 1926).

Kennedy, Charles, *The Future of Politics* (London: HarperCollins, 2001; first published 2000).

Laws, David, 'Reclaiming Liberalism', in Marshall and Laws (eds), *The Orange Book*.

Laws, David, 'Size Isn't Everything: Debating the State', in Margo (ed.), *Beyond Liberty*.

Liberal Democrats, *Our Different Vision: Themes and Values for Social and Liberal Democrats* (Hebden Bridge: Hebden Royd, January 1989).

Liberal Democrats, *Economics for the Future* (Dorchester: Liberal Democrat Publications, August 1991).

Liberal Democrats, *Facing up to the Future: Enduring Values in a Changing World* (Dorchester: Liberal Democrat Publications, June 1993).

Liberal Democrats, *It's About Freedom* (London: Liberal Democrats, June 2002).

Liberal Democrats, *Quality, Innovation, Choice* (The Report of the Public Services Commission) (London: Liberal Democrats, August 2002).

Liberal Democrats, *Trust in People: Make Britain Free, Fair and Green* (London: Liberal Democrats, July 2006).

Liberal Party, Liberal Party Papers, British Library of Political and Economic Science, London.

Liberal Party, *Britain's Industrial Future: The Report of the Liberal Industrial Inquiry* (London: Ernest Benn, 1928; reprinted 1977).

Liberal Party, *Ownership for All: Report of the Liberal Party Ownership for All Committee* (London: Liberal Publication Department, 1959).

Liberal Party, *Liberals Look Ahead* (The Report of the Liberal Commission) (London: Liberal Publication Department, 1969).

Liberal Party, *Liberalism Today* (London: Liberal Party Organisation, September 1975).

Luard, Evan, *Socialism without the State* (London: Macmillan, 1979).

Margo, Julia (ed.), *Beyond Liberty: Is the Future of Liberalism Progressive?* (London: Institute for Public Policy Research, 2007).

Marquand, David, *The Unprincipled Society: New Demands and Old Politics* (London: Jonathan Cape/Fontana Press, 1988).

Marquand, David, *The New Reckoning: Capitalism, States and Markets* (Cambridge: Polity Press, 1997).

Marquand, David, *The Progressive Dilemma: From Lloyd George to Blair*, 2nd edn (London: Phoenix, 1999).

Marquand, David (ed.), *John P. Mackintosh on Parliament and Social Democracy* (London: Longman, 1982).

Marshall, Paul and Laws, David (eds), *The Orange Book: Reclaiming Liberalism* (London: Profile Books, 2004).

MacIver, Don (ed.), *The Liberal Democrats* (Hemel Hempstead: Prentice Hall/Harvester Wheatsheaf, 1996).

McManus, Michael, *Jo Grimond: Towards the Sound of Gunfire* (Edinburgh: Birlinn, 2001).

Meadowcroft, Michael, *Social Democracy – Barrier or Bridge?* (London: Liberator Publications, August 1981).

Meadowcroft, Michael, *Liberal Values for a New Decade*, 2nd edn (Manchester: North West Community Newspapers, September 1981).

Michie, Alastair and Hoggart, Simon, *The Pact: The Inside Story of the Lib-Lab Government, 1977–8* (London: Quartet, 1978).

Mill, John Stuart, *On Liberty* [1859] (Harmondsworth: Penguin, 1974).

Mole, Stuart, 'The Liberal Party and Community Politics', in Bogdanor (ed.), *Liberal Party Politics*.

Owen, David, *Face the Future* (abridged and revised edn) (Oxford: Oxford University Press, 1981).

Owen, David, *A Future That Will Work: Competitiveness and Compassion* (Harmondsworth: Penguin, 1984).

Owen, David, *Social Market and Social Justice* (London: Tawney Society, 1987).

Owen, David, *Time to Declare* (London: Michael Joseph, 1991).

Owen, David and Steel, David, *The Time Has Come* (London: Weidenfeld and Nicolson, 1987).

Pardoe, John, *We Must Conquer Inflation* (London: Liberal Publication Department, 1974).

Peacock, Alan, 'Welfare in the Liberal State', in Watson (ed.), *The Unservile State*.

Peacock, Alan, *The Welfare Society* (London: Liberal Publication Department, 1961).

Rasmussen, Jorgen, *The Liberal Party: A Study in Retrenchment and Revival* (London: Constable, 1965).

Rodgers, William, *The Politics of Change* (London: Secker & Warburg, 1982).

Rodgers, William, *Fourth Among Equals* (London: Politico's, 2000).

Russell, Conrad, *An Intelligent Person's Guide to Liberalism* (London: Duckworth, 1999).

SDP/Liberal Alliance Commission, *Defence and Disarmament* (Hebden Bridge: Hebden Royd, 1986).

Seear, Nancy, 'Relations in Industry', in Watson (ed.), *The Unservile State*.

Sell, Geoffrey, 'Liberal Revival; Jo Grimond and the Politics of British Liberalism, 1956–67', PhD thesis (University of London, 1996).

Steed, Michael, 'The Electoral Strategy of the Liberal Party', in Bogdanor (ed.), *Liberal Party Politics*.

Steed, Michael, 'The Liberal Tradition', in MacIver (ed.), *The Liberal Democrats*.

Steel, David, *The Liberal Way Forward* (London: Liberal Publication Department, 1975).

Steel, David, *Labour at 80: Time to Retire* (London: Liberal Publication Department, April 1980).

Steel, David, *A House Divided: The Lib-Lab Pact and the Future of British Politics* (London: Weidenfeld and Nicolson, 1980).

Steel, David, *The Decade of Realignment: The Leadership Speeches of David Steel 1976–1985* (ed. Stuart Mole) (Hebden Bridge: Hebden Royd, 1986).

Steel, David, *Against Goliath: David Steel's Story* (London: Weidenfeld and Nicolson, 1989).

Steel, David and Holme, Richard (eds), *Partners in One Nation: A New Vision for Britain 2000* (London: Bodley Head, 1985).

Stevenson, John, *Third Party Politics since 1945: Liberals, Alliance and Liberal Democrats* (Oxford: Blackwell, 1993).

Thomson, David, *The Shocktroops of Pavement Politics? An Assessment of the Influence of Community Politics in the Liberal Party* (Hebden Bridge: Hebden Royd, September 1985).

Thorpe, Jeremy, *In My Own Time: Reminiscences of a Liberal Leader* (London: Politico's, 1999).

Wade, Donald, *Towards a Nation of Owners* (London: Liberal Publication Department, 1958).

Wade, Donald, *Our Aim and Purpose*, 4th edn (London: Liberal Publication Department, 1967).

Wade, Donald and Banks, Desmond, *The Political Insight of Elliot Dodds* (Leeds: Elliot Dodds Trust, 1977).

Wallace, William, 'Survival and Revival', in Bogdanor (ed.) *Liberal Party Politics*.

Watkins, Alan, *The Liberal Dilemma* (London: MacGibbon & Kee, 1966).

Watson, George (ed.), *The Unservile State: Essays in Liberty and Welfare* (London: Allen & Unwin, 1957).

Watson, George (ed.), *Radical Alternative: Studies in Liberalism by the Oxford Liberal Group* (London: Eyre & Spottiswoode, 1962).

Wiles, Peter, 'Property and Equality', in Watson (ed.), *The Unservile State*.

Wilkinson, Richard, *The Impact of Inequality* (London: Routledge, 2005).

Williams, Shirley, *Politics Is for People* (Harmondsworth: Penguin 1981).

Wyburn-Powell, Alun, *Clement Davies: Liberal Leader* (London: Politico's, 2003).

Index